Sara Verskin

Barren Women

Islam – Thought, Culture, and Society

Volume 2

Sara Verskin

Barren Women

Religion and Medicine
in the Medieval Middle East

DE GRUYTER

Winner of the 2018 BRAIS – De Gruyter Prize in the Study of Islam and the Muslim World

BRAIS
British Association
for Islamic Studies

An electronic version of this book is freely available, thanks to the support of libraries working with Knowledge Unlatched. KU is a collaborative initiative designed to make high quality books Open Access. More information about the initiative and links to the Open Access version can be found at www.knowledgeunlatched.org

Knowledge Unlatched

The Open Access book is available at www.degruyter.com

ISBN 978-3-11-068162-8
e-ISBN (PDF) 978-3-11-059658-8
e-ISBN (EPUB) 978-3-11-059367-9
ISSN 2628-4286

Library of Congress Control Number: 2019957926

Bibliographic information published by the Deutsche Nationalbibliothek
The Deutsche Nationalbibliothek lists this publication in the Deutsche Nationalbibliografie; detailed bibliographic data are available on the Internet at http://dnb.dnb.de.

This volume is text- and page-identical with the hardback published in 2020.
Cover image: © Calligraphy by Osman Özçay. With friendly permission.
Printing and binding: CPI books GmbH, Leck

www.degruyter.com

For my mother and father

Acknowledgements

In the decade it has taken to produce *Barren Women*, I have been frequently struck by how, in weaving together the elements of this project, I keep reaching for old threads I first picked up long ago, handed to me by teachers and colleagues who at the time could not have known how much I would benefit from their knowledge and generosity. It is a pleasure to finally be able to offer them here some acknowledgement of their contributions to my scholarship.

Barren Women is based on the dissertation I wrote in the Department of Near Eastern Studies at Princeton University. It could not have been written without the guidance, patience, and good instincts of my adviser, Michael Cook. I am deeply grateful for his unceasing support for this project from start to finish. I am equally grateful for the scholarly culture he cultivated in the department and in the classes I took with him, from which I still continue to reap benefits long after having left the institution. He promoted an environment of academic good will in which senior and junior scholars respectfully solicited each other's help with their research, generously gave each other their time and expertise, and publicly acknowledged their intellectual debts. Moreover, he taught me to allow my scholarship to be defined by my sources, and to allow those sources to lead me in new directions, even when they directed me away from my initial areas of academic comfort. As students in his courses, my classmates and I often looked at each other with exasperation and even fear as we found ourselves delving into books of numismatics and exploring Sogdian etymology. But it was that experience which convinced me that, when my studies took me in unexpected directions, it was my responsibility and my privilege to acquire whatever new knowledge I needed in order to continue, and to do so without sacrificing precision or seriousness. Some people call this approach "interdisciplinary." From Professor Cook, I came to think of it as a mark of intellectual curiosity, playfulness, and tenacity.

This book is also marked by the instruction I received from my other teachers at Princeton University. It was in the stellar class on methodologies for studying the Middle East that M. Şükrü Hanioğlu and Abraham Udovitch first introduced me to the complexities surrounding the study of women's history, and the debates I first encountered there have stayed with me. Hossein Modarressi taught me family law and guided me through my first serious research project on Islamic law, family planning, and the contested right to have children. Mark Cohen introduced me to the joys of Geniza research and the uses of cross-confessional social history. I am grateful to all of them.

https://doi.org/10.1515/9783110596588-001

Prior to my arrival in Princeton, I spent four formative and blissful years at the University of Chicago. In my first undergraduate year, I happened to enroll in a Bible course taught by the now late Tikva Frymer-Kensky, who introduced me both to the academic study of religious texts and to women's particular experiences of organized religion. The infectious enthusiasm of the late Farouk Mustafa drew me to Arabic studies. Fred Donner's class on *Mukhtaṣar al-Qudūrī* served as my first introduction to Islamic law. But it was Wadad Kadi's combination of towering erudition, charisma, and remarkable kindness, that permanently brought me into the fold of Islamic studies and set me on my current path. I am also much indebted to Helma Dik and to a good portion of the faculty of the Classics department of the University of Chicago, who provided a second intellectual home for me outside the field of Near Eastern languages and civilizations. They encouraged me to sit in on department workshops and colloquia, providing me with my first taste of the social experience of academic research. I would also like to thank John Craig for introducing me to the study of social and economic history, and for teaching me how to be creative in figuring out ways to "do" social history when sources are limited. Lastly, my gratitude goes to Wendy Olmsted who, in addition to encouraging me to become an academic, cultivated an idyllic atmosphere of intellectual enterprise in her classes. Her remarkably deft teaching of literature remains a model which I aspire to emulate.

Several people were kind enough to read my dissertation and provide recommendations for reshaping it into a book. I would particularly like to thank Eve Krakowski, Shaun Marmon, and Avner Giladi for their enthusiasm for the subject and for their thorough and thoughtful critiques and useful suggestions. I would also like to thank Andras Hamori and Monica Green for reading early drafts of what would later become chapters 6 and 7. I am grateful to all of them for their encouragement, wisdom, and collegiality. I would also like to acknowledge the members of a remarkable online community of scholars of medieval medicine, MedMed, led by Monica Green. I have benefited from their expertise in countless ways. Of course, any errors in my work are a reflection of no one else's shortcomings but my own.

In the course of my research I have greatly benefited from the support of my colleagues, classmates, students, and the administrators at my home institutions in the Near Eastern Studies department at Princeton and in the History department at Rhode Island College. I owe special thanks to the many librarians who went above and beyond the call of duty to help me along my way, especially at Princeton University. I would also like to acknowledge the librarians at the University of Minnesota, Columbia University, Brown University, the University of Rhode Island, and Rhode Island College who have aided me, especially those who patiently filled my seemingly inordinate number of interlibrary loan requests.

The publication of this book would not have been possible without the intellectual efforts and financial sponsorship of the British Association for Islamic Studies (BRAIS) and De Gruyter Publishers. I am grateful to the many BRAIS members who welcomed my scholarship and who received me so warmly when I was a stranger in their midst. I would particularly like to thank Omar Anchassi, Amira Bennison, Katrin Mittmann, Ayman Shihadeh, and Sophie Wagenhofer. I am also grateful to the Knowledge Unlatched organization for providing open access to this book.

When I first began my research, I was 23 years old and represented the youngest generation of my family. At the time, I had four living, beloved grandparents and great-grandparents, each of whom encouraged my work in their own way. Now I have only one grandparent still living and I have three children of my own, all of whom are now old enough to read the words of this book themselves, if not to fully understand their import. Through it all, I have benefited from my family's unceasing dedication and enthusiasm for my productivity, as well as for my fertility. In addition to providing me with love, support, space, and time for my work, my grandmother, brothers, father-in-law, and even a few more distant relatives have all read chapters of this book. Never once did I hear from them that my work was boring, inaccessible, or a waste of energy. Their patience with, and confidence in, me and my work has buoyed me up all this time.

My husband, Alan, has been my classmate, research assistant, discussant, and editor for the past seventeen years. Sometimes collaborating, sometimes working on parallel projects side-by-side, we have spent our professional lives reading, translating, writing, and teaching together. As wonderful as he has been in the role of live-in colleague, Alan has been even better in the role of baby-daddy-with-academic-benefits. When I was exhausted by my pregnancies, or buffeted and overwhelmed by the activities of motherhood, he kept me tethered to my scholarly life. And when I have been too engrossed in my work to respond to the demands of family and household, he has absorbed the impact of those demands himself. For this, and for all the joy and pleasure he brings into my life, I am filled with love and gratitude.

Daniel, Hannah, and Maya have already proven to have inherited their father's sweetness, humor, and inquisitiveness. I thank them primarily just for being their lovable selves, but also for ushering me into the experience of motherhood and generation-building, giving me a participant's perspective on the phenomena I study as a spectator.

My parents read and commented upon every section of this book. As historians in their own right, they taught me to love the people of the past, to desire to understand the broad contours of their societies, and to seek out their individual stories whenever possible. My mother taught me to interview and to write, my father to explore and sincerely appreciate the intellectual systems and moral calculus of people who hold a worldview different from mine. Moreover, just as they showed me the rewards of what would become my profession, my parents also showed me the delights offered by family and the intellectual stimulation it can provide. In honor of both those legacies, and in recognition of their unstinting love for me, my husband, and our children, I dedicate this book to them.

Contents

Studying Infertility in the Medieval Islamic World: Why and How — 1
Why study the experiences of barren women? — **2**
The importance of infertility as a phenomenon — **3**
Studying infertility to shed light on related issues in Middle Eastern and Islamic history — **7**
Methodological considerations and the nature of the sources — **8**
Previous studies as methodological models — **8**
The nature of the primary texts, and the promises, limitations, and pitfalls of studying intellectual history using sources spanning vast periods and topographies — **11**
Parallels between communities separated by religion and time — **15**
Sources excluded from this study which merit further inquiry: fictional literature, magic, and pilgrimage literature — **16**
Chapters and structure — **19**
Infertility as a locus for ambiguity, uncertainty, and compromise — **20**

Part I: **Infertility and Islamic Law Throughout the Life Cycle**

Introduction to Part I — 25

1 Infertility and the Purposes of Marriage in Legal Theory — 26
The childless marriages of the Prophet Muḥammad and the depiction of infertile spouses in the *ḥadīth*: two conflicting views — **26**
Mothers of the believers — **26**
Infertility in the *ḥadīth* — **28**
Infertility in the Islamic legal framework of sex and marriage, with comparisons to Christianity — **31**
Marriage annulment due to infertility and genital defects — **35**
Statements in favor of permitting *khiyār* (spouse's choice to pursue annulment) in cases of infertility — **39**
Objections to including infertility among the grounds for annulment — **41**
Ḥanbalī views — **41**
Ḥanafī views — **44**
Shāfi'ī views — **45**
Mālikī views — **46**

Genital defects, "female impotence," and their relation to infertility — **47**
A case from 17th-century Catholic Spain at the intersection of early marriage, marriage annulment, genital defects, and infertility — **53**

2 Law and Biology: Menstruation, Amenorrhea, and Legal Recognition of Reproductive Status — 57
Menarche: the legal ramifications of the onset of menstruation — **57**
Hypothesizing average age at menarche and marriage and the fertility of young brides — **58**
Amenorrhea — **67**
'idda and irregular menstruation — **69**
The extended *'idda* as a potential burden on women — **74**
A case study of irregular menstruation and the laws of *'idda* — **75**
The extended *'idda* as a potential boon to women — **80**
Women's testimony, privacy, and expertise — **85**

3 Islamic Law and the Prospects of Women Presumed to be Infertile — 93
Marital prospects — **93**
Childlessness and inheritance — **100**
Death of the childless wife — **101**
Death of the husband of the childless woman — **105**
Claiming inheritance against male kin without the benefit of sons — **107**

Conclusion to Part I: The Intersection of Islamic Law and Women's Biology — 111

Part II: Arabo-Galenic Gynecology and the Treatment of Infertile Women

Introduction to Part II — 117

4 **Gynecological Theory in Arabo-Galenic Medicine — 123**
The importance of the Greco-Roman medical tradition in Arabic medicine — **123**
Greek antecedents to medieval gynecological concepts — **128**
Moisture, menstruation, and health in Hippocratic texts — **128**
Women's anatomy and the female contribution to the embryo — **131**
Infertility and its treatment in Greek medicine — **136**
Etiology and treatment of female infertility in Arabo-Galenic medicine — **144**
Infertility in the *Firdaws al-ḥikma* (Paradise of Wisdom) — **144**
The intersection of infertility with other gynecological concerns — **151**
Menstrual retention and hysterical suffocation — **153**
Childless couples and the assessment of each spouse's fertility — **161**
Acknowledgement of male-factor infertility — **161**
The garlic test: A case study of recapitulated tradition and innovation — **164**

5 **Physicians, Midwives, and Female Patients — 175**
Non-gynecological interactions between male medical professionals and female patients — **177**
Gynecological care and interactions between male physicians, female patients, and female intermediaries — **185**
Theory, practice, and women's access to Arabo-Galenic medical knowledge — **198**

Conclusion to Part II: Medicine and Sexism — 203

Part III: **Healing and Religious Vulnerability**

Introduction to Part III — 207

6 Religiously Classifying the Medical Marketplace of Ideas — 211
Intellectual eclecticism and the pursuit of medical knowledge — **211**
Lack of classification of medicine in the *ḥadīth* collections — **215**
Jurists on the "medicine of the physicians" — **217**
Jurists on resorting to folk medicine — **230**

7 Heterodoxy and Healthcare Among Women — 237
Muslim female patients, male practitioners and the preservation of sexual boundaries — **242**
Muslim female patients, non-Muslim female practitioners, and the preservation of sexual and intellectual boundaries — **245**
Shielding Muslim women from heterodox gynosocial contexts — **252**
Ibn al-Ḥājj on women's networks of knowledge — **262**
Heterodoxy and women's medicine — **268**

Conclusion to Part III: A Tafsīr about the First Woman's Fertility and Theological Vulnerability — 271

Epilogue: Infertility and the Study of Women's History — 276
Infertility and family law — **277**
Medieval gynecology and its significance — **280**
The quest for conception: women's access to medical practitioners — **281**
Infertility and choice — **283**

Bibliography — 285
Primary Sources and Translations — **285**
Secondary Scholarship — **291**

Index — 303

Studying Infertility in the Medieval Islamic World: Why and How

This study began with an assumption and a question. Assuming that producing children was the primary source of women's value and women's power in medieval Islamic societies, what happened when women failed to produce children? There were good reasons to make this first assumption. After all, anthropological and sociological accounts from many modern Middle Eastern communities describe the importance of motherhood for women and the anxiety surrounding infertility; and members of these modern communities often ascribe such values and anxieties to religion and to centuries-old tradition. Moreover, throughout the contemporary world, arguments in favor of "traditional" or "patriarchal" practices, as well as those rejecting them, have hinged upon the notion that the limitations placed on women exist to either confine them or support them in their role as producers and nurturers of children.[1] Surely this was also true of the experiences of women in medieval Islamic societies? It raises the question of how those women who could not fulfill that role were treated.

From the start, it has also been clear that this line of reasoning is problematic. There are the definitional problems, such as what do we mean by "power," when should communal practices be labeled "Islamic," and what is the significance of the plural in the phrase "Islamic societies"? These concerns are real, but they represent a detour from the discussion at hand, not an actual contradiction or problematization of the supposition that motherhood was the primary role assigned to women, around which the traditional system, particularly as enshrined in Islamic law, was organized. Here, however, even a cursory knowledge of Islamic family law suggests a possibly fatal flaw with this argument: Islamic law barely mentions infertility and in no way overtly penalizes barren women.[2] Indeed, it makes rather little mention of maternity itself.[3] How then could it play

---

1 For some examples of the ambiguities of measures which serve to support and constrict women in their roles as producers of children, see Remke Kruk, "Pregnancy and Its Social Consequences In Mediaeval And Traditional Arab Society" *Quaderni Di Studi Arabi* 5/6 (1987):418–30.

2 The case of slave women represents something of an exception to this rule, as such women stood to gain some legal protections if they bore their masters' children. See Y. Mirza, "Remembering the *Umm al-Walad*," in *Concubines and Courtesans: Women and Slavery in Islamic History*, ed. M. Gordon and K.A. Hain (Oxford: Oxford University Press, 2017), 297–337.

3 The most recent scholarship on motherhood in the medieval Islamic world, Kathryn Kueny's *Conceiving Identities: Maternity in Medieval Muslim Discourse and Practice* (Albany: State University of New York Press, 2013), does not include any extended discussion of Islamic law.

https://doi.org/10.1515/9783110596588-002

a role in shaping the experiences of infertile women? Ultimately, it is the answer to this question which constitutes the subject of this book.

Why study the experiences of barren women?

For students of medieval Islamic societies, the study of barren women offers two benefits. First, it illuminates a phenomenon that is important in and of itself, as it was experienced by women in all eras and places, and with life-changing consequences. Secondly, in exploring the factors that shape the peculiar experience of infertility, we shed light on broader issues in Middle Eastern and Islamic history. In studying reproduction, we gain insight into the interplay between the medical and religious explanations of biological events and the significance attributed to them. In studying medical interventions, we gain insight into the remarkably diverse marketplace of ideas about health that existed in some medieval communities, and the anxieties some people felt as a result of the multiplicity of authorities and forms of knowledge. We see competition and anxiety expressed by religious authorities against medical authorities and practitioners of healing magic, male medical practitioners against female ones, and male religious culture against female religious culture. In studying women's sources of healthcare, we gain new insights into the meaning behind regulations governing women's modesty and social interactions. Finally, in studying the options available to childless women throughout their life cycles, we can fine-tune our understanding of some aspects of the institutions of Islamic marriage, divorce, and polygamy in ways that make us re-examine, and at times contradict, certain assumptions about patriarchy, paternity, motherhood, and women's vulnerability and empowerment within the Islamic legal system.

The picture of patriarchy that emerges from this study of infertility is a complex and somewhat surprising one. While much ink has been spilled by others in describing patriarchal attempts to exert male control over women's sexual organs so as to ensure fathers' confidence in their own paternity, this study shows the extent to which men depended upon and trusted women to individually monitor and interpret their own reproductive statuses. It also shows both the legal and medical willingness to tolerate, and even embrace, reproductive uncertainty and ambiguity. However, it also suggests that the social constraints urged upon women were understood by many jurists as existing for reasons beyond the need to guard against sexual and reproductive violations. Rather they were also put in place to guard against the threat of religious and intellectual syncretism, a threat to which some jurists thought women were particularly at risk, and particularly so during their experiences of events connected with health, birth, and death.

The importance of infertility as a phenomenon

Writing in Tunis in the 1970s, the sociologist Abdelwahab Bouhdiba produced a lengthy, dramatic, and damning depiction of the importance of fertility and the prospect of sterility for women in what he termed contemporary "Arabo-Muslim" society.[4] His *La Sexualité en Islam* highlights the role played by Islamic legal norms in making the fate of women contingent upon their reproductive success. Because of the weakness of a woman's position as a wife, a woman must seek safety through the institution of motherhood, he claims. Polygamy, divorce, and inheritance law all conspire to pressure women into producing children, as a means of obtaining loyalty, respect, care, and financial security in a system which is otherwise lacking in those things.[5] He concludes:

> Having children in the traditional Arabo-Muslim society is the fundamental element of security for a woman. Woe betide the sterile woman . . . Motherhood, then, was a protection. It was the only security for a woman – there was practically no other . . . So, given the "system" and the structures of the environment, the Arab woman tries to increase her chances by having as many pregnancies as possible. Hence that obsession with children – have children, more children and still more children!

Bouhdiba argues that even in *The Thousand and One Nights*, the classic story of the triumph of feminine brains over masculine brawn, what enables Shahrezad to survive is not her storytelling abilities, but rather her providing the king with three sons in the space of thirty-three months. "One of them walked, one of them crawled, and one was at the breast."[6]

Other sociologists and ethnographers describing their findings in twentieth-century Iran, Turkey,[7] Palestine,[8] Jordan,[9] Egypt,[10] and Morocco[11] have empha-

4 A. Bouhdiba, *Sexuality in Islam* (London: Saqi Books, 2004), 215f. *La Sexualité en Islam* (Paris: Presses Universitaires de France, 1975), 263f.

5 For an overview of Islamic texts that refer to the honor due to mothers, see A. Giladi, *Muslim Midwives: The Craft of Birthing in the Premodern Middle East* (New York: Cambridge University Press, 2015), 37–56.

6 Bouhdiba, *Sexuality in Islam*, 216.

7 C. Delaney, *The Seed and the Soil: Gender and Cosmology in Turkish Village Society* (Berkeley: University of California Press, 1991), 59. Of all the accounts of women's experiences in the Middle East that I have come across, Delaney's places the least emphasis on the stresses caused by in-

sized the role familial honor and social pressure play in shaping the experience of childless women, in addition to the fear of divorce. The French sociologist Paul Vieille, based on interviews with urban and rural women living in Iran in the 1960s, vividly depicts the shame associated with infertility and the pressure brought to bear in compelling young women to take measures to demonstrate their own fertility.

> After marriage all those who surround a young wife await with anxiety the announcement of a pregnancy. The event releases an anxiety; thenceforth the young wife will be cherished by her husband and her in-laws. If, on the contrary, there is a delay, anxiety grows on all sides. The father of the young girl has given a product for reproduction; he is discredited by his daughter who does not immediately promise a child. The husband's family, on its side, has acquired a young wife to increase its descendants; if her sterility continues, the husband loses interest in his wife and threatens to send her back or to take a second wife. The household is constituted to procreate; sterility is a broken contract. The young wife who is, habitually and without proof, taken to be responsible for the sterility of the couple, will do everything to change her state: pilgrimages, magic practices, potions, and so forth. If she does not succeed, she will have only a diminished status, and her family will feel dishonored by it.
>
> Social incitements to childbirth continue after the first birth. There are, notably, the uncertainties of the position of the wife in the household; the marriage is easily broken by the will of the husband alone. Even if this does not happen in the countryside,[12] the op-

fertility and the anxiety to have children. Writing about her fieldwork in a Turkish village in the early 1980s, she also mentions that abortion is common, and quite dangerous for the mother. However, she does note that, "If a child is not produced within a reasonable amount of time, the man is free to divorce or take a second wife. Although polygyny is forbidden in modern Turkish law, it sometimes occurs in villages where traditions of the Seriat (Islamic law) still operate. The system of beliefs implies that the marriage bond is less important than physiological paternity." Ibid., 53.

8 H. Granqvist, *Marriage Conditions in a Palestinian Village*, 1:117; 2:116, 244–6, and idem, *Child Problems Among the Arabs* (Södorström, 1950), 76–7, 224. T. Canaan, "Unwritten Laws Affecting the Arab Woman of Palestine," *Journal of the Palestine Oriental Society* 11 (1931), 175.

9 R. Antoun, "Social Organization and the Life Cycle in an Arab Village," *Ethnology* 6.3 (1967), 302–3.

10 Ḥ. ʿAmmār, *Growing up in an Egyptian village; Silwa, Province of Aswan* (New York, Octagon Books, 1966), 94. S. Morsey, *Gender, Sickness, and Healing in Rural Egypt* (Boulder, CO: Westview Press, 1993), 48, 54, 75. and "Sex Differences and Folk Illness," in *Women in the Muslim World*, L. Beck and N. Keddie (Cambridge, Mass.: Harvard University Press, 1978), 604–605. M. Inhorn, *Infertility and patriarchy: the cultural politics of gender and family life in Egypt* (Philadelphia: University of Pennsylvania Press, 1996).

11 V. Maher, "Women and Social Change in Morocco," in *Women in the Muslim World*, ed. Lois Beck and Nikki Keddie (Cambridge, Mass: Harvard University Press, 1978), 104.

12 Erika Friedl's account of a remote Iranian mountain village in the 1970s and early 1980s confirms this: "There aren't many childless couples in Deh Koh, and of the few not one ever split up,

> tion left to the husband to send back his wife easily leads the latter to look for means to attach her to her home. Children are reputed to be "nails" that attach the wife to the home. After marriage, women hasten to multiply these ties which guarantee them against repudiation.
>
> . . . the group of women: they actively surround the young wife, initiate her, guide her through the first pregnancies, welcome the newborn, and combat sterility. In them are transmitted ancient popular practices regarding magic, pharmacy, and medicine. They help the young wives and exert a considerable pressure in favor of fecundity.[13]

The effects of such pressure lead women to engage in a "quest for conception," memorably depicted by Erika Friedl in *Women of Deh Koh*, which includes a chapter portraying the experience of a childless young wife seeking aid in the wake of the Iranian Revolution,[14] and by Marcia Inhorn, in her books *The Quest for Conception: Gender, Infertility, and Egyptian Medical Traditions* and *Infertility and Patriarchy: The Cultural Politics of Gender and Family Life in Egypt*. In the course of such quests, infertile women seek assistance from ethnomedical practitioners, religious saints, and practitioners of biomedicine. A study from modern Egypt shows that concerns about infertility, and the perception that pregnancy is not occurring quickly enough, account for more than half of all women's medical visits, whether to biomedical physicians or practitioners of indigenous medicine.[15]

As depicted in modern accounts, in the course of this "quest for conception," women encounter and navigate Islamic legal culture in complex ways. The delivery of medical attention and care to women is potentially fraught as a result of modesty concerns. Moreover, medical systems and treatments, such as biomedical healing, humoral healing, magical healing, prayer, and pilgrimage rituals to attain saintly blessing, *baraka*, are subject to religious categorizations on the basis of theological orthodoxy and heresy. Whether a form of medical intervention meets with approval or disapproval from religious authorities is not dependent on whether such interventions are "traditional," validated by either

---

and no husband ever took a second wife because of his first wife's barrenness. Indeed after the first few rough years of crushed expectations, attempted cures, amulets and accusations, pilgrimages, travels to doctors, fights, sneers, and humiliating pity, and after hope has dimmed to a faint flicker deep in the couple's hearts, they tune in to each other as companions in misery and live more peacefully and leisurely than most of their neighbors harassed by large families." E. Friedl, *Women of Deh Koh* (London: Penguin Books, 1991), 48.

13 P. Vieille, "Family Alliance and Sexual Politics," in *Women in the Muslim World*, ed. Lois Beck and Nikki Keddie (Cambridge, Mass: Harvard University Press, 1978), 457.

14 Friedl, *Women of Deh Koh*, 47–65.

15 H. Khattab, N. Younis, and H. Zurayk, *Women, Reproduction, and Health in Rural Egypt* (Cairo: American University in Cairo Press, 1999), 65.

historical precedent or indigeneity. Indeed, among some devout Muslims, centuries-old medical systems are viewed with more suspicion than the more recent biomedicine. As Inhorn writes with respect to Egypt:

> Interestingly, contemporary Islamists tend to condone most biomedical therapies as the creation of God – as being "God's medicine." Yet, it is truly ironic that only modern, Western-based biomedicine is deemed religiously acceptable, given the rich history of *Yūnānī*-inspired Islamic and prophetic medicine in Egypt. As we shall see, many of the contemporary ethnomedical practices found in Egypt derive from these early, religiously acceptable medical traditions, which are now viewed as unorthodox by Islamist elements in Egyptian society.[16]

All of these characterizations of modern Muslim women's experiences highlight the importance of the Islamic legal tradition for understanding contemporary familial relations, gender roles, and attitudes toward medical treatment.[17] And yet, due to the paucity of scholarship,[18] anthropologists have largely skipped over the medieval Islamic period when describing the significance and consequences of infertility, reaching instead for literature from the Greco-Roman or even Biblical periods.[19]

Where scholarship about the intersection of Islamic law, science, and gender exists, it has been very useful. Thus Basim Musallam's work on the approaches of medieval Islamic physicians towards the "one-seed" and "two-seed theories" of conception, and the intertwined relationship between Islamic holy texts and those medical theories, has become the go-to text, almost the only one, for those wishing to provide some medieval Islamic context for contemporary conversations about the intersection of gender, medicine, and Islamic legal orthodoxy.[20] Still lacking, however, are studies of medieval interactions between male physicians and female patients, medieval attitudes toward the "quest for conception"

16 M. Inhorn, *Quest for Conception: Gender, Infertility, and Egyptian Medical Traditions* (Philadelphia: University of Pennsylvania Press, 1994), 94.
17 Inhorn, *Infertility and Patriarchy*, 26.
18 In an unusual dissertation, Egyptologist Nicole Hansen attempted to study 5000 years worth of fertility rituals in Egypt, from the Old Kingdom to the present. The pre-colonial Islamic era is the most sparsely sourced period. N. Hansen, "Motherhood in the Mother of the World: continuity and change of reproductive concepts and practices in Egypt from ancient to modern times" (PhD diss., University of Chicago, 2006).
19 E.g., Taufik Canaan, "Unwritten Laws Affecting the Arab Woman of Palestine," 175, 203. R. Patai, *Sex and Family in the Bible and the Middle East* (New York: Doubleday, 1959), 76–84.
20 B. Musallam, "The Human Embryo in Arabic Scientific and Religious Thought," in *The Human Embryo: Aristotle and the Arabic and European Traditions*. ed. G. R. Dunstan (Exeter: University of Exeter Press, 1990), 32–46.

and orthodox and heretical forms of medical treatment, and the extent to which modern women's experiences of disempowerment or fear of disempowerment as a result of infertility were shared by their medieval counterparts. This study represents a first foray, among what I hope will be many future ones, into filling those gaps in our knowledge.

Studying infertility to shed light on related issues in Middle Eastern and Islamic history

The exploration of infertility has much to offer students of medieval Islamic communities generally, well beyond specific information about barren women. Infertility represents an extreme case in which a woman's multiple roles as a mother, as a possessor and object of sexual desire, and as a conduit that binds families together (genealogically and financially) through marriage, are in direct conflict with each other. By examining this extreme case, we can gain insights into the relative significance of, and tensions between, those roles.

As other scholars have demonstrated, analyzing the ramifications of a marginal biological phenomenon and the rather specialized legal discourse surrounding it can yield fruitful and clarifying insights about more common experiences and pervasive social structures. For example, Paula Sanders's study of the treatment of hermaphrodites in medieval Islamic law not only provides information about what hermaphrodites might have experienced, but also illuminates the process, purpose, and scope of gender differentiation in Islamic law more generally.[21] The above-mentioned article by Basim Musallam, on medieval embryology, not only explains specific claims about genetics, but also makes a broader point, showing just how important scientific beliefs were in framing large branches of Islamic law, as it pertains to sexuality, contraception, and abortion.[22] Moreover, he shows that existing Islamic texts and laws favored and promoted certain scientific theories over others. My own study of infertility sheds light on a host of issues surrounding the physiology of pubescence, menstruation, and amenorrhea and their importance for understanding Islamic marriage and divorce law.

Exploring infertility also draws our attention to medieval medical treatment, both generally and with regard to women specifically. Because infertility was a

---

21 P. Sanders, "Gendering the Ungendered Body: Hermaphrodites in Medieval Islamic Law," in *Women in Middle Eastern History: Shifting Boundaries in Sex and Gender*, ed. Nikki R. Keddie and Beth Baron (New Haven: Yale University Press, 1991), 74–95.
22 Musallam, "The Human Embryo in Arabic Scientific and Religious Thought," 37–8, 42–3.

long-term problem, rather than an emergency, and because it was perceived as an affliction which could be attributed to multiple sources, in theory a medieval childless woman would have had ample time to seek an array of treatment options, just as modern childless women do today. And, just as they do today, the practitioners offering treatment existed in an environment in which they competed for the exclusive trust of their patients, while their patients often availed themselves of a hybrid system for understanding what, precisely, was wrong with their bodies. An analysis of infertile women's treatment options therefore leads us to examine who was offering explanations and treatments for ill health, the relationship between patients and those offering them treatment, and the relationship between competing practitioners. The information about competing practitioners further leads us to consider the question of the extent to which male authorities expected their views and writings about women's bodies to reach and influence women themselves.

Finally, studying infertility provides us with an opportunity to re-examine aspects of Islamic law which are regularly mentioned in medieval texts, but which have been ignored or at times misinterpreted in modern scholarship. For example, a great deal of attention has been paid to juristic concerns about interaction between women and unrelated men. However, little attention has been paid to the frequently expressed medieval concerns about women interacting with their fellow women. Similarly understudied are the frequent mentions of the legal outcomes of biologically unexpected circumstances – wives who are not old and yet do not menstruate regularly, husbands and wives who are in some way impotent and unable to engage in normal sexual activity, and women who claim to be pregnant with a fetus for years on end. Studying infertility brings to the fore and helps to contextualize the significance of these legal discussions.

Methodological considerations and the nature of the sources

Previous studies as methodological models

At the end of his life, the historian of medicine Michael Dols, produced a magnum opus, *Majnūn: The Madman in Medieval Islamic Society* with the objective of placing "the subject of insanity in its historical context, to examine its significance, not only within the fields of medicine, theology, magic, and law, but also within the social milieu of Islamic society."[23] In his book, Dols traces the history of medical thinking about the causes and treatments of mental illness in the Greek medical tradition and the Arabic one, as well as in Jewish, Christian, and Islamic texts. He goes on to describe the institutions built to provide care for the mentally ill. He then addresses moral perceptions of the significance of madness, as depicted by poets, mystics, and belle-lettrists. Finally, he explores the legal significance and consequences of insanity. In its ideal form, a study of medieval infertility would be structured using a similar template. My own study is far more limited than Dols's book, focusing specifically on the medical and legal discussions of the condition at hand. It is, however, written with Dols's scope in mind, both in terms of the larger questions it seeks to illuminate, and in terms of its handling of recondite source materials.

The similarities between infertility and madness are striking. The causes of both were simultaneously attributed to both "natural" biological dysfunction and divine intervention, and the onset of the disease was difficult to pinpoint. Both posed long-term problems, and therefore there was opportunity in the course of a single patient's lifetime to attempt multiple forms of treatment. Both affected not just the ill person themselves, but the families and communities that surrounded them. And for both, the historian lacks first-person narratives of the experiences of the unfortunate patients.

In his introduction, Dols describes the ways in which the nature of the sources available shaped his project, its methodology, and its limitations; much of what he writes is also transferable to the study of infertility. He notes that the paucity of descriptive resources necessitates pulling together sources that come from a wide range of locations and times. This means that "the fragmentary nature of the source material makes it quite difficult to delineate the subtle changes in the beliefs and practices concerning insanity or, conversely to avoid a static view of the subject."[24] Moreover, in both the medical and legal literature, the depictions of mental disturbances are "prescriptive rather than descriptive,"[25] meaning that the depictions of the phenomenon in these texts are there to provide a rationale for a particular method of treatment, rather than a clinical description, and therefore mapping contemporary diagnoses onto medieval medical descriptions requires making some interpretive assumptions.[26] The

---

23 M. Dols, *Majnūn: The Madman in Medieval Islamic Society* (Oxford: Clarendon Press, 1992), vii.

24 Dols, *Majnūn*, 2.

25 Ibid., 1.

26 Among Dols's assumptions are: (a) That mental illnesses found in medieval Islamic societies are similar to the ones recognized by modern medicine. (b) That based on biology, geography,

medical data also does not lend itself to quantification at all. Most importantly, "nor are there, to my knowledge, any reliable personal records of the insane that would allow them to speak for themselves; the rarity of authentic voices robs this work of immediacy, comfortably distancing us from what was often, surely, a painful reality."[27]

All of these methodological complications also pertain to the study of the treatment of barren women in the medieval Middle East. For Dols, these complications do not preclude scholarly analysis. He writes, "What can be expected, however, is a relatively firm grasp of the interpretations of irrationality, and a tessellated picture of the madman in medieval society."[28] This is also my task – to explore how infertility was understood and learn about the experiences of and attitudes towards infertile women from as many perspectives as are available to us.

Discussions of infertility include several unique components, not present in discussions of madness. Infertility is one place where social and religious expectations of gendered roles, scientific disputes about conception and reproduction, and familial dynamics, all intersect. For this reason, I have also looked to Basim Musallam's *Sex and Society in Islam: Birth Control Before the Nineteenth Century* as a model for my own work. There Musallam uses the specific issue of contraception as an entry point into a broader analysis of Islamic attitudes generally toward sexual activity and marriage. In doing so, he demonstrates

---

trade, and war, we can assume that mental illness caused by tropical diseases, malnutrition, and narcotics caused mental illness to be widespread and to probably increase over time. (c) That certain sociological factors pertaining to the segregation of minorities and women "may have produced a greater incidence of psychoneuroses and personality disorders than would be found in modern Western society" (p.3n5). My assumptions for my own work are similar to (a) and (b), but have nothing comparable to (c). Medieval infertility was due to the same sorts of causes as modern infertility, though most likely the prevalence of each particular cause was different (e.g. infertility or diminished fertility due to malnutrition or anemia would have been more prevalent in the past when more communities experienced periods of famine). In our own era, a common cause of infertility is sexually transmitted infections. Some of these infections are known to have existed in the past. For example the bacillus which causes gonorrhea, which was rampant in the pre-modern world, in particular is known to cause female infertility, even in women who have had only limited exposure to the infection and who are otherwise asymptomatic. At the moment, there is insufficient scholarship to make an argument as to whether such infections were more or less prevalent in various medieval populations in the Middle East. For an example of what such scholarship might look like, consider a study with respect to Japan. W. Johnston, "Sexually Transmitted Diseases and Demographic Change in Early Modern Japan." *East Asian Science, Technology, and Medicine* 30 (2009):74–92.

27 Dols, *Majnūn*, 2

28 Dols, *Majnūn*, 2.

how very large a role negative and positive evaluations of sexuality played in defining the institution of marriage, in both the Christian and Islamic worlds, even though this might not be intuitive given that both Christianity and Islam ultimately permit sexual activity within the confines of marriage. Additionally, he shows how Islamic law responded to competing medical theories of conception and to the biological reality that contraceptives were known to not always be reliable. His book also offers insights into how having children or avoiding childbirth were alternately understood as potentially both desirable and undesirable from the point of view of women's well-being. All of this stems from the discussion of contraception, which is to say, the voluntary decoupling of sexual relations from reproduction. My contribution to these topics stems from the study of the involuntary decoupling of sexual relations from reproduction.

The nature of the primary texts, and the promises, limitations, and pitfalls of studying intellectual history using sources spanning vast periods and topographies

The scope, methodology, and precision of this study have been influenced by the sources currently available. None of the medieval sources upon which I draw were produced by Muslim women. As Kathryn Kueny noted in her study of maternity, "it is impossible to assume that [women's] voices and contributions to Muslim discourse and practice, if any, may be fully uncovered."[29] In recognition of the nature of the texts, the goal of this research is not to extract or "liberate" women's voices from men's writings, but rather to explore how certain men, belonging to particular sectors of society, perceived women's experiences, vulnerabilities, and choices. Most of my sources are medical encyclopedias, religious advice books, and legal manuals.

From the medical texts, I have attempted to draw out information about the Arabo-Galenic gynecological heritage. Among the questions I ask are: what did physicians think it signified when a woman did not bear children? What did they think could have gone wrong? Were men blamed for infertility? Did gynecology serve as a field of discourse for reinforcing socially-approved gender roles? What sort of treatment options did physicians and pharmacists offer? How much contact did male medical practitioners have with female patients and female practitioners? Did male physicians expect that their writings on gynecological issues

29 Kueny, *Conceiving Identities*, 3.

would ever be read, known, or applied by women themselves? The answers to these questions are described in chapters four and five of this book.

The bulk of this study is based on the writings produced by the *fuqahā'*, Muslim jurists. The genres I make use of include theoretical law codes, *fatwās* (in which specific cases, whether theoretical or drawn from an individual life, are addressed by a jurist who clarifies the relevant points of law for the case at hand), books of advice and ethics based on Islamic sources (legal *adab*), *ḥisba* manuals (which instruct market inspectors how to go about ensuring public well-being), and anti-*bid'a* literature which decries "innovations" in social or religious life which are at odds with the author's views of Islamic orthodoxy.

The jurists' writings contain a treasure trove of information and yet are also full of shortcomings from the point of view of the social historian. The law was an institution which could potentially touch everyone, rich and poor, male and female, the educated and the uneducated – in a way which perhaps the Arabo-Galenic medical tradition did not. Even better, in their moralistic writings, the jurists reflect on the behaviors of people whom they feel they are unable to reach. Their writings thus, in theory, provide a window on to the lives of a broad swath of society. However, legal writings give us little information about those who were not in legal conflict and did not fear potential future conflict. When childless couples and their extended families took care of each other, they had no reason to have encounters with the legal system. Because this study utilizes legal material, it necessarily focuses on areas of conflict, the assertion or curbing of (usually male) power, and the transactional trading of familial privileges. That does not mean, of course, that in the communities described marriages and families necessarily lacked harmony or functioned on an entirely transactional basis.

Even more overtly inspirational moralistic literature, such as Ibn Mufliḥ's *al-Adāb al-shar'iyya*, Ibn al-Jawzī's *Aḥkām al-nisā'*, or Ibn al-Ḥājj's *Madkhal*, which describes ideal behavior (while emphasizing the prevalence of misbehavior), tends to depict ideal marital life in terms of the assertion of a husband's responsibility and noblesse oblige, which is requited by his wife's surrender of power to him. This too should not be taken as indicative of typical family dynamics. Indeed, the authors themselves complain that both husbands and wives blithely ignore their advice on marital relationships. However, the unfortunate result is that this study does not and cannot address what are surely some of the most salient features of the experience of infertility: love, pity, and companionship.

A second significant shortcoming in the legal material I use is that, unlike court records, it is not locale and time specific. Legal manuals, and even *fatwās* and *nawāzil*, do not privilege the accurate depiction of local and contemporary practices. The scholars who produced the legal analyses and moralistic literature upon which much of my research is based were also not primarily concerned with producing an accurate account of the prevalent behavior or local customs found in their own communities. Rather they were more concerned with categorizing various behaviors as commendable or reprehensible and establishing an intellectual pedigree for those categorizations. When it comes to legal matters that affect infertile women, the legal scholars do depict diversity, but generally with respect to intellectual strands and schools of thought, rather than with respect to locality and period.

There are a few types of cases in which these authors do focus on changes over time or place. This occurs most prominently when there is a significant break between the views attributed to the Prophet Muḥammad himself and the dominant position within a subsequent school of Islamic law. For example, on the issue of the desirability of women's prayer in mosques the Islamic authorities frequently acknowledge that while the Prophet permitted attendance, they themselves discourage it and justify that change on the grounds that contemporary women behave in a different (worse) fashion than the virtuous women of Medina.[30] The opposite situation is also attested to, in which a previously disliked practice becomes widely permitted. For example, al-Sarakhsī (d. ca. 490 A.H./1096 A.D., in Transoxania) writes that in spite of 'Ā'isha's condemnation of women who make use of bathhouses, "the correct position according to us is that there is no problem with having baths for either men or women because they have need of it, especially in our country."[31] References to changes over time and place also appear frequently in anti-innovation treatises, in which the author distinguishes between "the pure law" and the degenerate practices which he attributes to his own local community. In this literature, the diversity of practice is depicted as a novel occurrence, a recent deviation from a previously univocal norm, rather than a product of deeply-rooted multivocal traditions. Confirming whether the so-called "degenerate" practices are common, rare, or entirely hypothetical is not always possible.[32]

This brings the reader back to the concerns about the fraught use of the adjectives "medieval" and "Islamic" societies. The problems with such terms are

---

30 M. H. Katz, *Women in the Mosque: A History of Legal Thought and Social Practice* (New York: Columbia University Press, 2014), 97.

31 Behnam Sadeghi, *The Logic of Law-Making in Islam: Women and Prayer in the Legal Tradition* (Cambridge: Cambridge University Press, 2013), 114.

32 E.g. In Ibn al-Ḥājj al-'Abdarī's *Madkhal* written in the early 8th/14th century in Egypt, the author claims that Muslims women in Egypt, under the influence of their Christian and Jewish counterparts, have started observing "sabbaths" three days per week. Ibn al-Ḥājj al-'Abdarī, *Madkhal* (Beirut: Dār al-Kutub al-'Ilmiyya, 1995), 1/2:201–2.

manifest: they refer to communities separated by vast gaps in time and space, and which themselves draw on local traditions which may vary considerably, traditions that may have little relation to any one notion of "Islam." The texts I cite span from the 3rd/9th centuries through the 8th/14th centuries, and from Spain in the West, to Iraq in the East, and sometimes beyond. Can it be appropriate to write a sweeping overview of a topic through the use of sources from such diverse populations? The question becomes even more challenging because discourses on Islamic law and women are so often associated with attempts to depict the women of the Islamic world as universally "subjugated" and in need of "liberation" at the hands of the "modern West." In raising such concerns, Lila Abu-Lughod specifically cautions against writing in broad strokes.

> Much of the best recent literature in Middle East women's history and anthropology can be conceived of as working against universalizing discourses about patriarchy, Islam, and oppression. Scholars have been seeking to specify, to particularize, and to ground in practice, place, class, and time the experiences of women and the dynamics of gender.[33]

It is doubtless worthwhile to examine how infertile women experienced Islamic law in specific communities; however, it would be a mistake to therefore conclude that our knowledge of history cannot benefit from engaging in "universalizing discourses." Broad discussions, such as those featured in Michael Dols's *Majnūn: the Madman in Medieval Islamic Society*, Avner Giladi's *Children of Islam: Concepts of Childhood in Medieval Muslim Society* and Basim Musallam's *Sex and Society in Islam: Birth Control Before the Nineteenth Century* lay out the contours of the intellectual landscape. They provide a framework which helps us to begin to answer what was *important*, what was *axiomatic*, what was *conceivable*, what was *widespread*, and what was *controversial*, even if they may potentially mislead us as to relative frequency of different modes of dealing with any particular issue. Indeed, it is only in the context of such a framework that we can hope to pinpoint and appreciate the extent to which local practices represent a deviation from, an alternative to, or a renegotiation of, the norms propounded by juristic writings. My choice to study "barren women in the medieval Islamic world" is therefore not intended to elide over or ignore the significant differences between and within populations, but rather to engage in the prerequisite work necessary for those differences to be recognized and appreciated.

---

33 L. Abu-Lughod, "Feminist Longings and Postcolonial Conditions," in *Remaking Women, Feminism and Modernity in the Middle East*, ed. L. Abu Lughod (Princeton: Princeton University Press, 1988), 22.

Parallels between communities separated by religion and time

While the experiences of medieval Muslim women constitute the main topic of study, I also cite parallels and divergences between medieval Islamic Middle Eastern communities and medieval Christian European ones, as well as between Muslim and non-Muslim communities in the Middle East. My reasons for doing so are three-fold. First, there are some forms of historical data available from certain communities in medieval Christian Europe which are currently not available from any medieval Middle Eastern community. For example, scholars of European history have been able to start drawing conclusions about the age at which women in certain medieval communities reached various stages of physical maturity, based on data from exhumed skeletons. Secondly, because medieval Christian and Jewish communities in the Middle East shared both medical beliefs and economic conditions with their Muslim peers, but had different legal options when it came to infertility, at times it is easier to parse the concerns motivating non-Muslim women's legal strategies, and to thereby gain some sense of what mattered most to them. These are concerns which they may have shared with their Muslim neighbors, and they therefore shed light on what may have been women's concerns more broadly, regardless of religious boundaries.

Thirdly, it is worthwhile to note that many of those aspects of medieval women's experiences which modern egalitarian readers find most distasteful crossed confessional boundaries. In all three of the Abrahamic religions, women could be married off at very young ages. All three in some respect subordinated unmarried daughters to their fathers, and wives to their husbands. All three claimed that women's biological functions both determined and reflected their spiritual and social inferiority. This will come as no surprise to even the most casual student of medieval history and theology. However, it bears repetition given the contentious history of people denigrating Islam by drawing attention to the "plight" of Muslim women. It is my hope that if I can demonstrate the commonalities and peculiarities of the attitudes manifested by the different religious communities, honest assessments of women's comparative vulnerabilities and sources of power in those communities will not be viewed as a weapon to be wielded in contemporary ideological battles.

This study also makes extensive references to sources from other time periods, including from the modern Middle East. In particular, in the tradition of such historians of medieval social history as S. D. Goitein and Avner Giladi, I draw on modern ethnographies.[34] Where I have located a legal or social strategy

34 E.g. S. D. Goitein, *A Mediterranean Society: the Jewish Communities of the World as Portrayed*

that is employed by both modern women and medieval ones, I draw attention to how modern women characterize their thought process in employing that strategy. For example, women in medieval and early-modern Islamic societies sometimes made the choice to forfeit the inheritance which was their legal due, without providing an explanation for their doing so. Women living in twentieth-century societies also sometimes make this choice, but we have interviews with those women in which they offer explanations of the social purpose and motivations behind their individual choices. These must necessarily be used with caution; they in no way offer proof of what motivated medieval women. But they can offer us perspectives and analysis that are worth our consideration. Similarly, I do not assume that the biological ideas espoused by rural Turkish women in Carol Delaney's *The Seed and Soil* or by urban lower-class Egyptian women in Inhorn's *The Quest for Conception* necessarily coincide with the beliefs of Anatolian or Egyptian women from centuries ago. It would be highly problematic to assume that ethnographic accounts from Morocco, Egypt, Iraq, and Iran depict age-old social practices in those respective regions, and I do not use them to project modern practices back in time. But modern women's experiences and perspectives are not less valuable and thought-provoking for being ungeneralizable.

Sources excluded from this study which merit further inquiry: fictional literature, magic, and pilgrimage literature

There are several genres is medieval literature which can perhaps provide us with insights into the topic at hand, but which have been excluded from this particular study. These include magical texts and artifacts, pilgrimage literature and histories describing festival observances, and popular literature. In a future book, I intend to examine these genres for evidence of women's fertility rituals. However, for the most part, I have excluded these genres from this work because of the methodological complications involved. Among these complications is the difficulty of evaluating the veracity of what are often vague or unsympathetic descriptions of women's fertility rituals, written by men who view such rituals with disdain. Should we reject the outraged depictions of women's rituals that come from medieval moralists, on the grounds that outrage indicates lack of credibility? Or should we accept them at face value or, somehow, stake out a middle

in the Documents of the Cairo Geniza (Los Angeles: University of California Press, 1978), 3:7. Giladi, *Muslim Midwives*, 137.

ground? Even modern academic and sympathetic observers of fertility rituals are often quite shocked by them, yet it would be a mistake to dismiss their descriptions altogether.[35] Determining the meaning of ritual performances is even more fraught, and it requires a greater degree of openness to speculation than the rest of this study does. Hence, it will be saved for a future one. The attractions and pitfalls of such speculation can be observed in Nicole Hansen's dissertation, "Motherhood in the Mother of the World: Continuity and Change of Reproductive Concepts and Practices in Egypt from Ancient to Modern Times."[36]

Other complications stem from the repetitions of tropes and the expectations of certain literary conventions, which in turn make it more difficult to explore fictional stories in search of clues to historical reality. However, certain celebrated stories may be useful in further illustrating concerns and phenomena regarding infertility which we also find in other genres. For example, the story of "Dalīla the Crafty" in *One Thousand and One Nights*, depicts infertile characters using elements that will appear over and over again in the legal literature too. Consider Dalīla's victim Khātūn, the childless wife of a wealthy emir.

> The chief of the caliph's officers . . . was married to a beautiful girl whom he loved. On their wedding night she made him swear to take no other wife and to spend no single night away from home.
>
> One day, when her husband went to the caliph's court, he noticed that each of the emirs was accompanied by one son or two, and then, when he went into the baths and looked at his face in the mirror, he saw that there were more white than black hairs in his beard. He said to himself: 'God took away your father and will He not provide you with a son?' He was in an angry mood when he went back to his wife, and when she wished him a good evening, he said: 'Get away from me. From the day that I first saw you nothing has gone right for me.' 'Why is this?' she asked, and he said: 'On our wedding night you made me swear to take no other wife. Today I saw that every single emir had one or two sons. I thought about dying without issue, and a man who leaves no heir will not be re-

35 A useful example of discomfort on the part of the anthropologist can be found in Inhorn's description of her observations of a fertility ritual at the tomb of Shaikh al-Khibari near Alexandria. Inhorn, *Quest for Conception*, 228 – 231. For an example of an unsympathetic medieval description of popular rituals, consider Ibn al-Ḥājj's claim that women hollow out bread, fill it with mouse dung, and eat it to facilitate easy childbirth. Ibn al-Ḥājj, *al-Madkhal*, 3/4:221.

36 Hansen, "Motherhood in the Mother of the World," 41. Throughout her work, Hansen notes the similarities between aspects of ancient and current fertility rituals in Egypt. She notes the similarity between circumambulation rituals, segregation of post-partum women, celebrations of week-old newborns, and the use of honey in medicines. However, without information as to what the women believe they are achieving through the use of these rituals it is virtually impossible to tell whether we are seeing an inherited continuity, a faux-continuity (in which rituals which originated in the modern period are backdated), or simply the convergence of practices which are common to many societies.

> membered, and I am angry because you are barren and cannot conceive by me.' His wife invoked God's Name against him and said; 'I have worn away mortars by pounding powders and medicines, and the fault is not mine but yours. You are a flat-nosed mule with watery and infertile sperm that cannot inseminate and produce children.' 'I am going on a journey,' he told her, 'and when I come back I shall take another wife.' 'It is God Who determines my fortune,' she told him. He then let and each of them was sorry or having blamed the other . . .
>
> Khatun [told Dalila] 'on my wedding night I made my husband swear that he would take no other wife. Then he looked at other men's son and, in his longing for them, he accused me of being barren, while I told him he was an infertile mule. He went off in a fit of anger, promising to take another wife when he came back from his journey. I am afraid that he will divorce me and marry another, as he is a man of property with a large income, and if he has sons by another wife it is they who will take the wealth and the property instead of me.' 'Daughter,' said Dalila, 'don't you know about my master, Abu'l-Hamalat?[37] If any debtor goes to him as a pilgrim, God will free him of his debt, and any barren woman who visits him will conceive.' . . . Khatun told her that since the day of her wedding she had not left her house [not even] to offer condolences or congratulations.[38]

As shall be shown in the subsequent chapters, many elements of this story correlate with what we see in the medical and legal literature. As part of his marriage contract, the husband commits himself to monogamy, a very common stipulation in medieval Islamic marriage contracts.[39] The pain of the emir's childlessness is deepened by the fact that he is also fatherless and stems from the sense that no one will remember him after his own death. At this point the husband blames the wife not only for being barren, but for closing off the possibility of a second marriage, and he seeks to renegotiate this part of the contract. This too is attested to elsewhere. The wife in turn blames her husband for their childlessness. The belief that infertility could stem from either husbands or wives is also well-attested to in medieval medical literature. The wife's concern that her husband's children by another wife would eventually appropriate her share of his estate is also reflected in the legal sources. And finally, the wife's remark that she has been constrained from seeking a treatment for her infertility at the hands of a holy man because she is so virtuous that she does not leave the

---

37 The name is a pun, referring to both pregnant women and debtors.

38 M. Lyons (translator), *The Arabian Nights: Tales of 1,001 Nights Volume 2* (Penguin Classics: New York, 2010), 804.

39 K. Ali, "Marriage in Classical Islamic Jurisprudence: A Survey of Doctrines," in Frank Vogel and Asifa Quraishi, ed., *The Islamic Marriage Contract* (Cambridge: Harvard University Press, 2009) 23–25. A. Sonbol, "Shari' Court Records And Fiqh As Sources Of Women's History," *Religion & Literature*, 42 (2010) 238. Goitein, *Mediterranean Society*, 3:149–50.

house even for women's social activities, such as wedding celebrations and the paying of condolence calls, is also described in the jurists' writings.

Chapters and structure

Part I of this book explores the ways in which Islamic law could influence the experiences of infertile and childless women over the course of a lifetime, excluding the experience of medical intervention. The first chapter examines the significance of fertility as it is depicted in the early Islamic non-legal religious sources, particularly in the *sīra* and the *ḥadīth*, and explores the contrast between those texts and legal discussions of the role of fertility in marriage. The second chapter explores aspects of the reproductive life cycle that were the subject of a great deal of legal thought, including adolescent maturity, menarche, amenorrhea, and menopause. It shows how legal expectations of the reproductive cycle were in some ways at odds with the biological realities of many women. This, in turn, confused legal expectations about who was and was not likely to be infertile, pregnant, or potentially pregnant. The chapter further explores the prospects and the mechanisms of divorce and remarriage, and how reproductive dysfunctions complicated those procedures. Chapter 3 concludes this section with an exploration of the marital prospects of childless women and how childlessness affects the application of Islamic inheritance laws.

The second part of this book examines the perspectives we can gain on infertility from the Arabo-Galenic gynecological tradition. Chapter 4 describes the gynecological theory found in medieval medical texts and its relationship to the Greek medical tradition which it references. This choice of topic is based on the fact that the Arabic medical texts explored here explicitly claim Greek physicians as their primary authorities and, as will be shown in Part III, this had significance from the point of view of certain Islamic jurists. Chapter 5 discusses gender segregation, modesty concerns, medical interactions between the sexes, and the extent to which it was possible for gynecological ideas contained in medical books to have ever made a real impact on women's medical care. It aims to shed light on a question which has garnered attention from other scholars of the history of science and gender and society: whether specifically Islamic religious attitudes toward women's roles and towards gender-based separation are reflected in the Arabic medical writings about women's bodies.

The final part addresses attitudes toward medical treatment found in the writings of certain medieval jurists. Chapter 6 examines juristic depictions of the relationship between Arabo-Galenic medicine, the "medicine of the Prophet," and folk medicine. It argues that some jurists were concerned by the intellectual hybridity found in the medieval medical scene. They believed that people's desire for healing potentially led them to leverage supernatural forces other than God's, or to esteem as infallible truth pronouncements other than the Islamic revelation, or to put their trust in and offer their intimacy to non-Muslims. Chapter 7 argues that these same jurists were even more concerned about the potential for heterodoxy among women patients, particularly those seeking medical and ritual aid in dealing with significant moments in the life cycle and reproductive cycle. I argue that the jurists' stated preferences when it comes to who provides medical care to Muslim women demonstrate a concern with more than just modesty and the sexual dangers of female-male contact. Rather, they are motivated by a concern about intellectual influence, the dangers of female-female contact, and the rise of what they believe to be a gulf between Muslim women's culture, particularly as it relates to biology and the management of life cycle events, and the culture propagated by the jurists.

Infertility as a locus for ambiguity, uncertainty, and compromise

Among the most salient aspects of infertility is the way in which it foregrounds the uncertainty that people often lived with, on a biological, social, legal, and theological level. With regard to diagnosis, there was a pronounced resistance across the medieval Islamic world to legally or socially labeling either female infertility or male sterility as a permanent condition. One could not legally label one's spouse as infertile in the way one could, for example, label them as leprous. One could not be certain that a person who did not reproduce while they were young would also fail to reproduce while they were old. Indeed, as we shall see, even more obvious labels pertinent to reproduction, such as that of *yā'isa* (the post-menopausal woman) were often not conferred upon women until very old age. The significance of diagnostic uncertainty is also readily apparent when we analyze how, in both the medical and legal realms, the symptoms of pregnancy and infertility were conflated. So too were the therapies intended to promote conception and those intended to promote abortion or contraception. This resulted in both legal and medical ambiguity and hence confusion, but that ambiguity also provided potentially vulnerable women with room to maneuver in their own perceived self-interest, both legally and medically.

There was also uncertainty about the marital consequences of infertility. In many Muslim communities, infertility could potentially precipitate polygamy, divorce, remarriage, social disconnection, or disinheritance, but it did not have to.

These uncertainties also provided a broad range of opportunities for individuals to exercise choice, and to be influenced by the choices of their spouses and family members. This provided a flexibility which was not present to the same extent in societies dominated by Jewish or Christian views of marriage.

There was a tremendous amount of debate, ambivalence, and compromise surrounding healing itself, particularly for women. What constitutes effective medicine and what quackery? When does the pursuit of health constitute the reasonable exploitation of the cures set on earth by the beneficent God, and when does it suggest a lack of trust in that God? To whom should female patients turn for guidance? To male or female practitioners? To Muslims or non-Muslims? How much of a concern should avoiding physical immodesty be when seeking gynecological care? How much concern should there be to avoid heterodoxy, superstition, and dependency on those foreign to the household or to the religious community? The literature I have pieced together suggests that male physicians interacted with female patients and had few compunctions in doing so, yet there is also evidence that this interaction was viewed as suboptimal. Not only were interactions between male practitioners and female patients fraught, so also were interactions between female practitioners and their female patients, especially but not exclusively when the healers were non-Muslims.

Finally, this study highlights the multiple legal areas, pertaining specifically to women, in which there appears to be a significant tension between legal theory and social practice in many locales and time periods. These areas include: female socializing and ritual practices in gender-segregated settings, the role of women in transferring and preserving property between generations and families, the public demonstration of menstrual status, and the extent of interactions between men and women in medical settings. This tension is profoundly important when attempting to understand the ways in which Islamic law helped to shape the experiences of Muslim women, and when considering the malleability of religious discourse about gender and family roles. It has often been assumed that medieval Islamic law promoted a framework which placed intense pressure on women to have children and encouraged dissatisfaction with those who could not. Upon closer examination, however, we see that this pressure and dissatisfaction was not a one-way street. Islamic law did not condemn barren women, but rather had a disparately negative impact on them. Such disparate impact, combined with the fierce cultural desire for children, placed a strain on religious norms. It spurred individual women, their families, their medical practitioners, and their religious leaders to develop exceptions, reinterpretations, stratagems, and compromises in their negotiation of Islam.

Part I: Infertility and Islamic Law Throughout the Life Cycle

Introduction to Part I

'Ā'isha said: I asked the Prophet,
'What person has the greatest claim
over a woman?' He said, 'Her husband.'
I said, 'What person has the greatest claim
over a man?' He said, 'His mother.'[40]

Classical Islamic law does not grant infertility a particular legal status.[41] A prepubescent girl, a virgin, a pregnant woman, a breastfeeding woman, and an old woman all have special laws attached to their situation, but neither infertility nor childlessness is a legal category. Nevertheless, in a variety of areas, Islamic law had potentially distinct consequences for medieval infertile women, in part because infertility often correlated with other physical and social conditions, such as irregular menstruation, which in turn had legal implications. These laws did not target infertile women and, indeed, infertility rarely entered into Islamic legal discourse. Each area of the law was its own unit, defined by its own set of scriptural bases (*nuṣūṣ*) and its own principles (*maqāṣid*), onto which one can map individual cases. As a result, they are rarely considered together as contiguous topographical features that combine to form a legal landscape which an individual person, such as an infertile woman, might traverse over the course of a lifetime. This section attempts to lay out just such a grand landscape by piecing the discrete units together.

40 Al-Haythamī (d. 807/1405), *Majma' al-zawā'id* (Beirut: Dār al-Kutub al-'Ilmiyya, 2001), 4:405.
41 Only in the modern period are there exceptions. See Aharon Layish, *Marriage, Divorce, and Succession in the Druze Family* (Leiden: Brill, 1982), 205 and Vardit Rispler-Chaim, "Ḥasan Murād Mannā: Childbearing and the Rights of a Wife," *Islamic Law and Society* 2 (1995), 92. The article refers to a *fatwā* which can be found in Ḥasan Murad Mannā, *Fatāwā wa-tawjīhāt* (Cairo: Dār al-Ṣafwa, 1990), 201–2.

https://doi.org/10.1515/9783110596588-003

1 Infertility and the Purposes of Marriage in Legal Theory

The childless marriages of the Prophet Muḥammad and the depiction of infertile spouses in the *ḥadīth*: two conflicting views

Some Islamic laws concerning women are traditionally considered to have been derived from the Prophet Muḥammad's family life. These include laws pertaining to seclusion and veiling, adoption and kinship, sexual etiquette and negotiation within polygamous marriages, the procedure for dealing with accusations of marital infidelity, and others. Women's forms of purification from menses in preparation for prayer are also traced back to the practices of the Prophet's own family.[42] The tradition of permitting young girls to play with dolls is based on 'Ā'isha's (d. 58/678[43]) childhood in the Prophet's home.[44] Some have attributed the willingness to allow Muslim women to participate in the transmission of *ḥadīth* to the precedent of the Prophet's wives and daughters transmitting them.[45] However, not all aspects of the Prophet's household became precedents for deriving Islamic law. For example, the number of the Prophet's simultaneous marriages is held to be exceptional rather than paradigmatic for the Islamic laws of marriage.[46] With this in mind, the question arises as to whether Islamic legal attitudes toward infertility have any relation to the Prophet Muḥammad's personal example.

Mothers of the believers

Most of the Prophet Muḥammad's marriages were childless but there is a remarkably scant record of people commenting on that fact. Only two of Muḥammad's

---

42 M. H. Katz, *Body of the Text* (Albany: SUNY Press, 2002), 85, 97. A. Sayeed, *Women and the Transmission of Religious Knowledge in Islam* (Cambridge: Cambridge University Press, 2013), 30.
43 Here as elsewhere, Islamic calendar dates (A.H.) are followed by Christian ones (A.D.).
44 Al-Bukhārī (d. 256/870), *Ṣaḥīḥ al-Bukhārī* (Vaduz, Liechtenstein: Thesaurus Islamicus Foundation, 2000), 78 (adab):81 = no. 6130.
45 This too had its limits, as there were those who believed that the Prophet's wives represented the exception rather than the rule. Sayeed, *Women and the Transmission of Religious Knowledge in Islam*, 63 ff.
46 Katz, *Body of the Text*, 73.

https://doi.org/10.1515/9783110596588-004

many marriages and liaisons resulted in children and, of the children he did produce, no son survived childhood and only one daughter, Fāṭima (d. 11/633), survived her father.[47] Muḥammad is reported to have impregnated two women, his first wife Khadīja (d. 619) and Māriyya the Copt (d. 16/637).[48] Some of the other women with whom he had sexual relations did have children from previous husbands, but not from him. With the exception of ʿĀ'isha, all of his wives had been previously married, although some of those marriages were of short duration and during times of war. In total, approximately half of the wives and concubines associated with Muḥammad had no children at all, or there are conflicting reports about them.[49] In part, this can be attributed to the unusual patterns of fertility that occur in a society with high rates of divorce, premature death, and warfare.[50] For all of these reasons, it is difficult to determine the exact reason for the high number of childless unions in Muḥammad's family.

The Prophet Muḥammad does not appear to have devalued his childless marriages, quite the contrary. With some exceptions, his wives were held in high esteem in their own lifetimes and in the subsequent generations. Although a well-known *ḥadīth* has the Prophet praising his late wife Khadīja to his beloved but jealous wife ʿĀ'isha on the grounds that Khadīja gave him children, there is otherwise but little mention of childlessness as a source of strain in his mar-

---

47 In addition to his descendants through Fāṭima, Muḥammad also had two grandchildren from his daughter Zaynab and one from his daughter Ruqayya. The marriage between the Prophet's daughter Umm Kulthūm and ʿUthmān was childless. Zaynab's son ʿAlī died young while her daughter Umāma survived into adulthood and married ʿAlī ibn Abī Ṭālib, after the death of her aunt Fāṭima. She bore him a son, Hilāl. Muḥammad's grandson, from the union between his daughter Ruqayya and ʿUthmān, died in childhood. The household thus remained small. Ibn Sa'd (d. 230/845), *al-Ṭabaqāt al-kubrā* (Beirut: Dār Iḥya' al-Turāth al-ʿArabī, 1996) 8:252–262. On Muḥammad's children, see Ibn Qayyim al-Jawziyya (d. 751/1350), *Zād al-maʿād fī hady khayr al-ʿibād* (Beirut: Mu'assasat al-Risāla, 1998), 1:101.

48 There are some traditions in which ʿĀ'isha is said to have told Muḥammad that Māriya's son Ibrāhīm was not his. Some Shīʿī commentaries on Q. 24:11, e.g. *Tafsīr al-Qummī* say that the verse refers to this incident. Al-Qummī, *Tafsīr al-Qummī* (Qum: Mu'assasat al-Imām al-Mahdī, 2014) 2:702.

49 These are ʿĀ'isha, Ḥafṣa, Zaynab bt. Khazayma, Zaynab bt. Jaḥsh, Juwayriyya, Ṣafiyya, Maymūna, and Rayḥāna.

50 There is a large body of scholarly literature about the extent to which polygyny, as it is practiced in the twentieth century, itself reduces the fertility of women in such marriages in comparison to women in monogamous marriages. The correlation between depressed fertility in polygynous families is sometimes attributed to chemical-biological factors and sometimes to socioeconomic factors, while other scholars deny that there is a significant correlation at all. See K. Effah, "A Reformulation of the Polygyny-Fertility Hypothesis," *Journal of Comparative Family Studies* 30 (1999), 381–408.

riages.[51] While there are many traditions which report discussions between Abū Bakr and his daughter 'Ā'isha, and 'Umar and his daughter Ḥafṣa (d. 45/665), regarding their relationships with Muḥammad, I have not found one that addresses their childlessness.[52] Similarly, there is no record of Muḥammad's wives or enemies overtly accusing the Prophet himself of diminished fertility.[53] Some modern feminist Muslims have pointed to the example of Muḥammad's wives, revered in the Islamic tradition as the "mothers of the believers," as icons demonstrating the value of childless women[54] although, to my knowledge, no medieval source makes this positive connection.[55]

Infertility in the *ḥadīth*

In spite of the Prophet's personal example, many *ḥadīth*s associated with Muḥammad and 'Umar (d. 23/644), father of Muḥammad's childless wife Ḥafṣa, reference fertility as an essential trait to seek out in a spouse. Fertility is correlated with several other desirable traits, including virginity and amiability. Other *ḥadīth*s suggest that even when an infertile woman is otherwise desirable, her inability to conceive disqualifies her as a prospective spouse.

The following are some of Muḥammad and 'Umar's statements about infertile women.

---

51 E.g. Al-Bukhārī, *Ṣaḥīḥ al-Bukhārī*, 63 (*manākib al-ansār*):20 = no. 3818. Another exception occurs in a tradition where 'Ā'isha says of Māriya Umm Ibrāhīm: "Then God granted him a child through her and kept us from having one." Ibn Sa'd, *Ṭabaqāt*, 8:213. One could also perhaps interpret the following passage from Ibn Sa'd's biography of 'Ā'isha, a passage which is immediately preceded by discussions of the consummation of her marriage, as a request for a child: "I said to him, 'O Messenger of God, women are supposed have a *kunya*, so give me a *kunya*.' He said, 'Take on as your *kunya* your son 'Abdallāh,'" i.e. her nephew's name. Ibn Sa'd, *Ṭabaqāt*, 8:274, 275. See D. Spellberg, *Politics, Gender and the Islamic Past* (New York: Columbia University Press, 1994), 41.

52 E.g. al-Bukhārī (d. 256/870), *Ṣaḥīḥ al-Bukhārī*, 46 (*bab al-maẓālim*):25 = no. 2468.

53 The one time Muḥammad's fertility is addressed is in a *ḥadīth* in which he argues that he has proof that he is not the anti-Christ (*dajjāl*). Muḥammad says that whereas the anti-Christ is infertile and cannot sire children, he (Muḥammad) has sired children. Muslim ibn al-Ḥajjāj (d. 261/875), *Ṣaḥīḥ Muslim* (Beirut: Dār Iḥyā' al-Turāth al-'Arabī), 4:1783 = no. 2927.

54 See, for example, A. Chaudhry, "Unlikely Motherhood in the Qur'ān: Oncofertility as Devotion" in *Oncofertility: Reflections from the Humanities and Social Sciences*, ed. T. K. Woodruff et al. (New York: Springer, 2010), 287–94.

55 See Kueny, *Conceiving Identities: Maternity in Medieval Discourse and Practice*, 110–14. Kueny shows that even those medieval commentators who had positive attitudes toward 'Ā'isha still noted her infertility as an imperfection.

> Ma'qil b. Yasār (d. 59/679 in Baṣra) said: A man came to the Prophet and said "I have found a noble and beautiful woman, but she is infertile. Should I marry her?" He said: "No." Then he came to him a second time and he [again] forbade him. Then he came to him a third time and [the Prophet] said: "Marry amiable, fertile women so that I [God] may make you abundant among the nations."[56]
>
> From Ibn Jurayj (d. 150/767 in Mecca): A man came to the Prophet and said: "O Messenger of God, I have a cousin who is the most noble-minded of women but she is barren." The Messenger of God said: "Do not marry her." Then he said. "Marrying a fertile black woman is better than marrying a fair woman who is infertile. I taught you that a miscarried fetus who is the offspring of Muslims is told: 'Enter Paradise!' He remains, full of indignation, at the gate of Paradise and says: 'I will not enter paradise until my parents do.' So he is told: 'Then enter Paradise, by the grace of the mercy of God.'"[57]
>
> From Anas b. Malik (d. 91/709 in Baṣra): [The Prophet] said, "Marry amiable, fertile women and multiply, for I will make great the number of prophets among you on the Day of Resurrection. Beware of the barren woman, for [one married to] her is like a man ensconced at the top of a well, who waters his land daily, but whose land does not bloom, the stream [of water] is not absorbed.[58]
>
> Abū Dāwūd said: 'Umar said: "A mat in the house is better than a woman who does not produce children."[59]

The attitude manifested in these statements is summarized in Abū Ḥāmid al-Ghazālī's (d. 505/1111) *Iḥyā 'ulūm al-dīn.*

---

56 Abū Dāwūd (d.275/889), *Sunan* (Riyadh: Maktab al-Ma'ārif lil-Nashr, 1996), 311–12 = no. 2050, al-Nasā'ī (d. 303/915), *Sunan* (Riyadh : Maktab al-Ma'ārif lil-Nashr, 1996), 499 = no. 3227.

57 'Abd al-Mālik ibn Ḥabīb (d. 238/852), *Kitāb adab al-nisā' al-mawsūm bi-kitāb al-ghāya wa'l-nihāya* (Paris: Dār al-Gharb al-Islāmī, 1992), 152. This statement indicates that the cousin in question is unable to conceive and the Prophet responds that she is useless, even in comparison to a lowly wife. He says that conception is itself useful even if no live baby results, since the fetus can compel God to allow his parents into heaven. In so doing, the Prophet differentiates between a woman who is unable to conceive and a woman who is unable to carry a fetus to term, even though in almost all other places in Arabic and Islamic literature, the diagnosis of infertility encompasses both conditions. See, for example, al-Shaybānī's (d. 189/804) commentary on Q. 19:5 in which he glosses the word "barren woman" (*'āqir*) saying, "she does not menstruate, does not get pregnant, and does not give birth." Muḥammad ibn al-Ḥasan al-Shaybānī, *Nahj al-bayān 'an kashf ma'ānī al-Qur'ān* (Tehran: Nashr al-Hādī, 1998) 3:303.

58 Ibn Ḥabīb, *Kitāb adab al-nisā' al-mawsūm bi-kitāb al-ghāya wa'l-nihāya*, 152–3. There are many versions of this *ḥadīth* which do not include the final sentence or which have a different conclusion, see al-Bayhaqī (d. 458/1066), *al-Sunan al-kubrā* (Beirut: Dār al-Kutub al-'Ilmiyya, 2003), 7:131.

59 Abū Dāwūd, *Sunan*, 589 = no. 3922.

> The second purpose [of having children] is endearing oneself to the Messenger of God and pleasing him by increasing that which he takes pride in. For the Messenger of God stated this explicitly, and everything which is said of ʿUmar clearly indicates an emphasis on the obligation of procreation. For he married a lot and said, "I marry for procreation." In the *akhbār* regarding the disparagement of the barren woman (*madhammat al-mar'a al-ʿaqīm*) it is reported that he, peace be upon him,[60] said "A mat in the corner of the house is better than a woman who is infertile." He also said, "The best of your women are those who are fertile and amiable (*al-wulūd al-wudūd*). He also said, "A fertile black woman is better than a fair woman who does not produce children."[61] This indicates that procreation is a superior virtue of marriage [in comparison to the virtue of] taming sexual excess, since fair women are more suitable for securing chastity, lowering one's gaze, and curbing desire.[62]

All of the above *ḥadīth*s point to a tradition of forbidding, discouraging, and disdaining marriage to infertile women. It should be noted, however, that fertility is certainly not the only, or even the most common, virtue attributed to a good prospective wife. Other *ḥadīth*s instruct men to seek out wives who are, among other things, believers, modest, beautiful, well-born, thrifty, wealthy, appreciative, and soft spoken.[63] Among the most commonly mentioned, highly-prized attribute is that of virginity, which will be discussed below.

We thus have Muḥammad's personal legacy of contracting and remaining in non-procreative marriages standing in contrast to the statements attributed to him and to ʿUmar, father of the celebrated but childless Ḥafṣa, that disparage and forbid such marriages. These negative statements are frequently found in *adab al-nisā'* (etiquette or religious guidance pertaining to women) literature, but their legal potential never seems to have been exploited in the formulation of Sunnī family law. Instead, the *ḥadīth* most often cited in legal literature concerning infertility pertains to a sterile man:

> [Reported from] Ibn Sīrīn: ʿUmar b. al-Khaṭṭāb sent a man on a tax collecting mission, and he married a woman. But he was infertile (*ʿaqīm*), and when he was brought before ʿUmar

60 I have included the benediction here as there is some disagreement as to whether al-Ghazālī attributes this statement to ʿUmar or to Muḥammad himself. This formulation would indicate that the Prophet himself is meant, however the statement is elsewhere attributed to ʿUmar. It is possible that the benediction was inserted by a later copyist, rather than by al-Ghazālī himself.

61 See al-Ṭabarānī (d. 360/971), *al-Muʿjam al-kabīr* (Cairo: Maktabat Ibn Taymiyya, 1983), 19:416 and Ibn Ḥibbān (d. 354/965), *al-Majrūḥīn min al-muḥaddithīn* (Aleppo: Dār al-Waʿy, 1975), 2:111.

62 Al-Ghazālī, *Iḥyā ʿulūm al-dīn* (Cairo: Mu'assasat al-Ḥalabī, 1967), 2:26.

63 See Amāl Qarāmī, *al-Ikhtilāf fī al-thaqāfa al-ʿarabīya al-islāmīya* (Beirut: Dār al-Madār al-Islāmī, 2007), 37.

this was mentioned to him and he said. "Did you inform her that you are infertile?" He said, "No." ['Umar] said, "Then divorce her and inform her, then give her the choice."[64]

Although this *ḥadīth* is often cited in legal manuals, in discussions of laws pertaining to marital defects, it is usually immediately circumscribed or circumvented so as to limit or negate its impact, as will be explained later in this chapter.

In order to appreciate the significance of the radical divergence between Islamic law on the one hand, and the *adab al-nisā'* literature culled from these *ḥadīths* on the other hand, it is worth examining the consequences of infertility in other religions.

Infertility in the Islamic legal framework of sex and marriage, with comparisons to Christianity

In *Sex and Society in Islam: Birth Control Before the Nineteenth Century*, Basim Musallam began his study of Islamic attitudes toward contraception by highlighting the contrasts between Christian and Islamic premises regarding sexuality and its role in marriage. It would serve us well to reiterate these contrasts when considering attitudes toward infertility. Musallam noted the following elements of Islamic sexual morality: marriage could be polygynous, and legitimate sexual intercourse could be had not only with wives, but also with concubines. Marriage was not viewed as a necessarily permanent relationship because divorce was easy to obtain and could occur at any point. Finally, marital sexual intercourse was based on the right to sexual fulfilment; it needed no procreative justification, and therefore contraception and abortion were tolerated.[65]

Musallam contrasted these features of Islamic thought with Christianity's repressive approach to sexual intercourse, except as a prerequisite for reproduction, and Christianity's dedication to the idea of permanent, monogamous marriages. Looking at these same features with respect to infertility and marriage law, one can see that, in a Christian framework, one of the tragedies of childlessness was its seeming permanence and the remarkably few options that were available to a childless Christian couple, due to the restrictions on divorce and

---

64 The *ḥadīth* is found in a section on marriage to an impotent man, but the *ḥadīth* text is ambiguous as to whether this is so in the case in question. Logically, it is doubtful that the man is impotent because the issue seems to hinge upon the question of disclosure rather than consummation. Sa'īd b. Manṣūr (d. 227/843), *Sunan* (Bombay: Dār al-Salafiyya, 1982) 2:81= no: 2021.
65 B. Musallam, *Sex and Society in Islam: Birth Control Before the Nineteenth Century* (Cambridge: Cambridge University Press, 1983), 11.

remarriage.[66] In some cases the childless couple might be able to enter a religious order, or possibly remarry following the death of one of the spouses, or retroactively annul their marriage on the basis of either impediments or consanguinity, but otherwise they were unlikely to experience a change in their marital status. They could not hope to procreate with someone else or to leave a marriage that was marred by childlessness. Thus the late-7th-century East Syrian bishop of Fārs, Īšōʿbōkt, noted that many people think that the Christian ban on divorce is harsh, especially in cases where, "because of sterility or sickness ... a woman is unable to sleep with her husband, [and] he remains deprived of sons." Īšōʿbōkt acknowledged the sentiment but highlighted that the law's severity was at least egalitarian. For "when a man is taken hold by similar infirmities, a wife is compelled to bear this affliction."[67] Infertility thus accentuated the inherent rigidity of Christian concepts of marriage, as understood in most Christian communities.[68] By contrast, due to the very same factors that Musallam outlines, in Islamic societies much of the tragedy associated with childlessness was the very fluidity and precariousness of the childless woman's situation. Infertility highlighted the inherent flexibility, and hence uncertainty, embedded in Islamic marriages.

Two factors in Islamic family law played a particularly significant role in shaping the legal position of infertile couples: easily obtainable divorce and the acceptability of polygamy. Because infertility was acknowledged to have multiple potential causes, including sexual dissatisfaction and incompatibility (as will be seen in chapter four), spouses in childless marriages could hope that a different pairing would be more fruitful. The fact that husbands were legally able to divorce their wives for any or no cause, so long as they had the financial and social wherewithal to do so, meant that a childless wife could hope that her husband would divorce her. For then she would be free to marry someone else with whom she could conceive. A childless wife in that same situation, however,

66 There is a history of Catholics criticizing Middle Eastern Christians for practicing bigamy in order to obtain a child, in spite of their own religious precepts. For an example involving polygamy due to childlessness (after the death of an only child) see A. Jaussen, *Coutumes des Arabes au pays de Moab* (Paris: V. Lecoffre, 1908), 15 – 16. See also, J. P. Thompson, *Photographic Views of Egypt, Past and Present* (Boston: J. P. Jewett, 1856), 139.

67 L. Weitz, "Syriac Christians in the Medieval Islamic World: Law, Family, and Society," (Ph.D. Dissertation: Princeton University, 2013), 258. Cf. V. Garver, "Childbearing and Infancy in the Carolingian World," *Journal of the History of Sexuality* 21 (2012), 214.

68 Historians of the medieval Catholic church in Europe have noted that many of the restrictions on the dissolution of marriage became formalized and enforced in a process which began only in the eleventh century and continued through the thirteenth. R. M. Karras, *Sexuality in Medieval Europe: Doing Unto Others* (New York: Routledge, 2005), 62, 68.

could just as easily fear that her husband would divorce her and marry another woman, leaving his childless divorcée without long-term support.

The existence of the institution of polygamy similarly meant that a childless wife could hope that her husband would not divorce her, but would rather keep her and supplement her with a more fertile spouse.[69] In this way, polygamy could blunt the impact of the religious duty to produce children, for a man could hope to fulfil that requirement through some of his marriages and not through others.[70] This, of course, was true of the Prophet Muḥammad himself. Equally, a childless wife could fear that her husband would not set her free but would instead have her supplanted with a more fertile wife with whom she would be in (losing) competition.

In addition to divorce and polygamy – institutions explicitly enshrined in Islamic law – a third factor had a substantial role in defining the legal experience of infertile women in their marriages, which I will call the legal distaste for nebulousness. The Sunnī framework for marriage is marked by specific points in the timeline of a marriage. At the beginning of a marriage these include the transferal of the dower, the transferal of the bride to the groom's custody, and the act of consummation. At the dissolution of a marriage, defining points occur when a husband pronounces a formula of repudiation, when a wife renounces a debt owed her or returns a property to her husband, the death of the spouse, the menstrual cycles marking the *'idda* waiting period in which both spouses still have financial claims upon each other, and the end of the *'idda* when the ties between them have been severed. However, the realization that a marriage will likely not yield children does not occur as a legal assumption at any particular point in an Islamic marriage. Legal sources point this out frequently, particularly when citing the above-mentioned *ḥadīth* about the 'Umar's "sterile" tax-collector and denying that he could be labeled as such. By contrast, in the Rabbinic Jewish tradition, the ten-year anniversary of the marriage marks a point at which the marriage itself is considered sterile, and there are attendant legal consequences including, theoretically, legally-mandated divorce.[71]

69 See A. Bouhdiba, *La Sexualité en Islam*, 263. This is not to say that polygamy was the predominant form of marriage.

70 Muḥammad b. Muḥammad al-Ḥaṭṭāb, *Mawāhib al-jalīl* (Beirut: Dār al-Fikr, 1992), 3:404.

71 Mishna *Yevamot* 6:6, and Babylonian Talmud, *Yevamot*, 65b-66a. See J. Baskin, "Rabbinic Reflections on the Barren Wife," *Harvard Theological Review* 82 (1989), 101–14. This theoretical requirement was likely not often practiced as such. Cf. Yevamot 64a. However, there is some evidence that it could be brought to bear on practical matters when the wife wanted to obtain a divorce from a reluctant husband. A legal question was addressed to Hai Ben Sherira (939–1038), the gaon of the Yeshiva of Pumbedita in Iraq: "Regarding one who has lived with his

No medieval Islamic legal school has a binding test for either male or female fertility, and some medieval jurists note the particular difficulty of establishing the fertility of a sexually inexperienced woman.[72] For example, in commenting on the *ḥadīth*, "Marry amiable and fertile women," early Shīʿite writers explain that one predicts the fertility of a virgin based on the fertility of her kinswomen.[73] This is summarized in the *Jawāhir al-kalām:*

---

wife for ten years, which are not continuous, and who was intermittently in a different city and intermittently with her, and by whom she has not had children, is he obligated to divorce her when she asks for a divorce, and to give her her ketubba when she claims "[I want a child] to be a support for my hand and an axe to bury me"? Or does there need to be ten years in which he continuously lived in the same city with her?" Judeo-Arabic fragment in Friedman, *Jewish Polygyny in the Middle Ages*, 169 ff. The requirement is also cited in cases brought by medieval Jewish plaintiff husbands, who wanted to use it to override the clauses in their marriage contracts which stipulated that if they were marry a second wife, they would divorce the first and pay her the money due to her in her *ketubba* and to return her trousseau. These husbands wanted to either engage in bigamy or to divorce their wives without penalty. The argument was that the clause was invalid if it necessitated them violating the Biblical commandment to be fruitful and multiply. See, for example, Shimon b. Tsemah Duran (d. 1444 in Algiers), *Sefer ha-Tashbets* (Lemberg: Uri Ze'ev Salat, 1891), §94–95. In those places where the "Ban of Rabbenu Gershom," the 11th-century prohibition on both polygamy and unwanted divorce, was enforced there were medieval attempts to override it in cases of infertility. In response, the late 12th/early 13th-century German rabbi, Eliezer b. Yoel ha-Levi (Ravyah) wrote that Jewish communities no longer even promote divorce in cases of infertility, let alone use the commandment of being fruitful to override the polygamy ban. He notes that this is due in part to the prevalence of infertility: "We are not at liberty to waive the Ban of the illustrious Rabbenu Gershom, for there are so many unhealthy and barren women, yet no one opens his mouth to complain." Translation from E. Westreich, "Infertility as Ground for Polygamy in Jewish Law in Italy: Interaction among Legal Traditions at the time of the Renaissance," in *Olir – Osservatorio delle libertà ed istituzioni religiose* 2 (2003), 12.

72 ʿAbd al-Karīm Zaydān, *al-Mufaṣṣal fī aḥkām al-mar'a wa'l-bayt al-Muslim fī al-sharīʿa al-Islāmīya* (Beirut: Mu'assasat al-Risāla, 1994) 6:51.

73 There are many more shīʿī *ḥadīth*s attributed to both Muḥammad and ʿAlī disparaging marriage to infertile women, as well as providing advice on how to promote fertility. Interestingly, among the modern Druze community which banned polygamy a millennium ago but which does permit divorce, these *ḥadīth*s have formed the basis for some significant legal disagreements. A. Layish writes: ". . . the Druze Court of Beirut held that proven barrenness of the wife was a *sharʿī* ground for divorce, without the husband being liable (as to the financial consequences), on the strength of two religious-legal rules which provided that 'the supreme purpose of marriage is the production of offspring' and 'a barren wife should be avoided.' A majority of the Lebanese Druze Supreme Court of Appeal also held, in one case in which the wife's barrenness had been proved by medical documents, that the question of offspring was of great importance in a marriage; the husband might invoke barrenness as a ground for dissolution because he has a legitimate right to children 'for the preservation of the name and continuance of the memory [of the family] and the retention of the family property by the agnates in accordance with established tradition'; the court decided by a majority of votes that the husband

> It is said that the combination of [fertility] and virginity occurs in one who is not too young nor menopausal, and who has nothing in her temperament which indicates a tendency to barrenness, such as absence of menstruation. I say, the primary way of knowing whether a virgin is fertile is referring to [the reproductive history of] her kinswomen, her mothers and sisters.[74]

A similar concept of gauging the fertility of virgins based on their kinswomen is found in some late-medieval Sunnī sources such as the *Asnā al-maṭālib fī sharḥ Rawḍ al-ṭālib* and the *Kashshāf al-qinā'*, but none of these suggests that there exists a specific or formal means of implementing this concept.[75]

Marriage annulment due to infertility and genital defects

To what extent did Islamic legal theory acknowledge and privilege the desire for children as particularly important in a marriage? And to what extent did it treat the frustration of not being able to reproduce as any different from any other form of marital disappointment? We can begin to answer these questions by examining the sparse legal discussions of whether the prospect of childlessness due to a spouse's infertility can serve as a basis for either a husband or a wife to ask that their marriage be annulled, on the grounds that their spouse's infertility constitutes a defect that cheats the fertile spouse of a marital right. We can also examine legal discussions about injuries to a person's reproductive organs. Within these discussions are debates about whether the law allows someone to be designated as infertile, whether either spouse has a legal right to expect reproduction from a marriage, the sexual rights of spouses to each other and the extent to which those sexual rights can be disentangled from reproductive rights, and the extent to which the loss of one's own reproductive capacities con-

---

might divorce the wife without this being regarded as arbitrary repudiation entitling her to compensation. On the other hand, the minority of the court held that sterility of the wife (or husband) was not a secular or religious-legal ground for divorce because it did not constitute non-fulfilment of a marital duty the fulfilment of which depends on the will; in fact, in the particular case in question, the wife had done all she could: she had undergone prolonged medical treatment to become fertile." Layish, *Marriage, Divorce, and Succession in the Druze Family*, 205.

74 Al-Najafī (d. 1266/1855), *Jawāhir al-kalām fī sharḥ Sharā'i' al-Islām* (Beirut: Mu'assasat al-Murtaḍā al-'Ālamiyya, 1992), 10:360.

75 Zakarīyā ibn Muḥammad al-Anṣārī (d. 926/1520), *Asnā al-maṭālib fī sharḥ Rawḍ al-ṭālib* (Beirut: Dār al-Kutub al-'Ilmiyya, 2000), Chapter 14, no:263. Al-Bahūtī (d. 1051/1641), *Kashshāf al-qinā'* (Beirut: Dār al-Fikr, 1982) 5:9.

stitutes an injury and a harm deserving of a compensation over-and-above the loss of one's capacities for sexual intercourse and pleasure.

The concept of marital defects and annulment can only be understood in the context of the two far more common ways of ending a marriage in Islamic law. These means of dissolving a marriage are: *ṭalāq* (male-initiated repudiation) and *khul'* (in which the wife buys herself out of the marriage). Unlike in Christian ecclesiastical law, there was no Islamic legal case in which annulment was the only option a couple had for ending a marriage. In all cases a husband could legally choose to end a marriage via *ṭalāq* rather than annulment, since male-initiated divorce did not require any grounds whatsoever. And a wife could seek out a *khul'* arrangement to end her marriage, although her power was circumscribed to a greater extent than her husband's. Annulment was thus a lesser-used means of ending a marriage, one subset of which is known as *tafrīq lil-'ayb* (separation due to defect).[76] This form of annulment is significant for our purposes because medieval discussions about which defects ought to serve as grounds for annulment provide insights into what jurists believed were the minimum expectations of marriage, and sometimes these discussions suggest when legal understandings conflicted with other social or cultural expectations.

Annulment was established by the pronouncement of a judge, rather than the couple. While its use was not common, since it could be invoked in only very few circumstances, there were particular cases in which annulment had practical advantages over the more usual forms of divorce. Repudiation, *ṭalāq*, was a husband's privilege that had few intrinsic limits but did burden him with potentially heavy financial obligations. These included the support due to the wife during the *'idda* (the waiting period that follows a divorce, usually calculated as three menstrual periods), the repayment of the delayed, outstanding portion of the *mahr* (i.e. the dower paid by the groom to the bride as part of a marriage contract, often in an initial and a later installment) and, in some communities, the giving of a *mut'a*, a "divorce gift." However, if the marriage ended through *khul'* rather than *ṭalāq*, the wife, with her husband's consent, bought herself out of the marriage by either forfeiting the money the husband already owed her or otherwise compensating her husband. From a husband's perspective, a *khul'* divorce had some financial advantages and it is thought, for that reason, that *khul'* was a common form of marriage dissolution. The existence of this wife-initiated form of divorce was potentially empowering to a wife, but it also created a perverse incentive that could harm her. It could motivate a husband

76 Other grounds for annulment included the discovery that the marriage was illicit, e.g. due to incestuous kinship or to a wife's previous marriage having never properly ended.

not to offer *ṭalāq* even if the marriage was an unhappy one because, if the husband could pressure his wife into officially initiating the end of the marriage, he stood to save himself money.[77] Thus, while the costs of *ṭalāq* often served as a measure of protection against unwanted divorce, and *khul'* often served as a means for a woman to assert her independence, these factors also set up an opportunity for potential exploitation.[78] These concerns made annulment a potentially useful way to end the marriage. From the perspective of a husband, if he could obtain an annulment, he could potentially avoid paying for the maintenance of his former wife during the *'idda* waiting period that followed a divorce.[79] He could also avoid paying a divorce gift[80] and possibly (although not usually) he could also avoid paying the delayed portion of the *mahr*.[81] From

---

77 Rapoport, *Marriage, Money, and Divorce*, 72.

78 E.g. Ibn Rushd al-jadd was asked about a man who consummated marriage with his virgin wife and then, for the next eleven months, "harmed her" in a way which insults women, which Ibn Rushd understands to mean that he did not have sexual relations with her since the consummation. The wife "cannot stand him" and the man refuses to divorce her unless she gives him everything she owns. Ibn Rushd tells the court to warn the man that he has one year to have relations with his wife and if he does not by the end of that time, the court will end the marriage by decree and the wife will owe the husband nothing. Ibn Rushd, *Fatāwā Ibn Rushd*, 1:185. A similar form of extortion is mentioned in another *fatwā*, but in that case the wife capitulates to the demand and then sues afterward. Ibid., 2:952. Cf. al-Wansharīsī, *al-Mi'yār al-mu'rib*, 4:141. The Shāfi'ī jurist Ḥusayn ibn Muḥammad al-Marwarrūdhī (d. 462/1069) responds to a case where a woman whose husband never paid the *mahr* initiates a *khul'* divorce, paying a sum twice as much as the *mahr* to get out of the marriage. She then attempts to have the marriage retroactively annulled so as to recuperate the money she paid, but the jurist rules against her. See al-Marwarrūdhī, *Fatāwā al-qāḍī Ḥusayn ibn Muḥammad al-Marwarrūdhī* (Amman: Dār al-Fatḥ, 2010), 325. F. Zarinebaf-Shahr writing about Ḥanafī court cases in 17th-century Ottoman Istanbul writes that "often, in order to retain the *mehr*, men forced their wives to initiate divorce" and provides examples of ex-wives (successfully) attempting to retroactively sue for the exploitation. F. Zarinebaf-Shahr, "Women, Law, and Imperial Justice in Ottoman Istanbul in the Late Seventeenth Century" in *Women, the Family, and Divorce Laws in Islamic History*, ed. Amira El Azhary Sonbol (Syracuse: Syracuse University Press, 1996), 92.

79 Al-Haytamī, *Tuḥfat al-muḥtāj fī sharḥ al-minhāj* in *Ḥawāshī al-Sharawānī wa-Ibn-Qāsim al-'Abbādī 'alā tuḥfat al-muḥtāj bi-sharḥ al-minhāj li-Ibn Ḥajar al-Haytamī* (Beirut: Dār Iḥyā' al-Turāth al-'Arabī, 1988), 8:229.

80 *Mut'a*. This was not always a practical component of Islamic divorce. See Y. Rapoport, "Matrimonial Gifts in Early Islamic Egypt," *Islamic Law and Society* 7.1 (2000), 18–21 and D. Little, "A Fourteenth-Century Jerusalem Court Record of a Divorce Hearing: A Case Study" in *Mamluks and Ottomans: Studies in Honour of Michael Winter*, ed. D.J. Wasserstein and A. Ayalon (London: Routledge, 2006), 66–85.

81 Consider, for example, the above-mentioned case from the Druze Court of Beirut in Layish, *Marriage, Divorce and Succession in the Druze Family*, 205. See also Ibn Ḥazm, *al-Muḥalla* (Cairo: Idārat al-Ṭibā'a al-Munīriyya, 1928), 10:112–114, which discusses partial restitution of the *ṣadāq*

the perspective of a wife seeking to end her marriage, a key advantage of an annulment over other types of marriage dissolution was that she could use it to circumvent a husband who was reluctant to set her free, or who was trying to pressure her into a financially exploitative *khul'* divorce.[82]

Jurists identified only a few defects which could serve as legitimate grounds for annulment. Some jurists drew an analogy between marriage contracts and sales contracts and argued that the same (or similar) circumstances that would nullify a sale would also nullify a marriage. Others maintained that only those specific circumstances mentioned in *ḥadīth*s about marriage annulment could justify such a step. However, regardless of which avenue the jurists pursued, there was a marked tendency to limit the extent to which spousal defects could serve as grounds for annulment. This tendency is remarked upon by the Cordoban jurist and philosopher Ibn Rushd (d. 595/1198) who explained that while contracts of sale and contracts of marriage are similar up until the point of the consummation of the marriage, there are significant differences when defects are found after consummation. Moreover, he wrote, whereas in a sale any defect may be grounds to rescind the contract, there exists a "unanimity of the Muslims on the point that not every defect can lead to the nullification of marriage."[83] The physical and physiological defects most commonly recognized as grounds for annulment were leprosy, elephantiasis, insanity and, most importantly for our purposes, missing or abnormal genital organs.

In the premodern period almost all Sunnī legal discussions of whether infertility is a defect – one which constitutes grounds for the non-sterile spouse to have the marriage nullified – have a uniform conclusion that extends across the legal schools: female infertility is *not* considered to be such a condition.[84] There is slightly more debate as to whether that is true for infertile husbands married to potentially fertile wives, with Ibn Taymiyya (d. 728/1328) representing

to the husband. The 5th/11th-century Shāfiʿī jurist al-Marwarrūdhī rules that under particular circumstances the husband would not pay the *mahr.* Al-Marwarrūdhī, *Fatāwā*, 323.

82 The Mālikī treatise *al-Nawādir wa'l-ziyādāt* includes a chapter on husbands who become aware of a defect in their ex-wives following a *ṭalāq* divorce and attempt to retroactively convert it into an annulment, and on wives who become aware of a defect in their ex-husbands following a *khul'* divorce and attempt to do the same thing. Ibn Abī Zayd al-Qayrawānī, *Kitāb al-Nawādir wa'l-ziyādāt* 4:36.

83 Ibn Rushd, *Bidāyat al-mujtahid* (Cairo: Dār al-Salām, 1995), 3:1348. Translation from Imran Ahsan Khan Nyazee, *The Distinguished Jurist's Primer: A Translation of Bidāyat Al-Mujtahid* (Reading: Garnet, 2000), 2:59.

84 al-Buhūtī, *Sharḥ muntahā al-irādāt* (Beirut: Dār ʿĀlam al-Kutub, 1993), 2:678.

the minority medieval opinion that a woman may have a legal right to procreative sex.[85]

Statements in favor of permitting *khiyār* (spouse's choice to pursue annulment) in cases of infertility

Arguments in favor of including infertility among the list of defects permitting a spouse to exercise the choice (*khiyār*) to have the marriage annulled are quite rare in Sunnī legal literature. The above-mentioned instruction from 'Umar b. al-Khaṭṭāb to the sterile man to "inform her, then give her the choice" is widely cited, but it is then almost uniformly circumvented using the argument that it is impossible to determine with certainty that a man really is sterile. Among the exceptions to this rule is Ḥasan al-Baṣrī (d. 110/728), who is reported to have held the view that infertility in either spouse is grounds for annulment if the non-infertile spouse so desires. His opinion is cited by the Ḥanbalī jurist Ibn Qudāma (d. 620/1223) as follows, "If one [spouse] has found the other to be sterile, [the non-sterile spouse] is given the choice."[86]

The Shāfi'ī jurist al-Māwardī (d. 450/1058) states that there is an opinion within the school that a woman has a right to *khiyār* in the case of a husband who is able to have intercourse, but who lacks testicles, "because he is missing something without which there cannot be offspring."[87] While it is common among jurists to view genital defects as a legitimate reason for annulment on the grounds that such defects interfere with sexual intercourse, al-Māwardī's phrasing, which emphasizes offspring rather than intercourse, is unusual.

Ibn Taymiyya makes a novel argument for considering infertility, at least male infertility, as grounds for annulment. Rather than rooting the argument in definitions of defect, he draws a legal analogy between sterility and contraception: "If a husband is proven to be sterile, we rule by analogy that the woman has [the right of] choice, since she has a right to a child. It is for this reason that we say one cannot practice coitus interruptus with a free woman with-

---

85 This generalization about the literature is also confirmed in Vardit Rispler-Chaim, "Ḥasan Murād Mannā: Childbearing and the Rights of a Wife," 95–6. However, in 1995, a Saudi muftī, citing 'Umar's statement about the '*aqīm*, ruled that the wife of an infertile man could have her marriage annulled on the grounds that women marry for the purpose of having children. V. Rispler-Chaim, *Disability in Islamic Law* (Dordrecht: Springer, 2010), 61.

86 Ibn Qudāma, *al-Mughnī*, 10:59.

87 al-Māwardī, *Kitāb al-ḥāwī al-kabīr* (Beirut: Dar al-Kutub al-'Ilmiyya, 1999) 9:340.

out her permission."[88] Ibn Taymiyya's argument is based on the premise that there is a consensus (within the Ḥanbalī school) that it is not permitted for a man to practice coitus interruptus without his wife's consent. Building upon this premise, he argues that the reason that unilateral coitus interruptus is not permitted is because a free woman has a right to a child, and contraception would violate that right. Since a husband's sterility would also violate that right, logically it too may not be imposed upon a wife without her consent. Ibn Taymiyya's argument is not unproblematic; other jurists who also believe that a man has to obtain his wife's consent before practicing withdrawal argue that the legal right being violated is her right "that he ejaculate in her when having sexual relations with her,"[89] but that is a right to sexual fulfilment rather than a right to procreative sex. Ibn Taymiyya's understanding of the legal rights underlying the laws of consent and coitus interruptus is unusual but not unique. It is also found in the writing of the Ḥanafī jurist al-Kāsānī. The latter says that it is disliked for coitus interruptus to be practiced without the woman's consent, "because sex culminating in ejaculation is the way of getting a child, and she has a right to a child."[90] Within Ibn Taymiyya's own school, Ibn Qudāma agrees with him with regard to contraception though not with regard to actual sterility. I.e. a wife has a right to demand procreative sex rather than coitus interruptus, because she may want a child, but he does not extend that logic so as to support the notion that a wife may demand an annulment of her marriage to a sterile man.

Ibn Qayyim al-Jawziyya, Ibn Taymiyya's disciple, provides a long and detailed list of defects which are grounds for *khiyār* and that list does not explicitly include infertility. However, he makes an unusual argument that could be read as implicitly in favor of viewing infertility as a defect. After concluding his list he writes:

> It is preposterous to limit defects to two, six, seven, or eight to the exclusion of those which are inferred from them or are equivalent to them, such as the blind, the mute, the deaf and the woman whose hands and legs have been amputated either one or both. . . . The Commander of the Faithful, 'Umar b. al-Khaṭṭāb, told someone who had married a woman despite not being able to sire children: "Inform her that you are sterile and give her the choice." What would he ['Umar] say about defects which for her are complete, rather than partial? The analogy is this: that for every defect which repels the other spouse – and as a result of which mercy and benevolence, which are goals of marriage, cannot be

88 Ibn Taymiyya, *Fatāwā al-kubrā*, 5:464.
89 Aḥmad b. Muḥammad al-Ṭahāwī, *Sharḥ maʿānī al-āthār* (Beirut: ʿĀlam al-Kutub, 1994), 2:30 – 31.
90 Al-Kāsānī, *Badāʾiʿ al-ṣanāʾiʿ* (Beirut: Dār al-Kutub al-'Ilmiyya, 1986), 2:334.

> attained – *khiyār* is mandated. This is inferred from [the law of] sales, just as the conditions which are stipulated in marriages are based on the fulfilment of the conditions of sales. God and His Prophet did not subject one who is misled and deceived to the one who misled and deceived them.[91]

Ibn al-Qayyim seems to be using the example of male sterility as the initial premise in an *a minori ad maius* argument, i.e. if ʿUmar mandates *khiyār* in the case of sterility which is a "partial" defect, all the more so must *khiyār* be mandated in cases of a "complete" defect, such as blindness, muteness, etc. However, nowhere does he explicitly state or prove the initial "minor" premise implied here; he does not include sterility in the formal list of defects which have scriptural standing. Instead, he argues that there are many defects in addition to scriptural ones which could contravene the goals of marriage and thus may serve as grounds for annulment, and sterility falls into at least one those categories.

Objections to including infertility among the grounds for annulment

There are three different, frequently mentioned objections to including infertility as grounds for annulment: first, the (disputable) claim that it is not mentioned in any revealed text (*naṣṣ*) as grounds for annulment, and only those specifically revealed grounds are acceptable. Second, that logically the only acceptable grounds for annulment are ones that bar sexual intercourse and infertility does not do that. And third, that it is impossible to know for certain whether someone is sterile and so no one, particularly no man, can be labeled as such.

Ḥanbalī views

Of all the legal schools, the Ḥanbalīs permit marriage nullification for the most diverse set of reasons. They grant the choice to pursue annulment to both husbands and wives of spouses who suffer from insanity, leprosy, and elephantiasis; to wives of impotent[92] or castrated men or those without functioning testicles;[93]

91 Ibn Qayyim al-Jawziyya, *Zād al-maʿād*, 5:182.

92 There is some disagreement among Ḥanbalīs regarding the man who is able to consummate the marriage once but then becomes impotent, see Spectorsky, *Chapters on Marriage and Divorce*, 113. The two opinions are either that the wife has no grounds to annul the marriage, or that the husband is given one year to prove himself able to have intercourse. If he does not have sexual intercourse in that time, there appears to be a judicially mandated *ṭalāq:* the wife is given the full dower and must then begin her *ʿidda* period.

and to husbands of women who suffer from *'afl*, *qarn*, *fatq*, or *baḥr*, which refer to abnormalities of the female genitals.[94] Such genital abnormalities will be addressed later in this chapter. Ibn Qayyim al-Jawziyya describes the contrast between the schools of law thus:

> Dāwūd (d. 270/884), Ibn Ḥazm (d. 456/1064), and those who agree with them say that there is no nullification at all.[95] Abū Ḥanīfa says that there is no nullification except for castration and impotence. Al-Shāfi'ī and Mālik say: insanity, leprosy, elephantiasis,[96] vaginal blockage, castration, and impotence are bases for annulment. Imām Aḥmad [ibn Ḥanbal] added to [al-Shāfi'ī and Mālik's grounds for annulment]: also if the woman has been ruptured such that [the flesh] between the two orifices has been torn. According to his colleagues: also if there is a putrescence of the vagina and the mouth,[97] or if the openings for urine and semen in the vagina have been torn, or if there is an oozing wound in them, as well as hemorrhoids and fistulae. [They also include the conditions of] *istiḥāḍa* (constant menstruation), leaking of urine and such, lack of testicles, tuberculosis of the testicles, and *waj'*, i.e. one whose testicles are crushed, and if either [spouse] is a *khuntha* (intersex) in appearance.[98]

In the Ḥanbalī school, this list of defects is arrived at through the logic of sales/returns and the logic of the goals of marriage, rather than being understood simply as a matter of divine decree.[99] As to whether this list is an exhaustive one, there exists a difference of opinion between Ibn Qayyim al-Jawziyya and Ibn Taymiyya on the one side, and Ibn Qudāma on the other. Ibn al-Qayyim argues that these grounds for annulment are examples illustrating a general principle that, when the purpose of marriage is itself thwarted, the non-defective spouse may choose to end the marriage through annulment. Thus, in his view, there could be grounds beyond these examples. By contrast, Ibn Qudāma uses the same

---

93 Manṣūr b. Yūnus al-Buhūtī, *Sharḥ muntahā al-irādāt*, 2:676.
94 Ibn Qudāma, *al-Mughnī*, 6:651 and al-Buhūtī, *Sharḥ muntahā al-irādāt*, 3:86.
95 These jurists are associated with the Ẓāhirī school of Islamic law. Ibn Qayyim al-Jawziyya quotes Ibn Ḥazm's tongue-in-cheek argument that if the marriage contract describes the wife as healthy, and she is found to have any medical problem whatsoever, including infertility, he has technically not married her at all but rather some theoretically healthy person. He does not have the option of remaining married or dissolving the marriage because they are not spouses. Ibn Ḥazm, *al-Muḥallā* (Beirut: Maktab al-tijārī lil-tibā'a, 1969) 1:115.
96 See Rispler-Chaim, *Disability in Islamic Law*, 64, and R. Shaham. *The Expert Witness in Islamic Courts* (Chicago: University of Chicago Press, 2010), 42.
97 There seems to be some disagreement in the commentary tradition as to whether this is the literal mouth or the vaginal orifice or both.
98 Ibn Qayyim al-Jawziyya, *Zād al-ma'ād*, 5:165.
99 This is the argument in the *Mughnī*, in the *Zād al-ma'ād*, and *Sharḥ muntahā al-irādāt*.

starting point (that the above-listed defects are based on the logic of threats to the purpose of marriage) to come to the opposite conclusion:

> Any defect outside of these does not thwart the purpose of the marriage bond, which is sexual intercourse, as opposed to the various defects which are included in these. If one was to say, "leprosy and skin lesions do not thwart sexual intercourse," we would say: "in fact it does thwart it, because it produces an aversion which altogether prevents him from approaching, for he fears that he and his offspring will contract it." So too, one is afraid of an attack from a madman, and that serves as a palpable barrier [to intercourse].[100]

Ibn Qudāma's argument assumes that the purpose of marriage is sexual intercourse, and that all the canonical grounds listed for *khiyār* are in fact related to the ability to engage to intercourse. In Ibn Qudāma's view, there is no other purpose of marriage which, if thwarted, could be addressed through annulment. Since infertile people may still engage in sexual intercourse, infertility cannot be considered to be among the conditions that thwart the purpose of marriage and thus cannot serve as the basis for annulment.

In a similar vein, al-Buhūtī (d. 1051/1641) argues that infertility should be rejected from the list of legal defects because it does not preclude sexual enjoyment. He writes:

> Regarding defects other than those previously mentioned, none of these are grounds for either one of the spouses to exercise *khiyār*. For example, one-eyedness, lameness, lacking a hand or a foot, blindness, muteness, deafness, baldness, or one of them being infertile or menopausal [none of these may serve as grounds for nullification] . . . because none of these prevent sexual pleasure or threaten to infect [the other spouse].[101]

A different objection raised within the Ḥanbalī school against infertility being included among grounds for nullifying a marriage is that it is impossible to prove for certain that someone is infertile. In spite of the tradition in which 'Umar instructs a sterile man to divorce his wife and give her the choice of whether or not to re-enter the marriage, Ibn Qudāma says that it is impossible to categorically state that someone will never produce children.

> We do not know of any scholar who disagrees with [the view that infertility should not count] other than Ḥasan [al-Baṣrī] who said, "If one found the other to be infertile, they give them a choice." Aḥmad [Ibn Ḥanbal] tended to explain his words saying, "Perhaps his wife would like a child." But this is at the beginning of the marriage, so on what basis could it be nullified when [infertility] itself cannot be proven? One might prove it

100 Ibn Qudāma, *al-Mughnī*, 10:56.
101 al-Buhūtī, *Sharḥ muntahā al-irādāt*, 2:678.

> on the basis of menopause but, on the other hand, it is known that there are men who do not produce offspring when they are young, but then have offspring when they are old.[102]

In summary, there is a minority opinion within the Ḥanbalī school that a diagnosis of infertility, or at least male infertility, can serve as grounds for annulling marriage. However, the majority view is that infertility in either husbands or wives cannot be used in this way. However, among those espousing such a view, there is a disagreement as to whether infertility is excluded on the grounds that it is irrelevant since it does not preclude engaging in sexual relations, or whether it is excluded because one cannot actually label a spouse as infertile in the first place.

Ḥanafī views

Of the four main Sunnī legal schools, the Ḥanafī one has the most restricted definition of marital defects. Ḥanafī discussions of *'ayb* (defect) and *faskh* (nullification) are unique in that a wife's defects are *never* grounds for nullification. Instead, a husband has only one option for ending his marriage: traditional divorce. A wife, by contrast, may be able to have her marriage annulled if her husband is defective. However, a husband's defectiveness is determined solely on the basis of whether he has ever succeeded in penetrating his wife anytime during the marriage. No other aspects of his physical or mental state enter into the matter. The position is summarized by al-Kāsānī (d. 587/1191).

> With regard to the circumstances in which [a wife is entitled to] a choice [to have her marriage nullified]: the first and foremost consideration is whether he has had intercourse with this woman in this marriage. To such an extent is this the case that, if he had intercourse with her only once, then the choice to exercise that right has been passed up and no longer exists.[103]

If the husband lacks a penis, the nullification can take place immediately. If a woman claims that her husband is impotent, the husband may have up to one year to attempt to penetrate his wife after the complaint is brought to the court's attention.[104] If a woman finds herself married to a man whose testicles have been

---

102 Ibn Qudāma, *al-Mughnī*, 10:59–60.

103 Al-Kāsānī, *Badā'i' al-ṣanā'i'*, 2:325. Zaydān, *al-Mufaṣṣal fī aḥkām al-mar'a wa'l-bayt al-Muslim fī al-sharī'a al-Islāmiyya*, 9:24.

104 In *al-Fatāwā al-sirājiyya* the text specifies that this is a lunar year, eleven days shorter than a solar year. al-Ūshī, Sirāj al-Dīn Abū Muḥammad 'Alī ibn 'Uthmān, *al-Fatāwā al-sirājiyya* (Lenasia, South Africa: Dār al-'ulūm Zakariyyā, 2011), 205.

severed but who retains a penis (*khaṣiyy*) the case is treated as one of impotence, on the grounds that such a man may yet achieve an erection and penetrate his wife. This last scenario is significant because it allows us to differentiate between sterility and impotence. The man without functioning testicles is (in the jurists' view) necessarily permanently sterile but not necessarily permanently impotent. If he is able to overcome his impotence and penetrate his wife, he possesses no legal defect. The fact that he is still sterile has no legal consequence.

Even though Ḥanafī jurists often rule that a wife has a right to insist upon sex that is not curtailed by coitus interruptus, they do not make the argument that she has a right procreation. Usually, it appears that jurists understand "her right to obligate him to ejaculate into her"[105] as a right to intercourse itself, nothing more. Al-Kāsānī, by contrast argues that a wife's rights are not limited to sex. She has a right to the kind of sex that would allow her to conceive. "It is disliked for a husband to engage in *'azl* (coitus interruptus) with his free wife without her consent, because sex culminating in ejaculation is the way of getting a child, and she has a right to a child. With *'azl*, the [conception of a] child is thwarted and therefore her right is thwarted."[106] However, even if her husband ignores her prerogatives by practicing non-procreative sex, his behavior is categorized as either permitted or disliked – it is not forbidden and it certainly does not serve as grounds for nullifying a marriage. Moreover, al-Kāsānī never takes the next logical step Ibn Taymiyya articulates; that is to say, he does not argue that a woman may choose to request an annulment of a marriage to a sterile husband.

Shāfi'ī views

Al-Shāfi'ī argues that a man cannot know for certain that he is sterile. He therefore denies that the frequently-mentioned case of the sterile man being ordered to give his wife a means to exit the marriage has any practical application.

> If he married her and said, 'I am infertile,' or he said nothing about it until the contract had been completed and then he acknowledged it, she would still not have a choice. That is because he himself cannot know that he is infertile until he dies, because a man may be slow to have a child when he is young and yet he will have progeny when he is old. She does not have a right to choose on the basis of progeny. This is because the right to choose is reserved for loss of the ability to have sex, not the loss of the ability to have progeny."[107]

---

105 Al-Ṭahāwī, *Sharḥ ma'ānī al-āthār*, 3:30–31.
106 Al-Kāsānī, *Badā'i' al-ṣanā'i'* 2:334.
107 Al-Shāfi'ī, *Kitāb al-umm* (Beirut: Dār al-Ma'rifa, 1990), 5:43.

This view that one cannot consider infertility as a defect because one can never be sure that it will not eventually be overcome is echoed by subsequent Shāfiʿī jurists such as al-Māwardī, who explicitly extends the argument to the reverse case, when it is the wife who is accused of infertility. Al-Māwardī articulates this position in the context of a discussion about a wife who suffers from *ifḍāʾ*, a rupture in the genitals which can cause infertility. He writes regarding this injury: "Because he can have complete intercourse – even if she is infertile and cannot have offspring, or even if he, the husband, is sterile and cannot beget children – there is no *khiyār* for either one of them because this [sterility] is speculative, and perhaps it will end."[108] The same conclusion, that neither rupture nor infertility constitutes grounds for annulment, is also articulated by al-Nawawī.[109]

While this idea that infertility is not a defect because it cannot be proven is repeated frequently, Shāfiʿīs also refute the claim that a woman has a right to offspring. This is consistent with the *madhhab*'s view of a husband's decision to engage in coitus interruptus without the wife's permission.[110] With the exception of al-Shīrāzī (d. 476/1083), the Shāfiʿīs permit a husband to engage in this contraceptive practice regardless of his wife's consent, because she has a right to sexual intercourse, not to progeny.

Mālikī views

The majority Mālikī position regarding what constitutes grounds for annulment is similar to the Ḥanbalī one, with some minor distinctions with respect to specific kinds of defects, such as leprosy and forms of male castration.[111] There is, however, some disagreement as to whether a woman can ever exercise *khiyār* after the consummation of a marriage. The topic of female infertility specifically is barely considered in Mālikī texts. In Ibn Abī Zayd al-Qayrawānī's (d. 386/996) *al-Nawādir wa'l-ziyādāt*, the matter is dispensed with in one sentence: "As for one who is deceived by an infertile woman who cannot give birth, or a woman who is deceived by a sterile man, neither one of them has a [legal] argu-

108 Al-Māwardī, *Al-Ḥāwī*, 9:341.

109 Al-Nawawī, *Rawḍat al-ṭālibīn wa-ʿumdat al-muftīyīn* (Beirut: al-Maktab al-Islāmī, 1991), 7:178.

110 Al-Nawawī (d. 676/1227), exceptionally, disapproves of *ʿazl* even with a wife's consent. Abdel Rahim Omran, *Family Planning in the Legacy of Islam* (Routledge: New York, 1992), 159 ff.

111 Khalīl ibn Isḥāq al-Jundī, *Mukhtaṣar* (Cairo: Dār al-Ḥadīth, 2005), 1:102 and al-Qarāfī, *al-Dhakhīra* (Beirut: Dār al-Gharb al-Islāmī, 1994), 4:419 – 20.

ment."[112] Male infertility receives slightly more attention elsewhere. In the *Mawāhib al-jalīl*, in the context of a discussion of men's responsibilities when seeking a spouse, the Libyan jurist al-Ḥaṭṭāb (d. 954/1547) writes about the extent to which a prospective husband has an obligation to disclose to his prospective spouse his own proclivities toward asceticism with respect to fasting and to sex, especially if fasting leads to diminished sexual capacities or to a diminished ability to earn a living. Turning specifically to the question of procreation, al-Ḥaṭṭāb writes that a man ought to disclose in advance that he will not or cannot engage in marital sexual relations, but he has no responsibility of disclosure if he simply believes himself to be infertile. The first two situations, i.e. sexual asceticism and diminished earning capacity, are deemed to be harmful to the wife and to jeopardize their marriage, but the prospect of childlessness is not so deemed.[113]

Genital defects, "female impotence," and their relation to infertility

We have seen that while the jurists consider the possibility that a person might wish to annul their marriage to an infertile spouse, for the most part they ultimately reject the legality of doing so. However, with the exception of the Ḥanafīs (who reject altogether the notion of husbands annulling marriages on the basis of defects) most jurists do recognize a category of legal defect which is related to female infertility. They recognize defects to women's sexual and reproductive organs as constituting grounds for annulment.

Such defects are described using the following vocabulary:

a) *ʿafl:* A piece of flesh inside the vagina, resembling a man's scrotal hernia. This may correspond to the biomedical diagnosis of a vaginal prolapse.
b) *qarn:* A tissue or bone that blocks the vagina. This may correspond to the biomedical diagnosis of a vaginal septum.
c) *ratq:* Usually this is described as a piece of flesh partially or fully blocking the opening of the vagina, thereby rendering it so narrow that a penis can penetrate only with difficulty or not at all. This seems to correspond to the biomedical diagnosis of an imperforate hymen. It is also sometimes described as a piece of flesh within the cervix which partially or fully blocks

112 al-Qayrawānī, *al-Nawādir wa'l-ziyādāt*, 532.
113 al-Ḥaṭṭāb, *Mawāhib al-jalīl* 3:404.

off the uterus. This growth within the cervix may correspond to a number of modern biomedical diagnoses.[114]

d) *ifḍā'* or *fatq:* Rupture. This is described in the legal literature as a hole or fistula in the flesh dividing two organs, either the vagina and the rectum, or the vagina and the bladder, such that they are no longer completely separated.

The first three female sexual defects are all treated in the legal literature as being similar. Ibn Qudāma suggests that *'afl, qarn,* and *ratq* be understood as nearly synonymous.[115] They all refer to a vaginal passage too narrow for normal forms of sexual intercourse due to some blockage. From a medieval standpoint, unlike the male sexual defects (castration and impotence), all four of these female "defects" are adjacent to the traits considered to be desirable in women. The intact hymen is itself understood as an obstruction and as the very symbol of virginity. Similarly, in medieval dictionaries, *afḍā* means both to deflower a virgin and to "make the woman's two orifices [the rectum and the vagina] one."[116] According to some Egyptian jurists, *ratq* was also known as a potential complication associated with female circumcision, a ritual which those jurists generally viewed in a positive light and which was often performed when a girl was on the cusp of marriage.[117] For example, the Cairene Mālikī jurist al-Qarāfī (d. 684/1285) cites the Sicilian jurist Ibn Yūnus (d. 451/1061), citing the Alexandrian jurist Muḥammad ibn al-Mawwāz (d. 281/894), discussing marriage annulment in cases "where the imperforate hymen is caused by circumcision" (*al-ratq min al-khitān*).[118]

In Arabo-Galenic medical literature, all of the first three conditions were thought to be curable, unlike the non-sexual medical defects that were grounds for annulment, such as insanity or leprosy.[119] For example, the 4th/10th-century

114 al-Rāzī, *al-Ḥāwī fī al-ṭibb* (Beirut: Dar al-Kutub al-'Ilmiyya, 2000) vol. 3, book 9:16.

115 Ibn Qudāma, *Mughnī*, 10:56.

116 Lane, *Arabic-English Lexicon*, s.v. *f-ḍ-ā*. Cf. Al-Fayyūmī, *Al-Miṣbāḥ al-munīr fī Gharīb al-Sharḥ al-kabīr*, s.v. *f-ḍ-ā*. Al-Fayyūmī states that it can also refer to a rupture which unifies the vagina with the urethra.

117 J. Berkey, "Circumcision Circumscribed: Female Excision and Cultural Accommodation in the Medieval near East, *International Journal of Middle East Studies* 28. 1 (1996), 30.

118 Al-Qarāfī, *al-Dhakhīra*, 4:421. Also cited in Ibn Abī Zayd al-Qayrawānī, *Kitāb al-Nawādir wa'l-ziyādāt*, 4:529. Some modern medical journals have also noted that female circumcision can cause imperforate hymen as well as making it more difficult to identify and more dangerous to treat. E.g. M. Alsammani, "Imperforate Hymen Complicated with Genital Mutilation: A Case Report," *Journal of Clinical Case Reports*, 2 (2012), 107.

119 The *Mukhtaṣar Khalīl* also mentions this, but does not seem to attach any significant legal consequence to this fact. Khalīl ibn Isḥaq al-Jundī, *Mukhtaṣar*, 1:103. The relative ease or difficul-

Andalusian physician and surgeon al-Zahrāwī describes *ratq* as potentially causing retention of the menses or making intercourse, conception, and delivery difficult, and then he details methods for curing it. Al-Rāzī, writing in 3rd/9th-century Iraq and Iran, describes much the same thing. Such well-known authorities as Galen, Celsus, Paul of Aegina, al-Majūsī and Ibn Sīnā all wrote on the subject.[120] To cure *ratq*, writes al-Zahrāwī, one should instruct a midwife to break through the barrier using either a probe or her fingers or, in extreme cases, a scalpel. Al-Rāzī suggests the physician use a probe.

Unfortunately, this procedure could very well cause the fourth genital defect which, in some schools, could serve as grounds for annulment. This defect is known as *ifḍā'* or *fatq*, rupture. Outside of legal literature, both terms have a broad spectrum of meaning, with *fatq* also including non-feminine-specific medical conditions such as hernias, and *ifḍā'* also referring to the defloration of a virgin.[121] However, both the terms *ifḍā'* and *fatq*, when used in legal discussions of marital defects and injuries, seem to be used interchangeably and refer not to defloration, but to severe injury, usually in the context of rape or early marriage. For example, the Ḥanbalī jurist Ibn Qudāma glosses the word *fatq* saying:

---

ty of treating each of these conditions is discussed by Muḥammad ibn ʿAbd al-Bāqī al-Zurqāni (d. 1099/1710) in his commentary on the *Mukhtaṣar*. Al-Zurqāni, *Sharḥ al-Zurqānī ʿalá Mukhtaṣar Sayyidī Khalīl* (Beirut: Dār al-Kutub al-ʿIlmiyya, 2002), 3:421.

120 M. S. Spink and G. L. Lewis, *Albucasis on Surgery and Instruments* (Berkeley: University of California Press, 1973), 458–59. In Ibn Sīnā, *Qānūn fī al-ṭibb* (Būlāq: al-Maṭbaʿa al-Āmira, 1878) 2:594 = *kitāb* III: *fann* 21: *maqāla* 4: *faṣl fī al-rutqā'*. Al-Rāzī, *al-Ḥāwī fī al-ṭibb* vol. 3, bk. 9:16. The Mālikī jurist Asbagh ibn al-Faraj in Ṣaʿīd (d. 225/840), also mentions the possibility of curing the *ratq*. Cited in al-Qayrawānī, *Kitāb al-nawādir wa'l-ziyādāt*, 4:529. There it mentions the treatment taking anywhere between several months and up to a year. Cf. al-Majusī, *Kāmil*, 488.

121 In medical literature, *futuq* can refer to a variety of injuries in which the muscular wall of a bodily cavity is split or perforated or compromised, such that something outside protrudes through it, e.g. a hernia. It can also mean something that was closed or narrow and has been split open. For example, when clouds in the sky are parted or split asunder so that the sun shines through. With regard to a woman, the *Lisān al-ʿarab* defines *fatqā'* as "a woman with a widened vagina, the opposite of a *ratqā'*." But the same dictionary also includes the definition that appears in legal literature a that is: *fatqā'* "a woman whose two exits [vagina and rectum] have become one." *Ifḍā'* too seems to have a wider spectrum of meaning outside legal writings, including defloration of a virgin. The definition in the *Lisān al-ʿarab* that corresponds to medieval legal usage is this: "A woman who is *mufḍā:* one whose two exits have become connected . . . as a result of coitus."

> He said, regarding one who has sexual relations with his minor wife[122] and ruptures her, he owes one-third of the *diyya*. [I.e. he must pay one third of the sum he would pay for manslaughter.]
>
> Meaning of *fatq* (rupture): a perforation of [the barrier] between the passages for urine and semen. And it is also said: instead, it means a perforation of [the barrier] between the vagina and rectum. But that [second definition] is unlikely, because it is unlikely that the wall between the two spaces would be eliminated through sex, for this wall is strong and tough.[123]

The term *ifḍā'* when used in *ḥadīth* and legal literature with reference to compensation for injury or genital defects also seems to refer to a similarly severe condition with disastrous repercussions.[124] In an early *ḥadīth* collection the injury is described as one that may result in an inability to maintain a pregnancy or retain urinary and fecal continence.

> Zayd b. Thābit said, "Regarding a woman whose husband ruptured her: If fertility and both forms of continence are retained, a third of the *diyya* [is owed] for it. If fertility and both forms of continence are not retained, a full *diyya* [is owed] for it.[125]

The full *diyya*, or "bloodwit," refers to the amount of compensation owed to a victim's family in case of manslaughter. Compensation for non-fatal injuries is calculated as a fraction of the *diyya* and is paid to the living victim.

> Regarding a man who was spurned by a woman. He then ruptured her. 'Umar imposed the *ḥadd* punishment upon him and [further] penalized him with a sum of one third of her *diyya*.[126]

---

122 Medieval Islamic legal sources mention the dangers of intercourse, but not of childbirth, for young brides. By contrast, Jewish law in the late antique and medieval period seems to take into account the dangers of birth, but not of intercourse, for young brides. Hence it mandates the use of contraceptives for intercourse (but not abstinence) with girls. B.T. Yevamot 12b. Some Ḥanafī jurists also mention the concern that women given in marriage be robust enough to "tolerate the pain of circumcision," e. g. Ibn Nujaym (d. 970/1563) in his *Baḥr al-ra'īq* and Maḥmūd ibn Aḥmad al-Marghīnānī, (d. 1220) in his *Muḥīṭ al-burhānī fī al-fiqh al-Nu'mānī* (Beirut: Dār Iḥyā' al-Turāth al-'Arabī, 2003), 3:163.

123 Ibn Qudāma, *al-Mughnī*, 12:169–70.

124 It is possible that a somewhat less violent but similar injury is being described in al-Wansharīsī, *Mi'yār al-mu'rib* 3:234–5. It tells of a man who, in the course of consummating marriage to his virgin bride, did something which made her wet the bed, and she continues to do so nightly. He wishes to return her to her father, who refuses on the grounds that she had no such condition before.

125 'Abd al-Razzāq, *Muṣannaf* (Beirut: Dār al-Kutub al-'Ilmiyya, 2000), 9:262 = no. 17667.

126 Musannaf Ibn Abī Shayba #27325.

> Al-Ṣādiq was asked about a man who came upon a girl and ruptured her such that since then she excreted in this organ. She could not give birth.[127]

> He beat a woman and ruptured her (*afḍāhā*): meaning, he made the orifice from where her urine comes out and the orifice where her menses come out one; or [the orifices of] her menses and excrement one. This coitus was like a beating. Regardless of whether this is an unrelated woman who fights against it, or a wife whom he tears up during coitus, if she is rendered incontinent by it [he pays a penalty].[128]

> Regarding *ifḍā'* (rupture), which is when the barrier between where the penis enters and where the urine exits is punctured . . . he is able to have complete intercourse, even if she is infertile and cannot have offspring.[129]

> There is no *khiyār* as a result of either him or her being sterile, nor for her being *mufḍā'*. *Ifḍā'* is the elimination of that which is between where the urine exits and where the penis enters.[130]

These descriptions of injuries most closely resemble the conditions known in modern biomedicine as vesico-vaginal fistulae and recto-vaginal fistulae, in which there is a hole in the tissue separating either the vagina from the urinary tract, or the vagina from the rectum, such that excreta leak into the vagina. In modern medical literature, gynecological fistulae are most often discussed as a common obstetrical complication in the developing world, particularly among women whose bodies are too underdeveloped to healthily deliver children.[131] It is less frequently associated with sexual trauma in modern medical literature,[132] although it has received some attention from advocacy groups publicizing the problem of wartime rape.[133] Until the advent of modern surgery,

---

127 Muḥammad al-Najafī, *Jawāhir al-kalām*, 15:450.

128 Ibn ʿĀbidīn, *Radd al-muḥtār ʿalā al-Durr al-mukhtār* (Beirut: Dār al-Kutub, 1994), 10:221.

129 al-Māwardī, *Kitāb al-ḥāwī al-kabīr*, 9:341.

130 Al-Nawawī, *Rawḍat al-ṭālibīn*, 7:176.

131 For information about vesico-vaginal fistulae and recto-vaginal fistulae, see L. Wall, "Dead Mothers and Injured Wives: The Social Context of Maternal Morbidity and Mortality among the Hausa of Northern Nigeria," *Studies in Family Planning* 29 (1998), 341–59.

132 For an exception, see: M. Muleta and G. Williams, "Postcoital Injuries Treated at the Addis Ababa Fistula Hospital, 1991–97," *Lancet* 354, no. 9195 (1999), 2051–2 and A. M. Abasiattai et al., "Vaginal Injuries During Coitus in Calabar: A 10 Year Review," *Nigerian Postgraduate Medical Journal* 12.2 (2005), 12:140–4.

133 E.g., A. Longombe et al., "Fistula and Traumatic Genital Injury from Sexual Violence in a Conflict Setting in Eastern Congo: Case Studies," *Reproductive Health Matters* 16.31 (2008), 132–14.

fistulae were largely incurable, always debilitating, but usually non-fatal.[134] In the 11th/17th-century *Durr al-mukhtār* and in its 12th/18th-century commentary, the condition is described as being so severe as to make the possibility of sexual intercourse so remote that rules of gender segregation between unrelated members of the opposite sex may no longer apply. It has been argued that *ifḍā'* and *fatq* sometimes refer to fourth-degree perineal tearing, which is when the skin and muscle between the vagina and anal sphincter, and the sphincter itself, are torn, usually in the course of childbirth.[135] In modern medical diagnosis, the most salient feature of such injuries is fecal incontinence. Unlike these modern diagnoses, however, the injuries known as *ifḍā'* and *fatq* are described by medieval jurists as being the result of sexual intercourse, not of childbirth. *Ifḍā'* is also a term used in the legal literature to indicate rape.[136] Some legal works also mention that *ifḍā'* can occur by means of an instrument, such as a stone or tool, but even so it is still understood as a sexual act.[137]

All four of the genital-related defects mentioned in the legal sources correlate very strongly with physical immaturity. Moreover, the interventions used to attempt to cure these defects could lead to long-term infertility. I.e. treating a woman who has the defect of having a narrow or obstructed vaginal passage (*ratq*) may lead to a woman becoming a *fatqā'* whose vaginal wall has been damaged resulting in a fistula. Intriguingly, there is some evidence from Catholic Spain that such genital defects were considered to be a form of "female impotence," and that accusations of this sort of female impotence sometimes served as a legal cover for accusations of infertility since, in Catholicism too, impotence was grounds for annulment whereas infertility was not. This may or may not be true in the Islamic context, given that in Islam there were more avenues available for ending a marriage.

---

134 On the social effects of fistulae in a modern community see A. I. Islam and A. Begum, "A Psycho-Social Study on Genito-Urinary Fistula." *Bangladesh Medical Research Council Bulletin* 18.2 (1992):82–94

135 Hina Azam translates the injury, in the context of violent sexual assault, as "perineal tearing." However perineal tearing is a term with a wide valence (i.e. the injury can be superficial or more serious) but it is primarily used in regard to the relatively minor injuries to the surface of the body that often coincide with healthy childbirth, whereas in the context of medieval Islamic claims for damages, it refers to an injury that primary effects internal organs and that may result in multiple forms of incontinence. H. Azam, *Sexual Violation in Islamic Law* (New York: Cambridge University Press, 2015), 100.

136 For the use of the term to indicate rape see, D. Serrano, "Rape in Maliki Legal Doctrine and Practice," *Hawwa* 5 (2007), 166–207, esp. 167..

137 E.g. Al-Kāsānī, *Badā'i' al-ṣanā'i'* (Beirut: Dār al-Kutub al-'Ilmiyya, 2003), 10:445–6.

A case from 17th-century Catholic Spain at the intersection of early marriage, marriage annulment, genital defects, and infertility

The multi-layered connections between infertility and accusations of female genital defects are dramatically illustrated in a court case from 17th-century Catholic Spain. In this case, the husband seeks to end his marriage on the grounds that his wife is incapable of sexual intercourse due to genital defects. As the case unfolds, it becomes clear that he is in fact concerned about his wife's infertility, and that her infertility was itself the final consequence of a series of events stemming from his marriage to a physically immature girl who, it seems, was not initially acknowledged to be so young. Many of the social concerns and actions described here echo the technical language and seemingly obscure medical situations found in Islamic legal texts and flesh them out. At the same time, we must keep in mind the obviously divergent legal and social attitudes toward divorce in the Christian and Islamic worlds.

The following summary of the case is derived from the original scholarship of Edward Behrend-Martínez.[138] Magdalena Fernández de Valasco Sáenz's husband Pedro brought her to the court of Calahorra in 1697 to enter a plea for annulment on the charge of her impotence. Pedro's lawyer alleged that the previously-married father-of-three had found that his sixteen-year old bride's vagina was too narrow "for reception of the material that serves for the preservation of the species."[139] He complained to her natal family and her mother then attempted "to open and/or expand [Magdalena's] vagina using hands and instruments."[140] This, however, did not remedy the problem so Pedro turned to the court to put an end to the marriage.

In court, Pedro's lawyer complained that Magdalena was incapable of conceiving. The judge ordered an expert medical examination which concluded that Magdalena was small and had not yet reached menarche. It also found that Magdalena's genitals had been forced open by an instrument, leaving her mutilated and sterile. Magdalena's lawyer accused Pedro of injuring her by having intercourse with her when she was of "such a tender age."[141] The lawyer then said she only needed time to sexually mature and then she would be able to con-

---

138 See E. Behrend-Martínez, "Female Sexual Potency in a Spanish Church Court, 1673–1735," *Law and History Review* 24.2 (2006), 297–330. Also, E. Behrend-Martínez, *Unfit for Marriage: Impotent Spouses On Trial In the Basque Region of Spain, 1650–1750* (Reno: University of Nevada Press, 2007), 71–73. I have not studied the primary sources in their original languages.

139 Behrend-Martínez, "Female Sexual Potency in a Spanish Church Court, 1673–1735," 318.

140 Behrend-Martínez, *Unfit for Marriage*, 72.

141 Behrend-Martínez, "Female Sexual Potency in a Spanish Church Court, 1673–1735," 318.

summate the marriage and produce children. The lawyer said that this had also happened in his own family.[142] A second medical examination was ordered which found that Magdalena was not sixteen years old, but "about twelve." The court declared Magdalena impotent and annulled the marriage.

As with Sunnī law, in Spanish law infertility was not considered to be grounds for annulment, however, the inability to consummate the marriage due to genital defects did constitute such grounds. Canon law acknowledged "female impotence" as grounds for annulment beginning in the twelfth century.[143] Definitions of female impotence in the Catholic context closely resembled Islamic discussions of legal defects pertaining to women's genitals, particularly as both focus on purported vaginal blockages.[144] For example, Gratian's *Decretals* described three types of female impotence: a narrow vagina, a blocked vagina, or a tumor which has closed the entrance to the uterus.[145] Charges of female impotence were sometimes brought to court only after several years of marriage, indicating that the problem experienced by the couple was one which took years to surface, and thus was not likely to be a problem in actually consummating the marriage,[146] and sometimes these lawsuits, ostensibly about the charge

---

142 The scenario in which at first a woman is labeled as impotent (impossible to penetrate), and then later on is able to have normal sexual relations, is dealt with in the law code Sieta Parditas. *Las Siete Partidas*, tr. Samuel Parsons Scott (Chicago: The Comparative Law Bureau of The American Bar Association, 1931) 4:914. This condition seems to be one which resolves itself with the passage of time.

143 Behrend-Martínez, "Female Sexual Potency in a Spanish Church Court, 1673–1735," 316.

144 P. Darmon, *Trial by Impotence: Virility and Marriage in Pre-Revolutionary France* (London: Hogarth Press, 1985), 16. In the 12th-13th centuries A.D. there appears to have been some intellectual tension between the desire of Catholic religious authorities to encourage those stuck in marriages with an impotent partner to live "as brother and sister," and their reasoning that annulment would prevent more licentious forms of behavior (i.e. alternative forms of sexual behavior between spouses, or adultery.) This briefly culminated a decision by Pope Celestine IV, whose papacy lasted for less than 3 weeks of 1241, to issue a decree which allowed a husband, whose wife's genitals were too narrow, "both to keep her in his house and to remarry." Darmon, *Trial by Impotence*, 65. There is no evidence that such permission to engage in bigamy was ever legally implemented. For more on the religio-legal problems associated with such conditions see, C. S. Pinheiro, "The Medical Sources in the Chapters about Sterility of Rodrigo de Castro's *De universa mulierum medicina*," in Gayle Davis and Tracey Loughran, *The Palgrave Handbook of Infertility In History: Approaches, Contexts and Perspectives* (London: Palgrave Macmillan, 2017), 302.

145 *Corpus iuris canonici* Lib. 4, Tit. 15, Cap. 1 "De frigidis et maleficiatis, et impotentia coeundi."

146 This is not to suggest that charges of female impotence never occurred towards the beginning of a marriage. In fact, they seem to have often been leveled in response to charges of male impotence. In part, this can be attributed to canon law, which would have permitted the non-impotent spouse in an annulled marriage to remarry, but would have forbidden the other spouse from doing

of female impotence, were focused on the ability to become pregnant[147] Behrend-Martinez writes:

> Regardless of canon law, however, which did not allow for annulments based on sterility, one of the rhetorical concerns that the prosecution expressed in this case was that Magdalena was useless for the propagation of the species. Again, court rhetoric conflated female potency with fertility. Her vagina "could [not] permit the introduction of the material that serves for reproduction." After being mutilated by either her mother or husband, Magdalena's defect was probably no longer whether she could have sex or not but whether she could bear children. Therefore, the concern for the lack of sexual "potency" was specifically anxiety over reproductive capacity: she could not give Pedro any more children than he already had.
>
> The ability of an individual to reproduce was an issue in impotence cases, even though sterility was not an allowable cause for annulment under the law. The fact that sterility could not be directly considered was clear to the court and prosecutors; there were no annulment cases in which sterility was the central plea and very few mentioned it at all, but this did not prevent sterility from becoming a fundamental trial issue.[148]

Such cases demonstrate the connection between legal discussions of theoretical vaginal blockages and the practical desire to dissolve marriages to barren women.

In Magdalena's case, the accused wife really does seem to be physically unable to consummate the marriage. The testimonies suggest that this might be because she is very young. In addition to being small, she is premenarchal, and it seems that she, her parents, or her husband or perhaps all of them are either ig-

so. However, this phenomenon also occurd among Jews. Thus in a case addressed to Bezalel b. Avraham al-Ashkenazi, a 16th-century rabbi born in Jerusalem and educated in Egypt, we are informed that "Reuven was wed to Dina, but was unable to have normal intercourse with her. He went around saying that she was sealed closed and needed to be opened with a lancet, while her relatives went around saying that Reuven was impotent. When the two engaged in fights [the community?] sought to correct/rebuke the woman but did not succeed. And so Reuven initiated Jewish court proceedings and brought women with expertise in this matter as witnesses, but nonetheless the woman's relatives would not give in to the law. Instead, they went to the gentile law and removed from Reuven's possession the trousseau and all the gifts, and then they convinced him to divorce her – according to the testimony of widespread knowledge coming from those who know of the outrage done to Reuven." Ashkenazi, *She'elot u-teshuvot Rabenu Betsalel Ashkenazi* (New York: Feldman, 1955), folio 31, question 15. Cf. T. Rosen and U. Kfir, "What Does a Father Want?: An Unpublished Poem and Its Intertexts," in *Studies in Arabic and Hebrew Letters in Honor of Raymond P. Scheindlin*, ed. J. Decter and M. Rand (Piscataway, NJ: Gorgias Press, 2007), 129–53. Pp. 136–137 include the case of a twelve-year-old Jewish bride who is brutalized by both her impotent young husband and her parents for her perceived sexual faults.

147 Behrend-Martínez, "Female Sexual Potency in a Spanish Church Court, 1673–1735," 317.

148 Ibid., 319–320.

norant, or pretending to be ignorant, of her true age. In attempting to consummate the marriage, either her husband or her mother, and possibly her medical examiner, injure and mangle her internal sex organs, thus rendering her infertile as well. In this case, therefore, female infertility is both the central fear motivating concerns about female sexual impotence, and it is also the product of attempts to cure that impotence. "Impotence" is in turn a result of, or at least highly correlated to, marriage consummation at an early age, a topic we shall return to in the next chapter.

How much of this is relevant to an Islamic legal context? Several key aspects of the situation have parallels in the pre-modern Islamic world. As we shall see, Magdalena's age and pre-menarchal status at the time of marriage are similar to ages commonly found in the Islamic world. The disputes surrounding the need for patience for the young wife's physical immaturity are found in the Islamic context as well. The physical defect of which she is accused also has parallels found throughout Islamic legal theoretical literature about genital defects. So too do the interventions embarked upon by the mother, interventions which cause further damage to the girl's sexual organs. The description of the damage to Magdalena's sexual organs and fertility by these efforts also seems to match the condition of *ratq* as described in medieval Islamic texts. What is not clear, however, is whether we should read medieval Islamic allegations of female genital defects in light of this Catholic legal stratagem: i.e. those allegations of genital defects existed to provide legal cover for dealing with what was primarily a fertility complaint. The argument in opposition to such a reading is that a Muslim husband did not need such a strategy, since he had the option of divorcing his wife. The argument in favor of such a reading is that some Muslim husbands and some Muslim wives, or their families, clearly did want to end their marriages via annulment rather than by divorce. They attempted to do so by arguing retroactively that the wife was not in a position to marry, either because she had a genital defect, or because she had been married off when she was a minor in an improper fashion, or because she had not yet completed her *ʿidda* (waiting period) from a previous marriage.[149] We thus see that, while the jurists almost never granted official recognition of the notion that infertility itself constitutes a basis for ending a marriage, they did recognize as legitimate grounds for annulment physical defects that were highly correlated with infertility.

---

149 E.g. al-Wansharīsī, *al-Miʿyār al-Muʿrib*, 3:48–9, 245, 266.

2 Law and Biology: Menstruation, Amenorrhea, and Legal Recognition of Reproductive Status

Certain aspects of Islamic marital law had the potential to exacerbate or mitigate tensions surrounding fertility. As previously mentioned, this was true of Islamic legal tolerance for both polygamy and divorce. However, there were additional concepts which helped to shape the experience of infertility. The legal significance attached to menarche, menstruation, pregnancy, amenorrhea, and menopause also played a consequential role. So too did the legal dependence on, and distaste for, the mediating role played by midwives and other experts in female gynecology. In this chapter, we will examine medieval legal assumptions about what constitutes child-bearing age, the legal ramifications attached to a woman's menstrual cycles and their interruption, and how, counter-intuitively, social and legal flexibility regarding the length of gestation sometimes helped to protect and empower women who did not conceive at all.

Menarche: the legal ramifications of the onset of menstruation

The onset of menstruation was socially and legally significant in a number of ways that intersected with fertility and infertility. First, menarche triggered an expectation of fertility, i.e. the legal system operated under the assumption that, immediately following the onset of menarche, a woman was likely fertile and experiencing regular menstrual cycles. In post-menarchal adolescents, irregular menstruation was considered a defect, rather than normal.[150] However, from a biomedical standpoint, it is common now, and likely was even more common in the past, for menarche to be followed by a year or several years of irregular menstrual cycles, many of which may be anovulatory. There is little textual evidence from any medieval population in the Islamic world that there existed an awareness of the modern scientific notion of adolescent subfecundity. (However, there is some evidence from the learned medical literature that women were considered to reach the age of *peak* fertility at a later point than menarche.) The ear-

150 The 18th-century scholar Ibn ʿĀbidīn says, regarding the purchasing of a slave woman, that a girl who is between 15 and 17, and has not yet menstruated, is considered defective, since lack of menstruation is indicative of disease. He then says that if she menstruates, but only every 6 months, that too is a defect for which she can be returned to the seller. Ibn ʿĀbidīn (d. 1252/1836), *Ḥāshiyat Radd al-muḥtār* (Riyadh: ʿĀlam al-Kutub, 2003), 7:179.

https://doi.org/10.1515/9783110596588-005

lier women married, therefore, the more likely it would be that an extended period of time would elapse before they would get pregnant. Impatience with such an extended timeframe could potentially have negative, even disastrous, consequences, both medical and legal. A post-menarchal girl who was not pregnant might experience a desire or pressure to implement measures to cure her infertility, measures which themselves could damage her sexual organs.

The expectation of fertility meant that menarche also had the legal consequence of requiring post-menarchal divorcées and widows to experience three menstrual periods before remarrying, so as to establish that they were not pregnant with their former husbands' offspring. When women did not experience regular menstruation, it complicated their divorce and remarriage procedures, sometimes to the detriment of the women themselves and sometimes benefiting them.

Menarche was also consequential because it demarcated the end of legal minor-hood and the beginning of legal adulthood.[151] Minor girls who were virgins could be legally married and consummate their marriages but, in those cases where they had been given in marriage by their guardian other than their father, once they reached menarche they potentially had a limited window of time to choose to unilaterally end their marriages.[152] Unmarried minors who were not virgins (having been married and then either divorced or widowed all before reaching menarche) had to wait until legal majority to choose to remarry. This is significant for social historians because the women in this particular legal situation had reason to appear in court and thus to generate legal texts from which we can gather some information about the age and experiences of these adolescents.

Hypothesizing average age at menarche and marriage and the fertility of young brides

There was, and in some parts of the non-academic world still is, an incorrect presumption that North African and Asian girls mature and experience menarche at

151 Qarāmī, *al-Ikhtilāf fī al-thaqāfa al-ʿarabīyah al-islāmīya*, 328. Mahmoud Yazbak "Minor Marriages and Khiyār al-Bulūgh in Ottoman Palestine: A Note on Women's Strategies in a Patriarchal Society," *Islamic Law and Society* 9.3 (2002), 386–409.

152 If a girl was married off as a minor by anyone other than her father, then she could potentially exercise the choice to unilaterally end her marriage if she declared her desire to do so during the window of time between reaching menarche and engaging in post-menarchal sexual relations with her husband.

earlier ages than European girls.[153] There was also a presumption that, in premodern times, the onset of adolescence occurred even earlier than it does today. In an attempt to counteract such assumptions, Harald Motzki argued in 1985 that it was wrong to think that in the medieval Middle East (he specifically refers to 1st/7th-century Arabia, but also to later centuries and to a broader geographic region as well) females normally reached sexual maturity between age "nine to ten years," and instead he suggested that "the average was . . . for a girl, twelve to thirteen years, which corresponds approximately with modern European standards."[154] However, Motzki's suggested age range does not seem to be corroborated by either medieval texts or modern physical anthropology. In fact, late-antique, medieval, and Ottoman texts suggest that the average age of menarche was somewhat later than Motzki's suggested age of 12–13 years, with theoretical literature rarely if ever suggesting an average age of menarche younger than 14 years, and individual anecdotes referencing later ages. Moreover, studies of physical anthropology from other times and places suggest (though not definitively) a much later average age of menarche than what Motzki and other historians of the medieval Islamic world have assumed.

The medieval jurists understood menarche as being one of the ultimate signs of female legal physical maturity (*bulūgh*). The other indicators were: *iḥtilām* (wet dreams), pubic hairs, pregnancy, and reaching a preset age threshold for the onset of adulthood.[155] The minimum age for *bulūgh* in a girl was generally accepted to be nine years, and that was also legally considered to be the lowest

---

153 There is some evidence that the idea that "oriental" women living in hot climates reach puberty earlier than do European women is itself an "orientalist" fantasy in the Edward Saidian sense. Such claims were advanced by such noted 18th-century scientists as Boerhaave and Haller, and were refuted in the nineteenth and twentieth centuries. See K. Bojlén and M.W. Bentzon, "The Influence of Climate and Nutrition on Age at Menarche: A Historical Review and a Modern Hypothesis," *Human Biology* 40 (1968), 69. 20th-century scientific evidence about the role climate plays in menstruation suggests that either climate does not have much effect at all, or women in northern climes menstruate *earlier*, possibly due to vitamin-D deficiency, and those living closer to the equator tend to menstruate *later*. L. Zacharias and R. Wurtman, "Age at Menarche: Genetic and Environmental Influences," *New England Journal of Medicine* 280 (1969), 868–75.

154 H. Motzki, "Geschlechtsreife und Legitimation zur Zeugung im frühen Islam" in *Geschlechtsreife und Legitimation zur Zeugung* ed. Ernst Wilhelm Müller (Freiburg/Munich: Karl Alber GmbH, 1985), 493. My translation.

155 For references to the application of maximum-age rulings, see L. Peirce, *Morality Tales: Law and Gender in the Ottoman Court of Aintab* (Berkeley: University of California Press, 2003), 151.

possible age at which a girl can menstruate.[156] As for the ages at which women would be considered adults in the absence of physical signs of maturity, 17 is the most commonly mentioned number, with individual jurists setting the age between 15 and 19 years.[157] Such legal texts do not, however, imply that this number is meant to reflect an expected or average age of menarche. Several Roman and Byzantine physicians suggest that menarche and the onset of puberty begin at the age of 14, with some noting that "the best time for conception is about the eighteenth or the twentieth year."[158] The Tunisian physicain Ibn al-Jazzār al-Qayrawānī (d. 369/980) also cites the age of 14, though he says menarche can occur as early as age 12. Both the physician Abū Bakr al-Rāzī (d. 311/923) and Ibn Sīnā mention that it dangerous for girls younger than 15 to experience childbirth due to their small size, but otherwise they do not mention an expected age of menarche.

We have some anecdotal information about menarche from Ottoman court cases in which women exercise their *khiyār al-bulūgh* (their choice to unilaterally annul their marriage immediately upon reaching menarche, if they had been married off as minors by guardians other than their fathers). In a study of court records dating from 1600–1623 in the Anatolian city of Kayseri, Ronald Jennings finds records in which women who had been married as infants confirm, now that they were no longer minors, that they accept the marriages arranged for them and are not exercising their right of annulment. Ages are often not mentioned, but where they are, the age is listed as "more than 15 years old."[159] In his study of *khiyār al-bulūgh* in late-Ottoman Palestine, Mahmoud Yazbak cites the following information about ages. In 1871, a girl is married at 13, and reaches menarche at the age of 14; in another a 14 year old who has not reached menarche is married off. In 1911 a girl who is "more than 14 years old" testifies that she has just reached

---

156 Ibn Qudāma (d. 620/1223), *al-Mughnī* (Cairo: Maktabat al-Qāhira, 1968) 7:461. Al-Ḥaṣkafī (d.1088/1677), *Durr al-mukhtār* in *Hāshiyat Radd al-Muḥtār ʻalā al-Durr al-mukhtār* (Cairo: Muṣṭafa al-Ḥalabī, 1966) 3:507.

157 The 10th/16th-century Ottoman chef mufti Ebussuud Efendi considered children of both sexes to be of age as soon they demonstrated physical signs of maturity. "In the absence of such signs, females were considered to come of age at seventeen." L. Peirce, "Seniority, Sexuality, and Social Order: the Vocabulary of Gender in Early Modern Ottoman Society," in *Women in the Ottoman Empire*, ed. Madeline C. Zilfi (Leiden: Brill, 1997), 185. See also *al-Mawsūʻah al-Fiqhīyah* (Kuwait: Dawlat al-Kuwayt, Wizārat al-Awqāf wa-al-Shu'ūn al-Islāmīyah, 1987) 8:192 and Qarāmī, *al-Ikhtilāf fī al-thaqāfa al-ʻarabīya al-islāmīya*, 329.

158 Aetius of Amida, *The Gynaecology and Obstetrics of the VIth century*, tr. James Ricci (Philadelphia: Blakiston, 1950), 19.

159 R.C. Jennings, "Women in Early 17th Century Ottoman Judicial Records: The Sharia Court of Anatolian Kayseri," *Journal of the Economic and Social History of the Orient* 18 (1975), 78.

menarche. In 1884, a girl who is 15 and still a minor comes to court having been promised as an infant to two different people who now seek to consummate the marriage. Yazbak does not mention any case of a girl claiming to have reached menarche prior to the age of 14. It should also be noted, however, that the above-mentioned cases all come from several centuries after the medieval period and, for reasons that will be explored below, I argue that medieval living conditions would have likely meant that the average age of menarche would have been later than those mentioned in the Ottoman period in the same locales. In any case, to my knowledge, nowhere in the Middle East in any era of pre-20th-century history do we find evidence to suggest women commonly reached menarche prior to the age of 14.

Modern medical anthropology and European osteological historical records may give us more insight to the experience of women in the medieval Middle East. Studies of adolescence in living women from genetically similar but economically divergent populations have found that nutrition plays a significant role in determining the duration of adolescence and the onset of menarche. In developing countries, higher socio-economic status, higher caloric intake and, in particular, access to protein and fat from animal products, correlates with earlier menstruation, while underprivileged statuses, low caloric intake, and general malnourishment are associated with more prolonged puberty and later menstruation.[160] Thus, in the late-20th century, there is only moderate variation between the mean age of menarche of middle-class girls in European urban centers and their middle-class counterparts in Middle East and North African cities. The mean age ranges between 12.2 years and 13.4 years.[161] By contrast, the age of menarche ranges far more among those from varying economic backgrounds within the same region. For example, a 1982 study comparing wealthy urban adolescents in Kenya with their impoverished rural peers showed that, on average, rural girls experienced menarche more than two years later than wealthy girls.[162] Urban well-nourished girls reached menarche at the median age of 13.2 years, while their rural counterparts did so at the age of 15.3 years. Similarly, in a 1998 study from India, well-off girls experienced menarche at a median age

160 The reason for this correlation is not entirely clear, and the data is not clear-cut. See R. Sprinkle, "The Missing Politics and Unsettled Science of the Trend toward Earlier Puberty," *Politics and the Life Sciences* 20.1 (March 2001), 43–66.

161 J. M. Tanner, *Fetus Into Man: Physical Growth from Conception to Maturity* (Cambridge: Harvard University Press, 1990), 146.

162 H. Kulin et al., "The Effect of Chronic Childhood Malnutrition on Pubertal Growth and Development," *American Journal of Clinical Nutrition* 36 (1982), 527–36. The article cites similar results from studies of adolescents in the United States and in India.

of 12.1 years, while underprivileged ones did so at 15.4 years.[163] In Western populations, where there are historical statistics available, the mean age of menarche has fallen dramatically even in the past century, by about three years.[164] A similar decline of average age of menarche is currently being seen in populations in developing West African countries such as Gambia, Senegal, and Mali, where that age has declined from more than 16 years to less than 15 years in fewer than three decades.[165]

Turning to the medieval period, to my knowledge there are no studies of the physical maturity of adolescent human remains from anywhere in the medieval Middle East. However, in the past decade, there has been a great deal of osteological study of medieval and ancient European skeletons, especially in England and Italy, and there are also some studies comparing diets in medieval European and Middle Eastern populations. Studies of some individual European communities suggest that prior to the Black Death girls began puberty (i.e. breast development and growth spurts) at the same time as they did in the 20th century, but menarche (which occurs after peak height velocity has been reached and the growth spurt has begun to decelerate) occurred later, and the maturation and growth process occurred over a much longer timeframe.

> The ages at which individuals reached puberty, or achieved full adult maturity, were significantly different from those of modern people . . . In adverse conditions, juvenile growth can continue up to the mid-20s . . . Measurement of the length of the femoral shaft in children from Barton suggests that they lacked the growth spurt that is indicative of puberty, from which we can infer that puberty was not experienced until the later teens . . . The skeletal evidence suggests that young adults continued to grow into their early 20s, rather than reaching full physical maturity in their late teens. This has implications for our understanding of the lives of young medieval men and women. The age of menarche is assumed to have been around 15 years on the basis of medical texts from across medieval Europe . . . however, the age of menarche is determined principally by nutrition. It is likely that the poor nutrition experienced by young women in medieval Yorkshire and Lincolnshire would have delayed the onset of menarche until their late teens. In modern societies menarche is usually followed by up to three years of adolescent infertility."[166]

---

163 A.S Parent et. al. "The timing of normal puberty and the age limits of sexual precocity: variations around the world, secular trends, and changes after migration." *Endocrine Reviews* 24 5 (2003):673.

164 S. Scott and J. Duncan, Demography and Nutrition: Evidence from Historical and Contemporary Populations (Oxford: Wilson & Sons, 2008), 95.

165 S. Prentice et al. "Evidence for a Downward Secular Trend in Age of Menarche in a Rural Gambian population," *Annals of Human Biology* 37 (2010), 717.

166 R. Gilchrist, *Medieval Life: Archaeology and the Life Course* (Woodbridge: Boydell Press, 2012), 41–2.

Adolescent infertility is caused by irregular menstrual cycles, of which many may be anovulatory. In modern populations, the later the onset of menarche for an individual female, the longer the post-menarchal length of time for her menstrual cycles to become regular. Thus a girl who begins menstruating relatively late in her teen years will likely experience a longer post-menarchal period in which she is less prone to becoming pregnant. It is not currently known how to evaluate whether this correlation between late menarche and longer subfecundity held true for medieval populations.

The most comprehensive attempt to chart adolescent development in a medieval population comes from a study of four urban cemeteries in England with corpses from the years 900 to 1550, one with "high status" occupants and the rest with "low status" occupants. With a total of 994 skeletons of people aged 10 – 25, Mary Lewis and Fiona Shapland analyzed the stages and ages of pubertal growth. Their sample indicated that there is a mismatch between what the medieval European legal and literary sources imply about the age menarche, and the osteological record. I would argue that the same is likely true in the Middle Eastern context.

Lewis and Shapland's analysis shows that adolescents began puberty at a similar age to modern children at around 10 – 12 years, but the onset of menarche in girls was delayed by up to three years, occurring around 15 for most in the study sample and 17 years for females living in London.[167] Modern European males usually complete their maturation by 16 – 18 years; medieval males took longer with the deceleration stage of the growth spurt extending as late as 21 years.

> This period of physical and sexual development is at odds with medieval canon law, where the legal age at which boys and girls could consent to marriage was 14 and 12 years, respectively. This encompasses a time when both would have experienced the onset of puberty, but predates the period in which the majority of females would have been fertile (c.15 – 16 years). In practice, it seems males and females in 13th to 15th-century England married between 18 and 23 years . . . with urban females marrying slightly later . . .[168]

While there are no direct studies of skeletons in the medieval Middle East to compare with these findings, there have been some studies of medieval Middle Eastern diets. It may be hypothesized, based on evidence from medieval Europe, that nutritional factors had a significant effect on the maturation process for

---

167 According to this study, 86% of females reached menarche when they were 15 years old.
168 M. Lewis et al, "On the Threshold of Adulthood: A New Approach for the Use of Maturation Indicators to Assess Puberty in Adolescents from Medieval England," *Journal of Human Biology* 28 (2016), 48 – 56.

Middle Easterners just as they did for Europeans. Evidence from Iraq, Syria, and Egypt in the middle ages, both before and after the Black Death, suggests that – while there were significant differences in the specific diets of these populations, as compared to each other and as compared to the diets of those in Western and Southern Europe – certain nutritional elements were largely the same. Thus the content of bread differed quite substantially between the Middle East and Europe, but the high proportion of bread in the diet and in the budgets of most of the population did not. Prior to the Black Death, the price of meat, as well as other sources of fat and protein was so high as to be normally prohibitive for the working poor of Iraq, Syria and Egypt.[169] (However, poultry was available.) In comparison to their European counterparts, the lower and middle classes of Egypt are thought to have consumed a similar amount of calories, but less meat.

> The high cost of meat (mutton) in the Near East explains that the specialized workers (and probably also the small merchants) in the Near East had to allot one-fourth or even one-third of their income for it through all periods of the Middle Ages. In Southern and Western Europe the expenses for meat were relatively smaller. The nutritive value of the food which the working classes could afford was very small both in the Moslem East and in the Latin West. But since apparently until the Black Death, meat in Europe was much cheaper, the lower strata of the population had more proteins and lipids.[170]

There has been an interesting hypothesis based on skeletal evidence from England that children there had somewhat different diets from their parents, and that these diets consisted of even less meat. This would in fact be in keeping with Galenic humoral principles of the appropriate diet for the ages of man.[171] While such Ga-

---

169 A. Sabra, *Poverty and Charity in Medieval Islam: Mamluk Egypt, 1250–1517* (Cambridge: Cambridge University Press, 2000), 121–3 and E. Ashtor, "The Diet of Salaried Classes in The Medieval Near East," *Journal of Asian History* 4 (1970), 11. Ashtor estimates that in 11th-century (A.D.) Egypt, an adult male "worker" with a family could afford to buy approximately 1100 calories worth of food for himself, of which only 41 grams came from protein and 15 grams came from fats. By the 15th century, this had increased greatly to 1900 calories, 82 grams of protein, and 45 grams of fat.

170 Ashtor, "The Diet of Salaried Classes," 20.

171 Gilchrist, *Medieval Life*, 52: "The nutritional risk to children may have been further exacerbated by medieval childcare practices. Isotopic analysis of skeletal remains from Wharram Percy showed a lower level of nitrogen for children aged between four to eight years, in comparison with older children and adults. This result was interpreted as indicating that children in this age group were fed a diet which was more plant-based, with a lower proportion of marine foods and meat or animal-based products . . . In other words, medieval childcare practices may have spe-

lenic dietetic principles are mentioned in medical literature from the medieval Arab world, there is no evidence to either confirm or deny that such principles reflected or influenced common practice.

While it is not yet possible to draw definitive conclusions about the average age of menarche in any particular medieval Middle Eastern community, comparisons to modern populations and to medieval populations elsewhere in the world strongly suggest that in the Middle East, as in Europe, the average age of menarche was more likely to be 15 or 16 years or later, rather than the 12–13 year age suggested by previous historians.

How did age at menarche relate to age at marriage? We have no statistically-rich records available from any Middle Eastern community prior to the 19th century. The earliest census known to me which attempts to account for all women in the population comes from Egypt, in a government study conducted between 1846–1848. In his analysis of that census, focusing on Cairo, Philippe Fargues noted that the ages of women at the time of marriage were recorded only in one district, that of Old Cairo. There "the average age of women upon their first marriage is 13.8 years, compared to 20.3 years for men." Among women between the ages of 10–14, almost half (49.1%) had already married. For women between the ages of 15–19, 89% had ever been married. Kenneth Cuno, in his analysis of the census, noted that women younger than 15 were much less likely to be married in rural areas and, when they were, they tended to come from wealthier households.[172]

As for the pre-modern period, what anecdotal evidence we have suggests that it was not uncommon for women to marry at an early age. Yossef Rapoport attempted to make some statistical inferences about marriage patterns in Mamluk Cairo on the basis of the women mentioned in al-Sakhāwī's *Ḍaw' al-lāmi'* in which the 9th/15th-century writer chronicled the lives of 500 women. On the subject of the average age of first marriage for women, Rapoport wrote:

> The majority of girls were married off in their early or mid-teens . . . Sitt al-'Arab married Abū Shāma when she was fourteen. Rābi'ah the daughter of the scholar Ibn Ḥajar al-'Asqalānī, first married at the age of fifteen, and his granddaughter married at the age of sixteen. Some married earlier. Al-Sakhāwī married an eleven-year old girl. Al-Maqrīzī's mother

---

cifically denied children the foods rich in B12 which would have protected them from megaloblastic anaemia."

172 See P. Fargues, "The Stages of the Family Life Cycle in Cairo at the End of the Reign of Muḥammad 'Alī, According to the 1848 Census," *Harvard Middle Eastern and Islamic Review* 5 (2000), 12 and 33. K. Cuno, *Modernizing Marriage: Family, Ideology, and Law in Nineteenth- and Early Twentieth-Century Egypt* (Syracuse: Syracuse University Press, 2015), 66. The census is currently being digitized by Mohamed Saleh.

> first married when she was twelve. Orphan girls were usually married off while still minors, between ten and twelve. But it should be noted that some women were married at an older age. The historian al-Birzālī's daughter first married when she was nineteen. The virgin bride of Ibn Ḥajar was eighteen.[173]

Evidence from Jewish communities of Egypt indicates similar marriage patterns.[174] Women could experience their first marriage as late as their late teens or as early as their pre-teens, with marriage in the early teens occurring frequently. It is a mistake to assume that those ages correspond with either menarche or the level of physical maturity one would expect from a woman of the same age in the modern Middle East.[175] Based on the above considerations, it seems that first

---

173 Y. Rapoport, *Marriage, Money, and Divorce in Medieval Islamic Society* (Cambridge: Cambridge University Press, 2005), 38–9.

174 Child marriage within the Middle Eastern Jewish community is the subject of some scholarly debate between S. D. Goitein, M. Friedman, A. Grossman and R. Lamdan, with Lamdan and Grossman arguing that child marriage was so frequent as to be nearly the norm, and Goitein claiming that it was very rare. There appears to be little disagreement that 14–15 years was a common age for marriage, and the debate centers on just how frequent marriages were to girls aged 10 to 12 or younger. The age range suggested by the Geniza sources and medieval Jewish responsa literature seems similar to the one represented in the Muslim Mamluk sources. R. Lamdan, "Child Marriage in Jewish Society in the Eastern Mediterranean during the Sixteenth Century," *Mediterranean Historical Review* 11(1996), 37–59. Cf. T. Meacham, "Marriage of Minor Girls in Jewish Law: A Legal and Historical Overview," in *Jewish Legal Writings by Women*, ed. by M. D. Halpern and Ch. Safrai (Jerusalem: Urim Publications, 1998), 27. Eve Krakowski has argued that because Jewish marriages consist of two stages, *kiddushin* and *nisu'in*, which in the Geniza period were often separated by a substantial period of time, and because the timing of *nisu'in* is often not specified within the Geniza documents, there are fewer recorded incidents of consummated minor marriage than previously thought. E. Krakowski, *Coming of Age in Medieval Egypt* (Princeton: Princeton University Press, 2018), 123.

175 On the subject of whether Islamic law permits marriage to minors, there seems to be some confusion in English-language non-scholarly publications which sometimes cite al-Nawawī (d. 676/1277) as saying that it is forbidden to consummate a marriage before menarche. This claim seems to be based on a 1914 English translation of al-Nawawī's *Minhāj*. The English text by E. C. Howard is as follows: "A father can dispose as he pleases of the hand of his daughter, without asking her consent, whatever her age may be, provided she is still a virgin. It is, however, always commendable to consult her as to her future husband; and her formal consent to the marriage is necessary if she has already lost her virginity. Where a father disposes of his daughter's hand during her minority, she cannot be delivered to her husband before she attains puberty." *Minhaj et Talibin: A Manual of Muhammadan Law according to the School of Shafii*, tr. E. C. Howard (London: W. Thacker & Co., 1914), 284. A more literal translation of the Arabic text reads, "A father can marry off his virgin [daughter], whether a minor or an adult, without her consent; but it is commendable that he consult with her. He cannot marry off a non-virgin [daughter] except with her consent; so if she is a minor she is not married off until she reaches

marriages for many medieval Muslim, Jewish, and Christian women in the medieval Middle East would have occurred at a time when the woman was unlikely to be either fertile or experiencing menstrual regularity, due to physical immaturity.

Amenorrhea

The literary evidence of the widespread practice of mid-teenage marriage. coupled with skeletal evidence that mid-teens were often not as physically developed as they are at the present day, has a number of ramifications for understanding fertility. The first is that it must have been common in women's first marriages for them to not experience regular menstruation at all, due to being pre-menarchal or to experiencing the irregular and anovulatory menses associated with post-menarchal adolescence.[176] If and when a woman became fertile, it would also have been common for her not to experience regular menstruation due to pregnancy and lactation. This is, to some extent, borne out by evidence from *fatwās*, in which women who have born multiple children and are not old, testify that they have not experienced regular menstrual cycles in years, or indeed ever in the course of their marriage.[177]

Regular menstrual cycles are of supreme importance in Islamic divorce law, because they are used to determine the *ʿidda*, the mandatory period which must elapse after a first marriage has dissolved before a second marriage can legally take place. The *ʿidda* is significant in that a woman may not remarry until it is completed, ought not to leave the lodging provided to her by her former husband, and during that time her former husband has both financial obligations to her as well as sexual rights over her (if the divorce is not a triple, final one). The *ʿidda* period for a divorced woman is determined to last either for

puberty." As his commentators explain, he means that a non-virgin must give consent to be married, and she is legally capable of consent only once she has reached menarche, therefore the non-virgin minor cannot remarry until that point. Al-Nawawī, *Minhāj al-ṭālibīn* (Beirut: Dār al-Minhāj, 2005), 375–6. On medieval legal attempts to define the minimum physical requirements for consummation, see Kecia Ali, *Marriage and Slavery in Early Islam* (Cambridge: Harvard University Press, 2010), 76 and Yazbak, "Minor Marriages and Khiyār al-Bulūgh in Ottoman Palestine: A Note on Women's Strategies in a Patriarchal Society."

176 See, for example, *al-Fatāwa al-hindiyya* (Būlāq: al-Maṭba'a al-Kubrā al-Amīriyya, 1892), 1:531: "A minor woman whose husband has divorced her, and three months minus one day has elapsed, and who then menstruates once, but does not menstruate three times – her *ʿidda* has not been fulfilled."

177 See, for example, Ibn Taymiyya, *Majmūʿ fatāwa* (Medina: Majmaʿ al-Malik Fahd li-Ṭibāʿat al-Muṣḥaf al-Sharīf, 2004), 34:23.

three menstrual cycles or three months, depending on her menstrual status. If she is pregnant at the time of the divorce, the *'idda* lasts until she gives birth. If a woman is of reproductive age but has irregular or absent menstrual cycles, the *'idda* may be prolonged far longer than the usual three months. It is not uncommon for legal discussions of *'idda* to consider such prolonged periods, although to my knowledge such cases have not been studied systematically in the secondary literature.

Because the legal system was based on the assumption that women who reach menarche menstruate regularly and are thus potentially fertile, the circumstances of pregnancy and infertility looked identical to each other from the legal standpoint, since either may correlate with disrupted menstrual cycles! This meant that at the end of a marriage an infertile woman who failed to regularly menstruate could be tied to her ex-husband in much the same way as a woman who was pregnant at the time of her divorce. Her *'idda* could be extremely protracted. This is oddly the mirror image of the medical situation in which the use of fertility drugs and abortifacients, i.e. tools of "menstrual regulation," also looked profoundly similar. (As will be shown in the next chapter, lack of menstrual bleeding could be taken as a medical indication that the woman was already in the early stages of pregnancy, i.e. experiencing a missed period. Or, lack of menstrual bleeding could be a medical indication that the woman was not experiencing normal, healthy reproductive cycles and thus could not conceive until menstruation was restored. Drugs that produced menstrual bleeding could thus either be construed as producing an abortion in a pregnant woman or as jump-starting a menstrual cycle in a barren woman. Some drugs and treatments which were supposed to result in the expulsion of blood from the uterus, in one context appear as abortifacients, and in another appear as fertility agents.)

Amenorrhea was thus associated with both fertility and infertility, and it seems to have thrown a wrench into the legal system bent on establishing paternity and sexual belonging. For amenorrhea legally indicated that a woman's body could have been impregnated by a relationship with a previous man, even as it indicated an inability to become newly pregnant. This problem is directly and repeatedly attested to in *fatwā* literature. Women who were not menstruating regularly could find it difficult to complete their *'idda* and so could not permanently sever old marital ties and establish new ones. A "positive" flip-side to this problem also existed: in some legal schools a divorced woman who could claim amenorrhea (a claim which was difficult to legally dispute) could argue that she was, in fact, pregnant and thus argue that her ex-husband still owed her support or, if the ex-husband was deceased, inheritance. In this situation, presenting amenorrhea as indicative of pregnancy, rather than infertility, was a viable strategy for an infertile woman who wished to retain a legal and financial relationship with her former husband.

'idda and irregular menstruation

Legal literature rarely makes explicit reference to women who are experiencing infertility. After all, infertility cannot be legally proven. However, there are many references to women who are experiencing amenorrhea and irregular menstruation. These references are found in the context of legal discussions of divorce and widowhood, since such conditions affected the length of the *'idda* period. Given that the symptoms of amenorrhea and irregular menstrual periods in women of reproductive age correlate strongly with infertility and diminished fertility, it is worth delving into these discussions of the legal experiences of non-menstruating women in order to shed light on the legal landscape for infertile women.[178]

The length of the *'idda* period for divorcées is usually counted as three menstrual cycles.[179] However, for women who are post-menopausal (*āyisāt*), or who are minors who have not yet begun menstruating, the *'idda* is calculated as three lunar months.[180] From a legal perspective, a woman is considered to have reached menopause only once she has met two requirements: she has both ceased to menstruate and has reached a certain minimum age. The *Fatāwā al-hindiyya* notes that even if a woman who has met those criteria and has therefore observed an *'idda* based on months later appears to menstruate, then "the portion of her *'idda* which has elapsed is canceled and she must recommence by calculating her *'idda* by menstrual cycles."[181] The minimum age required to be considered past the age of menstruation is set between 50 and 62 years old

178 It is, of course, impossible to obtain statistics about the relative predominance of various causes of female infertility in different medieval contexts. However, research in MENA countries in the past 20 years suggests that tubal problems currently account for between 26% and 42% of female infertility, whereas pituitary, ovarian, and uterine disorders accounted for the remainder. Irregular menstruation is not usually a symptom of tubal blockages, but it is a symptom of the other kinds of disorders. In other words, if infertile medieval women in the Middle East suffered infertility from the same causes as do modern Middle Eastern women, between 58% and 74% of would have also potentially experienced irregular menstruation. See G. I. Serour et al., "Infertility: A Health Problem in the Muslim World" *Population Sciences* 10 (1991), 41–58.

179 By comparison, the waiting period in Jewish law is three months, not menstrual cycles, regardless of the circumstances. *Mishna Yevamot* 4:10.

180 If a minor is divorced, and during her three-month-long *'idda* she menstruates for the first time, her *'idda* begins anew, and is counted by menstrual cycles.

181 Shaykh Niẓām, al-*Fatāwā al-hindiyya*, 1:526–7.

and varies both between and within legal schools.[182] Among the Mālikīs the minimum age of menopause is set at either 50, or "one should ask women who are between the ages [of 50 and 70] about the blood which flows from women. If they say there is no menstruation at her age, she counts using months."[183] Most Shāfiʿī authorities consider the minimum age of menopause to be 62 years, with al-Qalyūbī also citing opinions in favor of age 50 and age 60. The minimum age of menopause is a matter of dispute among Ḥanafīs. Both 50 and 55 years are cited in the *Durr al-mukhtār.*[184]

Of course, in many medieval communities, precise birthdates went unrecorded for ordinary people, and thus there may not have been a practical opportunity to verify that a woman was, for example, 49 rather than 50 years old. Nevertheless, a woman who was said to be 49 and who had not menstruated recently would not, in theory, have been labeled menopausal by most scholars, with the exception of Ibn Taymiyya and his disciple Ibn Qayyim al-Jawziyya.[185] That this could be a practical problem even for some relatively older women is suggested in a passage from the *Masā'il* of Ibn Ḥanbal transmitted by Ibn Hāni' (d. 275/888).

> I asked Abū ʿAbdallāh [Ibn Ḥanbal] about a forty-year-old woman who married a man and remained with him for three years without menstruating or seeing any form of blood. Then the husband divorced her, and her *ʿidda* from this first marriage was determined to be three months, upon which she married another husband. She remained with him for four years, more or less, and did not menstruate. How should her *ʿidda* be determined, now that she has been divorced again?[186]

182 Similar ages are also found in medieval European literature. See D. W. Amundsen and C. J. Diers, "The Age of Menopause in Medieval Europe," *Human Biology* 45 (1973), 605–612.

183 Aḥmad ibn Muhammad al-Dardīr, *al-Sharḥ al-saghīr* in *Bulghat al-sālik li-Aqrab al-masālik ilā madhhab al-Imām Mālik* (Cairo: Muṣṭafa al-Bābī al-Ḥalabī, 1952) 1:497.

184 Al-Ḥaṣkafī, *Durr al-mukhtār* in *Hāshiyat Radd al-muḥtār ʿalā al-Durr al-mukhtār,* 2:606

185 Their explanation hinges upon the root meaning of the *yā'isa*, which is the word used for post-menopausal women but which literally means "hopeless" or "without expectations or prospects" in some particular regard. Ibn al-Qayyim explains. "Ibn Taymiyya said: Menopause is different for different women, and there is no cut-off point to apply to women. The intention of the verse is that each woman is without prospects with respect to herself. For menopause is the opposite of expectation, so when a woman becomes without prospect of menstruating, and she does not expect it, then she is menopausal, even if she is forty years old or thereabouts, though another woman will not be without prospect of menstruating even if she is fifty years old . . ." Ibn Qayyim al-Jawziyya, *Zād al-maʿād*, 5:583.

186 Ibn Ḥanbal, *Masā'il al-Imām Aḥmad bin Ḥanbal riwāyat Isḥaq ibn Ibrāhīm ibn Hāni' al-Nayṣābūrī* (Beirut: al-Maktab al-Islāmī, 1979), 207. Parallel cases can be found in Ibn Taymiyya, *Fatāwā*, 34:19. Similar situations are mentioned briefly in the *Fatāwā al-hindiyya*, 1:528.

In this instance, the divorcée is now in her forties, and has not menstruated in at least seven years. After her first divorce, three years prior, she waited three months before remarrying. If she could be legally considered post-menopausal, those three months would have been sufficient to finalize her first divorce, and she could go through the same procedure to finalize her second divorce. But Ibn Ḥanbal does not accord her that legal designation for either her first divorce or her second. Instead he cites several different opinions.

> There is disagreement. There are those who say that her *'idda* from the first [husband] should have been one year, such is the opinion of 'Umar.
>
> But Ibrāhīm says, "If she has ever menstruated, even if only once, then the *'idda* must be according to menstrual cycles and will last forever until she menstruates [again].
>
> But Ibn Mas'ūd says: in the case of 'Alqama's wife,[187] who fell ill and menstruated [only] twice and then died, 'Alqama inherited from her. The ruling of 'Umar b. al-Khaṭṭāb was that if she does not know what has made her stop [menstruating], e.g. sickness or breastfeeding, she should wait 12 months, and then remarry.
>
> Abū 'Abdallāh [Ibn Ḥanbal] said: My opinion is that they should be separated, that is, she and the husband who divorced her last, and then her *'idda* from the first [husband] should be set at 12 months, and afterwards the *'idda* from the second husband should be set at one year.

The first two opinions conflict with each other. In Ibrāhīm's view, in the absence of menstruation such a woman must wait twelve months between marriages. In Ibn Mas'ūd's view, in this situation she must wait three menstrual cycles regardless of how much time must elapse for that to occur. The third opinion, Ibn Ḥanbal's, suggests that Ibrāhīm's approach is correct under some circumstances, while Ibn Mas'ūd's approach is correct under others. A twelve-month waiting period is appropriate if menstrual cycles have stopped for no discernable reason, but if the amenorrhea can be attributed to a particular trigger, then the waiting period must be counted according to menstrual cycles regardless of how much time elapses. Ultimately, Ibn Ḥanbal concludes that the woman must now observe two years' worth of waiting, one year for each divorce.

Most later Ḥanbalī jurists take the position that if a woman stops menstruating for reasons unknown, her *'idda* is set at twelve months. This timeframe is usually explained as the combination of a nine-month-long waiting period to establish lack of pregnancy, at which point the lack of menstruation is attributed to menopause, followed by the three-month-long wait of a post-menopausal woman. However, under certain circumstances the delay in completing the *'idda* could be longer than one year. This occurs when the onset of amenorrhea corre-

187 The story of 'Alqama ibn Qays is explained on p. 72.

sponds to a known condition such as lactation or sickness, even possibly mental illness due to distress. Under such circumstances the woman must wait until her menses recommence or until she reaches the age of menopause, and only at that point may she begin calculating the three-month-long *ʿidda*.[188] On this point, early Ḥanbalī scholars refer to a case where the circumstance causing the amenorrhea is "known" and, as a result, the *ʿidda* is prolonged indefinitely, or until those circumstances change. The case is a story about ʿAlqama (d. 62/681), a companion of the Prophet. ʿAlqama divorced his wife whereupon she became ill and stopped menstruating. Seventeen months later, she died. In that case Ibn Masʿūd, another companion of the Prophet, ruled that ʿAlqama inherited from her, thus indicating that she died while still within her *ʿidda* period, proving that the *ʿidda* can last for more than a year.[189] There is a debate as to what motivated Ibn Masʿūd's ruling. Ibn Ḥanbal's son ʿAbdallāh (d. 290/903) seems to understand the story to mean that since amenorrhea coincided with ʿAlqama's wife having fallen ill, one could hope that menstruation would resume once the illness ended, and hence the *ʿidda* could last as long as the triggering illness and for three menstrual cycles thereafter.[190] Others interpreted the ruling in a different light, saying that the reason that the woman was still considered to be in her *ʿidda* nearly a year and a half after her divorce was because Ibn Masʿūd thought pregnancy could last for two years:

> Isḥāq[191] said . . . The meaning of the ruling about ʿAlqama and his wife's illness is that Ibn Masʿūd favored the opinion that pregnancy could last two years, as ʿĀʾisha said: "A child does not remain in the womb more than two years."[192]

Those who attributed to Ibn Masʿūd the logic that, although gestation is usually nine months long, it is possible for it to last up to two years, and hence the *ʿidda* can last that long, also argued that under all circumstances of amenorrhea, once the two years have passed and it is clear that there is no pregnancy, the divorcée can remarry immediately, without needing to undergo the three-month-long

---

188 Ibid., 7:465.

189 Al-Sarakhsī, a Ḥanafī, would later use the story to illustrate a point about the rights of a husband to revoke a divorce even during a prolonged *ʿidda*. Al-Sarakhsī (490/1096), *al-Mabsūṭ* (Beirut: Dār al-Kutub al-ʿIlmiyya, 1993) 6:19.

190 Susan Spectorsky, *Chapters on Marriage and Divorce* (Austin: University of Texas Press, 1993), 133.

191 Isḥāq b. Manṣūr al-Kawsaj (d. 251/865).

192 Aḥmad ibn Muhammad al-Dardīr (d. 1201/1786), *Sharḥ al-kabīr ʿalā Mukhtasar Khalīl* in *Ḥāshiyat al-Dasūqī ʿalā al-Sharḥ al-kabīr* (Beirut: Dār al-Fikr, n.d.) 2:471.

waiting period of the post-menopausal woman.[193] The notion that gestation could last so long will be addressed later in this chapter.

Ḥanafīs and most Shāfiʿīs take a very different position on the question of how a woman experiencing amenorrhea completes a divorce, a position which largely side-steps the question of whether the woman is possibly pregnant. Instead they maintain that a woman remains in her *'idda* until such time as she had bled three times or reached the minimum age required to be legally considered post-menopausal. Once she reaches menopause, her *'idda* is calculated as lasting three months, at the end of which she is free to marry. In theory, such laws would mean that an *'idda* could last many years indeed.[194] Interestingly, although the view that a non-menstruating woman must remain in her *'idda* until old age is endorsed in the *Durr al-mukhtār*, the Ḥanafī author also suggests that it would be prudent in such a situation to direct a woman to a Mālikī judge, so that she may complete her *'idda* in a single year.[195] And in the *Radd al-muḥtār* Ibn ʿĀbidīn quotes al-Zāhidī (d. 658/1260) as saying that one fellow Ḥanafī jurist issued a *fatwā* based on the view of Mālik on this matter "because of need."[196]

Mālikīs follow the nine-months-plus-three-months formula if menstruation seems to have ceased entirely. However, if menstruation occurs intermittently, the waiting period may be longer.

> If the woman who is waiting for a year menstruates during that year, even if it is on the last day of that year, then she must wait again for a second menses, or until the end of [another] year. When the year ends without her menses appearing, her *'idda* is over. But if her menses do appear within that year, even if it is on the last day, she must wait for a third menses, or a complete "white" year in which there is no blood, if she is free. If she is a slave, she stops at the second year.[197]

Such a situation, in which menstruation is highly infrequent, could theoretically delay a divorcée's remarriage for up to three years.

193 Ibn Qudāma, *al-Mughnī*, 7:463. Ibn Ḥanbal, *Masā'il al-Imām Aḥmad ibn Ḥanbal wa-Isḥāq ibn Rāhwayh* (Medina:ʿImādat al-Baḥth al-ʿIlmī, 2004), 4:1705–1707. A translation of the latter can be found in Spectorsky, *Chapters on Marriage and Divorce*, 189

194 al-Ūshī, Sirāj al-Dīn Abū Muḥammad ʿAlī ibn ʿUthmān, Al-Fatāwā' al-Sirājīya (Lenasia, South Africa: Dār al-ʿulūm Zakariyyā 2011), 232.

195 Ibid., 3:508; and al-Kāsānī (d. 587/1191), *Badā'iʿ al-ṣanā'iʿ*, 2:195. The adoption of Mālikī practice in regard to this issue would be enshrined in the Ottoman "Law of Family Rights" in 1917. See N. J. Coulson, *A History of Islamic Law* (Edinburgh: Edinburgh University Press, 1964), 192.

196 Ibn ʿĀbidīn, *Ḥāshiyat Radd al-muḥtār*, 5:186.

197 Aḥmad ibn Muhammad al-Dardīr (d. 1201/1786), *Sharḥ al-kabīr 'alā Mukhtasar Khalīl* in *Ḥāshiyat al-Dasūqī 'alā al-Sharḥ al-kabīr* (Beirut: Dār al-Fikr, n.d.) 2:471.

The extended *ʿidda* as a potential burden on women

Fatwās, particularly those of Ibn Taymiyya, shed some light on the negative consequences of long *ʿidda* periods from the point of view of women seeking to end a marriage. (For the usefulness of the extended *ʿidda* to women see the section below.) In one *fatwā*, Ibn Taymiyya addresses the case of a young, married woman who seems to have stopped menstruating altogether, with no indication of when or if she will begin menstruating again. Her husband decides to divorce her. The petitioner asks: "Is the *ʿidda* for her divorce measured by months or must she wait until she reaches the age of menopause?" Ibn Taymiyya responds by highlighting the plight of a woman stuck in this situation.

> If it is possible that her menses will return, and it is possible that they will not return, then she should wait one year and marry, as ʿUmar b. al-Khaṭṭāb ruled regarding the woman whose menses had stopped without her knowing what had stopped them. She waits one year, and that is the common view, for example the view of Mālik and al-Shāfiʿī. As for one who says that she must be of the age of menopause, that is a very weak view, with so much harm in it as to be unparalleled in the law. For it keeps her from marriage at the very time of her need of it and would only permit [marriage] to her once she no longer needs it [i.e. in her old age].[198]

In another *fatwā*, Ibn Taymiyya reiterates the same logic and explicitly characterizes it as *maṣlaḥa* (arrived at on the basis of the public interest). In this case, a woman's second husband has divorced her upon realizing that she had menstruated only once during her *ʿidda* following her divorce from her first husband. In an effort to remarry her second husband, the wife then declares that she has reached menopause. As part of his answer, Ibn Taymiyya concludes with an attack on the Ḥanafī view.

> According to [Abū Ḥanīfa] a woman in this precarious situation would remain in her *ʿidda* until she grew old and reached the age of menopause, even though according to their opinion she would have to remain unmarried until 50 or 60. But that would be such a hardship as to be an exception to the law, and so the *maṣlaḥa* of the Muslims abolishes it.[199]

Ibn Taymiyya's *fatwās* also include a response to a case about a woman in her *ʿidda* whose menses are "delayed" as a result of breastfeeding and who resorts

---

198 Ibn Taymiyya, *Majmūʿ Fatāwā*, 34:20.
199 Ibid., 34:17.

to drugs in order to bring on menstruation. He notes that such menstruation does indeed qualify, so that the woman can be free to remarry.[200]

A case study of irregular menstruation and the laws of *'idda*

If Ibn Taymiyya's *fatwās* seem relatively clear-cut, a *fatwā* attributed to the Mālikī Qāḍī 'Iyāḍ (d. 544/1149) demonstrates the complicated nature of calculating the *'idda* and the significant resulting problems that an irregularly menstruating woman could have in entering and leaving a marriage. It also foregrounds the role of husbands and of other women in mediating an individual woman's encounter with the law. The case begins as follows:

> When [Muḥammad b. Aḥmad] married his wife Fāṭima bt. Muḥammad (known as Ibn Najjūma), he learned[201] that she had a condition which delayed her blood. It concerned him that he might have contracted his marriage with her before the completion of her *'idda* following her husband's, 'Alī b. Muḥammad's, divorce from her. Muḥammad therefore questioned and interrogated her, and informed her about what was required of her, whereupon she acknowledged to him that her blood had only come twice since her divorce from 'Alī, and that she was ignorant of [the requirements]. Muḥammad withdrew from her and consulted with some trusted men of learning, who instructed him to divorce her, for she is not permitted to him. He therefore separated from her . . .[202]

The *istiftā* begins with Muḥammad realizing that his wife is not menstruating as expected. This, he realizes, may have been the case prior to the marriage and he gets her to acknowledge that, in fact, she had menstruated only twice since her divorce after her previous marriage. He tells her "what was required of her." She says that she was ignorant of the requirement. He divorces her, apparently surprised by her confession.

The judge is then told that Muḥammad, even before his marriage, was aware of the possibility that the requirements of *'idda* were not being fulfilled. During his courtship, he had requested of a male intermediary, who in turn requested of his wife, that she educate the potential fiancée about the rules of *'idda*.

200 Ibid., 34:19.
201 Lit. "it was revealed to him." This is the version that appears in al-Wansharīsī, *al-Mi'yār*. The version that appears in Ibn Rushd's *Fatāwā* says "to her."
202 Ibn Rushd, *Fatāwā Ibn Rushd* (Beirut: Dār al-Gharb al-Islāmī, 1987), 2:1085–7 and Aḥmad ibn Yaḥyā al-Wansharīsī, *al-Mi'yār al-mu'rib wa'l-jāmi' al-mughrib 'an fatāwā ahl Ifrīqiya wa'l-Andalus wa'l-Maghrib* (Rabat: Wizārat al-Awqāf wa'l-Shu'ūn al-Islāmiyya lil-Mamlaka al-Maghribiyya, 1981) 3:401–3.

> Muḥammad testified . . . that he had addressed Ḥājj Ḥaḍḍūr . . . to propose marriage between himself and Fāṭima b. Muḥammad b. Najjūma, and Muḥammad said to him: "Tell her to fear almighty God, her Lord, and to wait by herself until her *'idda* is completed. Inform her that if she is of the sort who sees blood, then [she must do so] three times. If she does not see [blood], then [the *'idda*] is three full months. She is not permitted to marry or to become engaged until after what I told you. Warn her against doing what she did with the Fāsī who proposed to her, when she decided to contract the marriage with him prior to the end of her *'idda*."
>
> . . . Umm Qāsim, the wife of Ḥājj Ḥaḍḍūr, met with Fāṭima b. Muḥammad Ibn Najjūma to inform her of all that Muḥammad b. Aḥmad mentioned above. [Umm Qāsim said that] she said all of this and informed her of it, and that Fāṭima told her that her *'idda* had been completed, and that she had seen blood three times since her divorce from her first husband.

This passage shows that that before his engagement Muḥammad had warned Fāṭima (via intermediaries) to keep to herself and not to do what she did in the past, which was to become engaged to a man (the Fāsī, who may or may not have been her previous husband 'Alī) before she had completed her *'idda*. It seems that Fāṭima has a history of attempting to enter into marriages before she has completed her *'idda*.

Throughout this history Fāṭima is frequently informed by others about the laws of *'idda* and yet she maintains that she was ignorant of what she is supposed to do.

> . . . The husband seeks to take back the dower, but the woman is keeping it. She claims ignorance, but the husband has female witnesses saying that they informed her of what he said verbatim, and that the matter had been clarified to her during her *'idda* from the first husband, which incidentally, according to one of them, was the second time [they had done so?]. The husband says that with this clarification, there is no possibility of her being ignorant . . .

The husband seeks to annul his marriage and retrieve the dower he gave to his wife, on the grounds that by not menstruating three times since her previous marriage she had not completed her divorce and thus was not free to marry. He further claims that the woman must have lied in saying that she was free to marry, since multiple people had provided instruction to her about how the laws of *'idda* work. The jurist disagrees, however, saying that she may well have thought she had fulfilled her *'idda* obligations, and that if she is willing to issue a sworn oath that that was her state of mind, she may keep the dower like any other divorcee.

The answer:

> . . . It has not been confirmed what the Ḥājjī's wife said to/about[203] her: i. e. whether – when [the Ḥājjī's wife] informed her that the *'idda* is three menses, and warned her against marrying before its completion – [Fāṭima] then said that her *'idda* had been completed and that she has seen blood three times since her divorce from her first husband. My view is that since
>
> [a] she denies that she was informed that the *'idda* is three menses, and she was not informed of that, and
>
> [b] she married only because she thought her *'idda* from her first husband had been completed, and
>
> [c] since she denies this within the limits of the law
>
> she is not required to return any part of the dower to him. But if she refuses to swear [that this was the state of her marriage], she does not receive from him anything except the price of her vulva,[204] and the rest returns to him . . .

Everyone involved in the case assumes that Fāṭima must be confused about the rules of *'idda*, at least initially. Her husband-to-be assumes that Fāṭima must be warned to keep to herself until she menstruates three times, and that she needed to be enlightened by Ḥājj Ḥaḍḍūr. Umm Qāsim makes the same assumption. The other women affirm that they explained everything to her not once, but twice. Finally, the muftī seems to agree that there is room for ignorance here. There seems to be something truly complicated about the law of *'idda* in this case such that it would make sense for the men and women involved to check and double-check the situation.

In David Powers's analysis of this case, he maintains that Fāṭima's failure to comply with the laws of *'idda* is motivated by selfishness, and that her claim of ignorance of those laws is obviously false. However, the most plausible way of accounting for the actions of all the people mentioned in the legal document is to take seriously the fact that Fāṭima's menstrual cycles were infrequent ("her blood was delayed"). This means that when Muḥammad instructed her, by way of Ḥājj Ḥaḍḍūr and Umm Qāsim that "if she is of the sort who sees blood, then [she must do so] three times; if she does not see [blood], then [the *'idda*] is three full months," Fāṭima's status really was potentially ambiguous. The complicated nature of the situation seems to stem in part of from the legal dichotomy differentiating between those who menstruate and those who

203 There are a number of textual variants among the manuscripts in this section. It might say "to her" or "about her."

204 On the use of this phrase see Kecia Ali, *Marriage and Slavery in Early Islam*, 151.

do not. (The language of the instructions issued here is mostly Qur'ānic. It is possible, of course, that this language is used for official purposes in the legal document but does not reflect the actual wording used to instruct the woman.) Fāṭima believed she fell into the category of those who do not menstruate, and so she thought her *'idda* ought to be calculated as three months long. The point of contention between the parties to the lawsuit is not whether Fāṭima knew that she was not allowed to marry during her *'idda*. She was not ignorant of that. She says that "she only married someone thinking that her *'idda* from her first husband had been completed" but, she claims, she never said that she had "seen blood three times" and did not know that she had to. The point of contention is whether Fāṭima knew that she still fell into the category of the menstruating woman, regardless of her lack of regular menstrual cycles. This, according to Fāṭima and Qāḍī 'Iyāḍ, she could plausibly claim not to know. She did not know that a woman with oligomenorrhea such as herself had to see blood three times, rather than simply wait the three months. Muḥammad and the other witnesses, for their part, testify that they explained the laws of *'idda* many times and that she must thus have known that she was in the category of women who must calculate their *'idda* by menstrual cycles.

Fāṭima's situation appears to have been further complicated by the semi-public and semi-private nature of menstruation, at least in this particular community. This attitude toward menstruation can be inferred from details from the *fatwā*. Prior to the marriage, it seems that Fāṭima was publicly known to have a menstrual problem – hence the women's repeated counseling of her regarding the laws of *'idda* and Muḥammad's warning that he knows about her and the Fāsī.[205] So, in this community, there is a public dimension to menstruation. But there is also a private dimension to menstruation, hence the public's ignorance of the fact that Fāṭima had menstruated only twice since her most recent divorce. The public aspect of menstruation might have been somewhat obscured by the legal requirement that a woman remain at home during her *'idda* period. Muḥammad's message to Fāṭima at the time of the proposal includes the caution to keep to herself, indicating that this theoretical requirement was expected (by

205 One could make the argument that the public knew nothing about her menses at the time of the Fāsī relationship, and that they knew she had not completed her *'idda* simply because not enough time had elapsed, e. g. she had been divorced only one or two months prior. However, if that were the case, then Muḥammad's concerns would have been allayed with the passage of time. Given his concerned behavior at the time of his own engagement, one would have to argue that Muḥammad and the women's concerns shifted from counting time to counting menses, and it just so happened Fāṭima had a menstrual problem too. This strikes me as a plausible, if not the most likely, scenario.

at least some) in this community to be put into practice. This would account for the fact that no one is sure how many times Fāṭima menstruated until she supplies the information herself.

So, at the time of her relationship with the Fāsī, Fāṭima was known to have a menstrual problem, but for some reason at the time of Muḥammad's marriage both the female witnesses and Muḥammad believed that the danger was past and, perhaps, so did Fāṭima. There are at least two scenarios in which this could happen. Perhaps at the time of her engagement to the Fāsī, Fāṭima had not experienced menstruation at all, or had only menstruated once and then stopped, and so the public image of Fāṭima was as someone experiencing amenorrhea. Once she menstruated again, it was mistakenly believed that she was now having regular cycles. Only once Muḥammad and Fāṭima had been married for a while did it become clear that this was not the case.

Alternatively, at the time of her engagement to the Fāsī, Fāṭima had menstruated twice, and so the public image of Fāṭima was of a person who had regular, though long, cycles. By the time Muḥammad proposed, he and the women thought that a sufficient interval had elapsed for her to have completed three cycles, and so they then did their due diligence and were satisfied when she affirmed that she had completed her *ʿidda*. Meanwhile, Fāṭima believed that since she was no longer seeing blood she simply had to wait three more months. Only once she was married did it become clear to Muḥammad that his wife did not have predictable menses. In either case the misunderstanding, deliberate or feigned, came to light only once the husband realized his wife menstruates only intermittently instead of having cycles and he chose to ask her how many times she had menstruated prior to her marriage.

In his article about this case, David Powers concludes that it showcases a woman craftily using faux-naiveté to manipulate the judicial system.[206] However,

206 D. Powers, "Women and Divorce in the Islamic West: Three Cases," *Hawwa* 1 (2003), 29–45. Powers' analysis leaves out the vital piece of information that the wife has delayed menses. He argues, "Clearly knowledgeable about the rules of marriage and divorce, Fāṭima manipulated these rules, apparently for the purpose of lining her pockets with dīnārs and dirhams. She used her knowledge of the law to deceive not one but two husbands, in succession. Ironically, she defended her action with the claim – surely disingenuous – that she was ignorant of the law. The strategy appears to have worked." He also suggests that, in addition to being motivated by greed, "Fāṭima may have had other motives, e.g., to extricate herself from a marriage that had been forced upon her by her marriage guardian, fear of pregnancy, or hatred of men." Powers' only evidence for his claim that Fāṭima is "clearly knowledgeable" is that she appears to avoid losing the lawsuit. There is no evidence that she wanted either divorce. If her purpose was to avoid marriage to this husband or to avoid pregnancy in general, it seems that by merely disclosing her menstrual state she could have avoided both.

a more straightforward analysis of the *fatwā* – especially when read together with the laws of menopause and with Ibn Taymiyya's *fatwās* – suggests that the confusion, miscommunication, and frustrations experienced by Fāṭima and Muḥammad make sense within the context of the application of the laws of *'idda* for those with disrupted menstrual cycles. Moreover, since infertile women often experience such menstrual disruptions, infertile women would have been more likely than others to suffer from this frustrating legal situation, making it more difficult for them to conclude a divorce and to initiate a remarriage.

The extended *'idda* as a potential boon to women

Medieval jurists, especially Mālikī ones (as well as 19th-century French colonial administrators and 20th-century anthropologists) also recognized that the extended *'idda* could potentially be beneficial both to divorcées and to widows. This is so in situations when the former wife uses her extended *'idda* to retain the rights due to her from her former husband. Two writings from the Andalusian jurist Ibn Rushd al-Jadd (d. 520/1126) illustrate this point. The first is a *fatwā* he writes in response to the case of a woman whose husband divorced her. As legally required, she lived in her former husband's house during her *'idda*. After some time, when the "*'idda* for one such as her ended," the former husband attempted to evict her from the house, at which point she declared that she was pregnant, and her former husband claimed that she was lying.

> Ibn Rushd received a query from Badajoz about a woman whose husband divorced her, and she observed her *'idda* in the house in which she had been divorced. The *'idda* for one such as her ended and the husband, wanting to remove her from his house, told her that her *'idda* had already ended. She declared that she was pregnant, in [the house], while her husband claimed she was lying and he wishes her to be examined by women. Must she swear that she suspects she is pregnant or not?
>
> Answer: I have pondered the question and lingered over it. If she declared this after four months or so, she is to be believed without an oath. If she declared this after six months or so, she is believed so long as she swears. There is disagreement if she declared this near to the end of the year, and some say that she should be believed so long as she swears, while others say that she is not to be believed unless there was a hint of this previously. But if she declares this after the year has ended she is not to be believed unless the women examine her and corroborate what she declared.[207]

207 Ibn Rushd, *Fatāwā*, 3:1278–79, also in al-Wansharīsī, *al-Mi'yār al-mu'rib*, 4:482.

Here, the divorced woman argues that she is still in her *'idda* by virtue of suspecting that she is pregnant, and as a result she still has a right to lodgings paid for by her former husband. Her former husband denies that there is reason to believe that she is pregnant and wishes the matter to be settled by female experts, while the court considers whether she should be forced to swear an oath in order to be believed. Nowhere in either the question or the answer is it explicitly stated what indications the woman has that she is pregnant. Most likely it is the absence of menses but, particularly in North Africa, menstruation was still considered compatible with pregnancy.[208]

In his book of jurisprudence *al-Bayān wa'l-taḥṣīl* the same jurist, Ibn Rushd, addresses another set of (hypothetical) scenarios, in which a woman is divorced and her former husband dies some unspecified time later. She then seeks to inherit from him as a widow, on the grounds that she never menstruated after her divorce.[209] The jurist is asked to consider the following situations, "in regards to a man who divorces his wife while she is [a] breastfeeding or [b] not breastfeeding, and then he dies. She claims that she has not menstruated and is seeking a share of the inheritance [i.e. the share normally due to a widow]." Since we are studying the potential legal options of infertile women we shall focus on his response to the situation in which the ex-wife/would-be widow claims to be experiencing amenorrhea unconnected with breastfeeding.

Ibn Rushd begins by citing the opinion of the Andalusian jurist al-'Utbī (d. 255/869). "He said, regarding a woman who is not breastfeeding: she is believed until one year has elapsed, whether or not she mentioned [her lack of menstruation] before, but she must swear to it – unless there is a rumor that she has already menstruated three times." Ibn Rushd explains that this means that if her divorce has occurred within the past year, and she is willing to swear that in that time she has not menstruated, then she is believed and hence inherits as a widow would.

He then addresses the situation if more than a year has elapsed since the divorce. If "she then seeks the inheritance, alleging that her *'idda* has not ended due to there being a sensation present in her womb," then she is not believed until women examine her and corroborate her statement. Here Ibn Rushd explicitly connects the reason for the extended *'idda* to the notion that the woman might yet be pregnant. Citing another authority, he says that if the examining

208 E.g. al-Wansharīsī, *al-Mi'yār al-mu'rib*, 4:524.
209 Ibn Rushd, *al-Bayān wa'l-taḥṣīl* (Beirut: Dār al-Gharb al-Islāmī, 1984) 5:419.

women do find "suspected" pregnancy,[210] she may remain in the lodgings provided for her *ʿidda* for up to five years. If, after five years, she still claims to feel pregnant and to not be menstruating she is no longer believed. From the divorced woman's point of view, that means she can potentially obtain for herself up to five years of housing, if her lack of menstruation can be interpreted as pregnancy rather than infertility.

Ibn Rushd then mentions a debate as to whether her former husband had to be aware, prior to his death, that she was not menstruating (and thus that they were not fully divorced). He seems to subscribe to the opinion that the husband's knowledge is not requisite. However, he also mentions other opinions. He cites the opinion of Damascene Mālikī jurist Ibn al-Mawwāz (d. 281/894) who rules that she can only inherit if her former husband was aware during his lifetime that she had not menstruated yet. He further mentions an alternative construction of the relevant timeline: if her claim comes only four months into the divorce, she is believed without swearing to it. After six months she is believed only with an oath. And if she claims "not to have completed three menses due to delayed menstruation," but that claim emerges only after a year or two has elapsed, and her husband is already dead, she is not believed. He concludes that in a situation where the woman's claim or oath will not suffice, she should be examined by other women, who may provide expert testimony.[211]

The practical upshot of Ibn Rushd's discussion is that if a woman makes it known that she has not menstruated since her divorce, then she may claim the benefits due to a pregnant woman without any external corroboration, though she may need to swear an oath as to her status. It is not clear whether this oath is about only her lack of menstruation or also her "sensation" of pregnancy, or whether those are considered to be one and the same. If her claim to be experiencing amenorrhea or pregnancy is made late in the *ʿidda* process, it is not rejected outright as impossible, but rather it is subjected to a higher standard of proof. The more expediently timed the woman's claims are, the higher the burden of proof required to substantiate them. That proof, however, need not be the eventual birth of a child, but rather testimony from expert women that the ex-wife exhibits some symptoms of pregnancy.

---

210 The language used here for suspicion of pregnancy is *mustarāba* and *rība*. This idiom is also used elsewhere in Ibn Rushd's writings in regard to a woman who claims to be pregnant while her ex-husband denies it. E.g. al-Wansharīsī, *al-Miʿyār al-muʿrib*, 4:482. The term also appears in the *Miʿyār* in at least one place where it is not attributed to Ibn Rushd. See *al-Miʿyār al-muʿrib*, 4:524 and 5:56.

211 Ibn Rushd, *al-Bayān wa'l-taḥṣīl*, 5:419–20.

Particularly in North Africa, the testimony of midwives could have enough force to compel a man to financially support his ex-wife for years, if the testimony supported the claim that the ex-wife was experiencing a prolonged pregnancy. In Moroccan lore, a fetus could go into a state of hibernation in which the mother can feel its presence but it does not grow until it "wakes up" or is "awakened." This hibernating gestation can last for up to five years. Midwives were responsible for diagnosing this condition, known as the "sleeping fetus," *rāqid*, and their help was also sought in "awakening" the *rāqid* and so that normal pregnancy could "resume." The *rāqid* is well known within secular scholarship of Islamic law as an instrument for protecting the reputation of women who birth children at inconvenient moments, moments that would indicate that they conceived when they were unmarried or their husbands were not present to impregnate them. However, the notion of *rāqid* protected not only women with awkwardly-timed pregnancies, but also women who did not appear to be pregnant at all. Multiple medieval *fatwā*s which reference extended gestations do not refer to situations in which the paternity and circumstances of the conception of a baby are suspect, but rather to a situation in which a woman claims to be pregnant despite not yet producing a baby.[212] Until recently,[213] the *rāqid* was understood by Europeans working in Morocco as primarily a coping mechanism for infertile women.[214] In reference to late 19th and early 20th-century Morocco, Ellen Amster writes:

> The raqid prevented unilateral divorce (*ṭalāq*), because according to the Qur'an, a man cannot divorce a pregnant wife before she gives birth, after which he owes her two years of maintenance for breast-feeding. A divorced woman could thus receive up to five years of maintenance by claiming a raqid pregnancy, and a widow could delay the division of her husband's succession by declaring herself pregnant at his funeral; any child born within the five-year delay period would consequently inherit. Shariʿa and Berber customary courts left the diagnosis of the raqid to the woman herself, her mother, or a midwife . . . In the Morocco of the twentieth century, French physicians were incredulous that shariʿa judges could believe such a "physiological absurdity." Doctors saw the raqid as a woman's

212 E.g. al-Wansharīsī, *al-Miʿyār al-muʿrib*, 3:224–25.
213 By the late-twentieth century, it had re-emerged as a way of coping with the pregnancies of North African women whose husbands were living in Europe as migrant workers.
214 F. Legey, *The Folklore of Morocco*, tr. Lucy Holtz. (London: Unwin, 1935), 105–106: "A barren woman will never admit her sterility. She believes that she has conceived, and that her pregnancy is delayed by a spell . . . she imagines that she was pregnant, and the child fell asleep . . . she then abandons herself to certain practices in order to wake it up . . . It is also thought that if this magic medicine does not wake up the child, it will facilitate its expulsion, and that the woman will then conceive normally."

ruse to avoid divorce, and Dr. Delanoe commented wryly, “Every sterile woman claims to have [sleeping child.]”[215]

Amster goes on to show that French doctors and the French legal system were seen as instrumental in upholding the prerogatives of living ex-husbands and the kin of deceased ex-husbands, who denied that their ex-wives and ex-in-laws were pregnant. By contrast, the courts based upon *sharīʿa* and customary law were perceived as being more protective of the rights of such women, and especially their right to lodging during the *ʿidda*. Similarly, Noel Coulson has noted that in modern Egypt too, efforts to reform the legal code along more European lines included provisions to protect ex-husbands from the demands of an extended *ʿidda* on the basis of long gestations.[216]

It should be noted that while the concept of the sleeping fetus is most commonly associated with Morocco, the notion that a fetus could gestate beyond one year is found in sources from Medina and is acknowledged by not only the Mālikī school, but also by the other three Sunnī schools, with the Hanafīs having the most narrowly defined limits of possible gestation, setting it at two years and other schools mentioning four, five, and seven year limits.[217] Sometimes even longer gestations are mentioned. In a remarkable account of his family life, a learned Cairene named Burhān al-Dīn Ibrāhīm al-Biqāʿī (d. 885/1480) describes the nine-year-long pregnancy of his concubine, Ḥasbiya Allāh, with his much-anticipated child. He mentions that a rival wife and some acquaintances scoff at the concubine's claim, but al-Biqāʿī asserts that his experience has the support of both medical authors and female midwives who have periodically examined the “pregnant” woman.[218]

---

215 E. Amster, *Medicine and the Saints* (Austin: University of Texas Press, 2013), 167–8.

216 Coulson, *A History of Islamic Law*, 176.

217 See al-Sarakhsī, *al-Mabsūṭ*. 4:45. Ibn Rushd the grandson (Averroes) takes exception to the notion of long gestations. He writes, “They disagreed about the longest period of pregnancy through which the father can be associated with the child. Mālik said that it is five years, while some of his disciples said it is seven. Al-Shāfiʿī said that it is four years. The Kūfīs said it is two years. Muḥammad ibn al-Ḥakam said it is a year. Dāwūd said it is six months. This counting is based on practice and experience. The opinions of Ibn ʿAbd al-Ḥakam and the Ẓāhirites are closer to the normal. The rule should be based upon what is normal, not upon what is rare, which would, perhaps, be impossible.” Translation from Imran Ahsan Khan Nyazee, *The Distinguished Jurist's Primer: A Translation of Bidāyat al-Mujtahid* (Reading: Garnet, 2000), 2:433.

218 al-Biqāʿī, *Iẓhār al-ʿaṣr li-asrār ahl al-ʿaṣr* (Riyadh: n.p., 1993) 3:43–4. Here both the “mother” and the “father” appear to be motivated in part by animus toward one of his wives and her child. See. L. Guo, “Tales of a Medieval Cairene Harem: Domestic Life in al- Biqāʿī's Autobiographical

Women's testimony, privacy, and expertise

One striking aspect of references to women's reproductive statuses is the extent to which they could remain private, unknown to anyone but the woman herself, at least in some communities. This is somewhat surprising given the close quarters in which people lived, the significance of menarche for women's legal and ritual identities, and the importance of purification after menstruation for all kinds of ritual activities. Despite the public significance of menstruation, all of the above-mentioned legal cases and hypothetical questions indicate that, in many places, it was possible for no one but the woman herself to be aware whether she was currently experiencing regular menstrual cycles.[219] Thus the biological fact of menarche and menstruation or lack thereof was, in some places, a private matter, such that an individual woman might exercise some control over the timing of its becoming a social fact.

For example, *al-Mi'yār al-mu'rib*, the famous collection of North African and Andalusian *fatwās* compiled by al-Wansharīsī (d. 914/1508), includes many cases where no one but a girl herself is aware whether she has reached menarche.[220] It also includes several cases in which a husband is surprised to find that his new wife is physically immature, and this is particularly true in the case of fatherless brides.[221] Sometimes this in and of itself causes a legal problem,[222] but in other cases we hear of it only because it is invoked as part of a legal counterclaim,

---

Chronicle," *Mamluk Studies Review* 9 (2005), 111. Interestingly, in addition to experiencing food cravings, Ḥasbiya Allāh's main form of signaling her pregnant status is by attempting and failing to complete the Ramaḍān fast. Al-Biqā'ī notes her attempts to fast and her becoming overcome by dizziness by noon, despite her self-care. Al-Biqā'ī further mentions that after failing to fast during Ramaḍān for two years in a row, the woman made up the fasts over the course of another two months, as religiously required, and both he and she engaged in other forms of expiation for her failure to fast. It may be worth investigating whether prematurely breaking the fast was considered to be a quintessential form of intentionally or inadvertently revealing a pregnancy, in the way that avoiding alcohol in social situations or vomiting unexpectedly is in American culture.

219 Cf. M. H. Katz, "Scholarly Authority and Women's Authority in the Islamic Law of Menstrual Purity," in F. Kashani-Sabet and B. Wenger, ed., *Gender in Judaism and Islam: Common Lives, Uncommon Heritage* (New York: New York University Press, 2014), 85–87; 93.

220 E.g., al-Wansharīsī, *al-Mi'yār al-mu'rib*, 3:245; 3:266.

221 For a summary of the legal ramifications of marrying off fatherless brides see Yazbak "Minor Marriages and Khiyār al-Bulūgh in Ottoman Palestine," 392–3. For an analysis of juristic opinions pertaining to minor marriage more generally see Nūr al-Dīn 'Abd Allāh ibn Ḥumayyid al-Sālimī, *Iḍāḥ al-bayān fī nikāḥ al-ṣibyān: aḥkām tazwīj al-ṣighār* (Beirut: al-Dār al-'Arabiyya lil-'Ulūm, 2006).

222 E.g. Ibn Rushd, *Fatāwā*, 294. al-Marwarrūdhī, *Fatāwā*, 323, 335. al-Nawawī, *Rawḍat al-ṭālibīn*, 246.

rather than because it is at the heart of a legal dispute. For example, a fatherless girl with a seemingly unscrupulous uncle is married off "when she was not even close to maturity" and dies in that state.[223] Her relatives sue for her estate on the grounds of her minority, and her husband sues on the grounds that he thought she was mature. Sometimes the bride herself seems to be pretending to be more physically mature than she is, and at other times the husband disputes with the bride's family and claims that she is in fact mature enough to endure sexual relations, while they claim that she is not.[224] We even have a case in which both occur: a fatherless girl being raised by her kin is married off and then, at the point of consummation, she tells her husband that she has not reached puberty (*bulūgh*), and he divorces her on the spot. He later regrets his decision because she is in dire need, but he is told she cannot remarry until she can prove puberty. Then the girl announces that she has reached puberty and officially proves to some unspecified powers-that-be that she shows breast-budding, which is a sign of maturity. The couple then remarry but at around the time of consummation she begins to "hate" her husband, and then tells him that she has not, in fact, reached puberty and flees. He denies her claim of immaturity. Both sides then each bring an expert woman (*bayyina*), who offer competing expert opinions about whether the girl shows signs of breast-budding.[225] All this suggests that these physical characteristics were often not a matter of public knowledge until such time as a legal dispute arose and progressed to the point where expert witnesses were required, and that even at this point physical characteristics were subject to interpretation and manipulation.

It should be noted here that numerous *fatwā*s in al-Wansharīsī's *al-Mi'yār al-mu'rib* indicate that while a father could marry off a virgin daughter who had not yet reached menarche, the jurists and Maghribi/Andalusi society in general were scrupulous about waiting to marry off a fatherless girl until she either reached menarche or displayed some other sign of pubescence. (Some Mālikī sources specifically list not menarche, but rather being physically tall enough to birth a child, as the minimum developmental requirement for a virgin orphan girl to marry.[226]) *Fatwā*s further demonstrate that at times these measures protected girls from exploitation and sexual trauma and, as we have seen, at other times orphan girls deliberately tried to circumvent these measures and pretend to be older in order to marry and thereby save themselves from deprivation.

223 al-Wansharīsī, *al-Mi'yār al-mu'rib*, 3:96–7.

224 Ibid., 3:8–9.

225 Ibid., 3:48–9.

226 Ibn Abī Zayd al-Qayrawānī, *Kitāb al-nawādir wa'l-ziyādāt* (Beirut: Dār al-Gharb al-Islāmī, 1999), 4:398.

A variation on this theme of strategic manipulation of menarchal status is alluded to in a 9th/15th-century slave-buying guide by an Egyptian Ḥanafī jurist. Obviously, the book is written with the interests of a male slaveowner in mind, and thus it may not be possible to take at face value its account of slave women's motivations. Nonetheless it is worth noting the book's claim that a female slave might engage in strategic misrepresentation of her menstrual status for legal purposes. "If a slave girl declares that she is not mature, do not trust her statement in this regard, whether it is [a claim to be] younger or older. For a slave girl might have entered puberty while subject to a [previous male owner] but has concealed it due to her desire for a child, so that she might be freed from the bondage of slavery. Many slave girls pretend to be infertile to deceive their owners. Therefore, whoever wishes to sell a slave girl should display her for sale only while she is menstruating."[227] The implication here seems to be that a slave woman might secretly hope to conceive, because a slave who is impregnated by her owner is entitled to certain privileges. According to most jurists such a woman, known as an *umm al-walad* (mother of a child), can never be sold away from her young child. The child is the property of her owner/the child's father and, if the enslaved mother is sold to a different owner, the sale is nullified according to most legal authorities. Moreover, there developed early on in Sunnī legal history a consensus that, upon the death of the owner, both mother and child would go free and the child would inherit from the father. For this reason, the author of the slave-manual suggests that a slave woman might resort to trickery to become an *umm al-walad*. The woman might pretend she is too young to get pregnant so as to "entrap" her new owner into impregnating her and to thereby improve her legal status. The slaveowner would have sexual relations with her thinking that he does not risk begetting a child because his slave is either too immature or is otherwise infertile. Or she could trick someone in the slave market, by being already pregnant but concealing her pregnancy at the point of being re-sold, knowing that once she is sold and reveals she has been impregnated by her former owner, she is no longer legally subject to the new owner.[228] Other slave-buy-

---

227 Maḥmūd b. Aḥmad al-ʿAyntābī, *al-Qawl al-sadīd fī ikhtiyār al-imā' wa'l-ābīd* (Beirut: Mu'assasat al-Risāla, 1996), 38.

228 The laws governing the position and rights of the *umm al-walad*, the slave who had birthed her master's child, were subject to a great deal of dispute, particularly in the earlier periods of Islamic legal development. See Mirza, "Remembering the Umm al-Walad." See also G. Lydon, and B. Hall, "Excavating Arabic Sources for the History of Slavery in Western Africa," in *African Voices on Slavery and the Slave Trade*, ed. A. Bellagamba et. al., (Cambridge: Cambridge University Press, 2016), 24. See also, S. Marmon, "Domestic Slavery in the Mamluk Empire: a Prelimi-

ing manuals, one from 5th/11th-century Iraq and another from 6th/12th-century Spain also mention misrepresentations of menstrual status, but emphasize the slave-dealers' role in promoting trickery, rather than attributing it to the enslaved women's own designs.[229]

Menstruation or lack thereof in the wake of a divorce or death also seems to have been a largely individual matter in many communities, such that the woman held the discretionary power to choose when to make others in her community aware of the end of her *'idda.*[230] We have seen an example of this phenomenon in the case of the woman whose husband divorced her after realizing that she had not menstruated thrice after her previous divorce. All those involved besides the woman herself were unaware of how many times she had menstruated, though they suspected that there was a problem. Judith Tucker comes to a similar conclusion in her analysis of menstrual status in 17th-century Damascus. She mentions a case that came before a Ḥanafī judge in which a wife claimed to have menstruated three times before entering her second marriage, while her second husband accused her of lying. The judge affirmed that her oath in this matter is accepted and the marriage is valid. Tucker writes: "A woman was empowered, within the limits of the feasible, to define her own waiting period, and it was her word, not that of her husband or others, that determined when the waiting period ended. A woman who was known to have irregular menstrual periods, for example, could also testify to the completion of three menstrual cycles, and her testimony would be accepted, so long as a reasonable period of time had passed."[231] The writings by Ibn Rushd about whether to believe claims about the presence of a sleeping fetus also indicate that, at least for the first few months, a woman's word was believed without any external check.

Midwives and similar experts do appear to have a role in this system, but it seems that their presence was not always thought desirable or welcome in the initial stages of a dispute. Such attitudes are particularly prominent among jurist

---

nary Sketch," in *Slavery in the Islamic Middle East,* ed. S. Marmon (Princeton, Markus Wiener Pub, 1999), 1–24.

229 Ibn Buṭlān, *Risāla fī shirā al-raqīq wa-taqlīb al-'abīd*, in *Nawādir al-makhṭūtāt* edited by 'Abd al-Salām Hārūn in *Nawādir al-makhṭūtāt* 4 (Cairo: Lajnat al-ta'līf wa'l-tarjama wa'l-nashr, 1954), 383. And al-Saqatī, *Fī adāb al-ḥisba = Un manuel hispanique de Hisba* (Paris: Leroux, 1931), 52.

230 The means by which such public signaling occurs seems to vary considerably. An interesting example of such signaling through the performance of a ceremonial bath can be found in a 20th-century fatwā from Timbuktu. See M. Mathee, "Women's Agency in Muslim Marriage: Fatwās from Timbuktu," *Journal for Islamic Studies* 31 (2011), 91.

231 J. Tucker, *In the House of the Law: Gender and Islamic Law in Ottoman Syria and Palestine* (Berkeley: University of California Press, 2003), 170.

in North Africa and Spain. There is mention of midwives being summoned to confirm the presence of genital defects and injuries to the genitals, as well as female claims of male impotence, but this was not uncontroversial. Particularly in the Mālikī school, modesty concerns complicated the assertion of sexual defects. The Mālikī school is unusual in that at least some jurists thought that proving the existence of a wife's sexual defects by means of direct examination might cause more harm than benefit to the husband.[232] For example, al-Wansharīsī quotes a question posed to the Cordovan judge Ibn Dhakwān (d. 451/1059) about a man who accuses his wife of suffering from the defect known as *ratq*. The judge consults with the Cordovan muftī Ibn 'Attāb (d. 462/1069) who responds that, in accordance with the legal opinion advanced by Saḥnūn (d. 240/854), the woman should be examined by other women. However, he notes that his fellow Cordovan muftī Ibn al-Qaṭṭān (d. 460/1068) rules that other women should not be examining her, on modesty grounds.[233] This is consistent with Mālikī views of modesty regulations in other contexts too, which severely limit the ability of anyone apart from the spouse to legally examine a woman's vagina. (Oddly, however, Mālik is said to have called for a rather public test of male impotence, which would preserve the man's modesty but not that of his sexual partner. In this case, the man's penis is daubed with saffron and he is secluded with his partner. Then two women examine her vagina for traces of the saffron.[234])

In addition to concerns about modesty, there were other objections to the testimonies of expert women. Some jurists expressed reservations not with examination per se, but rather in regards to investing midwives with too many simultaneous roles. For example, as Ron Shaham has explored in his book on expert witnesses, Ibn Sahl (d. 486/1093), a Cordovan jurist and judge, objected to midwives being responsible for examining sold slave women, looking for defects that might annul the sale. He objected on the grounds that such a practice effectively made the midwife "a witness, a physician, and a jurisconsult (*muftiyyah*) at

232 al-Qarāfī, *al-Dhakhīra*, 4:422.
233 al-Wansharīsī, *al-Mi'yār al-mu'rib*, 3:132. The opposite attitude is displayed in *al-Mi'yār al-mu'rib*, 3:139. Delfina Serrano mentions that while female slaves who were victims of rape might be examined by midwives, "there is a disagreement in the case of the free woman: Ibn al-Mawwaz and Ibn Habib transmitted from Mālik that the woman, regardless of her status, must be examined by a group of women in order to determine if she has been deflowered. According to Ashhab, the free woman is not subject to this exam." D. Serrano, "Legal Practice in an Andalusī-Maghribī Source from the Twelfth Century CE: The *Madhāhib al-ḥukkām fī nawāzil al-aḥkām*," *Islamic Law and Society* 7 (2000), 201.
234 Al-Qayrawānī, *al-Nawādir wa'l-ziyādāt*, 538.

the same time."[235] When it came to issues of paternity, there was a general reluctance to accept female testimony that could not be corroborated by a man, on the grounds that women's testimony was insufficient in most criminal cases.[236] On occasion we hear of midwives testifying that a divorcée or widow is pregnant but who are then shown to be lying or mistaken.[237] Here is such a case from North Africa:

> Sīdī 'Abdallāh al-'Abdūsī [d. 849/1445 in the region of Fez] was asked about a woman whose husband had died, and she said she was pregnant. Some midwives knowledgeable about such matters probed her womb and said it was indeed inhabited. She remained like that for longer than the period of the *'idda*, i.e. the *'idda* of the widow.[238] Later she wanted to marry [again] and her case was brought to the qāḍī al-Ḥaṣan. She said that her womb showed no indication of that which she had previously declared, and that she had menstruated twice in one month. The qāḍī ordered the knowledgeable midwives to probe her womb and they said, "To us, nothing which we previously saw appears to be in her womb now." Then the qāḍī ordered it be testified to, and [some males] testified to what the woman and the midwives had said. She then married, consummated the marriage, and remained with her husband for about six months. Then she said, "I appear to be pregnant and it is from my deceased husband." Her husband hit her and divorced her via *khul'*, and she remained so for about one month. Then the husband took her back, and she remained another eleven months and then gave birth. She said, "he is the offspring of my first husband." It was said to her, "did you not then marry while you were pregnant?" She said, "I feared for myself and for my money, when the Arab who asked me to marry him, because it is their custom to marry a woman to get her money." Then some of the people said to her husband: "Make her swear that the child is that of the first (husband) and leave her and her child, even if it is your son." So he made her swear and divorced her via *khul'* and reconciled(?) with the

235 Shaham, *The Expert Witness in Islamic Courts*, 96.
236 Giladi, *Muslim Midwives: The Craft of Birthing in the Premodern Middle East*, 113–132. In a Jewish *istiftā'* from eleventh-century Iraq addressed to Hayy Gaon, a husband being sued for divorce voices his disdain for midwives this way: "What does our master, the Head of the Yeshiva, say in the matter of a man who married a virgin and lived with her for about two years, and afterwards she brought him to court saying that he is impotent. She claims that she is still a virgin, while he says, 'I penetrated her and deflowered her [lit: I brought out the blood of virginity] at the time of the wedding.' She denies it and says, "Bring women who are midwives to me to check me, and they shall find that I am a virgin.' He says, 'She hates me and has set her sights on another man. I do not consider the words of midwives, and they cannot be trusted to the extent that they would make me lose, such that I would have to pay out the *ketubah*. For this is like witnessing, and women are unfit for witnessing.'" My translation of the medieval Hebrew translation of an only partially extant Judeo-Arabic original. Hebrew in *Otsar ha-ge'onim* ed. B. Lewin (Jerusalem: Hebrew University, 1928), 7:148. Discussion and Arabic fragment in M. Friedman, *Ribui nashim be-Yisrael = Jewish Polygyny in the Middle Ages Jewish Polygyny in the Middle Ages* (Jerusalem: Mossad Bialik, 1986), 169 ff.
237 Shaham, *The Expert Witness in Islamic Courts*, 88.
238 Four months and ten days.

> child. After this some of the people said to him, "the child is yours, notwithstanding the woman's vow." So now he seeks his son, but the relatives of the dead [first husband] are preventing him, saying "he is the son of our dead brother." Clarify for us to whom the son belongs.[239]

This case hints at several complicating factors which, without more detail, we cannot entirely confirm. Yet certain elements are clear: soon after becoming widowed, the widow decided that it was in her interest to be considered bound via pregnancy to her deceased husband. But then, at some later date (at least four and one-half months into her widowhood) she decided to marry again, at which point she no longer claimed to be pregnant. Six months into the second marriage, which was at least 11 months after the death of the first husband, the wife announced that she was gestating the first husband's child. This led to a *khulʿ* divorce, resulting in a month-long separation, followed by a reconciliation. This pregnancy claim was not soon followed by the actual birth of a child. Rather, a child was finally born 11 months after the reconciliation, and thus at least 22 months (if not much later) after the death of the first husband. Throughout this saga, the midwives' testimonies confirmed the wife's own claims about the matter. And, throughout most of this timespan, the woman clearly wished to be perceived as pregnant, though it took her quite some time to actually birth a child. Her reasons for wanting to be perceived as pregnant were, ironically, to avoid the entanglements of a new marriage. Initially she dissuaded suitors by claiming to be pregnant by her deceased husband, but then decided she had best remarry. If her statement about fearing for own safety is to be believed, she remarried because she thought it would protect her from the advances of other suitors whom she perceived as being a threat. Yet she clearly had mixed feelings about her second marriage, persuading her husband to divorce her, twice, by claiming to be pregnant with another man's child. Here the impetus for claiming to be pregnant and extending her *ʿidda* seems to be primarily that it gave her the space to be practically independent, by virtue of tying her to a dead husband rather than a living one.

This complex relationship between biological realities, legal definitions of biological phenomena, and marriage and divorce practices, meant that cultural practices influenced expectations of fertility, and that women could reframe their biological state to gain legal advantage. Sometimes legal and cultural factors created an expectation of fertility, even when biology pointed toward likely subfecundity or infertility. Such was the case when women experienced early first marriages, or when they experienced divorce somewhat early or late in life.

239 al-Wansharīsī, *al-Miʿyār al-Muʿrib*, 4:54–5.

When the distinctions in the legal system were difficult to apply to these nuanced biological realities experienced by subfertile and infertile women, it could be a source of confusion and frustration. On the other hand, the legal system and the community often placed a great deal of trust in women, such that they had the opportunity and flexibility to represent their reproductive status in ways that enhanced their legal position.

3 Islamic Law and the Prospects of Women Presumed to be Infertile

Marital prospects

On occasion, legal works provide us some insight into the marital prospects of women who had acquired a reputation for being infertile. For example, in his commentary on *Tuḥfat al-muhtāj fī sharḥ al-minhāj* the 19th-century Shāfi'ī scholar al-Shirwānī, reflects on the comparisons and contrasts between a theoretical post-menopausal woman and a theoretical sterile woman "whom a man who already had offspring decided to marry."[240] While al-Shirwānī is a late scholar, the family dynamic he alludes to is probably not limited to his time and place. The infertile woman seems to be someone who has experienced previous marriages, but who is nonetheless able to attract a proposal from a man who is content with her infertility because he already has offspring. In the household of a man who already has as many children or heirs as he desires, and who does not wish to have more, it makes sense that an infertile wife might well find a suitable home. However, al-Shirwānī goes on to say while at first it may seem that an infertile woman is "like a menopausal woman, since she does not conceive, for pregnancy is not a possibility for her, ordinarily" he then argues the contrary, saying that an infertile woman's case is different "since there is a possibility that she may yet become pregnant and her lack of pregnancy during her previous marriages was due to a cause other than infertility." He opts for the latter interpretation, saying that since one can never be sure that she really is infertile, she cannot be compared to a menopausal woman. There always remains a hope or fear that a barren woman may yet prove fertile.

This description of the possibilities and uncertainties surrounding a seemingly infertile woman on her second marriage bears quite a strong resemblance to the depiction of a childless widow contemplating her future in *Women of Deh Koh*, Erika Friedl's fictionalized anthropological account of life in a rural village in Iran in the 1970s and early 1980s. There she describes a middle-aged childless widow weighing the possibility of remarriage.

> She had been around a long time, yet she was not old. There were several middle-aged widowers in the village, a couple of them even eligible relatives. But perceptive as she was, she appreciated their problems very well. For a man who still wanted children she was a bad

240 al-Shirwānī, *Tuḥfat al-muhtāj fī sharḥ al-minhāj wa-ḥawāshī al-Shirwānī wa'l-'Ibādī* (Cairo: Maktaba al-tijāriyya al-kubra bi-Miṣr, 1983), 8:78.

https://doi.org/10.1515/9783110596588-006

> risk, even if there was a tacit understanding that her barrenness probably had been due to [her late husband]'s inadequacy and not hers. For a man with grown sons, on the other hand, she was not old enough; there was still just a chance she might have children, which would obviously not be in the interest of the older children. Against the opposition of his sons, an older man had little chance to take a youngish wife.[241]

As described by Friedl, infertile women could potentially be desirable as spouses, since some husbands would not want more children than they already had from a previous marriage. However, as both Friedl's account and statements such as the one by al-Shirwānī attest, infertility was something that people believed could not be determined with certainty. (This, despite the fact that medical literature frequently describes tests to diagnose fertility and infertility.)

In modern ethnographic literature, in addition to unmarriageability, another, much-feared consequence of infertility is polygyny. Conversely, apologists for polygyny point out that the institution protects infertile women from the prospect of divorce, and that it is a significant argument in favor of polygyny.[242] How then was polygyny as a consequence of infertility viewed in the medieval world?

The idea that polygamy may protect infertile women can be found in *ḥadīth* literature. A *ḥadīth* tells the story of a sixty-year-old convert to Islam, Nawfal b. Muʿāwiya, who had five wives prior to his conversion. Once he joins the Prophet, he learns that Islam limits him to only four wives, and he must divorce one. The woman whom he is forced to abandon is his elderly, barren wife. Here, the limitation placed on polygamy (only four wives) proves negative for the barren woman, whereas she was better off during the era of more expansive polygamy. Commentaries on Q. 4:128 also point to the notion that polygamy is good for barren wives. The Qur'ānic verse reads in part, "If a woman fears contempt on the part of her husband, or abandonment, it is no sin to them if they come to terms of agreement between them, for agreement is best." The verse was understood as referring to the practice of allowing a wife to cede to her co-wife the marital rights originally allotted to herself so as to avoid being divorced. The Prophet's wife Sawda, who ceded her conjugal rights to ʿĀ'isha to avoid divorce, is often cited in Qur'ānic commentaries as an example of this sort of trade off. Al-Ṭabarī (d. 310/923), in commenting on this verse, gives other examples of

---

241 Friedl, *Women of Deh Koh*, 32.

242 For a discussion of the modern defenses of the institution of polygamy, see S. Rank, "Polygamy and Religious Polemics in the Late Ottoman Empire: Fatma Âliye and Mahmud Es'ad's Ta'addüd-i Zevcât'a Zeyl" *Cihannüma: Tarih ve Coğrafya Araştırmaları Dergisi* 1/2 (Dec. 2015), 61–79.

women who might find themselves making this calculation. He writes, "If a woman has grown old, or does not give birth, and the husband wants to marry someone else, he can come to her and say, 'I want to marry a woman who is younger than you, so that she may birth children for me, and I will award her days and maintenance,' then, if she is satisfied with that, he will not divorce her . . ." Thus, in al-Ṭabarī's view, an infertile woman might find herself making the choice to either accept divorce or to accept a polygamous marriage in which the sexual rights due to her are ceded to another wife.

Here polygamy is explicitly associated with inequality, and the infertile wife who consents to it does so for fear of the alternative. Divorce, in this case, seems to be viewed as a worse prospect than polygamy. However, marriage contracts often suggest the opposite and indicate that in general a woman would prefer to be divorced than to be in a polygamous marriage. There is an abundance of medieval marriage contracts stipulating that a man who engages in polygamy may be compelled to divorce his first wife, which implies that many people considered divorce to be a better prospect than sharing a husband.[243] Other marriage contracts suggest a more flexible attitude toward polygamy. For example, a commonly discussed stipulation in a marriage contract was that the first wife, rather than be automatically divorced in the event of a second marriage, instead be given the power to divorce the second wife on her husband's behalf.[244] (Such marriage conditions are usually rejected by the jurists, except by the Ḥanbalīs.[245]) These sorts of conditions raise the question of whether infertility was a factor that changed the normal calculus and, if so, how. Among the three prospects of divorce, monogamous childlessness, and polygamy, which represented the worst case scenario for barren women and which the best? To the extent that women's families were wary of polygamy, and all evidence from marriage contracts indicates that many were, what was it about polygamy that they object-

243 E.g. A. Sonbol, "A History of Marriage Contracts in Egypt." In *The Islamic Marriage Contract*, ed. Frank Vogel and Asifa Quraishi (Cambridge: Harvard University Press, 2009), 102–5. See also, Ali, "Marriage in Classical Islamic Jurisprudence," 25 and 44n263–4 and Rapoport, *Marriage, Money, and Divorce*, 69, 74. A version of this clause is mentioned and permitted by Ibn Ḥanbal in the *Masāʾil ibn Ḥanbal* of Isḥāq b. Manṣūr al-Kawsaj. Ibn Ḥanbal, *Masāʾil al-Imām Aḥmad ibn Ḥanbal wa-Isḥāq ibn Rāhwayh*), 4:1682.
244 This is sometimes known as the "Qayrawān clause," though it was more widespread than the name implies. See Dalenda Larguèche, *Monogamie en Islam : l'exception kairouanaise* (Manouba: Centre de publication universitaire, 2011). E.g. Ibn al-ʿAṭṭār, *Kitāb al-Wathāʾiq waʾl-sijillāt = Formulario notarial Hispano-Arabe* (Madrid: Majmaʿ al-Muwaththiqīn al-Majrīṭī, 1983), 7. See also, A. Sonbol, "A History of Marriage Contracts in Egypt."
245 *Kashshāf al-qinā* 5:134. 4:1682.

ed to? What did barren women in polygamous marriages fear most, and what would make the prospect of polygamy more palatable?

Jewish documents from the Cairo Geniza, as well as some rabbinic legal responsa from the Geonim of Iraq, suggest some intriguing answers to the question of the circumstances under which an infertile woman facing the prospect of either divorce of polygamy might prefer one or the other. Jewish rabbinic family law as it was practiced in the medieval Middle East, in both its Palestinian and Babylonian forms, had many parallels with Islamic family law. Minor marriage was permitted, as was divorce. As was true among Muslims, among Jews divorce was accompanied by the payment of the delayed portion of the dower and with a divorce gift. Jews of the Middle East, like their Muslim counterparts, often wrote "monogamy clauses"[246] into their marriage contracts stipulating that a man cannot take a second wife or maidservant without his wife's permission – the violation of which would trigger the wife's right to force a divorce.[247] One of the differences between Jewish law and Islamic law, however, was that divorce was more often discouraged and more cumbersome to effect,[248] and polygamy was more strongly discouraged among Jews in much of the Arab world.[249] Anoth-

---

246 In an unusual example of such a clause from the 11th century, in a marriage agreement in which one of the parties is a man who comes from Ramle in Palestine (where Jewish polygamy seems to have been almost entirely absent), it seems to say that the husband promises to live monogamously or else to pay a fine, *except* if the wife does not become pregnant. Unfortunately, the document is badly preserved at precisely this spot. Friedman, *Ribui nashim be-Yisrael* 56. The designation for this Cairo Geniza document is ENA NS 18.27.

247 For examples see, Friedman, *Ribui Nashim be-Yisrael* 63–65, 71–73. For an example of a divorce settlement which actually cites this clause as the reason for the divorce, see pp.74–78. The settlement's lack of mention of children implies that the marriage is childless. For examples of marriage contracts in which the violation of monogamy results in the imposition of a fine, rather than a divorce, see ibid. 67–71, 73–4.

248 This is not to suggest that divorce was rarely practiced rather, as Goitein shows, "[i]n the Geniza world, divorce was disapproved but abundantly practiced." Goitein, *Mediterranean Society*, 3:260. However, unlike Islamic divorces, which in theory could come into effect through speech, even by an ill-considered slip of the tongue, Jewish divorces did not come into effect except through the delivery of a court-drawn-up document.

249 Ibid., 147–8, 150. Among Jewish communities in the Islamic world attitudes toward polygamy seem to have varied somewhat, with the Jews of Palestine seemingly not practicing polygamy at all in either the Islamic era or in late antiquity, while the Jews of both Christian and Muslim Spain seem to have practiced it until relatively late. In the documents and literary works from the Cairo Geniza, there are many anti-polygamy clauses, suggesting that polygamy was a practical concern for Egyptian Jewish women. Polygamy among the Jews of Iraq in late antiquity and the early Islamic era seems to have been associated with travel, and bears some resemblance to the Shīʿite institution of *mutʿa* (temporary marriage). In Spain and particularly in Egypt, polygamy seems to have been strongly associated with travel as well, with different

er difference was that rabbinic law strongly encouraged, or even compelled, couples who had not produced children in the first ten years of marriage to divorce.[250] Because continuing childless marriages, divorce, and polygamy were all actively discouraged among Jews, some questions addressed to rabbinic authorities about divorce and polygamy describe in detail the emotional, economic, and legal trade-offs that childless Jewish couples had to negotiate. These same trade-offs might very well also have applied to the petitioners' Muslim counterparts.

Several documents from the Cairo Geniza are quite detailed in their descriptions of what childless women had to gain and fear from polygamous marriages. A 12th-century document depicts a couple drawing up a new ketubba (marriage contract) to govern their marriage, after the original contract that had governed the first years of their marriage was lost. The new document reflects a change in their circumstances. The husband's perspective is described thus: "I ask to marry a woman in addition to her, for I have not had any offspring from her. I wish to see offspring in front of me, as is obligated upon us by Moses our Teacher, by being fruitful and multiplying, and in order that there be a remembrance of me, and my name and the name of my fathers will not be cut off." The woman agrees to her husband marrying a second wife if the following conditions are observed:

> I [the husband] agreed, and promised to follow all the conditions she chose, namely:
> I will take nothing out of her apartment which is currently in it, including furniture and dishes . . .

---

wives living in different regions of the world, rather than with the simultaneous maintenance of two households in close proximity. See Friedman, *Ribui nashim be-Yisrael*, 88–92; 205–240. Polygamy was also highly associated with spousal abandonment in the course of travel, to such an extent that Maimonides issued a ban prohibiting any local Jewish woman from marrying a foreign Jew unless he could prove that he was single, and simultaneously mandating that any foreign Jewish man who had married locally and planned to travel abroad again was to deposit a divorce document to be delivered if he did not return within a predetermined time of one, two, or three years. Maimonides, *Teshuvot ha-Rambam* (Jerusalem: Mikitse Nirdamim, 1960), 624 = #347.

250 Initially this rule also extended to allegations of male impotence, but by the 16th century there were a number of Jewish authorities of Spanish descent living in Egypt, Palestine, and Istanbul writing in favor of compelling divorces in cases of alleged impotence after substantially shorter periods of time. R. Weinstein, "Impotence and the Preservation of the Family in the Jewish Community of Italy in the Early Modern Period" (Hebrew) in *Sexuality and the Family in History = Eros, erusin, ve-isurim: miniyut u-mishpaḥah ba-historiyah*, ed. I. Bartal and I. Gafni (Jerusalem: Merkaz Zalman Shazar le-toldot Yisrael, 1998), 163. Cf. Babylonian Talmud, *Yevamot* 64b, which suggests that two and a half years is a more appropriate length of time to see if a marriage can yield children.

> No curse will ever be placed on her, neither a light curse nor a grave one, not even an oath, and not by means of magic.
>
> And that in everything I spend on [the two wives] and in everything that I am to buy to maintain them, I will not give preference to one over the other in any of these regards.
>
> But if there is [document torn] and she asks to be divorced, then I will be bound to pay her the 100 dinars of delayed dower and for [document torn] another 100 dinars." [251]

The woman in this document is hedging her bet. She conditionally agrees to her husband taking a second wife but expresses a fear that the husband might be tempted to reduce her own material standard of living. She also is fearful lest the new wife attempt to curse her or use magic against her. Elsewhere in the document, she promises not to curse the new wife or any children she might have. (The potential for rivalry and cursing in such circumstances is dramatized in a story in the *Thousand and One Nights*, in which a man marries his cousin "a girl of twelve, who reached womanhood only afterward" who for thirty years bore no children. The man then takes a mistress, who bears him a son. The childless wife then spitefully curses her rival and the child, turning them into a cow and calf to be slaughtered.[252]) The new document further stipulates that if the barren wife has reason to regret opening the marriage to a second wife, her husband will agree to divorce her and pay the remainder of her delayed dower and divorce gift.

A very similar document from al-Maḥalla, Egypt, from the year 1141, describes in minute detail an agreement between a Jewish apothecary, Sa'adya, and his wife, Na'ama, whom it seems he threatened with divorce before reconciling with her.

> The Elder Sa'adya said to us: I am sick of my life and have sworn a binding oath to get [re-] married. I have already reached an agreement with my spouse,[253] my current wife Na'ama bt. Abū Naṣr, that she will permit me to marry another woman. I had already offered her dower to her and to separate from her, but she did not choose this. Rather, I bound myself to the conditions that she asked of me. They are:
>
> That I not promote the woman I marry over her, rather I will be equitable with the two of them, with regard to sleeping arrangements, spending, and maintenance.
>
> I will not give preference to the other over her in any matter; rather, sleeping, night by night, on regular days, Sabbaths, and holidays, will be split equally between the two of them. So too with regard to spending and maintenance.

---

251 Friedman, *Ribui nashim be-Yisrael*, 177.

252 H. Haddawy, *The Arabian Nights* (New York: Norton, 1990) 22. One may perhaps also see parallels with the story of Abraham's childless wife Sarah and her ill-treatment of Hagar/ Hājar.

253 Lit: "with my tent." For this locution see Goitein, *Mediterranean Society* (Berkeley: University of California Press, 1999), 3:160 – 1.

> And if I am blessed with offspring from the wife I shall marry, be it male of female – once I die the [son or daughter] shall not do anything against my wife Na'ama bt. Abū Naṣr, nor will anyone else be empowered by him to take her to court or to utter any kind of curse or oath against her, for I have already made her loyal to me and to all of my heirs after me, in her words, in her house, and in her marriage document, in regards to everything . . .[254]
>
> And at any time while I am still alive, having married [a second wife], should my first wife become distressed by her life with me, I will be obligated to pay her the entirety of her delayed dower and will divorce her, and I will not impede her. And if I do not pay her delayed dower, the court will have the right to sell off the following household furnishings in order to pay her the delayed dower,[255] and I will pay her both the remainder of her dower and her alimony, and this is the list of furnishings . . . [256]

In this document the woman indicates that she too is concerned both about her standard of living and about potentially incurring a curse from the new wife, but here the division of time and sexual rights is also mentioned as a factor. Additionally, the document anticipates the end-of-life conflicts between the childless widow and the rest of the family and attempts to head off a potential lawsuit between the two sides. A third document similarly describes the reconciliation of a man and his barren wife who initially asked to be divorced. As part of their reconciliation he promises that his wife will be provided with a decent burial.[257]

---

254 S. D. Goitein explains that, "in reality, this agreement [to pay the delayed dower] frequently proved to be unenforceable simply because the husband was unable to acquire the means for the payments guaranteed. Consequently, when the end of life approached, we find settlements made in which the amount of the late marriage gift to be paid was reduced, sometimes to half the original amount or even less. The reductions involved concessions of on the husband's side, usually the granting to the wife the status of 'trustworthiness," . . . protected her from being troubled by heirs and courts with demands to render account of any property of her husband held by her." Goitein, *Mediterranean Society*, 3:251 and 254–58 describe the difficulty a widow might have in acquiring her due from the late husband's other heirs.

255 Friedman's *Ribui nashim be-Yisrael* includes an odd example of what appears to be some sort of settlement, in which a husband pays his first wife the delayed dower and transfers her trousseau entirely to her custody immediately prior to marrying a second wife, but the document does not explicitly say that he is divorcing her. Perhaps this represents a precautionary step similar to the above-described enumeration of the property which would be transferred in the event of a divorce. The document dates from 1130. The document is Bodl MS Heb. B 11, fol. 3, in Friedman, *Ribui nashim be-Yisrael*, 80–81. A similar document from the same decade appears on p.119 but, in this document, it seems that the first wife had forced her husband (also her cousin) to divorce his second wife, but is now agreeing to allow him to remarry his divorcee, on condition that the first wife receive her delayed dower in advance in case she has trouble collecting it later.

256 Friedman, *Ribui nashim be-Yisrael*, 185.

257 Ibid, 194.

These stipulations imply that for some childless women a good polygamous marriage was seen as a better alternative than divorce, and divorce was a better alternative compared to an unhappy polygamous marriage. In order to establish a good polygamous marriage, the contracts include the conditions that (a) the current wife not be forced to give up her current standard of living; (b) the husband treat his wives equitably with respect to sexual arrangements and financial support; (c) the current wife not suffer abuse from the new wife; and (d) the current wife will be given the means to support herself after the husband's death, with no attempts to withhold the money owed to her. One of the documents goes so far as to specify which valuables will be sold by the court in the event that the family of the deceased attempts to thwart the childless widow from collecting her money from the estate. Interestingly, none of these documents attempt to define a relationship between the childless wife and any potential child produced by the new spouse, other than to restrain hostilities between them. In no way is polygamy presented as a surrogate form of motherhood or as potentially expanding the circle of relations for the barren woman.

Of course, in many Islamic and Jewish communities, the practice of polygamy was either limited or practically non-existent.[258] For example, Leslie Peirce notes that polygyny is not mentioned at all in the court documents of the Anatolian town of Aintab, in the early modern period, even among childless families.[259] Presumably, remaining monogamous in a childless marriage must have been a practical option for many, if for no other reason than the potentially high financial and social costs of divorce. Of course, in such cases, legal literature can offer us few insights, since there was no reason for the relationship to receive scrutiny from the court. The experiences of childless spouses who remained married to each other did not draw the law's attention until such time as one spouse died and the other became a potential heir to the inheritance.

Childlessness and inheritance

Up to this point, we have examined the implications of infertility for those attempting to contract or dissolve a marriage. However, infertility was also signifi-

---

258 For a brief discussion of the high costs associated with polygamy in early modern Aleppo, and the court records which attest to this cost see A. Marcus, *The Middle East on the Eve of Modernity: Aleppo in the Eighteenth Century* (New York: Columbia University Press, 1989), 199–200, 368. He notes, however, that infertility was considered an exceptional circumstance, in response to which polygamy was potentially acceptable even among Jews.

259 Peirce, *Morality Tales: Law and Gender in the Ottoman Court of Aintab*, 150.

cant after the death of one of the spouses, since childlessness had a substantial impact on the rules of inheritance. Furthermore, the prospect of future inheritance had the potential to influence family dynamics while both spouses were still living. Women's childlessness had consequences in three different inheritance situations:

(a) When a married, childless woman died, leaving behind a living husband and her natal family as heirs. (If her parents have also died, then the inheritance distribution takes on added complications.[260])
(b) When a married, childless woman was widowed, thereby inheriting a portion of her husband's legacy without the legal possibility of her share returning back to her husband's bloodline. The legacy would thus be transferred from her husband's bloodline to that of her own birth family.
(c) When a childless woman was due to inherit or to collect from the estate of a relative by birth but had no husband or son to represent her interests during the legal proceedings.

The ability of women to take hold of property in their lifetimes, and their ability to pass on property to their own heirs upon their deaths, were intimately connected. Medieval Islamic law in no way distinguished between infertile and fertile women regarding their rights to inherit, benefit from, and manage their own property. But it did distinguish between women who had children and those who were childless when it came to their rights to pass along property to their heirs. The result was that a childless woman, who passed away before her husband, effectively handed over to her husband's family half of the property given to her by her natal family, with no chance of it going to her natal family's descendants. A childless woman who survived her husband handed over up to a quarter of her husband's property to her own natal family. This created potential incentives to postpone or impede childless women from gaining access to property during their lifetimes.

Death of the childless wife

In Sunnī legal theory, when a childless woman dies leaving only a husband and members of her birth family as heirs, the husband receives fifty percent of her

260 The situation of a person who dies without living ancestors or descendants to inherit from them is known as *kalāla*, a complicated topic that is beyond the scope of this book.

estate.[261] In those societies in which a woman's estate might include a substantial bridal trousseau as well as other property, this could represent a significant financial loss for her birth family. One way of mitigating fears of this sort of situation was to marry a woman to her paternal cousin who, for inheritance purposes, was also a member of her natal family.[262] Another way was to either pass off the woman's possessions (which she had received from her birth family) as life-time gifts which, upon her death, would revert back to her birth family, or to call into question the woman's marriage itself. Such scenarios are mentioned in some *istiftās* addressed to Ibn Taymiyya.

> He was asked about a mature woman who died, leaving a father, a mother, and a husband, and whose father then took possession of her trousseau, leaving nothing to her heirs . . .
> He was asked about a woman who died, leaving a husband and her two parents, and whose father then took hold of her possessions, saying that she was a minor. Does her husband inherit from her?[263]

Yossef Rapoport has analyzed Mamluk-era attempts by some women's families to take back the trousseau following her death if she produced no children.[264] Such families would either add clauses to the marriage contract which would finalize the transfer of the trousseau from parents to daughter only once she gave birth, or they would engage in legal proceedings to define her trousseau as a temporary gift.[265] Maya Shatzmiller notes that there was a practice in Muslim Spain

---

261 Based on Qur'ān 4:12.

262 "The structural means to prevent property passing out of the family is the marriage of paternal first cousins. In such a marriage, the husband inherits from the wife in two capacities: as a husband he is a Qur'ānic heir, who, in the absence of children, takes one-half of her estate (by the side of children he takes only one-quarter but there is no danger then of the property passing out of the family), and as an agnatic relative he takes the residue." A. Layish, "The Mālikī Family "Waqf" according to Wills and "Waqfiyyāt," *Bulletin of the School of Oriental and African Studies*, 46 (1983), 28.

263 Taqī al-Dīn Ibn Taymiyya, *Fatāwā al-Nisā'*, ed. Ibrāhīm Muḥammad al-Jamal (Cairo: Maktabat al-Qur'ān, 1987), 195, 203. Referenced in Rapoport, *Marriage, Money, and Divorce*, 17. The translation is mine.

264 Rapoport, *Marriage, Money, and Divorce*, 17.

265 Rapoport notes that since, in Jewish law, the bride's family would not inherit from her if she had a widower, there exist both Karaite and Rabbanite contracts from Mamluk Cairo which have a similar stipulation. Shraga Abramson notes that the stipulation that half of the estate of a childless wife return to her birth family can be found in the Jerusalem Talmud and was a matter of frequent debate. It was enshrined in law in the widely publicized thirteenth-century *takkanah* (decree) of Toledo, but apparently it was slightly different in its Arabic and Hebrew versions, which circulated simultaneously. Abramson, "On the Takkanah of Tuletula (Toledo) Regarding the Husband's Inheritance of his Wife's Estate," *Zion* 60 (1995), 201–224. For an example of this

of fathers maintaining ownership over property ostensibly given to their daughters until one to seven years into the marriage.[266] Al-Wansharīsī's *Mi'yār* has several such cases,[267] including a case of a mother and step-father suing their widower son-in-law to recover their late daughter's trousseau after she died. The widower launches a countersuit for the wedding expenses. It is not at all clear how much time had elapsed since the wedding.[268]

Multiple *istiftā*s and stipulations in marriage contracts indicate that childlessness was commonly understood by parents of the bride to represent an exception which prevented the marriage from being fully realized. Parents with such views strategized to interrupt the transfer of property from the wife's natal family to the husband and his heirs. Judith Tucker notes that in Ottoman Palestine the jurists accepted the popular notion that the property given to women at the time of their marriage was a life-time loan which would return to her parents if she died.[269] It is possible that the husbands of infertile women also viewed their marriages as not fully realized, given that there are many instances of a widower suing his deceased wife's family for the return of his wedding expenses; however, it is also possible that this was simply a legal tactic rather than an expression of social values.

In a later historical context, that of early-modern Ottoman Anatolia, the association between the production of children and a woman's achievement of status as an autonomous adult and householder with property of her own, was both physically manifested and embedded in language itself. Leslie Peirce describes how, in the town of Aintab, wives did not get their own residences until they birthed their first child:

---

clause in an 11th-century marriage contract found in the Cairo Geniza see T.S. 13 J 6.33, in Friedman, *Ribui nashim be-Yisrael*, 68–71. For an analysis of the prevalence of such stipulations in marriage contracts found in the Cairo Geniza see Eve Krakowski, *Coming of Age in Medieval Egypt* (Princeton: Princeton University Press, 2018), 246–251. Judith Olszowy-Schlanger has identified sixteen Karaite marriage contracts which stipulate that if a woman dies childless her possessions revert back to natal family, thus preserving their property, but the husband is also absolved of paying the delayed portion of the dower. J. Olszowy-Schlanger, *Karaite Marriage Documents From the Cairo Geniza: Legal Tradition and Community Life In Mediaeval Egypt and Palestine* (Leiden: Brill, 1998), 241–4.

266 *M. Shatzmiller, "Women and Property Rights in Al-Andalus and the Maghrib: Social Patterns and Legal Discourse," Islamic Law and Society 2 (1995), 229–30.*

267 Al-Wansharīsī, *al-Mi'yār al-Mu'rib*, 3:97, 221. 9:150. Cf. 4 Ibn al-'Aṭṭār, *Kitāb al-Wathā'iq wa'l-sijillāt*, 339.

268 Al-Wansharīsī, *al-Mi'yār al-Mu'rib*, 3:92 and 9:127–8.

269 Tucker, *In the House of the Law*, 56.

> It was generally [the *gelin*, new bride], not the young husband, who made the spatial transition into marriage by moving into the household of his parents (the term *gelin* derived from the verb *gelmek*, "to come" . . .) The word emphasized that the young bride had as yet no identity except as an affiliate to her husband's family . . . The female adult, in contrast – the *avert* or *hatun* – acquired her identity from the establishment of her own household unit with the birth of children. This event was often accompanied by a physical move into a separate residence . . . household-as-residence was seen as a fundamental constituent of full adulthood. This convergence of household and the production of children reflects the widespread view of parenthood as critical in establishing full personhood in the community. More than marriage itself, childbearing and child-rearing transformed men and women into socially mature adults. There was, however, a gender disparity in this signaling of adulthood, as the existence of two labels for the married woman – new bride and female adult – suggests. It was the female member of the marital pair – the bearer of the child – whose changing status marked the inception of the new household. Correspondingly, it was she who experienced greater pressure to bear children.[270]

In those communities in which the full-fledged acknowledgement of a woman's marriage and her right to pass property on to her heirs was subject to the birth of children, the prospect of childlessness had the potential to shape her familial life during her lifetime. Rapoport notes that parental attempts to stall the transfer of property sometimes meant that the younger generation had to take their parents to court. He writes, regarding the Mamluk period, "The vast majority of disputes over dowries were intergenerational rather than conjugal. In the legal literature the question is almost never usurpation of the dowry by the husband, but rather the parents' attempt to revoke the gift."[271] Mathieu Tiller mentions a similar pattern in his analysis of *Adab al-qāḍī* written by the 3rd/9th-century Ḥanafī jurist al-Khaṣṣāf.[272]

In those communities where this practice of delayed or revocable forms of dowry prevailed, such an arrangement might have compounded the frustrations of a childless marriage. When the financial benefits accruing from marriage only legally "took hold" once a marriage proved stable as evidenced by the presence of children, lack of children would have further contributed to lack of financial autonomy and hence to marital instability. I have found at least one source which uses the phrase, "the time it takes to produce two children from two pregnancies," as a proverbial idiom for establishing that a marriage originally con-

270 L. Peirce, *Morality Tales: Law and Gender in the Ottoman Court of Aintab*, 149–150.
271 Rapoport, *Marriage, Money, and Divorce*, 18.
272 M. Tillier, "Women before the Qāḍī under the Abbasids," *Islamic Law and Society* 16 (2009), 282.

tracted under questionable circumstances now has the longevity to be thought of as valid.[273]

Death of the husband of the childless woman

In a monogamous marriage, a woman with no descendants whose husband had died would theoretically receive one quarter of her husband's property in addition to any deferred dower still owed to her, according to all Sunnī schools of law.[274] (According to Twelver Shī'ites she would not inherit at all.[275]) If she was part of a polygynous but childless family, that quarter would be divided equally between all widows. Thus if there were three wives, each would receive one twelfth of the estate. If a man died leaving one or more widows and at least one son (e.g. from a different marriage), his widow(s) would receive a total of one eighth of the estate. In all of the above cases, the property inherited by any childless widow would effectively be removed from her husband's bloodline because, when she died, all of her heirs would be from her natal family. [276] The same cannot be said of a widow who has children with the deceased, since their mutual children would bring the greater part of their mothers' portion back into the paternal bloodline once they inherit from her.[277]

---

273 Al-Dasūqī, *Ḥāshiyyat al-Dasūqī 'alā al-Sharḥ al-Kabīr* (Beirut: Dār al-Fikr, n.d.), 2:224.

274 Based on Q 4:12.

275 Shī'ī legal literature which deals with recompense of injuries demonstrates a recognition of the financial loss associated with infertility. The Shī'a award a woman the full *diyya* in compensation if a man injures her in such a way as to cause her to prematurely lose her ability to menstruate thus rendering her barren. Sunnī schools do not usually award compensation for the loss of fertility, but only for damage to a body part. Ibn Bābawayh al-Qūmmī (d. 381/992) *Man lā yaḥḍuruhu al-faqīh*, § 5334.

276 Interestingly, according to Marcia Inhorn's studies of infertility in contemporary Egypt, those infertile women who were married to their cousins sometimes considered themselves to be in a much better position and to have happier marriages relative to other infertile women who were married to "strangers." M. Inhorn, *Infertility and Patriarchy* (Philadelphia: University of Pennsylvania Press, 1996), 130. Inhorn does not, however, mention issues of inheritance in any of her work.

277 The complicated nature of the partition of the property of childless men sets the stage for a riddle told in the fifteenth *maqāma* of al-Ḥarīrī (d. 516/1122): a man dies whose only living heirs are his full-brother and his widow, who herself has a full brother. Under what circumstance would the widow's brother legally come to inherit all of the property other than his sister's and disinherit the deceased's brother? See al-Ḥarīrī and F. Steingass, *The Assemblies of al-Ḥarīrī; Student's edition of the Arabic text; with English notes, grammatical, critical, and historical* (London: Sampson Low, Marston & Co. 1897), 112.

The awareness of conflicting interests between the widow and the rest of the deceased husband's relatives could lead the husband, the wife, or the other relatives to attempt to circumvent sharʿī inheritance laws through the establishment of *waqf*s (endowments), death-bed divorce[278] or, on occasion, the discovery of a *rāqid* i.e. "sleeping fetus." Some scholars argue that *waqf* endowments served in some communities as a means of disinheriting women, although that view has come under a great deal of scholarly criticism, and others have argued that endowments tended to supplement rather than detract from women's shares of inherited wealth.[279] Sometimes a *waqf* seems to have been put in place to safeguard the inheritance of existing children before a new marriage was embarked upon. For example, a case in al-Wansharīsī's al-*Miʿyār al-muʿrib* describes a man with two young children who, prior to marrying a new wife, creates an endowment for the benefit of his children. The new marriage lasts twelve years before the death of the husband and appears to be childless.[280] In this case, the widow takes control of the endowment for several years before her step-son, at the age of twenty-one, is finally able to take control of it himself. At that point, she has trouble extricating her delayed dower from her late husband's estate due to its being tied up in the endowment.

278 If the husband were to divorce his wife irrevocably, just before his death, she would not inherit any share of the estate, thereby preserving more money for the husband's other heirs. Rapoport, *Marriage, Money and Divorce*, 87. The legality of such a measure is a matter of dispute. There are many examples of medieval *istiftā*s which describe deathbed divorce but, unfortunately, such documents rarely describe who the husbands' heirs are who are competing with the (ex-)widow. For example none of the *fatwā*s in al-Wansharīsī's *al-Miʿyār al-muʿrib* specify who the competing heirs are. See volume 4:87–8. Modern *fatwā*s which address the deathbed divorce of childless women do specify the competing heirs, perhaps because there are fewer of them than there would have been in pre-modern periods e.g. ʿAllām Naṣār, "*Fatwā* – January 19, 1952," in *Fatāwā dār al-iftā' al-miṣriyya* (Cairo: Wizārat al-Awqāf, 1980), 5:114. The phenomenon of disinheriting childless widows through deathbed divorce is also mentioned by modern women's rights advocates, particularly in Pakistan. *Report of the Pakistan's Women's Rights Commission*, 1976 quoted in "Some Facts and Figures About Women's Situation In Pakistan," *Manushi* 12 (1982):5. There, there have been some efforts to ameliorate the position of childless women by allowing husbands to transfer property to them during their lifetimes, with the property reverting back to the husband (if he is alive) or his family (if he is deceased) after the wife's death. These efforts have often failed to succeed on the grounds that they are difficult to justify within the Islamic legal system.L. Carroll, "Life Interests and Inter-Generational Transfer of Property Avoiding the Law of Succession," *Islamic Law and Society* 8 (2001), 271.

279 P. Hennigan, *The Birth of a Legal Institution: The Formation of the Waqf in Third-Century A.H. Ḥanafī Legal Discourse* (Leiden: Brill, 2004), xvi.

280 Wansharīsī, *Miʿyār al-muʿrib* 7:261.

On occasion, particularly in the Mālikī *madhhab*, we read about heretofore childless women who have been widowed for years and are able to disrupt the inheritance system by giving birth to a *rāqid* who then inherits a portion of his deceased father's estate. Al-Wansharīsī describes jurists trading increasingly outlandish stories, such as this one:

> A woman came to us whose husband had died while her womb was occupied by a child. Then, after seven years, she brought forth the child. The aforementioned man had left other children and [this new child] inherited along with them, once they saw his resemblance to their father. They acknowledged him and did not deny it to him.[281]

Despite its farfetched nature, the case is important in terms of demonstrating the protracted impact of childlessness and fertility on the inheritance system.

Occasionally, we also hear of old age with the impending prospect of inheritance as a time for spouses to demonstrate care for each other regardless of their fertility failures. In the *Kitāb al-Umm*, al-Shāfiʿī relates the story of the daughter of Ḥafṣ ibn al-Mughīra. Her first husband ʿAbdallāh b. Abū Rabīʿa, divorced her, prompting ʿUmar b. al-Khaṭṭāb to marry her. But ʿUmar found out prior to consummating the marriage that she was infertile and could not bear children, and so he divorced her too. She remained single for several more years, long enough for ʿUmar to die and sometime into the caliphate of ʿUthmān. Then her first husband, ʿAbdallāh, remarried her when he fell ill so that she too could inherit from him along with his other wives, because "there was a kinship between them."[282] Here the kinship is likely both emotional and biological.

Claiming inheritance against male kin without the benefit of sons

In addition to inheriting from her husband and children, a woman also inherited from her birth relatives: her parents, and sometimes her siblings and paternal grandparents.[283] Islamic inheritance law, by recognizing a daughter's and sister's right to inherit property from her birth family, and to keep her finances separate

---

281 Ibid. 4:492.
282 Al-Shāfiʿī, *Kitāb al-umm* 4:108. The story is also told in ʿAbd al-Razzāq's *Muṣannaf*, #11132.
283 Throughout the Islamic world, customary law was often at odds with the sharīʿa's insistence on awarding women shares in inheritance. Rapoport, *Marriage, Money and Divorce in Medieval Islamic Society*, 20. See also, Annaliese Moors, "Inheritance: Contemporary Practice," in *Encyclopedia of Women in the Islamic Cultures*, ed. Suad Joseph (Leiden: Brill, 2003–2007), 2:300 and Y. Tobi, "Inheritance Rights of Jewish Women and Moslem Women In Yemen," *Proceedings of the Seminar for Arabian Studies* 24 (1994), 201–8.

from her husband's, provided a woman with a measure of autonomy but also placed a woman in a potentially awkward position in which her financial interests did not entirely coincide with those of either her birth family or her husband's family. The person whose financial interests most closely mirrored her own was her son. The mother of a young son could become the guardian of his share of his father's inheritance, should her husband choose to appoint her to that position. It was in her interest to protect her son's share of the property from her husband's kin and business partners. Later, an adult son could potentially be in a position to protect his mother's share of her birth-family's property, since it was in his interest to do so.

A woman's male kin from her natal family were often her de facto protectors[284] and representatives in legal proceedings,[285] but when it came to inheritance from the estates of her birth relatives, her share competed with those of her brothers and uncles.[286] Thus her usual representatives had financial interests which were directly opposed to her own. By contrast, in the person of her son, she would have a male family member who could effectively represent her because his financial interests coincided with hers, as he would inherit from her but would not inherit from her male relatives.[287] Such representation, however, would not be available to a childless woman.

There are at least three known ways in which women dealt with the threat of being deprived of their inheritance. They could sue their fellow heirs for their in-

284 On the high status of the bond between brothers and sisters see Goitein, *Mediterranean Society*, 3:21–24. For a contemporary anthropological perspective on the relationship between brothers and their widowed childless sister, see Friedl, *Women of Deh Koh*, 26–46.

285 "With regard to women and inheritance, the evidence suggests that women received their inheritance shares but probably were not present at the division of the estate. I do not know if it was a common practice for husbands to represent their wives or for male relatives to represent unmarried women, and I do not know if women in fact received their inheritances, although I strongly suspect that this was the case. The fatwās indicate that females were dependent on male relatives for the receipt of their shares . . ." M. Shatzmiller, "Women and Property Rights in Al-Andalus and the Maghrib: Social Patterns and Legal Discourse" *Islamic Law and Society* 2 (1995), 241.

286 Zarinebaf-Shahr, writing about seventeenth-century Ottoman Istanbul, notes that a large percentage of women's court petitions were about inheritance and property disputes: "Inheritance disagreements occurred among members of all economic strata, but mostly among members of the middle class, where women were left dependent on male relatives for the protection of their property rights. Zarinebaf-Shahr, "Women, Law, and Imperial Justice in Ottoman Istanbul in the Late Seventeenth Century," in *Women, the Family, and Divorce Laws in Islamic History*, ed. Amira El Azhary Sonbol (Syracuse: Syracuse University Press, 1996), 87 ff.

287 Ottoman-era court records show mothers on occasion suing their adult sons for their one-eighth share of the husband's estate.

heritance in court, they could sue for their inheritance from people who had bought their expropriated property from the rival heirs, or they could choose to forfeit their property. In practice, in appears that in some places the latter two were quite common. For example, in 16th-century Ottoman Anatolia, according to Leslie Peirce, a large percentage of women's court appearances revolved around inheritance disputes. But the defendants in these cases were not women's rival heirs to the family estate. "Women's rights," writes Peirce, "were infringed by a variety of male relatives – stepfather, uncle, even father, and, most frequently, brothers." In such cases, rather than suing their own relatives directly, women instead sued those to whom their relatives had sold the share of the property which "should" have gone to the sister or daughter. Peirce writes: "Female suits . . . were brought directly against the current owner and not against the male relative who had sold the land. The court's interest was to defend the women's claims; it did not concern itself with prosecuting the wrongful seller or compensating the loser."[288] The same process is described by Ronald Jennings, who examined early 17th-century court records from the Anatolian city of Kayseri.[289] The roundabout nature of such legal behavior suggests that women did not think it was in their own interest to attempt to formally sue their own male relatives.

Modern anthropological research in Palestine, Jordan, Pakistan, Bangladesh, and India suggests that, in those contemporary societies, women sometimes view forfeiting their inheritence rights (*tanāzul*) as a good strategy for securing their relationship with their brothers, a relationship which brings both material and social benefits.[290] This is particularly true of childless women, as is explained in this analysis of family dynamics in an Arab village in the newly-formed state of Israel:

> While women legally have the right to inherit (The Koran, iv, 13), no woman with a brother will demand her share of the property. In brief, a woman is always jurally and emotionally connected to her father's household and his patrilineage. At times of difficulty, quarrels, or maltreatment in her husband's household, as a young widow or as a childless older one, she requires the security of the house of her paternal relatives. Without such protection, and without her own kin to defend her rights, a woman is easily exploited. She will not risk in-

288 L. Peirce, *Morality Tales: Law and Gender in the Ottoman Court of Aintab*, 213.

289 R.C. Jennings, "Women in Early 17th Century Ottoman Judicial Records: The Sharia Court of Anatolian Kayseri" *Journal of the Economic and Social History of the Orient* 18 (1975), 67.

290 Widows sometime forfeit their rights to their husband's wealth as well, in order to benefit her son and to acquire his loyalty. However there is no perceived benefit accruing to the widow in cases where the widow is childless. S. Sait and H. Lim, *Land, law and Islam: property and human rights in the Muslim world* (New York: Zed Books, 2006), 123.

> curring the anger of her brother by requesting property and thereby reducing his share. Should she do so, she would be cut off from his household.[291]

In a summary of these studies of women's forfeiture of property, Siraj Sait and Hilary Lim write:

> It is an interesting example of 'God proposes, Man disposes' where pragmatic or socio-cultural considerations alter the impact of Shari'a rules, even though they take effect after the Shari'a formula is implemented. While gender rights advocates are justifiably concerned over women being forced to renounce their limited property rights, the reality may be far more complex. It may be a choice over empowerment through property or through enhanced family support.[292]

Based on these insights, we can see how a childless woman might have been both particularly vulnerable and empowered by her situation. By virtue of not having anyone whose financial interests coincided with hers, she had few natural allies when it came to matters of inheritance. Unlike women who had children, however, childless women could relinquish their share to their brothers, and thereby seek to win from them the support which they would have received from their children.

291 H. Rosenfeld, "Processes of Structural Change within the Arab Village Extended Family," *American Anthropologist* 60 (1958), 1130.
292 Sait and Lim, *Land, law and Islam: property and human rights in the Muslim world*, 121.

Conclusion to Part I: The Intersection of Islamic Law and Women's Biology

Islamic law rarely penalizes barren women or delegitimizes childless marriages. This is the case despite the fact that *ḥadīths* dating from the first centuries of Islam decry such marriages, and despite the economic and social problems that accompanied childlessness. Indeed, in Islamic legal theory women could not even be categorically labeled as infertile from the time they reached menarche until they reached old age. Yet this presumption of fertility did not always match up with either biological likelihood or socially constructed diagnoses. This is not to say that Islamic law was irrelevant to the experiences of medieval Muslim women, nor am I suggesting that legal theory represents the "true" place of women in Islamic societies. Rather, I would argue that it is the mismatch between Islamic legal theory, legal practice, biology, and other sources of cultural expectations that had the greatest impact in defining the situations in which medieval barren women found themselves.

This mismatch is evident on multiple fronts. Even though in *ḥadīth*-based advice literature, the legal-philosophical literature, and in the more theoretical sections of legal handbooks there are frequent mentions of the idea that reproduction is one of the primary goals of marriage (*maqāṣid al-nikāḥ*), this goal did not shape the development of laws of marriage. To a remarkable extent, it was a different goal of marriage, that of sexual pleasure, that shaped the law.[293] It was women's roles as possessors of female sexual desire and as objects of male sexual desire that defined their place when contracting a marriage. A woman's desire for sexual satisfaction, her utility as a sexual object, and her defectiveness if she becomes sexually unavailable to her husband, had far greater legal consequences than her desire for children, her utility as a producer of children, and her defectiveness if she was infertile. For this reason, the lower age limit of marriage was set not at the point when a woman would likely produce children, but rather at the point when she became capable of engaging in sexual intercourse. Similarly, a free woman could demand complete sexual intercourse rather than coitus interruptus (usually) not on the grounds of her right to a child, but rather on the grounds of her right to sexual satisfaction. For both sexes, it was not in-

293 Judith Tucker makes much the same point, with an emphasis on a slightly later historical context. J. Tucker, "Muftīs and Matrimony: Islamic Law and Gender in Ottoman Syria and Palestine," *Islamic Law and Society*, 1.3 (1994), 272.

https://doi.org/10.1515/9783110596588-007

fertility, but rather impotence, which served as legal grounds for marriage annulment.

We see a mismatch between law and biology in the laws pertaining to the *ʿidda* period, the ostensible legal purpose of which was to clarify that a womb is not "occupied" by the offspring of a previous husband. However, the *ʿidda* was measured via menstrual cycles, an imperfect proxy for reproductive capacity. Further muddying the situation was the biological possibility of oligomenorrhea and amenorrhea, which proved disruptive to the legal function of the *'idda* period. Moreover, the belief in multi-year-long pregnancies, a belief acknowledged both in law and in society at large, added another dimension to concepts of infertility, reproductive availability, and paternity. Finally, the seemingly straightforward biological facts of menarche, menstruation, conception and pregnancy were complicated by women's abilities to "shape" these facts by concealing them or swearing to their occurrence.

We see a mismatch between the legal and social expectations of the role women ought to play in conveying and enjoying the benefits of familial wealth. All women, both fertile and infertile, had the legal right to inherit and thereby the ability to divert wealth from their birth families, and this was a source of frustration which prompted legal intrigue. For infertile women, the frustrations were all the more palpable because even as they diverted wealth to other families, they did not produce multi-generational networks with them. Katherine Kueny, in her work on motherhood in Islamic thought, suggests that this incapacity was further magnified by the infertile woman's inability to create kinship ties through breastfeeding.

> Women who have no infant to breastfeed cannot create an expanded network of blood ties with their own children or others among their family or the community of believers. Without the ability to establish such an expansive network of familial relations, few will inherit from them. In the absence of offspring, the wealth of the family must be transferred laterally rather than linearly, a secondary provision put forth in the Qur'ān that stifles a husband's God-given right to sow his own legacy among future generations. Unmoored, barren women are left adrift in a world organized around kinship ties.[294]

Finally, there was a blatant mismatch between legal and social attitudes towards polygamy, and infertility further complexified the situation. In Islamic legal theory, a husband could engage in polygamy without reproach and with an expectation that all wives would receive equal treatment. However, in general practice, women, their families, and their communities frequently went out of their way to

294 Kueny, *Conceiving Identities*, 158.

protect women from the perceived evils of polygamy. Infertility, however, was an exception to that generalization. It was often acceptable for men in otherwise monogamous societies to engage in polygamy so as to be able to maintain a relationship with a barren wife, while attempting to nonetheless produce offspring. Women who were given the choice between polygamy and divorce might even view polygamy as the better option.

The result of all these mismatches was that the Islamic legal context provided infertile women and their families with a dizzying array of paths, rather than narrow dictates, within which they could maneuver and strategize. It is certainly the case that there were women whose childlessness rendered them particularly weak and in need of protection, and it is also true that as a result of not recognizing infertility as a source of particular social vulnerability, the legal system had no impetus to put in place safeguards to protect their interests. We also see, however, that there were women who could exploit the flexibility provided by the discrepancies highlighted here so as to secure their own well-being.

Part II: Arabo-Galenic Gynecology and the Treatment of Infertile Women

Introduction to Part II

Medieval gynecology as an intellectual field was shaped by male scientists' lack of direct access to women's reproductive organs, an obstacle rooted in female anatomy itself, in addition to cultural values of modesty. The internal and hence physically inaccessible nature of women's reproductive organs meant that any scientist would have to make some inferences when attempting to help people have children. The scientist had to infer what contribution mothers make to their offspring, given that there is no visible maternal equivalent to the father's semen. He had to infer what conditions made it likely that coitus would result in conception, given that not all sexual encounters produce a pregnancy. He had to infer what the early signs were that conception had taken place, given that the embryo must be growing for some time before it is large enough to be detected through quickening or maternal showing. He had to infer the reason behind the well-observed phenomenon that pregnant women do not tend to menstruate, and lactating women often do not either. He had to infer the causes of miscarriage, given that the triggers of early contractions resulting in the premature expulsion of still-growing fetuses are not obvious, and the same is true of the causes of intrauterine fetal death. He also had to infer the sources of breastmilk and its relationship to pregnancy.

There were additional, related questions that ancient and medieval scientists asked which may not seem intuitive to us but which do derive from universally observable phenomena. Among these were: why do women usually menstruate? Given that most women experience menstruation, what does it signify if a woman does not, or does not do so regularly? If menstruation is natural and healthy, is lack of menstruation a symptom, or perhaps a cause, of ill health? What makes it impossible for women to "self-pollinate" given that they obviously contribute to the make-up of the child (as indicated by hereditary similarity) and have the capacity to grow and nourish the fetus in their wombs? Do women manifest a physical indication of sexual desire and arousal, as men do in the form of erections? Do women experience impotence, as men do? Would a woman who is not aroused during a particular sexual encounter be unlikely to get pregnant, just as a man who experiences erectile dysfunction during a sexual encounter is unlikely to impregnate? Conversely, if a woman does conceive, does that indicate she was aroused at the time of conception and was thus a willing sexual partner? What makes an embryo develop as male or female, at what stage does sexual differentiation occur, and can one influence that bodily process, in the same way that one can influence the shape of one's body through eating and exercise? Is a male fetus an indication that its male parent has a stronger

https://doi.org/10.1515/9783110596588-008

"seed," i.e. a more powerful hereditary influence; and is a female fetus the product of a stronger, more influential female parent? And finally – given that the womb during pregnancy obviously expands, causes pain, compresses other organs such as the bladder and stomach, pulses so violently (in the form of contractions) as to be able to expel the fetus, and then shrinks postpartum – does the womb do such things when it is not occupied by a pregnancy?

Infertility was a particularly complicated gynecological issue because it was linked to theories of conception and embryonic development, and these theories carried significance beyond the realm of medicine. Many of the scientists, philosophers, and theologians who articulated a conception theory did not do so primarily for the purpose of describing where babies come from, but rather to describe the relationships between Creator and creation, soul and body, form and matter. In such descriptions, these binary relationships were mapped onto the male and female contributions to the embryo and, inevitably, it was the female contribution which constituted the junior or less sophisticated partner in the relationship. Some scientists also embraced more egalitarian-seeming theories of conception, not due to a commitment to the principle of gender equality, but rather due to its seeming consonance with Islamic religious texts and law, as well as empirical observations about heredity.[295]

In some ways, the significance of conception theory beyond the purely medical realm is analogous to the significance attached to the motions of the planets and celestial bodies, beyond the realm of physical astronomy. The cosmos hinted at truths about God Himself, His creation, His providence, His sovereignty, and the truths contained in His own book, the Qur'ān. But astronomical truths were also practically important. They helped people to orient themselves toward Mecca; and, to the extent that people put stock in the idea that the movements of the planets and stars impacted human life, astronomical insights were perceived as being practically useful.[296] Similarly, articulating the correct theory of conception mattered both because it was a metaphor or metonym for larger philosophical truths, and because it had a practical value.

In addition to the philosophical and theological ramifications that influenced medical thinking about fertility and infertility, there were more mundane concerns as well. The treatment of infertility potentially called for sexually-charged and immodest interactions. Medical diagnosis and treatment of infertility involved conversations about sexual technique, the physical examination of the

295 Musallam, "The Human Embryo in Arabic Scientific and Religious Thought," 37.
296 On the prominent role of astronomy in medicine, see P. Pormann and E. Savage-Smith, *Medieval Islamic Medicine* (Washington, DC: Georgetown University Press, 2007), 154–156.

genitals, the application of pessaries (suppositories) in the vagina and ointments within the uterus, vaginal fumigation, and the consumption of sexually suggestive foods and substances. It also possibly involved medicalized forms of genital rubbing or surgical correction of genital abnormalities.[297]

The confluence of these complications raises some interesting questions. How was infertility understood by the physicians of the medieval Islamic world? To what extent did their beliefs about women's bodies differ from the beliefs held by those physicians of antique and late-antique periods whom the medieval physicians esteemed? Did broader philosophical attitudes about female inferiority and social constructions of feminine virtues have an impact on how infertility was understood and treated? Most importantly, is there evidence that the theory and treatments espoused by classically-trained male physicians had any practical applications for female patients? Was masculine discourse about gynecology merely an intellectual exercise, which was neither informed by nor could hope to impact the secluded world of women? Or, perhaps, was the world of women and gynecological care not nearly as secluded and segregated as some have assumed?

The role and significance of gynecology in the medical literature produced by medieval Islamic civilization has been the subject of some debate. The great historian of Islamic science, Manfred Ullmann, devotes only four paragraphs of his *Die Medizin im Islam* to discussing medieval gynecology in the Islamic world, describing it as essentially underdeveloped as a result of medieval physicians having nothing to do with gynecological care.[298] Ullmann makes a two-fold claim: book-learned male physicians did not invest in the study of gynecology, and the reason they did not do so was because only midwives, who lacked all access to Arabo-Galenic medical theory, had the opportunity to treat gynecological conditions. Ullmann is somewhat obscure in his attribution of the source of this "underdevelopment," suggesting it might be due to "morality codes" or to some other aspect of culture, which he ambiguously terms "tradition." In any case, in Ullmann's view, learned gynecology must have been a moot and underdeveloped discipline, because all medically learned people were men, and gender segregation made gynecology an exclusively female domain. Men could not tread or have an impact in this domain, and so they took no interest in it.

297 Ibn Sīnā, *Qānūn fī al-ṭibb* 2:590 = *Kitāb* 3: *fann* 21: *maqāla* 4: *faṣl fī al-rutqā'*. al-Majūsī, *al-Kāmil*, 2:488. al-Rāzī, *al-Ḥāwī fī al-ṭibb* vol. 3, bk. 9:16.
298 Ullmann, *Medizin im Islam*, 250.

By contrast, in her book *Conceiving Identities: Maternity in Medieval Muslim Discourse and Practice*, Kathryn Kueny characterizes medieval gynecology as an arena for the assertion of male dominance and control over the incompetent bodies of women, specifically so as to wrest the power of reproduction from them. She writes:

> [T]he rhetoric and discourse appropriated by medieval Muslim physicians and scholars [cast] the female body as the passive, more dependent sex that must be controlled and dominated by men . . . to keep hazards at bay, medieval physicians assert knowledge of, or control over, every stage of the reproductive act by surveying and circumscribing the female body, and by working to cure any problem within it that might interfere with man's desire to replicate himself . . . Assuming the role of custodian and surveillant of women's bodies, male medical scholars and physicians, like the Qur'ānic God, claim both the knowledge and power to generate life.[299]
>
> Given their near-obsessive interest in concocting ways to prevent miscarriages, it is evident Muslim physicians believe in most cases that God does not destine the fetus to die but rather that women do not take proper caution for or care of what they are carrying, or that women's bodies are simply not well equipped for the task. Because women often failed to bring a pregnancy to fruition, men needed to be that much more vigilant in protecting the fetus from female ignorance, carelessness, or weakness, or in devising ways to overcome the female body's inherent deficiencies. As a result of their concern, elite scholars rendered women incapable of caring for their own bodies.[300]

Whereas Ullmann submits that gynecology was neglected by male physicians because it was not within men's purview, since that which was out of sight also was out of mind, Kueny makes a contradictory claim. She depicts physicians as attempting to artificially insert themselves into an area in which one would naturally expect women to be independent, competent, and dominant. Physicians did so for the purposes of asserting women's passivity, incompetence, and need for male aid. Kueny also claims that their depictions of the functioning of the uterus artificially use physiological notions to promote religious notions of chastity.[301]

The following two chapters argue in opposition to both Kueny's and Ullmann's characterizations of medieval gynecology. Both characterizations overemphasize the power and explanatory value of certain cultural tendencies. Neither a desire to use medicine as a tool of subjugation, nor a commitment to modesty and gender segregation account for the way infertility is discussed in medieval medical writings. Medical discourse on infertility reflects neither lack

299 Kueny, *Conceiving Identities*, 53.
300 Kueny, *Conceiving Identities*, 71.
301 Kueny, *Conceiving Identities*, 68.

of interest, nor an assumption of custodianship or surveillance of women's bodies, nor an intellectual assault on women's virtue or reproductive competence.

The answers that Arabo-Galenic physicians offered to genuinely perplexing questions about reproduction and female physiology were similar to those provided by their Greco-Roman predecessors. However, the Arabic writers modified the Greek medical tradition in two interesting directions. First, Arabic depictions of the role of the female body in the reproductive process were somewhat more egalitarian and less socially coercive than Hippocratic and Galenic – and especially Aristotelian – depictions. Second, there was an attenuation of the links between physiological theories, diagnostics, and therapeutics when it comes to gynecology, although this was also true to a lesser degree already in Galen's own time. Even when certain beliefs about anatomy and conception were jettisoned, nevertheless diagnoses, tests, and therapeutic measures, which had been based on the abandoned theories, continued to be propounded. Thus in many cases, practical aspects of gynecological care remained constant even as underlying theory varied. Sometimes the converse was true as well, and a diagnosis remained constant while the measures taken to respond to it varied considerably. Of course, incongruity between therapeutics and etiology is not unique to the medieval context. Consider that bloodletting remained a staple of European and American medical practice for two centuries after William Harvey proved that blood circulated and so the body was unlikely to have a superfluity of blood. Or, to offer a more modern example, recall that American parents, who theoretically know that "the common cold" is a virus, still frequently warn their children not to go outside in winter with wet hair or an insufficiently heavy coat, lest feeling cold cause them to "catch a cold."

The flexible relationship between etiology, diagnostics, and therapeutics meant that, despite the fact that scientists fiercely debated and held diverse opinions about embryology,[302] those debates did not result in correspondingly divergent sets of practical recommendations within the gynecological literature. Rather, we see the repetition of a relatively narrow set of practical recommendations which often had "ecumenical" value, easily integrated into diverse and conflicting scientific worldviews and appropriate to a wide range of gynecological needs.

302 For discussions of such debates see Musallam, "The Human Embryo in Arabic Scientific and Religious Thought." Also N. Fancy, "Womb Heat versus Sperm Heat: Hippocrates against Galen and Ibn Sīnā in Ibn al-Nafīs's Commentaries," *Oriens* 45 (2017), 150–175 and U. Weisser, *Zeugung, Vererbung, und pränatale Entwicklung in der arabisch-islamischen Mittelalters* (Erlangen: Hannelore Lüling, 1983).

Did the gynecological theories or advice found in medieval medical writings have any practical import? Would educated male physicians have advised women patients regarding their gynecological ailments and, even if they had, would women have been inclined to pay any attention to their book-learned knowledge? The extant literature we have suggests that, in some communities at least, the answer to both these questions is "yes." At the very least, the situation is much more ambiguous than Ullmann assumes.[303] Medical writings often depict male physicians as having close interactions with their female patients. They consistently show that physicians thought they ought to be involved in medical care and worked with midwives who mediated their interactions with female patients, and that at other times male physicians interacted with female patients directly, including in the management of gynecological matters. Moreover, the extant medical texts we have suggest that medieval writers assumed that the knowledge they and their readers possessed would be utilized by real female patients.

---

303 It should be noted that until recently historians of European medicine also assumed that in Christendom, prior to the early modern period, male physicians had little to do with childbirth or the treatment of gynecological conditions. This view has been challenged and undermined in recent years, particularly by Monica Green. See M. Green, *Making Women's Medicine Masculine: The Rise of Male Authority in Pre-Modern Gynaecology* (Oxford: Oxford University Press, 2008), particularly pp. 36–45 for the earlier period. Also, M. Green, "Caring for Gendered Bodies," in *Oxford Handbook of Medieval Women and Gender*, ed. Judith Bennett and Ruth Mazo Karras (Oxford: Oxford University Press, 2013), 345–61.

4 Gynecological Theory in Arabo-Galenic Medicine

The importance of the Greco-Roman medical tradition in Arabic medicine

In his *Shukūk ʿalā Jālīnūs* (Doubts About Galen) the famously independent physician Abū Bakr Muḥammad ibn Zakarīyā al-Rāzī (d. 311/923), known as Rhazes in the Latin tradition, writes:

> Galen says, "One who understands what is said in this section knows what renders men sterile and women infertile: that is, a man who has a balanced temperament is always fertile, but one who lacks balance will be fertile if he so happens to be coupled with his opposite in humoral temperament." This is not true, for I have seen many men such as this, cycling through women, hoping to reproduce, and it is of no use to them. One of them would buy slave girls according to our guidance to him, and I evaluated their humoral compatibility with him.[304] I also had a neighbor, whose warm and moist temperament could pass for that of a camel, who expended great efforts in his cycling through slave girls, but it was of no use to him – even though Galen says that this sort of temperament is strongest with respect to reproduction.[305]

Al-Rāzī's observations remind us of some peculiar aspects of infertility as an "illness." First, it was ongoing, and therefore a patient usually had the time to make a variety of attempts to fix the problem. This was not true of other types of ailments such as acute diseases or injuries. However, infertility was anomalous among other long-term conditions such as chronic pain, or diminished eyesight, in that there was a strong possibility that it could be resolved. Like fevers and other acute conditions, infertility could pass, whether due to effective intervention or despite neglect or harmful medical treatment. If it resolved and the former sufferer did produce children, having had ample time to attempt a variety of treatments, attributing the source of healing was a matter open to interpreta-

304 The Christian physician, Isḥāq ibn ʿAlī al-Ruhāwī (d. 931 A.D.), who lived in northwestern Iraq, seems to allude to the practice of physicians choosing sexual partners for their patients when he writes, "It is of value to distinguish between skillful shrewd practitioners and those who imitate them. You may see these two classes when they come into a city and plan to show what they claim about their work with various arts. Some of them butter up the sultan of that country with electuaries and in selecting women who are pretty and act well, which they claim have [health] value." This translation of al-Ruhāwī's *Adab al-ṭabīb* is from Martin Levey, "Medical Ethics of Medieval Islam with Special Reference to Al-Ruhāwī's 'Practical Ethics of the Physician,'" *Transactions of the American Philosophical Society* 57 (1967), 90.

305 al-Rāzī, *Kitāb Shukūk ʿalā Jālīnūs* (Tehran: Muʾassasah-ʾi Muṭālaʿāt-i Islāmī, Dānishgāh-i Tihrān, 1993), 79.

https://doi.org/10.1515/9783110596588-009

tion. Moreover, unlike most other types of long-term medical conditions, there was a clear line differentiating between success and the lack thereof in treating infertility. In the management and alleviation of pain, or even diminished eyesight, the patient's subjective perceptions dictated the extent to which a course of treatment was deemed successful. Not so for the treatment of infertility. When successful treatment was marked by the arrival of a child, one could make an empirical argument, or at least an anecdotal one, demonstrating the failure of a particular explanatory theory and course of treatment, which is precisely what al-Rāzī does.

Al-Rāzī's attack on Galen's statements about fertility respond to a medical culture which proudly described its theories as an intellectual inheritance from the Greco-Roman world. Hippocrates (fl. c. 5th century B.C.), Aristotle (fl. c. 4th century B.C.), Dioscorides (fl. c. 1st century A.D.), Galen (d. c. 216 A.D.), Paul of Aegina (fl. c. 7th century A.D.) and many others are cited as authorities in the medieval Arabic gynecological literature. Most of the gynecological beliefs described below entered into the Arabic medical corpus through the mediation of Galen and later figures such as Stephanus of Athens, Aetius of Amida, and Paul of Aegina.[306] It is not my intention to explore here the translation and reception history of individual Greek or Roman medical texts, or to trace the route through which they were transmitted to the Arabic-writing world, since others have already done so.[307] Instead, this chapter explores the substance of

306 For the importance of Galen in shaping the Arabic reception of Hippocratic texts, see M. Ullmann, *Die Medizin im Islam* (Leiden: Brill, 1970), 35–62; N. Fancy, "Womb Heat versus Sperm Heat: Hippocrates against Galen and Ibn Sīnā in Ibn al-Nafīs's Commentaries," *Oriens* 45 (2017), 150–175; and P. Pormann, "The Hippocratic Aphorisms in the Arabic Medical Tradition," *Aspetar* 2 (2013), 412–415.

307 There are several scholarly works which describe the transmission of Greco-Roman gynecology to the medieval Islamic world and to Latin Europe. Max Meyerhof and Dimitri Joannides produced three short monographs on the subject in the 1930s. D. Joannides, *Esquisse de la gynécologie et de l'obstétrique chez les égyptiens et les grecs* (Cairo, 1934); idem, *La gynécologie et l'obstétrique chez Avicenne (Ibn Sina) et leurs rapports avec celles des grecs* (Cairo, 1938); and idem, *La gynécologie et obstétrique de Paul d'Egine et son influence sur la médecine arabe* (Cairo, 1940). Ursula Weisser wrote an important study of medieval Arabic understandings of the physiology of reproduction and heredity *Zeugung, Vererbung, und pränatale Entwicklung in der arabisch-islamischen Mittelalters.* Monica Green's "The Transmission of Ancient Theories of Female Physiology and Disease Through the Early Middle Ages" (Ph.D. Dissertation: Princeton University, 1985) provides the best overview of the history of the translation movement with respect to gynecology. It includes an appendix with useful flowcharts depicting the translation movement with regard to individual gynecological texts on pp. 235–238. For a recent philologically-oriented analysis of the transmission, reception, and exegesis of Hippocratic aphorisms pertaining to gynecology see Rosalind Batten, "The Arabic Commentaries On The Hippocratic

Arabic medical writings about the causes and treatments of infertility and related gynecological issues.

This book uses "Arabo-Galenic medicine" as an infelicitous shorthand for a complex intellectual heritage as we know it from a certain set of highly influential texts which routinely refer to each other. These texts are all written in Arabic, though many of the texts' authors were also steeped in other linguistic traditions. Some of these texts reflect a variety of sources of local and global medical knowledge, especially Indian medicine and particularly Indian pharmacy, although this influence and inspiration is sometimes acknowledged only in vague or anonymizing terms by our authors. Most often, the medieval authors explicitly situate their own thinking and contributions to the medical field in the context of Greek thought, especially as mediated by Galen and Galen's disciples. They buttress their arguments by citing either texts translated from the original Greek and Syriac into Arabic, or by engaging with other original Arabic texts which also situate themselves within the same intellectual heritage.

As depicted by the medieval Arabo-Galenic authors themselves, the ancient theorists who exerted the most influence on their own framework for understanding gynecology were Hippocrates, Aristotle, and Galen.[308] Whereas in the medieval Latin world Soranus's (fl. c. 100 A.D.) famed *Gynecology* was continuously in circulation, there is little evidence that it was ever translated into Arabic. However, some of Soranus' gynecological thought became known to the Arabic world through Paul of Aegina (d. c. 690 A.D.).[309] The gynecological sections of many of the Byzantine medical encyclopedias, which were later transmitted to the Arabic world, also draw heavily on Soranus' treatments.

The extant Hippocratic treatises relating to gynecology are *Diseases of Women (I & II), Diseases of Young Girls, On Barrenness, Generation* and *Nature of the Child, Nature of Women, Seven-month Child, Eight-Month Child, Superfetation* and *Excision of the Embryo*. According to Manfred Ullmann, only two of the more minor works on gynecology, *Superfetation* and *Diseases of Young Girls*, are known to have been translated into Arabic in the medieval period, as was Hip-

Aphorisms: Arabic Learned Medical Discourse On Women's Bodies (9th-15th Cent.)" (Ph.D. Dissertation: University of Manchester, 2018). Scholarly discussions about which Greek gynecological works were available in Arabic versions has heavily relied on the work of Manfred Ullmann. Ullmann's *Die Medizin im Islam* is available in an accessible English summary: *Islamic Medicine* (Edinburgh: Edinburgh University Press, 1978).

308 Weisser, *Zeugung, Vererbung, und pränatale Entwicklung*, 53.

309 Ullmann, *Islamic Medicine*, 11, 14, 15 and Peter Pormann, *The Oriental Tradition of Paul of Aegina's Pragmateia* (Leiden: Brill, 2004).

pocrates' *Aphorisms,* which also includes gynecological material.[310] *On Generation* and *Nature of the Child* also exists in a modified form in Arabic as *Kitāb al-ajinna li-Buqrāṭ.*[311] A book attributed to Hippocrates called *Kitāb awjā' al-nisā'*, i.e. "Diseases of Women," is found in lists of books but, according to Ullmann, there is no evidence that it was ever extant in Arabic.[312] However, *Superfetation* has a broader gynecological scope than its title implies, corresponds closely with *Diseases of Women I,* and contains some passages which are identical to those found in *On Barrenness.* Of all of these, Hippocrates' *Aphorisms* is the most frequently cited text in the medieval Arabic medical literature pertaining to infertility.

Medieval gynecology, like other branches of medicine, was heavily influenced by Galenic thought.[313] The authority of Galen was so respected that a medieval physician might resort to *ta'wīl* (scriptural reinterpretation) in order to explain away his errors by arguing that his teachings had merely been misunderstood. Johann Christoph Bürgel notes the following example of such esteem:

> 'Abd al-Laṭīf al-Baghdādī discovered that the lower jawbone of the human body was not, as Galen had thought, composed of two parts, but that it was a single sutureless bone. This famous Egyptian scholar made his discovery in the course of osteological studies in an ancient cemetery in the northwest of Cairo – but not until he had investigated more than two thousand skulls did he realize that he had come across an error in Galen's teaching. In his account of this experience he expressed the conviction – which, self-evident as it may seem to us, was a bold statement in those times – that the evidence of the perception of our senses deserved more confidence that the teachings of Galen;[314] though having said so,

310 Green, "The Transmission of Ancient Theories of Female Physiology and Disease Through the Early Middle Ages," 79 and Ullmann, *Die Medizin im Islam*, 29.

311 Commenting on the relationship between the two texts, the modern editors of *Kitāb al-ajinna li-Buqrāṭ* write: "The text, as preserved . . . shows a mixture of translation, paraphrase, and comment . . . in many cases the distinctions between expanded translation, paraphrase and restatement are blurred." M. C. Lyons and J. N. Mattock, *Kitāb al-ajinna li-Buqrāṭ* (Cambridge: Pembroke Arabic Texts, 1978), ii.

312 M. Ullmann, "Zwei spätantike Kommentare zu der hippokratischen Schrift 'De morbis muliebribus'" *Medizinhistorisches Journal* 12 (1977), 245–262; M. Green, "The Transmission of Ancient Theories of Female Physiology and Disease through the early Middle Ages," 74.

313 Green, "The Transmission of Ancient Theories of Female Physiology," 235–7.

314 Al-Baghdādī's claims to originality were by no means well-received. See N. Peter Joosse, *The Physician as a Rebellious Intellectual: The Book of the Two Pieces of Advice or Kitāb al-Naṣīḥatayn by 'Abd al-Laṭīf ibn Yūsuf al-Baghdādī* (Frankfurt am Main: Peter Lang Edition, 2014). The biographer Ibn al-Qiftī's entry about him is both personally and professionally scathing. It concludes, "In 628, it occurred to him to travel to Iraq and to make the *ḥajj* pilgrimage. He fell sick in Baghdad and began to treat himself with his own medicine, and died – just as

> he added, typically enough that there might be found an interpretation of the words in question which would free Galen from the charge of error.[315]

A somewhat less diffident attitude can be found in the above-quoted *Shukūk ʿalā Jālīnūs* (Doubts About Galen) in which al-Rāzī anticipates that his criticism of Galen, and in particular of his humoral theory, will itself be met with consternation. Using terminology that is deliberately reminiscent of Islamic jurisprudential language, al-Rāzī compares the stance of his critics, who believe he should have a more reverential attitude toward Galen, to jurists bound by *taqlīd*. *Taqlīd* refers to the intellectual posture of a jurist who imitates or conforms to his predecessors' conclusions, rather than revisiting the premises on which they are based, due to his belief that he is bound by his predecessors' authority. Al-Rāzī instead calls on his fellow scientists to emulate the *sunna*, the exemplary tradition, of the great philosophers of old. His language echoes the religious value of emulating the *sunna* of the Prophet Muḥammad.

> As for those who censure me and call me ignorant for having produced this Book of Doubts – I do not call them philosophers. They have turned their backs on the tradition (*sunna*) of the philosophers. They have taken up the tradition of ignorant upstarts, through imitation (*taqlīd*), refraining from raising any objection against it. Aristotle says: 'Plato and the Truth are at odds, and both are friends to me – but the Truth is a friend dearer still than Plato.'[316]

Al-Rāzī's criticisms of Galen's theories were indeed alarming enough to inspire some of the great figures of medieval medicine such as Ibn Abī Ṣādiq al-Nīsābūrī (d. after 462/1068), Ibn Zuhr (Avenzoar, d. 557/1162) and Moses Maimonides (d. c. 1204) to write refutations of them. Ibn Zuhr accounted for this failing in al-Rāzī by claiming that either al-Rāzī did not author the book at all, or he wrote his book when he was an adolescent too young to understand Galen, or

---

God had wished – in the year 629. His books were sold in Aleppo. I happened upon some of them, and they were of the degree of inferiority which is furthest removed from perfection. God save us from the enticement of pretentiousness!" Ibn al-Qiftī, *Inbāh al-ruwāt ʿalā anbāh al-nuḥāt*, ed. Muḥammad Ibrāhīm (Cairo: Dār al-Kutub al-Miṣriyya, 1950), 2:196. Translation by A. Verskin, "A Muslim-Jewish Friendship in the Medieval Mediterranean: ʿAlī Ibn al-Qifṭī's Biography of Rabbi Yūsuf Ibn Shamʿūn," in *The Idea of the Mediterranean*, ed. Mario Mignone (Stony Brook: Forum Italicum Publishing, 2017), 189.

315 J. C. Bürgel, "Secular and Religious Features of Medieval Arabic Medicine," in *Asian Medical Systems: A Comparative Study*, ed. Charles Leslie (Berkeley: University of California Press, 1976), 45–6. The anecdote comes from ʿAbd al-Laṭīf al-Baghdādī, *Kitāb al-Ifāda wa'l-iʿtibār* (London: Allen and Unwin, 1965), 176 and 272–6.

316 al-Rāzī, *Kitāb Shukūk ʿalā Jālīnūs*, 2. The English translation is slightly modified from a passage in M. Mohaghegh's afterward to the book.

else he produced it as an old man whose great mind had become addled by exposure to arsenic and sulfur in the course of his alchemical studies.[317] This reverential attitude toward Galen is significant not only for comprehending gynecology and embryology in medieval learned medicine, but also for understanding the ambivalence and the criticisms leveled by some jurists against the culture of Arabo-Galenic medicine. Such attitudes will be explored in chapter 6.

Greek antecedents to medieval gynecological concepts

Moisture, menstruation, and health in Hippocratic texts

In their gynecological statements the Arabo-Galenic physicians explicitly drew on Hippocratic theory and practice, despite lacking direct access to some of the major Hippocratic gynecological texts. Hippocratic medical theory characterized women's health, and the difference between women and men, through the lens of polar opposites: dry and moist, right and left, hot and cold, etc.[318] Hippocratic gynecology in particular associated women with moisture, while Aristotelian and Galenic gynecology placed emphasis on characterizing women as colder than men. These opposites recur throughout Arabo-Galenic gynecological writings, with masculinity associated with heat,[319] dryness and the right side, and femininity associated with cold, moisture and the left side.[320]

The most obvious evidence of women's "moisture" was menstruation, but the characterization was not localized to the uterus, rather it defined women's entire physiology. According to Hippocratic gynecology, women are moist because their softer, porous flesh retains fluid more than does the less-porous flesh of men.[321] Men rid themselves of what excess fluid they have through per-

---

317 Mohaghegh, *Kitāb Shukūk ʿalā Jālīnūs*, 112.

318 On the internal consistency of the gynecological works and their relation to the rest of the Hippocratic corpus see, A. E. Hanson, "Continuity and Change: Three Case Studies in Hippocratic Gynecological Therapy and Theory," in S. Pomeroy *Women's History and Ancient History* (Chapel Hill: University of North Carolina Press, 1991), 76–7.

319 There is some inconsistency in the Hippocratic texts with regard to heat. *Diseases of Women I* says that "a woman has hotter blood, and because of this she is hotter than a man," while in *Regimen for Health* it says "Females, inclining more to water, grow from foods, drinks and pursuits that are cold, moist and gentle. Males, inclining to fire, grow from foods and regimen that are dry and warm."

320 Weisser, *Zeugung, Vererbung, und pränatale Entwicklung*, 275.

321 Text in A. E. Hanson, "Hippocrates: Diseases of Women 1," *Signs* 1 (1975), 572.

spiration. Women, however, must do so through menstruation, pregnancy (in which case menstrual blood nourishes the fetus) or lactation.[322]

Whereas biomedical gynecology understands menses as merely the shed lining of the uterus, the Hippocratics understood the menses as a large quantity of excess fluid which filled the uterus to capacity before being evacuated through menstrual bleeding. They estimated that a healthy woman discharges approximately one pint of blood each cycle, about seven or eight times as much as is estimated in studies of twentieth-century women.[323] The process through which all this fluid was evacuated could easily be impeded, so they thought, leading to a build-up of "retained menses." If the "retained menses" were not evacuated, the uterus would become overfull, thereby causing pain and serious disease.

The entire extant fragment of the Hippocratic treatise *Diseases of Young Girls* is devoted to describing the dangers risked by women whose excess moisture is not given a proper outlet.

> Afterwards blood is gathered into their wombs for evacuation. Yet, when the mouth of the exit is not opened and more blood flows in due to their nourishment and the increase of their body, then the blood, not having a way to flow out, rushes from the quantity towards the heart and the diaphragm. When these parts are filled, the heart becomes numb; then lethargy seizes them after the numbness, then after the lethargy, madness seizes them . . .
>
> When these things occur in this way, the young girl is mad from the intensity of the inflammation; she turns murderous from the putrefaction; she feels fears and terrors from the darkness. From the pressure around the heart, these young girls long for nooses. Their spirit, distraught and sorely troubled by the foulness of their blood, attracts bad things, but names something else even fearful things. They command the young girl to wander about, to cast herself into wells, and to hang herself, as if these actions were preferable and completely useful. Even when without visions, a certain pleasure exists, as a result of which she longs for death, as if something good . . .
>
> Release from this comes whenever there is no impediment for the flowing out of the blood. I urge, then, that whenever young girls suffer this kind of malady they should marry as quickly as possible. If they become pregnant, they become healthy. If not, either at the same moment as puberty, or a little later, she will be caught by this sickness, if not by another one. **Among those women who have regular intercourse with a man, the barren suffer these things.**[324]

---

322 Green, "The Transmission of ancient theories of female physiology," 16.

323 L. Dean-Jones, "Menstrual Bleeding according to the Hippocratics and Aristotle," *Transactions of the American Philological Association* 119 (1974), 181.

324 Ann Ellis Hanson and Rebecca Flemming "Hippocrates' 'Peri Partheniôn' (Diseases of Young Girls): Text and Translation," *Early Science and Medicine* 3 (1998), 251–252. My emphasis.

In this text, lack of regular menstruation is depicted not as menstrual absence but rather as menstrual retention, i.e. menstrual blood exists, but it is locked in and needs to be released or else it will overfill and damage the rest of the body. That release is best obtained through marriage and sexual intercourse. Sexual intercourse is itself credited with providing an outlet for menses. (There is some disagreement among classicists as to whether the Hippocratics thought of defloration as breaking a hymenal seal or stopper which then allows the menses to flow out, or whether sexual intercourse was thought to dilate the veins and the cervix, thereby providing a wider channel for the exiting menses.[325]) Thus irregular or absent menstruation is not understood as indicative of a girl being too young to have reached full physical maturity, or too young to be married, but rather lack of marriage is depicted as barring her from reaching full physical health, thereby causing disease. Moreover, an even better outlet for excess menses is pregnancy and lactation, since menses nourish the fetus, and excess blood is the raw ingredient that when "cooked" is transmuted into breastmilk. If pregnancy and birth are particularly salubrious then, by extension, those who are married but barren are particularly at risk of ill health.

The Hippocratic gynecological treatises are thus premised on the notion that women who have reached puberty are subject to diseases if they are not regularly menstruating, pregnant, or nursing. Not only are menstruating, pregnant, and nursing women considered to be healthy, but Hippocratic medicine claims that women who have given birth are subject to less pain while menstruating and less severe disease.[326] Such an understanding assumes that sexual intercourse and childbirth are necessary for women in order to avoid illness. Conversely, virgins, non-fertile women, and unattached widows are depicted as physically at risk. In this system, barren women are in a disadvantageous position not simply because they cannot produce children, but because they are thought to be suffering from injurious disease, one which may even lead to derangement and a propensity toward violence.

---

325 L. Dean-Jones, L. Dean-Jones, *Women's Bodies in Classical Greek Science* (Clarendon Press: Oxford, 1994), 50.

326 Ibid., 19. Cf. *Diseases of Women I*, 572 and *Diseases of Young Girls*. The latter is in Ann Ellis Hanson and Rebecca Flemming "Hippocrates' 'Peri Partheniôn' (Diseases of Young Girls): Text and Translation," *Early Science and Medicine* 3 (1998), 251.

Women's anatomy and the female contribution to the embryo

Three anatomically erroneous but significant assumptions with respect to female anatomy were passed from the Hippocratics to Galen and onward into Arabic medical literature. The first of these was the assumption that in a healthy woman there is a direct passage between the mouth, uterus, and vagina. Furthermore, 5th-century B.C. Greek anatomical thought implied that the uterus has olfactory capabilities, and thus a medical practitioner can attract or repel the uterus upwards or downwards within the body by introducing attractive or repellant substances to it via the vagina or mouth. Later Greek and Arabo-Galenic physicians rejected entirely the idea that the uterus can sense odor or move in response to it, yet the application of the same sorts of odorous substances continued to play a significant role in antique and medieval gynecology. Furthermore, Hippocratic gynecology assumed that a woman's fertility depended on her having an unobstructed channel between vagina, uterus, and nose. A blocked passage was understood as indicative of ill-health and sterility. A variety of medieval diagnostic practices continued to be predicated upon the existence of this passage but, as we shall see, medieval writers develop this line of thought in new and divergent ways.

The second anatomical error was the idea that the human uterus is "bipartite"[327] i.e. that the uterus is composed of two symmetrical cavities, a left one and a right one (as is true in the case of some animals).[328] This assumption was used to explain why male and female fetuses develop differently in utero. It continued to hold sway in Galenic and later Arabic medicine despite the fact that, through reports of dissections, and possibly from internal examinations, Galen himself was aware that the uterus did not have two cavities.[329] Me-

327 Modern biomedicine treats the bicornuate uterus as a rare and serious medical condition. A somewhat more common condition is the "uterine septum" in which a partition bifurcates an otherwise normally-shaped uterus. This condition often causes miscarriage.

328 The anatomists of Alexandria, Egypt, who performed dissections, correctly described the shape of the uterus. However, this information was not integrated into later gynecological theory. Alexandria seems to be the only place in the ancient Greco-Roman world where we know that dissection was performed. It seems it was tolerated there from the third century B.C. until the second century A.D. Ludwig Edelstein, *Ancient Medicine* (Baltimore: Johns Hopkins Press, 1967), 256.

329 Galen, *De Uteri Dissectione*, chap. 3, translated in Charles Mayo Goss, "On the Anatomy of Uterus," *The Anatomical Record* 144 (1962), 77–83.

dieval medicine referenced the left and rights "sides" of the uterus in discussions surrounding fertility and pregnancy tests, as well as fetal development.[330]

The third error lay in the belief that there was a passage connecting the uterus to the breasts. The explanatory value of this passage was that it meant that changes in the breasts could be used to monitor changes in the uterus, particularly during pregnancy. Drawing on Hippocrates' *Aphorisms* 5:37–38, al-Rāzī writes, "If she was pregnant and her breasts suddenly shrivel, then she has experienced a miscarriage. And if she was pregnant with twins and one of her breasts shrivels, she has miscarried the [fetus] which is on that side. The signs of conception, whether it is a male or a female: males are on the right side [of the uterus] and females are on the left side, and it is only rarely otherwise."[331] The connection between breasts and uterus also held out the possibility of treating uterine ailments by means of the more accessible body part, for example by applying cupping glasses under the breasts and drawing blood from there to prevent excessive blood loss during menstruation.[332] The passage between the uterus and the breasts was also useful for explaining lactational amenorrhea – it stood to reason that nursing women might not menstruate because their "excess" blood, which would otherwise be evacuated by menstruation, had been transformed into breastmilk. Finally, the existence of the connection between the breasts and the uterus suggested a biological relationship between the babies wet-nursed by women and those birthed by them, a relationship that fit in well with Islamic concepts of milk-siblinghood, which created legal ties of close kinship between a wetnurse and the nursing child.[333]

Notably missing from the gynecological teachings of Hippocrates and Aristotle is an awareness of the existence of the ovaries. Although ovaries are large enough to be visible without modern technology, it is thought that their existence only became widely known in the Greco-Roman scientific world in the 3rd century B.C. thanks to Herophilus, even though others in the Mediterranean world had long been using ovariotomy in animals (and sometimes in women)

---

330 For beliefs about the divided uterus see Weisser, *Zeugung, Vererbung, und pränatale Entwicklung*, 275.

331 al-Rāzī, *al-Ḥāwī fī al-ṭibb* vol. 3, bk. 9:75. This closely follows *Aphorisms* 5:37–38.

332 Ibn al-Jazzār al-Qayrawānī and Gerrit Bos, *Ibn al-Jazzār on Sexual Diseases and Their Treatment: a critical edition, English translation and introduction of Book 6 of Zād al-musāfir wa-qūt al-ḥāḍir* (London, Kegan Paul International, 1997), 149 (Arabic), 272 (English.) Cf.

333 Giladi, *Infants, Parents and Wet Nurses: Medieval Islamic Views on Breastfeeding and their Social Implications*, 119.

as a means of sterilization.[334] The physicians of late antiquity and the medieval world, by contrast, were very much aware of the existence of ovaries and surmised that they were the female equivalent of testicles. However human ova, the existence of which continued to be a matter of debate until the 18th century since they are almost too small to see with the naked eye, are entirely missing from both ancient and medieval gynecology. The lack of a detectable equivalent to semen raised the question of whether women produce a gamete, "seed," as men do.

The Hippocratic gynecological treatises did not explicitly lay out a theory of reproduction.[335] They were, however, clearly based on a two-seed understanding of conception. In Hippocratic texts, semen constitutes the male seed. Women also secrete seed into their womb, where it encounters semen. The "female seed" is also a fluid, just as semen is; and this fluid is secreted during sexual arousal, just as semen is. As Leslie Dean-Jones writes, this is not a substance which the physicians claimed to have directly observed. Rather, "the female seed was not necessarily a visible secretion as a man's was; it was postulated because of its explanatory value in a hypothesis, not because it had been empirically observed . . . the female seed is by nature emitted into the womb. It only appears outside the womb if the womb is open contrary to nature."[336]

Aristotle argued against the notion that women produce seed as men do. Instead, he posited that menstrual blood is itself the female contribution to the embryo. He compared the semen and the menses to a carpenter and a block of wood. The menses are a material to which the semen provides the form. When the semen acts on the menses, it thereby creates something new, an embryo, just as the carpenter acts upon the wood to create a bed.[337] This is known as the one-seed theory of generation. Aristotle offered a number of arguments against the idea that women produce a gamete. He claimed that women lack the "vital heat" necessary to concoct seed, that pre-pubescent boys resemble women and since the former cannot bring about conception the latter cannot either, and that women could not possibly be secreting seed because they are already secreting something else, namely menses. Among the arguments that have greatest implications for the treatment of childless women was his claim that male seed is secreted only where there is sexual pleasure and arousal, yet women get pregnant even when sexual intercourse is unwanted. This was

334 A. Preus, "Galen's Criticism of Aristotle's Conception Theory," *Journal of the History of Biology* 10 (1977), 67.
335 Dean-Jones, *Women's Bodies in Classical Greek Science*, 154.
336 Dean-Jones, *Women's Bodies*, 156.
337 Aristotle, *Generation of Animals*, 1, 18–22.

proof to him that whatever it is that women are contributing to the embryo, it is not seed, for they make that contribution with or without pleasure.

This assertion that women can conceive regardless of whether they are sexually aroused potentially had both quite negative and positive ramifications for the social treatment of women. Those physicians who, unlike Aristotle, subscribed to the two-seed theory of conception, encouraged men to become attuned to their wives' sexual desires so as to increase the likelihood of the woman secreting seed, resulting in conception.[338] On the other hand, in accordance with the two-seed theory, when a woman did become pregnant, the fact that conception occurred was evidence that the woman was a willing participant in the sexual act. Authors such as Soranus and al-Rāzī claimed that conception is possible only when women ejaculate,[339] thus indicating that impregnated women are willing sexual partners even in cases of purported rape.[340] Their view also implied that a woman's sterility can be blamed on her sexual frigidity. By contrast, Aristotle's position de-incentivized paying attention to women's sexual desires, since they are unimportant from the perspective of reproduction. However, it also supported the notion that conception can occur without impugning the virtuous intent of a sexually assaulted woman. It also absolved infertile women of the charge that their reproductive failure is attributable to a lack of sexual ardor for their husbands. The great adherent of Aristotelian thought among the medieval physicians, the philosopher Ibn Rushd (Averroes), drew a connection between Aristotle's assertion and listening to women's claims. "Aristotle has argued that a woman can get pregnant without ever experiencing emission. I too have pursued this matter by observation and found it to be true . . . I have also asked women about it, and they tell me the same. That is, they often become pregnant without experiencing pleasure."[341]

Five hundred years after Aristotle, Galen drew upon the discovery of ovaries and on Aristotle's own work to criticize Aristotle's reproductive theories. According-

338 See al-Rāzī, *al-Ḥāwī fī al-ṭibb*, vol. 3, bk. 9:66. Ibn Sīnā, *Qānūn fī ṭibb*, 2:550 = *Kitāb* III: *Fann* 20: *maqāla* 1: *fasl fī 'udhr al-ṭabīb fī mā yu'allim min al-taldhīdh*. Al-Baladī, *Tadbīr al-ḥabālā'*, 10. Weisser, *Zeugung, Vererbung, und pränatale Entwicklung*, 152. Cf. Aetius of Amida, "Sterile and useless (inane) are those women who are forced to have coitus against their will. For love presides over (is essential for) conception; and women in love conceive very often." Aetius of Amida, *The Gynaecology and Obstetrics of the VIth century*, tr. James Ricci (Philadelphia: Blakiston, 1950), 36.

339 Rāzī, *al-Ḥāwī*, 9:58.

340 Soranus, *Gynecology* 36–7.

341 Muḥammad ibn Aḥmad ibn Rushd, *Kulliyāt fī al-ṭibb* (Morocco: Ma'had al-Jinirāl Frankū, Lajnat al-Abḥāth al-'Arabīya al-Isbānīya, 1939), 30. Translation from Musallam, *Sex and Society in Islam*, 64.

ing to Galen, Aristotle was correct in claiming that women lack the quantities of vital heat found in men, but that inequality of heat accounts for why male and female reproductive organs are fundamentally similar (as ovaries and testes are) rather than categorically different. According to Galen, heat pushes the genitals of male fetuses outward, whereas relative cold keeps the genitals of female fetuses inside. What emerges from this theory is a conceptualization of female anatomy not as entirely different from male anatomy, but rather as the mirror of it. Galen writes:

> All the parts, then, that men have, women have too, the difference between them lying in only one thing, which must be kept in mind throughout the discussion, namely, that in women the parts are within [the body], whereas in men they are outside . . . Consider first whichever ones you please, turn outward the woman's, turn inward, so to speak and fold double the man's, and you will find them the same in both in every respect. Then think first, please, of the man's turned in and extending inward between the rectum and the bladder.
>
> If this should happen, the scrotum would necessarily take the place of the uteri, with the testes lying outside, next to it on either side; the penis of the male would become the neck of the cavity that had been formed; and the skin at the end of the penis, now called the prepuce, would become the female pudendum [the vagina] itself. Think too, please, of the converse, the uterus turned outward and projecting. Would not the testes [the ovaries] then necessarily be inside it? Would it not contain them like a scrotum? Would not the neck [the cervix], hitherto concealed inside the perineum but now pendent, be made into the male member? And would not the female pudendum, being a skin-like growth upon this neck, be changed into the part called the prepuce? It is also clear that in consequence the position of the arteries, veins, and spermatic vessels [the ductus deferentes and Fallopian tubes] would be changed too. In fact, you could not find a single male part left over that had not simply changed its position; for the parts that are inside in woman are outside in man.[342]

According to Galen, the heat possessed by men makes their bodies efficiently use up all of their nutrients through normal masculine activity. Due to women's diminished heat "the female is less perfect than the male . . . for if among animals the warm one is the more active, a colder animal would be less perfect than a warmer."[343] This imperfection creates an inefficiency that keeps women from using up all their nutrients and gives them an excess which can be used to nurture the fetus, whereas men in their efficiency cannot do so. In this model, the menses are both a raw material from which the fetus will be fashioned and the nutrient for the fetus, but they are not the female gamete. The female gamete

---

342 Galen, *On the Usefulness of the Parts of the Body*, 2:628–9.
343 Galen, *On the Usefulness of the Parts of the Body*, 2:628.

is a seed like the male seed, but thinner and colder and therefore less impactful. It is produced in the female testes (ovaries) and transmitted from them to the uterus through tubes that are analogous to the seminal vesicle. Galen claims to have observed this female sperm. From his descriptions, it seems he is referring to a mucus discharge in the uterus.[344] This Galenic concept of the male and female genitals as inside-out versions of each other is reiterated by the medieval physicians of the Islamic world,[345] as are modified versions of his two-seed theory.[346]

Infertility and its treatment in Greek medicine

Both the Hippocratics and Aristotle recognized that a couple's lack of children may be due to infertility stemming from either partner, male or female, or both.[347] However, in those authors' works, male infertility was not fully medicalized in the sense that the physician might want to look for it, diagnose it and suggest a course of action to correct it. As Rebecca Flemming writes:

> [References in Aristotle to male infertility] are all essentially theoretical, about causes not cures (though *GA* 747a3–22 provides diagnostic advice); and the first does not even refer to specific explanations for male infertility. Similarly, the few explicit Hippocratic engagements with male reproductive failure (the Scythians in *Airs Waters Places* 21,[348] and the

---

344 M. Boylan, "Galen's Conception Theory," *Journal of the History of Biology* 19 (1986), 62.

345 Cf. Ibn Sīnā, *Qānūn fī al-ṭibb*, 2:555–6 = *kitāb* III: *fann* 21: *maqāla* 1: *faṣl fī tashrīḥ al-raḥim*. Ibn Zuhr, *Kitāb al-taysīr* (Rabat: Akādīmiyyat al-Mamlaka al-Maghribiyya, 1991), 340. al-Majūsī, *Kāmil al-ṣināʻa fī al-ṭibb* (Cairo: al-Maṭbaʻah al-Kubrā al-ʻĀmira, 1877), 1:123. ʻAlī ibn Sahl Rabbān al-Ṭabarī, *Firdaws al-ḥikma*, 34.

346 B. Musallam, "The Human Embryo in Arabic Scientific and Religious Thought," in *The Human Embryo: Aristotle and the Arabic and European Traditions*, ed. G. R. Dunstan (Exeter: University of Exeter Press, 1990), 33–4.

347 R. Flemming, "The Invention of Infertility in the Classical Greek World: Medicine, Divinity, and Gender," *Bulletin of the History of Medicine* 87 (2013), 571.

348 The Scythians are said to have sterilized men by cutting a nerve behind the ear and thereby disrupting the production of semen, which was thought to occur initially in the spinal column. Interestingly, this notion made its way not only into the medical commentary tradition, but also in the *ḥisba* tradition. In his manual for market inspectors, the 6/12th-century *muḥtasib* al-Shayzarī, who practiced somewhere in the Syria / Palestine / Egypt region, writes that one should not permit phlebotomists to bleed the veins behind the ears because that causes sterility. He says there is a debate regarding whether cutting into the vein behind one ear only has a sterilizing effect. *Kitāb nihāyat al-rutba fī ṭalab al-ḥisba lil-Shayzarī* (Cairo: Lajnat al-ta'līf wa'l-tarjama wa'l-nashr, 1946), 92.

> enigmatic *Aphorisms* 5:63[349]) are never followed up therapeutically. All these authors are, of course, deeply committed to the importance of the male contribution to generation; but its dysfunction seems not to be medicalized.[350]

While these texts acknowledge the reality of male infertility, they have little to say about how to diagnose it and provide no information about how to remedy it. In part, this can be attributed to the perception that the easiest way to deal with a man's seeming lack of fertility is to have him attempt to reproduce with another woman. In *Generation of Animals*, Aristotle writes that one can test whether a man's semen is fertile by placing it in a vessel with water and seeing if it sinks to the bottom (in which case it is) or floats to the surface (in which case it is not).[351] However, he also writes, "in knowing the causes [of sterility] on the husband's side there are various signs to be taken, but taking those that are mostly easier, let him be observed to have intercourse with other women and to generate."[352] Although this attitude is later echoed in the *Qānūn* of Ibn Sīnā (d. 427/1037) as well as in al-Majūsī's (d. 384/994) *Kāmil al-ṣināʿa al-ṭibbiyya* with some modifications, medieval Arabic texts devote somewhat more attention to male infertility than did Greek ones.[353]

By contrast, female fertility and infertility is the subject of a great deal of medical diagnostic, prognostic, and therapeutic interest in ancient medicine. Remarkably, of the 1500 pharmacological recipes found in the Hippocratic corpus, 80% are gynecological and found in treatises devoted to women's fertility.[354] The

---

349 The aphorism is "[V:62] Women who have the uterus cold and dense (compact?) do not conceive; and those also who have the uterus humid, do not conceive, for the semen is extinguished, and in women whose uterus is very dry, and very hot, the semen is lost from the want of food; but women whose uterus is in an intermediate state between these temperaments prove fertile. [V:63] And in like manner with respect to males; for either, owing to the laxity of the body, the pneuma is dissipated outwardly, so as not to propel the semen, or, owing to its density, the fluid (semen?) does not pass outwardly; or, owing to coldness, it is not heated so as to collect in its proper place (seminal vessels?), or, owing to its heat, the very same thing happens." Translation by Francis Adams.

350 R. Flemming, "The Invention of Infertility in the Classical Greek World: Medicine, Divinity, and Gender," n. 23.

351 Aristotle, *Generation of Animals* II 7:747a, 3–7. Cf. Ibn Sīnā, *al-Ḥayawān* XVI = volume 8 of *al-Shifāʾ* (Cairo: al-Hayʾa al-Miṣrīya al-ʿĀmma lil-Taʾlīf, 1970), 2 :409 Cf. Weisser, *Zeugung, Vererbung, und pränatale Entwicklung*, 152.

352 Aristotle, *History of Animals Vol VII-X*, Tr. D. M. Balme (Cambridge: Loeb Series, Harvard University Press, 1991), 636b11.

353 al-Majūsī, *Kāmil al-ṣināʿa fī al-ṭibb*, 2:467.

354 L. Totelin, *Hippocratic Recipes: Oral and Written Transmission of Pharmacological Knowledge in Fifth- and Fourth-century Greece* (Boston: Brill, 2008), 2, 197.

Hippocratic treatises also include dozens of tests to diagnose fertility or lack thereof. These texts describe many causes of female infertility, which may be categorized as follows:

(1) The inability of semen to pass into the uterus due to a narrowness or blockage in the passage between the vagina and the cervix, or due to the abnormal shape or position of the uterus. The blockage may be attributed to the retention of "old" menses which have coagulated, having failed to be fully evacuated.
(2) The inability of the uterus to retain the male semen, and the subsequent "slipping out" of the semen due to either the failure of the uterus to "close" over the cervix or to an unhealthy smoothness and slipperiness in the uterus. This slipperiness may be caused by an excess of moisture, coagulated blood, or ulcers.
(3) An excess or deficiency of heat or moisture in the uterus which "overcooks" or "dries out" the seed.
(4) Dyskrasia, i.e. an overall humoral imbalance in the woman's body.[355]

Despite having a very different understanding of how reproduction occurs, both Aristotle's and Galen's descriptions of the potential causes of female infertility are quite similar to the Hippocratic ones, and Aristotle seems to draw heavily upon the Hippocratic treatise *On Barrenness.*[356] Aristotle describes the problem of the smooth, slippery uterus, deficient moisture in the uterus, and general humoral imbalance.[357] Galen explains that menstrual blood helps provide the uterus with texture, and lack thereof causes the uterus to be too slippery to retain the semen.[358] These all enter into the medieval medical literature as well.

On Barrenness also mentions diagnostic measures for establishing infertility based on physical touch. "If the mouth of a woman's uterus or its neck becomes hard, this will be recognized when she palpates with a finger, and also if her uterus is turned aside toward her hip. When the case is such, do not give any sharp suppository – for if the mouth of the uterus ulcerates after becoming inflamed, there is a great danger that barrenness will result."[359] Note that, in this phrasing,

355 Hippocrates, *Diseases of Women I,* §11, Cf. Galen, *On Hippocrates' On the Nature of Man,* §47–49.
356 A. Preus, "Biomedical Techniques for Influencing Human Reproduction in the Fourth Century B.C.," *Arethusa* 8 (1975), 246.
357 Aristotle, *History of Animals* VII.2–3 (582–3). Cf. Galen, *On Hippocrates' On the Nature of Man,* §48.
358 Galen, *On the Anatomy of the Uterus,* 81 (chapter 10).
359 Hippocrates, *On Barrenness* § 230. Translation by Paul Potter. *Hippocrates Vol. X,* 367.

it appears that the female patient herself conducts the intimate examination to find out whether the cervix is hard. While it seems that this information is meant to be communicated to the medical practitioner, it is not the practitioner himself who conducts the manual examination. Similarly, in *On Barrenness* the medical practitioner is instructed to prepare sitz-baths and pessaries for the patient, to lay out blankets for her, and to make sure she does not burn herself, but it is the patient herself who inserts the pessary.[360]

On Barrenness mentions several categories of treatments for those diagnosed with infertility: eating certain foods the utility of which is not always explained, clearing the passage between vagina and mouth by means of sitz-baths, pessaries, and fumigations, or introducing probes to change the width of the vagina; or changing the texture or environmental qualities of the uterus by inserting "fertilizing" substances or using probes. Some of the ingredients in Hippocratic fertility recipes are known to have been attached to specific qualities, for example boiled foods were thought to make the body more soft and moist, red wine to make it dryer and harder, etc. Other ingredients were associated with purgation and excretion: puppy and octopus meat, for example, were believed to have a laxative effect.[361] In *On Barrenness*, both eating boiled puppies and fumigating with them are recommended for removing blockages in the passage to the uterus.[362] Other fertility ingredients are those found in perfumes, which were themselves closely associated with sexual stimulation and intercourse in Greek antiquity.[363] These include frankincense, myrrh, cinnamon, cassia and styrax,[364] all of which also play a prominent role in the medieval period. Castoreum (a substance extracted from the glands of beaver foreskins) had a similar use and was associated almost exclusively with "women's medicine."[365] Known in Persian and

360 Ibid., § 221.
361 *Hippocratic Recipes*, 198.
362 Hippocrates, *On Barrenness* §218 and 230.
363 Totelin explains "Perfumes played an important role in sexual preliminaries in ancient Greece, and in *Assembly Women*, Blepyrus plaintively asks his wife οὐχὶ βινεῖται γυνὴ κἄνευ μύρου; (Can't a woman fuck without perfume?). Perfumes appear frequently in the Hippocratic gynaecological recipes . . . [many] pessaries in the Hippocratic collections of recipes, [had] to be dipped in perfume before being applied. This act of dipping a pessary in scented oil may be the equivalent of anointing the genitalia and other parts of the body before sexual intercourse; it serves as a preliminary to penetration. The perfume that is most commonly used in the Hippocratic recipes to facilitate the insertion of a pessary is rose oil. This again might not be a coincidence; ῥόδον (rose) was a slang term for the female genitalia throughout antiquity." *Hippocratic Recipes*, 204.
364 Totelin, *Hippocratic Recipes*, 150
365 Ibid., 161.

Arabic literature as *jundbādastar*, castoreum continued to be particularly associated with the treatment of uterine problems from ancient Greek antiquity through the modern period. (It continued to be used in the West until the early 20th century to treat spasms and hysteria and to induce labor after intrauterine fetal death.[366]) Others ingredients are associated with fertility due to their having shapes or names reminiscent of sexual organs, such as stag horns, figs, radishes, myrtle, squirting cucumber, and gourds. We know how they were viewed because many of the Hippocratic ingredients also appear in ancient plays where it is clear they have sexual connotations. Not all of these ingredients continued to have sexual association in later periods. This is true of celery, for example, which in the ancient Greek comedies represents female sexual organs, or barley and pennyroyal which connoted pubic hair. (Of all these ingredients, only pennyroyal is currently known to have chemical effects of pharmacological value. The essential oil of pennyroyal is lethally toxic and was used as an emmenagogue and abortifacient until the early 20th century. It also has muscular and hallucinogenic effects.) Other ingredients were believed to open the uterus and expel what it retained, whether menstrual blood which needed to be purged or a dead fetus which needed to be forced out. The drugs associated with this purgation included pennyroyal, silphium, squirting cucumber, and gourds.[367] In medieval texts, the squirting cucumber in particular became associated with these functions.[368] It is also known as wild cucumber, or *ecballium elaterium*, or in Arabic as *qiththā' al-ḥimār, qiththā' barrī or 'alqām.*[369] Of course, in the Arabic texts, the repertoire of materia medica is significantly expanded.

---

366 Michael J. O'Dowd, *The History of Medications for Women: materia medica woman* (New York: Parthenon Pub. Group, 2001), 88–89.
367 Totelin, *Hippocratic Recipes*, 214–19.
368 It appears, for example in Ibn al-Jazzār al-Qayrawānī's *Ṭibb al-fuqarā'* as an abortifacient in his chapter "On Treatment of Diseases of the Uterus, Menstrual Retention, and Bringing Down the Fetus," and in his *Zād al-musāfir* in three places (emmenagogue, abortifacient, and ingredient in a treatment for gout). Ibn al-Jazzār al-Qayrawānī, *Ṭibb al-fuqarā' wa'l-masākīn* (Tehran: Mu'assasah-'i Muṭāla'āt-i Islāmī, Dānishgāh-i Tihrān, 1996), 158. Ibn al-Jazzār al-Qayrawānī and G. Bos, *Ibn al-Jazzār on Sexual Diseases and Their Treatment: a critical edition, English translation and introduction of Book 6 of Zād al-musāfir wa-qūt al-ḥāḍir* (London, Kegan Paul International, 1997), 141, 195, 235.
369 See Dioscorides and T.A. Osbaldeston, *Dioscorides De Materia Medica: a New English Translation* (Johannesburg: IBIDIS, 2000), 707 (Bk 4:155). Ibn al-Jazzār, *Ibn al-Jazzār on Sexual Diseases and Their Treatment*, 291. According to John Riddle, modern medical testing has confirmed the contraceptive but not the abortive qualities of the squirting cucumber. J. Riddle, *Contraception and Abortion from the Ancient World to the Renaissance* (Cambridge: Harvard University Press, 1992), 54.

Lack of menstruation is also acknowledged in ancient and medieval texts as either an underlying cause or a sign of infertility. These texts often depict amenorrhea as a form of constipation, rather than menstrual absence. The woman produces menses, but the blood is retained by the uterus rather than evacuated from it, which results in infertility because the male semen is either physically blocked from reaching the uterus, or because the retained menses have congealed or rotted resulting in a toxic uterine environment. The first step, therefore, to promoting fertility is to supply an emmenagogue to "bring down" the retained menstrual blood from the uterus. A large number of the gynecological recipes, both ones associated with fertility and ones thought to be contraceptives, are described as promoting this menstrual "regularity." In the medieval period, the association of bleeding (in the form of menses) with the return of fecundity to barren women is so strong that virtually all medieval commentaries on the Qur'ān, and likewise Tales of the Prophets, describe the restoration of fertility to the barren wives of Abraham and Zechariah in terms of the sudden onset of menstruation.[370]

Importantly, whereas today a "missed period" is the classic first indication of pregnancy, the Greek physicians (and, it seems, later physicians as well) did not seem to view disrupted menstruation in quite the same manner, even though they were well aware that amenorrhea is a symptom of pregnancy.[371] This means that when a non-menstruating woman was given an emmenagogue or underwent a surgical procedure to trigger a menstrual cycle in the hopes of her getting pregnant, it is possible that the resulting blood was in fact an abortion.

One method of treating infertility was the insertion of wood, lead, or tin probes through the vagina and into the uterus.[372] Hippocrates suggests this form of treatment to cure amenorrhea and initiate a menstrual cycle and thus a fertility cycle, to widen the vagina or dislodge a blockage in the uterus, or to change the texture of the uterus and make it less smooth and thereby enable it to retain semen more easily. We have encountered the use of such a probe in chapter 1, in the case of Magdalena from 17th-century Catholic Spain. If con-

370 E.g., Ibn Kathīr, *Qiṣaṣ al-anbiyā'*, glosses Q. 21:90, which refers to God fixing Zakariyyā's wife for him, and explains that it means that previously she did not menstruate and then God made her do so. Cf. al-Shaybānī and Ibn Kathīr's *Tafsīr* on Q. 21:90 and Ibn al-Jawzī's Ibn al-Jawzī's *Zād al-masīr fī 'ilm al-tafsīr* on Q. 11:70.

371 H. King, *Hippocrates' Woman: Reading the Female Body in Ancient Greece*, 32 and Rebecca Flemming, *Medicine and the Making of Roman Women: Gender, Nature, and Authority from Celsus to Galen* (New York: Oxford University Press, 2000), 162. Cf. Hippocrates' *On Barrenness* §215. Although see *Aphorisms* IV:61.

372 Hippocrates, *Superfetation*, § 29; *On Barrenness*, §217, 221, 228, 238, 244.

ducted early in a pregnancy, before the existence of the pregnancy was evident to the woman, such probing would certainly have caused an abortion, which would have looked like the onset of menstruation.[373] The probe could also cause further damage to the internal organs, thereby creating even more impediments to fertility. In Arabo-Galenic medicine, probes or hooks (*ṣināra*) appear in the context of treating *ratq*, the condition in which the vagina is too narrow or is blocked by excess tissue.

Throughout Greek medical literature, and subsequently, there are substances and even surgical techniques that are mentioned both as abortifacients and as means for promoting fertility. It could be argued that this is simply due to the fact that many substances, such as wine, honey or frankincense, had multiple medical uses or were thought to be panaceas. However, certain substances such as wormwood, pennyroyal, and fenugreek were not simply general panaceas but rather seem to have maintained millennia-long reputations as "women's drugs." From a biomedical point of view, the conflation of abortifacients with fertility agents has a peculiar logic. Both first-trimester miscarriages and the beginning of the reproductive cycle (in the form of menstruation) are characterized by vaginal bleeding. Moreover, amenorrhea may be either a symptom of pregnancy or a symptom of hormonal disruption associated with infertility.[374] Therefore, a treatment which resulted in vaginal bleeding may have induced either menstruation, or hemorrhage, or fetal death or uterine contractions so as to cause an abortion. Moreover, because the fetus is so small in the early stages of pregnancy, the different phenomena would have been difficult to distinguish. Therefore, it seems likely that sometimes when women thought they were taking substances to begin a menstrual period so as to promote fertility, in fact they were prematurely ending an undiagnosed pregnancy. There were, of course diagnostic tools for determining whether a woman is already pregnant. For example, *On Barrenness* offers the following test: "Grind red ocher and anise very fine, dissolve in water, give (sc. to drink), and let the woman sleep. If colic comes on around her navel, she is pregnant: if this does not happen, she is not."[375] The same test, but with hydromel instead of ocher, is proposed in Hippocrates'

373 A. Preus, "Biomedical Techniques for Influencing Human Reproduction in the Fourth Century B.C.," 249.

374 Etienne van de Walle et al., *Regulating Menstruation: Beliefs, Practices, Interpretations* (Chicago, University of Chicago Press, 2001). This book explores the notion that discussion of the medical goal of "regulating" menstruation, in many cultures and periods throughout the world, has served as a device for communicating information about abortifacients.

375 Hippocrates, *On Barrenness*, §215. Translation by Paul Potter. *Hippocrates Vol. X*, (Cambridge, MA: Harvard University Press, 2012), 341.

Aphorisms 5:41. This diagnostic tool also appears frequently in medieval manuals, together with explanations as to why the test is effective (these explanations are not present in the Hippocratic treatise).[376]

Throughout antiquity and into the medieval period, the treatment of infertility related in some respects to the medical theories surrounding conception and female anatomy but did not altogether accord with them, since treatments were premised on ideas that stood apart from the theory. For example, diagnostic interest in menstrual blood and therapeutics intended to alter the qualities of menstrual blood remained a constant of medieval treatments of infertility, even though the significance of menstruation to the reproductive process was a matter of intense dispute and subject to diverse medical opinions. The importance of introducing pleasant smells into the uterus, for the sake of improving or maintaining reproductive health, remained constant, even after the medical community had come to the consensus that the uterus cannot move and does not have the olfactory capability to be attracted or repelled by odors. The disjuncture between conception theory and therapeutic practice can also be seen in attitudes toward male infertility, for though it was theoretically acknowledged that men could be the source of infertility, it was never fully embraced therapeutically. Moreover, therapeutic techniques were not limited to or grounded in conception theory. We see this, for example, in the emphasis on the use of sexually suggestive ingredients to promote reproductive health. All of this indicates that while treatment techniques could find justification in prevailing scientific theory, they were not dependent upon it.

376 E.g. ʻAlī ibn Sahl Rabbān al-Ṭabarī, *Firdaws al-ḥikma fī al-ṭibb*, 38 and al-Rāzī, *al-Ḥāwī fī al-ṭibb* vol. 3, bk. 9:51. In a fascinating Latin account, *De Secretis Mulierum* of Psudeo-Albertus Magnus (late thirteenth-century), the author describes this test as being surreptitiously administered, as a means of uncovering the truth when a woman would otherwise wish to the conceal whether or not she is pregnant. He warns that "some women, however, are so clever and so aware of the trick that they refuse to tell the truth." H.R. Lemay, *Women's Secrets: A Translation of Pseudo-Albertus Magnus's "De Secretis Mulierum" with Commentaries* (Albany: State University of New York Press, 1992), 125.

Etiology and treatment of female infertility in Arabo-Galenic medicine

Infertility in the *Firdaws al-ḥikma* (Paradise of Wisdom)

What follows is an analysis of the discussion of infertility found in the *Firdaws al-ḥikma* (Paradise of Wisdom), written around the year 236/850 by the physician ʿAlī ibn Sahl Rabbān al-Ṭabarī, a Syriac Christian convert to Islam who lived in Persia and Iraq. The relevant sections of the *Firdaws al-ḥikma* have the advantage of being both comparatively succinct and representative of the sorts of discussions of infertility found in many subsequent Arabo-Galenic medical works. Al-Ṭabarī begins his discussion of diseases of the uterus with the following list of gynecological concerns.

> Among the greatest of maladies afflicting the uterus are infertility, the slipping out of the seed, the miscarriage of the fetus, uterine suffocation, hemorrhage of menstrual blood, retention of menstrual blood, tumors, and dyscrasia.[377] For if there is an excess of heat the seed is burned. An excess of cold freezes it. If there is an excess of moisture, or the ability to hold on[378] to the seed is weakened, the seed slips out. If there is an excess of dryness it desiccates and dries up the seed.[379]

Al-Ṭabarī's list begins with infertility, and then proceeds to enumerate a variety of concerns ending with dyscrasia which, as he explains, leads to the "seed" – either the gametes or embryo – failing to thrive. In this list al-Ṭabarī seems to categorize infertility as both an illness in and of itself, and as a symptom and consequence of other conditions. He does not fully differentiate between causal factors for infertility, etiological types of infertility, and comorbidities associated with infertility. These topics are all discussed together.

Al-Ṭabarī begins by explaining the danger an adverse environment poses to the "seed." Like a literal plant-seed, the human seed can only thrive in environments with appropriate levels of warmth and moisture. Al-Ṭabarī does not specify whether "seed" refers to the embryo itself or to the male or female gametes

377 Cf. al-Majūsī, *al-Kāmil*, 1:388 and Weisser, *Zeugung, Vererbung, und pränatale Entwicklung*, 158.

378 *misāka* = holding in, retention. I have avoided translating the word as retention only because in this particular context it would be confused with *iḥtibās al-dam*, retention of the (menstrual) blood. *Misāka* was also the word used in the legal texts to refer to urinary and fecal continence.

379 al-Ṭabarī, *Firdaws al-ḥikma fī al-ṭibb*, 273. Cf. Ibn Sīnā, *Qānūn fī al-ṭibb*, 2:562 = *kitāb* III: *fann* 21: *maqāla* 1: *faṣl fī dalāʾil al-bard fī al-raḥim.*

prior to conception. Indeed, his guidance is not constructed upon a particular understanding of what constitutes the female contribution to the embryo or of the stages of embryonic development. Rather, his guidance is based both on humoral notions of achieving balance, and on analogical inferences about what conditions cause plant seeds to thrive or die.

The emphasis on the harmful effects of excessive heat, cold, moisture, and dryness is found in virtually all subsequent discussions of the pathologies of the uterus in Arabo-Galenic medicine. Such conditions are largely depicted as curable, through fumigations and foodstuffs meant to restore the correct balance of heat and moisture.[380] Sometimes these foodstuffs are described as directly impacting heat, and there are "warming" foods or "cooling" ones. At other times the treatments are meant to aid in the production of one of the four humors: blood (characterized by heat and moisture), phlegm (cold and moisture), yellow bile (heat and dryness), or black bile (cold and dryness).

Excessive heat and cold in the uterus, in addition to creating an inhospitable environment for the seed, are also depicted as potential impediments to conception because they affect the quantity and viscosity of menstrual blood. Menstrual blood that is too thin or thick does not flow out properly, and thus becomes stuck in the uterus or clogs blood vessels.[381] This old blood can impede pregnancy by coagulating into a barrier near the cervix, thereby preventing semen from reaching the uterus, or by coating the wall of the uterus thereby making it too slippery to retain the embryo, or by rotting and producing noxious fumes which poison the uterine environment. Infertility due to this menstrual retention is treated by ingesting drugs, applying pessaries, and using fumigation techniques, the purposes of which are to make the blood flow out more easily and evacuate from the womb.

Al-Ṭabarī explains that excessive moisture and other conditions can also cause infertility by making the uterus too smooth for the seed to adhere within the womb. He writes, "Among the things that prevent conception are conditions in the uterus itself, such as ulcers, stiffness, excessive coarseness, or viscous phlegm. These make it slippery such that it cannot retain the seed in it."[382] The concern that conditions within the uterus could make it physically unable to keep either semen or the embryo from slipping out is found throughout both Greek and Arabic texts. When this slipperiness is attributed to excessive moisture, it can be corrected by having the woman take measures to bring

---

380 al-Ṭabarī, *Firdaws al-ḥikma*, 40.

381 Cf. Ibn al-Jazzār, *Ibn al-Jazzār on Sexual Diseases and Their Treatment*, 263.

382 al-Ṭabarī, *Firdaws al-ḥikma*, 274.

about "dryness."[383] Such measures include ingested pills and decoctions, compresses, enemas, pessaries, and fumigations meant to absorb or draw out excess moisture. The recipes for these pessaries and fumigations, particularly as described by Ibn Sīnā, often combine one or two dozen ingredients.[384] Slipperiness can also be attributed to an unreceptive texture in the uterine wall, a result of the scarring over of previously healed ulcers and abscesses. While ulcers, tumors, and wounds to the uterine wall are considered to be treatable by medieval authors, the infertility that may result from them is usually not.[385]

Al-Ṭabarī continues his description of things that cause infertility by listing conditions that block the semen's path to the uterus.

> Also, blood or a fleshy growth which blocks the path [to the uterus], the uterus disappearing from its place,[386] or excessive fat in the part of the diaphragm nearest to the intestines.[387]

These conditions are treated by diet, to promote fat loss, as well as surgery to remove growths in the vaginal canal.[388]

Al-Ṭabarī's discussion of infertility also addresses the problem of miscarriage. In some respects, the failure to conceive and the failure to sustain a pregnancy are not entirely differentiated, especially when conception failure is attributed to the uterus failing to retain seed. Conflation between miscarriage and this kind source of infertility is typical of some other medieval discussions as well, particularly in the *Qānūn.*[389] Kueny characterizes these discussions as physicians' "near-obsessive interest in concocting ways to prevent miscarriage" based on their belief in women's carelessness and inadequacy. This interpretation is a mistake. The physicians do not pathologize healthy pregnancies so much as they elide over the distinction between a woman failing to conceive because the semen or embryo slips out of her uterus rather than embedding in it, and a woman failing to carry to term when the fetus detaches from the uterus and "falls out." In discussing the prevention of miscarriage, the authors are providing therapeutic advice to treat what is, in their view, a variant form of infertility.

---

383 Al-Baladī, *Tadbīr al-ḥabālā'*, 28–29.
384 E.g. Ibn Sīnā, *Qānūn fī al-ṭibb*, 2:577–8 = *kitāb* III: *fann* 21: *maqāla* 2: *faṣl fī ḥuqna jayyida*
385 Ibn Sīnā, *Qānūn fī al-ṭibb*, 2:565 = *kitāb* III: *fann* 21: *maqāla* 1: *al-tadbīr wa'l-'ilāj*
386 I.e. uterine prolapse. Cf. Ibn al-Jazzār, *Ibn al-Jazzār on Sexual Diseases and Their Treatment*, 177.
387 al-Ṭabarī, *Firdaws al-ḥikma*, 274.
388 al-Zahrāwī, *Albucasis on Surgery and Instruments*, 457.
389 Cf. Ibn Sīnā, *Qānūn fī al-ṭibb*, 2:577 = *kitāb* III: *fann* 21: *maqāla* 2: *faṣl fī ḥafẓ al-janīn*

Al-Ṭabarī views miscarriage primarily as the dislodging of the embryo from the uterus. Childlessness which is a result of miscarriage or the inability to retain the embryo is treated by shielding the pregnant woman from physical or psychological experiences or malevolent forces which can cause her to move in a way which might jolt the embryo. At various times in the pregnancy, the connection between the embryo and the uterus is seen as particularly fragile.

> Miscarriage can also result from excessive cold or indigestion, or grief, or a coarse wind, or an excess of phlegm in the veins of the uterus, or from a jump from a height to the ground, or a blow, or a strong jolt.[390]

Elsewhere in the *Firdaws al-ḥikma*, al-Ṭabarī explains:

> [Miscarriage may result from] diarrhea, or a blow to her breast, or from a severe shock or fright, or because she hears an alarming noise, or due to exhaustion or severe misfortune or because she approaches things which by their natures abort the fetus. Among stones and the like there are those which protect the fetus and those which eject it from the womb, whether it is alive or dead. You will find this in its own chapter . . . Hippocrates says, "Pregnant women, if they need treatment should receive treatment in the fourth through seventh month, but not before or after that." The reason for his statement is that during the first month the fetus is akin to a weak fruit which can be dislodged by a slight wind or movement, but in the eighth month it is akin to ripe fruit which is not dislodged by a slight wind or movement.[391]

Here, al-Ṭabarī lists a variety of direct and indirect causes of miscarriage.[392] Drawing on an image and timeline found in Hippocrates, he notes that, in the early stages of pregnancy, the fetus is attached like an "unripe fruit" which can thus be easily dislodged. Listed among the misfortunes which can cause a miscarriage are body blows and emotional blows. It is not entirely clear from these passages whether the emotional blows are dangerous because psychological distress itself triggers the miscarriage, or whether the physiological assumption is that, when enduring psychological distress, the internal organs physically move or shudder, and it is this movement which physically dislodges the embryo. Note that here diarrhea is thought to be able to cause a miscarriage, and

390 al-Ṭabarī, *Firdaws al-ḥikma*, 274.
391 al-Ṭabarī, *Firdaws al-ḥikma fī al-ṭibb*, 39–40. Cf. Ḥunayn ibn Isḥāq, *Kitāb al-mawlūdīn* (Baghdad: Majma' al-Lugha al-Siryāniyya, 1978), 38. Ibn al-Jazzār, *Ibn al-Jazzār on Sexual Diseases and Their Treatment*, 285–6 and al-Rāzī, *al-Ḥāwī fī al-ṭibb*, vol. 3, bk 9:49–50 and al-Baladī, *Tadbīr al-ḥabālā'*, 15–16.
392 Cf. Soranus, *Soranus's Gynecology* 45–46, which has a very similar list.

it is not uncommon for bowel movements to be associated with anguish or strong emotional responses.[393]

In the middle of this passage about the physical and psychological triggers of miscarriage, al-Ṭabarī includes a description of stones and plants which, without being ingested, can also trigger miscarriage or protect women from miscarrying.

> The head of the hospital of Jundīshāpūr informed me that there is, among a family in the village of Ahwaz,[394] a stone which protects the fetus if it is tied to the pregnant woman. Moreover, we have heard that, according to the son of a revered Christian woman in Rayy, if this pregnant woman with this stone inadvertently encounters another pregnant woman, the one who does not have the stone with her will miscarry. Daylamite women inform me that this protective stone is widely available in Jīlān. Dioscorides mentions a plant called the *fawflāfīqūs* (=qawqlāqimūs? =cyclamen?), which resembles the bindweed leaf. According to his information, it is a thorn which is placed on wounds . . . if this leaf is affixed to a woman who is not pregnant, she then conceives. But, if a pregnant woman glances at it, then she miscarries. Pregnant women must be careful during the eighth month because if they miscarry there is a risk they will die, and should therefore avoid acute exhaustion, poor food, excessive washing, and sneezing.[395]

In his description of these stones and plants that can exert power on women's bodies without being ingested, al-Ṭabarī cites as authorities female informants and male intermediaries for female informants. He mentions a physician at the famous hospital of Jundīshāpūr, who himself refers to the folk knowledge of people in the surrounding villages. He also cites the son of an unknown Christian woman, and then refers to some Daylamite women with whom he appears to have had direct contact. Each of these informants refers to a stone or plant that affects women who encounter it. The stone serves as a sort of shield, not only protecting pregnant women from miscarriage and deflecting the threat posed by other pregnant women, but making the threat rebound upon the woman lacking the stone.

393 Cf. Ibid., 38: "For the seed is evacuated through fright, sorrow, sudden joy and, generally, by severe mental upset; through vigorous exercise, forced detention of the breath, coughing, sneezing, blows, and falls, especially those on the hips; by lifting heavy weights, leaping, sitting on hard sedan chairs, by the administration of drugs, by the application of pungent substances and sternutatives; through want, indigestion, drunkenness, vomiting, diarrhea; by a flow of blood from the nose, from hemorrhoids or other places; through relaxation due to some heating agent, through marked fevers, rigors, cramps and, in general, everything inducing a forcible movement by which miscarriage may be produced."

394 I.e., near the hospital in Jundīshāpūr.

395 Al-Ṭabarī, *Firdaws al-ḥikma fī al-ṭibb*, 39–40.

As Manfred Ullmann notes, interest in the healing properties of stones, magical cures, and "sympathetic" cures is not divorced from "rational" medicine in Arabo-Galenic writings, but is it more prevalent in gynecology than in other areas of medicine.[396] It is not surprising, therefore, that the one magic square depicted in the entire *Firdaws al-ḥikma* is to be found in the section on childbirth.[397] (This is an early Arabic example of the ancient 3 x 3 *buduh* square, with the numerals in the rows and columns adding up to 15, and the numbers 2, 4, 6, and 8 at the corners.[398]) Ibn Sīnā too mentions many non-rational remedies for gynecological problems.[399]

Treatments involving the ingestion of the reproductive powers of animals are particularly common in the medieval (as well as ancient) gynecological literature. For example, Ibn Sīnā suggests that a woman experiencing infertility drink elephant urine at the time of coitus.[400] The 7th/13th-century Egyptian guide to pharmacy, *Minhāj al-dukkān*, describes using an enema made of rabbit rennet for hastening conception,[401] an ingredient which does not appear in other recipes in the book, but which is also recommended for fertility purposes in Dioscorides' *Materia Medica.*[402] Similarly, a 5th/11th-century book of pharmacy made by the physicians in the 'Aḍudī hospital in Baghdad, based on the pharmacological work of physician Sābūr Ibn Sahl (d. 255/869), explains that "if a woman drinks some of the testicle and the rennet of a hare, she will be blessed with a male child."[403]

Treatments of infertility sometimes also reflect the influence of particular conception theories. The "two-seed" theory of conception, which posited that women secrete a semen-like seed, implied a therapeutic corollary: to increase

---

396 Ullmann, *Islamic Medicine*, 109 and *Medizin im Islam*, 253.

397 al-Ṭabarī, *Firdaws al-ḥikma fī al-ṭibb*, 281.

398 On the history of the *buduh* magic square, including its obstetrical uses see, V. Porter, L. Saif, and E. Savage-Smith "Amulets, Magic, and Talismans" in *Companion to Islamic Art and Architecture* (Wiley-Blackwell, 2017), 538.

399 Ibn Sīnā, *Qānūn fī al-ṭibb*, 2:566 = *kitāb* III: *fann* 21: *maqāla* 1: *al-tadbīr wa'l-'ilāj.*

400 Ibn Sīnā, *Qānūn fī al-ṭibb*, 2:566 = *kitāb* III: *fann* 21: *maqāla* 1: *al-tadbīr wa'l-'ilāj.*

401 L. Chipman, *The World of Pharmacy and Pharmacists in Mamluk Cairo* (Leiden: Brill, 2010), 262. Al-Rāzī too recommends it for the same purpose. *Al-Ḥāwī*, 9:58. Cf. al-Majūsī, *al-Kāmil*, 2:436.

402 This is one of only three ingredients which Dioscorides recommends to aid conception, but it is also a contraceptive. He writes that rabbit rennet "aids conception, but if drunk after menstruation, it causes barrenness." Translation from J. Riddle, *Goddesses, Elixirs, and Witches: Plants and Sexuality throughout Human History* (New York: Palgrave Macmillan, 2010), 69.

403 Ibn Sahl and O. Kahl, *Sābūr Ibn Sahl's Dispensatory in the Recension of the 'Aḍudī Hospital* (Leiden: Brill, 2009), 210.

the likelihood of conception, women ought to be stimulated so as to secrete more seed, and therefore husbands should make efforts to become more satisfying lovers. Ibn Sīnā advises:

> There is no shame for the physician if he speaks about enlarging the penis, narrowing the entrance, and female sexual pleasure, because these two things occasion the production of offspring. Often, a small penis becomes a concern because the woman cannot be pleasured by it and so she does not ejaculate. Since she does not ejaculate there is no child. It may also become a concern because it might alienate his wife and she might seek someone other than him. Likewise, if she is not narrow, her husband will not satisfy her and she too will not satisfy her husband, and this must all be offset. Similarly, sexual pleasure encourages quick ejaculation, and in most cases of women whose ejaculation is delayed, and who are left with their desire unsatisfied, there is no offspring.[404]

In this way Ibn Sīnā argues that a physician may need to discuss sexual matters or recommend sexually enhancing alterations, in order to protect against infertility, as well as concupiscence.

The second theory of conception is sometimes called the "seed and soil" model. According to this theory, male sperm constitutes the only or main gamete, and the role of the female body is to serve as a space to grow and nourish the embryo. This image is found in the Greek tradition, including in Hippocratic writings, and seems to have coexisted with the two-seed theory of conception. This same is true in Ayurvedic texts such as the *Charaka Samhita*.[405] The two coexist in the Islamic tradition as well. An example of reproductive organs being compared to a tilled field can be the found in the Qur'ān, in a passage frequently cited in legal discussions of intercourse. "Your women are a tillage for you; so come unto your tillage as you wish" (Q. 2:223). A similar image is evoked by the *ḥadīth*, cited previously, "Beware of the barren woman, for one married to her is like a man ensconced at the top of a well, who waters his land daily, but whose land does not bloom, the stream [of water] is not absorbed.[406]

The classicist Ann Ellis Hanson has argued that this "seed and soil" model is also reflected in the practice of treating infertile women with fertilizer-like substances. Such methods of treatment are prevalent in Greek medicine and are closely associated with gynecology. For example, the following recipe comes from the Hippocratic text, *Diseases of Women I:*

---

404 Ibn Sīnā, *Qānūn fī al-ṭibb*, 2:549–50 = *Kitāb* III: *Fann* 20: *maqāla* 1: *faṣl fī 'udhr al-ṭabīb fī mā yu'allim min al-taldhīdh.*

405 P. Rây and H.N. Gupta. *Caraka Samhita; A Scientific Synopsis* (New Delhi: National Institute of Sciences of India, 1965), 7–8.

406 Ibn Ḥabīb, *Kitāb adab al-nisā' al-mawsūm bi-kitāb al-ghāya wa'l-nihāya*, 152–3.

> If the mouth <of the womb> is closed, let her apply fig juice until it opens; and let her wash herself immediately with water. And crush hawk's excrement in sweet wine and give to drink whilst she is fasting, and let her immediately sleep with her husband. Or, whenever the menses are stopping, crush excrement of the Egyptian goose in rose perfume, and anoint the vagina and let her sleep with her husband.[407]

The fig juice has symbolic associations with fertility and the excrement used in this recipe has literal use as agricultural fertilizer. In the Hippocractic corpus, mention of dreckapotheke ("dung therapy") is limited to gynecological texts.[408] In Arabic texts, the use of dung is not limited exclusively to gynecological and fertility-related matters, but it is particularly pronounced in those areas.

The intersection of infertility with other gynecological concerns

Female infertility is depicted in medieval medical texts as the potential consequence, or byproduct, of several other gynecological conditions and concerns, concerns which are also of great interest to physicians for reasons other than infertility. As a result, discussions of infertility also veer off into several other distinct, but intersecting, medical areas. These include the ascertainment of fetal sex and development, diagnosis of menstrual retention and uterine suffocation, and assessment of male and female reproductive history and prospects.

An example of these intersecting discussions can be seen in the continuation of a passage from the *Firdaws al-ḥikma* on the damage inflicted on the seed by excessive heat and cold. Al-Ṭabarī writes:

> Hippocrates says, if the breasts of pregnant women shrivel, they miscarry. If one breast shrivels, she miscarries the fetus which is on the side of the shriveled breast. If the color of the woman is good, that indicates that the fetus is male. If her color is ugly it indicates that the fetus is female.[409] The reason for [Hippocrates'] statement is that the male is warm and the female is cold, and warmth improves coloring whereas cold makes it uglier and greener.[410]

Here we see the influence of the Hippocratic notion of the connection between the breasts and the bifurcated uterus, onto which has been mapped the Aristotelian concept that the male fetus is warmer (thereby providing healthier color-

407 This translation is from *Hippocratic Recipes*, 213.
408 Ibid., 212.
409 Hippocrates, *Aphorisms*, V. 38.
410 al-Ṭabarī, *Firdaws al-ḥikma*, 37. Cf. al-Baladī, *Tadbīr al-ḥabālā*, 18.

ing) and the female is colder (producing a sickly color in the mother). The discussion of infertility and the proper environment for the seed moves into a discussion of miscarriage which is intermixed with a discussion of fetal sex diagnosis. Conception, pregnancy, and sex differences are all part of the same continuum of concerns and even the same continuum of diagnosis. We see this even among physicians with substantial disagreements as to the causes of sex variation,[411] and even among those who express skepticism about the connection between heat and gender. This continuum of infertility and fetal sex diagnoses is articulated by al-Rāzī, accompanied by his characteristic caveats. In his experience, many men and women do not conform to humoral type.

> Signs of conception: Apollonius said: if the menses are retained without fever or trembling or shortness [of breath] then she is pregnant. For menses which are retained due to illness present with the above [symptoms], but if the uterus shows no [sign of illness] then she is indeed pregnant. If she is pregnant with a male, then her color is good; if with a female then her color is pallid in comparison to her usual color prior to conception, for the female is colder while the male is warmer. This is so only in general, for it is possible for someone pregnant with a female [fetus] to improve her regimen after conception thus improving her color, and the opposite is possible too. There are many other signs of a male [fetus], such as having many and forceful movements. These signs are also only general ones, for if she is carrying a very weak male or a tremendously strong female one it is possible that [the female fetus's] movements will be greater and more forceful. [Galen?] said: the fetus cannot be cold unless both the sperm of the man and the uterus of the mother are cold at the same time. But as for me [al-Rāzī], I consider this to be ridiculous because it arbitrarily assigns categories for nature's actions . . . but we have indeed seen many women with humoral temperaments that are warmer than are those of many men. This indicates masculinity and femininity are not determined by warmth but rather by predominance of one type [of seed].[412]

Al-Rāzī combines into a single discussion what might seem to the modern reader to be entirely separate topics: recognizing and differentiating between amenorrhea due to pregnancy and amenorrhea due to illness, differentiating between healthy pregnancy and unhealthy pregnancy, and differentiating between pregnancy with a male fetus from pregnancy with a female fetus.

---

411 See S. Gadelrab, "Discourses on Sex Differences in Medieval Scholarly Islamic Thought," *Journal of the History of Medicine and Allied Sciences* 66 (2011), 40 – 81 and N. Fancy, "Womb Heat versus Sperm Heat: Hippocrates against Galen and Ibn Sīnā in Ibn al-Nafīs's Commentaries," 150 – 175.

412 al-Rāzī, *al-Ḥāwī fī al-ṭibb*, vol. 3, bk. 9:50 – 1. Cf. Al-Baladī, *Tadbīr al-ḥabālā'*, 20.

Menstrual retention and hysterical suffocation

Menstruation and the qualities of menstrual blood occupy a central role in medieval discussions of both fertility in particular, and women's health in general. With regard to fertility, the significance of menstruation is two-fold. First, menstrual blood itself is understood to be either a female gamete or the source of nourishment for a fetus. Insufficient menstrual blood can also mean that the body lacks nourishment for the fetus.[413] Second, menstrual blood is also understood as potentially blocking conception or rendering the environment of the uterus noxious if it is not flushed out correctly and regularly.

Infertility is not, however, the only problematic consequence of irregular menstruation. Rather, the medieval physicians continue the tradition of emphasizing the importance of menstruation to women's general health. They also continue to warn of the danger of retained menses and the disease known as "uterine suffocation." However, whereas Hippocratic descriptions of these illnesses pathologize the bodies of women who are not fulfilling the socially expected roles of marrying and producing children, and the treatments of these diseases appear to coerce women into fulfilling socially-approved roles, this is less true in medieval Arabo-Galenic discussions of these conditions.

5th-century B.C. Greek texts describe uterine suffocation, also known as "hysterical suffocation," or "the wandering womb," as a disease in which the uterus expands or moves and in so doing displaces or crushes a woman's other vital organs, potentially causing a variety of dire symptoms, including insanity, epileptic-like fits and deathly faints.[414] The phenomenon is famously described in Plato's *Timaeus:*

> The seed [semen in males] having life, and becoming endowed with respiration, produces in that part in which it respires a lively desire of emission, and thus creates in us the love of procreation. Wherefore also in men the organ of generation becoming rebellious and masterful, like an animal disobedient to reason, and maddened with the sting of lust, seeks to gain absolute sway; and the same is the case with the so-called womb or matrix of women; the animal within them is desirous of procreating children, and when remaining unfruitful long beyond its proper time, gets discontented and angry, and wandering in every direction through the body, closes up the passages of the breath, and, by obstructing respiration,

413 Ibn Sīnā, *Qānūn fī al-ṭibb,* 2:567–71 = *kitāb* III: *fann* 21: *maqāla 1.*

414 The phenomenon of the "wandering womb" has received a great deal of scholarly attention. See, for example, C. Faraone, "The Rise of the Demon Womb in Greco-Roman Antiquity," in M. Parca and A. Tzanetou (eds.), *Finding Persephone: Women's Rituals in the Ancient Mediterranean* (Bloomington: Indiana University Press, 2007), 224–37; and S. Gilman et al., *Hysteria Beyond Freud (*Berkeley: University of California Press, 1993).

> drives them to extremity, causing all varieties of disease, until at length the desire and love of the man and the woman, bringing them together and as it were plucking the fruit from the tree, sow in the womb, as in a field, animals unseen by reason of their smallness and without form; these again are separated and matured within; they are then finally brought out into the light, and thus the generation of animals is completed.[415]

This description of sexual reproduction attributes to the uterus an independent "lust" equivalent to the "disobedient" lust subsisting in the male genitals. But the uterus diverges from its male counterpart by attacking its "host" when it is discontented by lack of children. It wanders up into the woman's body thereby suffocating her. In an effort to pacify it, man and woman engage in sexual intercourse. Implicit in this physiology is a message that women who do not engage in sexual intercourse and reproduction put themselves in mortal danger.

The Hippocratic treatise *Diseases of Women I,* describes hysterical suffocation thus:

> When the womb is near the liver and the abdomen and when it is suffocating, the woman turns up the whites of her eyes and becomes chilled; some women become livid. She grinds her teeth and saliva flows out of her mouth. These women resemble those who suffer from Herakles' disease.[416] If the womb lingers near the liver and the abdomen, the woman dies of the suffocation.[417]

The ultimate cure for hysterical suffocation is pregnancy, which weighs down the womb and keeps it from moving into other parts of the body. Sexual intercourse also helps because the moisture and weight provided by semen anchor the womb in place. Alternatively, sweet smelling substances can be applied to the vagina to "lure" the "animal" uterus down to its proper place, and foul-smelling substances can be applied to the nose to repel the uterus away from the upper body cavities. This last treatment is based on the previously mentioned premise that the mouth, uterus, and vagina are all part of one continuous channel.

In Aristotle's thought and in later Greek and Roman medicine, uterine suffocation continues to be an accepted diagnosis despite the widespread acknowledgement that the uterus is anchored in place by ligaments and so cannot

415 *Timaeus* 91b-d. Translation by B. Jowett. Galen's synopsis of the Timaeus was available in Arabic and there may have been other sources as well. On the Arabic reception of the *Timaeus*, see A. Das, "Galen and the Arabic traditions of Plato's Timaeus" (Ph.D. thesis: University of Warwick, 2013). For the reception of this specific passage see also, Weisser, *Zeugung, Vererbung, und pränatale Entwicklung*, 146–7.

416 I.e., epilepsy.

417 Translation in A. E. Hanson, "Hippocrates: 'Diseases of Women 1,'" §10.

move into the regions occupied by other organs.[418] Such knowledge was confirmed by human dissections undertaken in Alexandria in the generations after Aristotle's death.[419] By the second century, Soranus and Galen are well aware that the uterus is moored in place by tissue connecting it to other organs with the result that it cannot wander. Soranus rejects the notion that the uterus can move upward and mocks the idea that the uterus possesses olfactory capabilities. But he does not reject the existence of the disease that was thought to be caused by the womb's wandering, claiming instead that inflamed ligaments pull the uterus in the wrong direction, thereby triggering the symptoms known as uterine suffocation. Moreover, although he entirely rejects the notion that the uterus is an animal-like being with a sense of smell, he still prescribes the same use of smells as therapy, on the grounds that they make the uterus contract.[420]

Galen too objects to the idea that the uterus can wander upward and yet he too takes for granted the existence of the condition described as uterine suffocation.[421] He says that it occurs when retained menses and female seed rot, which in turn causes congestion in the blood vessels entering the uterus, which in turn distends the adjacent ligaments, which in turn pulls on the uterus such that the uterus rises, expands, or twists. Furthermore, the rotting of the retained menses creates a noxious fluid which poisons and chills the woman's whole body, thereby causing the severe symptoms. He attributes this disease particularly to widows and prescribes odor therapy as well as measures to "release" the build-up of female "semen."[422] Moreover, although as an anatomist Galen was well aware of the impossibility of hysterical suffocation, as a therapist he, as Monica Green puts it, "displayed his medical conservatism by retaining the odoriferous therapy even though, with his new etiology, it would have lost any semblance of a rational basis."[423] Galen prescribes the use of both cupping and the application of strong smelling substances to the mouth and vagina to treat a woman whose

---

418 Aristotle, *Generation of Animals* 720a, 12–14, denies the wandering womb phenomenon. Aristotle, *History of Animals* 582b, 22–6, nonetheless says that an empty womb can rise upwards and cause suffocation.

419 C. Faraone, "Magical and Medical Approaches to the Wandering Womb in the Ancient Greek World." *Classical Antiquity* 30 (2011):6.

420 H. King, *Hippocrates' Woman: Reading the Female Body in Ancient Greece* (London: Routledge, 1998), 231.

421 Galen, *On the Usefulness of the Parts of the Body*, tr. Margaret Tallmadge May (Ithaca: Cornell University Press, 1968), 2:653.

422 See Green, 'The Transmission of Ancient Theories of Female Physiology and Disease' 48. Also Helen King, 'Galen and the widow: towards a history of therapeutic masturbation in ancient gynaecology.' EuGeStA: *Journal on Gender Studies in Antiquity* 1 (2011): 205–235.

423 Green, "The Transmission of Ancient Theories of Female Physiology," 50.

"uterus rises or experiences deviations." Like the Hippocratics, he appears to subscribe to the notion that sweet smells attract the uterus to its proper place and fetid smells repel it from its current abnormal place. We thus see in Soranus' and Galen's writings that the anatomical premise has changed drastically, since they know the uterus cannot sense smell, nor is it free to float about, much less to roam about the body like an animal desiring to satisfy its cravings. But the symptomology of the illness previously thought to be caused by the uterus moving does not change, only its etiology. Moreover, even though the etiology changes, the therapies, including odor therapy, do not change.

In medieval Arabic texts, the causes and cures for *ikhtināq al-raḥim* (uterine suffocation/strangulation) are subtly reinterpreted in significant ways. Whereas in the Hippocratic texts both menstrual retention and hysterical suffocation are described as resulting from a person's status as a virgin, widow, or barren woman, over time, particularly in the Byzantine and Islamic periods, these conditions become attributed to a wider variety of causes, and suggested treatments varied just as widely. Al-Ṭabarī writes:

> Retention of menses may be due to heat, dryness, severe fatigue, or nosebleed because this diminishes the blood, or [it may occur in] one who is fat for her blood departs due to her fat, or because the veins of her womb are narrow, or from a rupture. As a result of retention of the menses or lack of coitus, there may occur vapors, asthma, damage to the liver and stomach, heart palpitations, vile thoughts, headache, uterine suffocation, inability to conceive, abscess, and dropsy, because when the [uterus] retains the menstrual blood, [the blood] will coagulate in its veins and disperse its vapors into the entire body, thereby causing these maladies.[424] Sometimes the uterus is stretched by a tumor or coagulated, sticky superfluities, such that it inclines to one side and is therefore lacking in height or width. Sometimes the uterus rises upwards towards the diaphragm thereby causing suffocation, and it overcomes the woman such that she may lose consciousness. In which case, a wool flake should be placed on her nose so as to learn whether she is alive or dead. If the wool moves, then she is alive. The cause of this is either an excess of coitus or the lack of it. For, if there is much seed it might rot and become like a poison, and sometimes it spreads and so the diaphragm convulses and the woman suffocates . . . Sometimes an itch accompanied by swelling also occurs in the uterus due to the intensity of desire for sexual intercourse, just as in a male there is an itch and swelling due to desire.[425]

Much of al-Ṭabarī's above description has Greek antecedents. We see the Galenic assimilation of uterine suffocation into the framework of retained menses. The use of a flake of wool to ascertain whether a woman is still breathing, having lost consciousness as a result of a uterine ailment, comes from an anecdote

424 Cf. Bos, *Ibn al-Jazzār on Sexual Diseases and Their Treatment*, 264.
425 al-Ṭabarī, *Firdaws al-ḥikma fī al-ṭibb*, 273–5.

found in several different Galenic texts. It is also found in Aetius of Amida's gynecological treatise.[426] In some versions the woman is described as a longtime widow, but al-Ṭabarī makes no reference to the marital status of the unconscious woman here.[427] As in the *Timaeus*, the uterus is depicted as swelling with sexual desire, comparable to male tumescence. Like Galen, al-Ṭabarī describes excessive female seed as needing to be removed, or exorcised. Menstrual blood needs to be exorcised as well, and he does not clearly differentiate between menses and seed. The menses or seed can potentially endanger a woman if they are not evacuated and instead coagulate and rot. When it putrefies it makes the uterus uninhabitable for any embryo and sends vapors or fumes throughout the rest of the body, especially upwards towards the head. This retained menstrual blood or seed may indeed be attributed to a woman's failure to engage in sexual relations with a man, but al-Ṭabarī also suggests it can be attributed to the woman engaging in too much sexual activity. (The notion that sexual excess causes hysterical suffocation can also be found in the works of pre-Islamic authors as well, such as Paul of Aegina and Aetius, who writes that it is most prevalent among lascivious women and those who make use of contraceptive drugs.[428]) Furthermore, al-Ṭabarī also believes that these maladies can also be attributed to a host of other problems, some psycho-social (such as shock or depression) and others more physical, such as cold or hemorrhoids.[429]

The extent to which these conditions are associated with unattached women varies somewhat in medieval medical texts. Ibn al-Jazzār, like al-Ṭabarī, conflates hysterical suffocation (which he very much associates with sexual deprivation) with menstrual retention, which he does not particularly associate with sexual deprivation. He writes:

> [Hysterical suffocation] occurs [to a woman] by reason of a surplus and corruption of her sperm when she is withheld from sexual intercourse. For then the sperm increases, corrupts and becomes like a poison. This happens mostly to widows, especially when they have

426 Aetius of Amida, *The Gynaecology and Obstetrics of the VIth century*, 70.

427 The story of Galen's use of wool to test whether a sexually-deprived widow has fainted or died is found in several sources, including Galen, *On the Usefulness of the Parts*, K. VIII, 414–15. It appears to have entered into the Arabic corpus via Paul of Aegina, appearing in al-Rāzī, Ibn al-Jazzār, and Ibn Sīnā's works. For interpretations of this anecdote see Helen King, 'Galen and the widow: towards a history of therapeutic masturbation in ancient gynaecology.' *EuGeStA: Journal on Gender Studies in Antiquity* 1 (2011), 205–235.

428 S. Gilman et al., *Hysteria Beyond Freud.* (Berkeley: University of California Press, 1993), 47.

429 Cf. al-Rāzī, *al- Ḥāwī fī al-ṭibb*, 9:37. Cf. Ibn Sīnā, *Qānūn fī al-ṭibb*, 2:600 = *kitāb* III: *fann* 21: *maqāla* 4: *'alāmāt* (*ikhtināq al-raḥim*).

> given birth to many children. It can also happen to women when they have reached sexual maturity without knowing any man. For when the sperm has collected in them, they need its emission just like men, which is a natural act. But when the woman does not have a man, the sperm is collected in her and a cold vapour arises from it to the respiratory diaphragm because of its connection to the uterus. This causes asthma, and because the diaphragm is connected with the throat and with the places of [origin] of the voice suffocation occurs to her, as we have explained. This disease can also be caused by retention of the menstruation, for when the retained menstrual blood and the sperm collect in them, the disease called "hysterical suffocation" occurs to them with extreme force, especially in autumn or in winter.[430]

Here hysterical suffocation is identified as particularly prevalent among unattached women, not because the uterus is searching for reproduction, but because both sexes require sexual release in order to be healthy, lest "cold vapors" arise from the retained male and female sperm.[431] It can also occur due to the lack of evacuation of the menses.[432] The diseases at hand are more prevalent among adult virgins and widows, according to Ibn al-Jazzār, but despite many pages of detailed instructions as to how to alleviate the problem, neither he nor al-Ṭabarī recommend that the problem be fixed through marriage. This is also true of Paul of Aegina and Aetius of Amida's treatment of the subject.[433] In other words, hysterical suffocation and menstrual retention are diagnoses that no longer necessarily serve to pathologize unattached women.

This is also somewhat true of al-Rāzī's pronouncements on the topic. The exception can be found in his treatise dedicated to enumerating the medical virtues of sexual activity, in which he describes it as a potential cure for hysterical suffocation.[434] He also quotes other people's opinions about the medical value of intercourse for treating these conditions. In his *Ḥāwī*, he lists a dozen different authorities, citing both their descriptions of hysterical suffocation and their cures for it, and among them he cites the opinions of older authorities who do recommend marriage for curing the malady. There he quotes Hippocrates as saying "if she does not have a husband then one marries her off quickly"[435] and "this suffocation does not occur to pregnant women. Therefore my [recommendation] is

---

430 Bos, *Ibn al-Jazzār on Sexual Diseases and Their Treatment*, 274–275. Bos' translation.
431 Cf. Ibn al-Quff.
432 See also Ibn Sīnā, *Qānūn fī al-ṭibb* 2:589 = *Kitāb* 3: *fann* 21: *maqāla* 3: *faṣl fī a'rāḍ [iḥtibās al-ṭamth]*
433 See Green, "The Transmission if Ancient Theories of Female Physiology and Disease," 106.
434 Peter E. Pormann. "Al-Rāzī (d. 925) on the Benefits of Sex: A Clinician Caught between Philosophy and Medicine." *O ye gentlemen: Arabic studies on science and literary culture, in honour of Remke Kruk* 2 (2007), 124
435 al-Rāzī, *al-Ḥāwī*, 9:43.

that it is treated with what brings down the blood and thins out the semen, or with much sexual intercourse . . . If she becomes pregnant, the situation is obviated altogether, for the womb is weighed down and moves back and is made moist."[436] He also cites al-Masīḥ's commentary on *Diseases of Young Girls*, "When a woman matures to the point of menstruation and is a virgin, blood is diverted toward her uterus . . . and it causes something like insanity in her. If that has happened, it [?] should be removed and then one should marry her off, for if she becomes pregnant she will become healthy."[437]

Both Ibn Sīnā and al-Majūsī explicitly recommend marriage if the patient is a virgin. Al-Majūsī writes, "If the woman is a virgin, then she must marry. If she rarely engages in intercourse, she should do so. For intercourse voids the semen which is retained in its passages and unblocks the blockage which was caused by it['s retention] and, in so doing, makes it cease, God willing."[438] If the cause of hysterical suffocation is found to be "retention of semen," Ibn Sīnā recommends marriage as one possible cure. Note that the assumption in this case is that the woman is not currently engaging in sexual relations because she is unmarried. Thus it appears that the "semen" in this case is female semen, which has not found an outlet.

> If the cause of the [hysterical suffocation] is retention of the semen, then it is necessary to get started on marriage. Until that time, she should engage in exercise and [make use of] those things which dry out the semen, such as rue, mint . . . as in the [aforementioned] recipe. The midwife must insert her hand in the vagina and rub it with oil of lily or nard or laurel, and massage the entrance to the vagina, and she should massage the entrance to the uterus a great deal. [The patient] must be given both pleasure and pain, so that it will be like the experience of sexual intercourse.[439]

Although Ibn Sīnā encourages marriage to cure hysterical suffocation, unlike in the Hippocratic texts, marriage is not recommended for the purpose of curing the woman's wandering womb by weighing it down with pregnancy or with male

436 Ibid., 9:44.
437 Ibid., 9:45. This is ʿĪsā b. Ḥakam al-Dimashqī, known as al-Masīḥ. Ibn Abī ʿUṣaybiʿa says he lived during the time of Harūn al-Rashīd. Ibn Abī ʿUṣaybiʿa does not mention him having written this treatise. He is referred to extensively by al-Baladī in *Tadbīr al-ḥabālā'*.
438 al-Majūsī, *al-Kāmil*, 2:438–9.
439 Ibn Sīnā, *Qānūn fī al-ṭibb* 2:602 = *Kitāb* 3: *Fann* 21: *maqāla* 4: *faṣl fī al-muʿālajāt*. Cf. Ibn Sīnā, *Qānūn fī al-ṭibb*, 2:599 = *Kitāb* III: *fann* 21: *maqāla* 4: *faṣl fī ikhtināq al-raḥim*. The phrase is reminiscent of Galen's *On the Affected Places*. For an analysis of the history of the interpretation of this passage in modern scholarship see H. King, "Galen and the widow: towards a history of therapeutic masturbation in ancient gynaecology." *EuGeStA: Journal on Gender Studies in Antiquity* 1 (2011), 203–235.

semen. Rather, it is recommended to give her the opportunity to rid herself of her own pent-up female semen. The alternative he offers appears to be medical masturbation as a means of evacuating female semen in much the same way that men do. (Some of the language here, including the reference to "pleasure and pain" is reminiscent of the language of Galen and the widow.)

In other medieval texts, the potential causes of menstrual retention and hysterical suffocation are so numerous and varied that the diagnoses no longer function as a means of reinforcing particular gender roles. Rather the diagnoses serve as an intermediary step, providing a rational basis for linking almost any precipitating factor with a treatment which promises cleansing, purgation, relaxation, or release. Ibn al-Jazzār, for example, writes that retained menses can be caused by nosebleeds, hemorrhoids, excessive fat, exercise, sorrow, fear, anxiety, and anger. The symptoms of menstrual retention are similarly non-specific. It can manifest in the form of emaciation, nausea, fever, and lack of sexual appetite.[440] As for treatment options, Ibn al-Jazzār recommends several different ways to evacuate or exorcise the retained blood, fumigation being the preferred technique. Other therapies include pessaries, back and foot massage, rubbing the genitals (performed by a midwife),[441] bleeding, and cupping.[442]All of these techniques involve the creation of intimate and sensory-rich experiences, the purpose of which is to effect a form of release and relief by breaking down and expelling whatever is frustrating the normal menstrual and reproductive cycle.

One can see the cross-over appeal of such a diagnosis. It can be understood in strictly biological terms – the blood is being blocked in the uterus and, as a result, is undergoing a natural process of decay and so it must be evacuated and the uterus cleaned of the rot by means of incense burning and intimate touch to break down or remove the decay. But it can just as easily fit into worldviews that posit that a woman can be inhabited by a malevolent force, a ghost twin, or an evil eye, which must be released, driven out, or exorcised so that the body can resume its normal functions, possibly by means of rituals involving strong scents and intimate touch. Christopher Faraone has demonstrated that, in the Roman and Byzantine worlds, there was a great deal of intellectual compatibility of medical understandings of the wandering womb and magical concepts exhibited in material culture. Amulets and magical recipe books have been found from the first, second, and fourth centuries (the most recent, from

440 Bos, *Ibn al-Jazzār*, 263–4.

441 Ibn Sīnā makes the same suggestion, *op. cit.* al-Rāzī does so as well and quotes previous authorities for doing so in *al-Ḥāwī fī al-ṭibb*, 9:38, 40 and 44. al-Majūsī also writes that the midwives do this, see *al-Kāmil*, 2:428.

442 Bos, *Ibn al-Jazzār*, 275. Cf. al-Rāzī, *al-Ḥāwī*, 41 and 44.

Upper Egypt) which abjure the womb itself to stay in place, and both of these accord with the demonic exorcism practices of the time.[443] It may be argued that echoes of this notion can be seen in modern Egyptian fertility rituals as described by Marcia Inhorn and others.[444]

Childless couples and the assessment of each spouse's fertility

Acknowledgement of male-factor infertility

Throughout the Arabo-Galenic medical corpus, male-factor infertility, female-factor infertility, and "incompatibility" between the humoral temperaments of a couple are all recognized as potential reasons for a woman to fail to become pregnant. Male infertility receives somewhat more attention in the Arabic tradition than in the Greek, though still not nearly to the extent of female infertility. Male infertility is generally attributed to one of three failings: humoral imbalance, producing too little sperm, and erectile difficulties. Some authors also claim that male infertility can be caused by defective sperm or by a problem with the angle of the penis such that it cannot project semen "in a straight line."[445] However, the inability on the part of the man to produce offspring is rarely classified as a disease to be treated in and of itself in medical encyclopedias. Rather, male infertility is addressed as a subsection of discussions about undesirable sexual performance. Often male infertility is conflated with impotence, small penis size, and lack of sexual prowess. The is less true in Ibn Sīnā's *Qānūn* where, in several places, male and female infertility are described in similar terms and addressed at the same time.[446] There the terminology for male and female fertility-related difficulties is so similar that it is sometimes difficult to tell which partner is under discussion. Ibn Sīnā repeatedly uses the term

443 Faraone, "Magical and Medical Approaches to the Wandering Womb in the Ancient Greek World." 19 – 22.
444 M. Inhorn, *Quest for Conception*, xxiii; R. Natvig, "Liminal Rites and Female Symbolism in the Egyptian Zar Possession Cult," *Numen* 35 (1988), 57 – 68; and J. Boddy, *Wombs and Alien Spirits: Women, Men, and the Zar Cult in Northern Sudan* (Madison: University of Wisconsin Press, 1986).
445 Ṭabarī, *Firdaws al-ḥikma*, 37 – 38. Cf. Philip J. van der Eijk, *Diocles of Carystus*. (Leiden: Brill, 2001), 1:87 – 91 and 2:93 – 97.
446 Ibn Sīnā, *Qānūn fī al-ṭibb*, 2:562 = *kitāb* III: *fann* 21: *maqāla* 1: *faṣl fī dalā'il al-yabūsa.*

manī to refer to both men's and women's "sperm,"[447] by which he means male semen and, it seems, female ejaculate. Another, unusual expression of egalitarianism with respect to male and female infertility can be found in al-Majūsī's brief discussion of the topic. While other physicians prescribe surgical treatments for female infertility, in his *Kāmil* al-Majūsī does the same with respect to male infertility: "If instead [his infertility] is due to a blockage within the vesicles of the penis, then he must be treated by unblocking that blockage by using a blade, which we will discuss in the chapter on surgery."[448]

One reason the diagnosis of sterility and fertility in men received comparatively little attention in medical texts is due to the fact that men who wanted to prove themselves fertile even if they failed to conceive with their spouses had ample opportunity to do so, whereas women did not. In a society where divorce, polygamy, and concubinage were options, a man could potentially have multiple sexual partners, and thus multiple opportunities to attempt to procreate. Ibn Sīnā makes a point similar to Aristotle's about the inegalitarianism of medicine in this regard: while a husband may be medically advised to have sexual relations with another woman, such is not the case with respect to a wife. He writes:

> Regarding the infertile [woman] and sterile [man] by nature: a person with a humoral temperament contrary to that of his partner needs to replace them. As for a person with a short penis, there is no remedy. Similarly, [there is no remedy for] a woman whose orifice for menstruating has become plugged up as a result of ulcers which have since healed over and become slippery. Regarding a woman who needs to replace her husband, the physician is not in a position to help her. But regarding the rest of the cases, there are [treatments].[449]

In other words, for husbands with a "incompatible" sexual partner, a physician might medically advise him to take on a new one. (We have encountered physicians offering help in choosing sexual partners for their male patients in al-Rāzī, *Kitāb Shukūk 'alā Jālīnūs*, and his contemporary al-Ruhāwī mentions something similar.[450]) It is socially unacceptable for physicians to offer such advice to women who are having difficulty conceiving with their husbands. Like Aristotle and Ibn Sīnā, al-Majūsī too suggests that a man's apparent sterility might simply be due to incompatibility, and so it is appropriate for the physician to recommend that the man attempt to procreate with someone new.

---

447 Ibn Sīnā, *Qānūn fī al-ṭibb*, 2:562 = *kitāb* III: *fann* 21: *maqāla* 1: *faṣl fī al-'uqr wa-'usr al-ḥabl*
448 al-Majūsī, *Kāmil al-ṣinā'a fī al-ṭibb*, 2:437.
449 Ibn Sīnā, *Qānūn fī al-ṭibb*, 2:565 = *kitāb* III:*fann* 21: *maqāla* 1: *al-tadbīr wa'l-'ilāj.* My italics.
450 E.g. al-Rāzī, *Kitāb Shukūk 'alā Jālīnūs*, 79 and al-Ruhāwī's *Adab al-ṭabīb*, in Levey, 'Medical Ethics of Medieval Islam,' 90.

> If lack of conception is due to the husband, and that is due to his sperm having little compatibility with some women, then he must switch women so that he may encounter what will be compatible with the humoral temperament of his sperm.[451]

Since medieval authors acknowledge that childlessness could be a result of either incompatibility or a difficulty subsisting in either the man or woman, naturally the medical literature includes many tests of assessing individual fertility and infertility. Some tests assess both partners simultaneously, while others test only the woman for fertility. In the Arabic medical corpus these diagnostic measures appear to be employed only after a woman has failed to conceive, rather than to distinguish fertile from infertile women prior to marriage. To my knowledge, these texts do not suggest a standard amount of time that should elapse before medical attention is sought.

One commonly described means of establishing whether the male or female partner in a sexual relationship is responsible for that union's childlessness is by examining the qualities of their urine. Al-Ṭabarī writes:

> If the woman does not produce children, and you want to know whether that is due to the woman or due to the man, then take some of the man's urine and sprinkle it on a growing lettuce root, and sprinkle the urine of the woman on another lettuce root.[452] The next day whichever root is found to have dried up, then that seed is the corrupt one.[453] Or take some of both their seeds and put them [this likely refers to the lettuce upon which each has urinated] in a vessel in which there is water, and whichever of the seeds floats to the surface of the water, that is the one in which there is infertility and corruption. Or take some peas, lentils and beans, and plant them in the ground, and have woman urinate on them for two days. If any of them germinate as a result, then she can conceive. And if not, then she cannot.[454]

Such urine tests seem to be common across a wide variety of cultures and appear in ancient medical and magical texts throughout the Mediterranean world.[455] In-

---

451 al-Majūsī, *Kāmil al-ṣināʿa fī al-ṭibb*, 2:437.

452 Cf. Ibn Sīnā, *Qānūn fī al-ṭibb*, 2:564 = *Kitāb* III: *Fann* 21: *maqāla* 1: *faṣl fī al-ʿalāmāt* [*ʿalāmāt al-ʿuqr*].

453 Like the garlic test, this too will become a tool for diagnosing virginity (though only on the part of women). E. g., whereas in the Greek texts this is either a pregnancy or a fertility test, in the *Sefer ahavat nashim* the author maintains "The sages of Greece do this experiment: the girl must urinate over marshmallows in the evening, and bring them in the morning; if they are still fresh she is modest and good, if not, she is not." Caballero-Navas, *Book of Women's Love*, 142.

454 al-Ṭabarī, *Firdaws al-ḥikma fī al-ṭibb*, 38.

455 For an attempt to draw a direct connection between ancient Egyptian versions of this test and late medieval Egyptian versions, see A. Bayoumi, "Survivances Egyptiennes," *Bulletin de la Société royale de géographie d'Égypte* 19 (1937): 279 – 287.

terestingly, what is tested is not the parents' gametes, but rather a broader quality of being nurturing versus poisonous that subsists even in urine. Such a test is particularly adaptable because it does not require that one subscribe to any particular theory about what constitutes the female contribution to the embryo.

The garlic test: A case study of recapitulated tradition and innovation

Among the many procedures for diagnosing fertility is one that stands out both for its longevity and for the perspective it can offer us on the transmission and reinterpretation of ancient medical heritages. The test appears in a wide variety of medieval Arabic-language literary genres, including medical compendia, obstetrical treatises, erotica, slave-buying guides, and encyclopedias. It also appears in other languages and eras, spanning three continents and 3000 years. It can be found in some of the oldest Egyptian medical papyri, Hippocratic gynecological treatises, the writings of the Roman and Byzantine physicians, the Babylonian Talmud, and in medieval Hebrew and Latin texts up through the early modern period.

The procedure appears in a number of variations within the Hippocratic corpus.

> If a woman does not conceive, and you wish to ascertain whether she can conceive, having wrapped her up in blankets, fumigate below, and if it appears that the scent passes through the body to the nostrils and mouth, know that of herself she is not unfruitful.[456]

> Test for fertility: boil a head of garlic and apply it to the uterus; on the next day have the woman examine herself by palpating with a finger; and if her mouth smells, the sign is positive. If not, make another application.
>
> Test for fertility: enclose a little oil of bitter almonds in a piece of wool, apply it [as a vaginal suppository], and see what the woman's mouth smells of.[457]

> Apply a suppository of a little oil of bitter almonds wrapped in wool: then at dawn examine whether the suppository has given off an odor through the woman's mouth: if it has, she will become pregnant, but otherwise not . . . Another: thoroughly clean a head of garlic, snip it off, and apply as a suppository against the uterus: on the following day, see whether it has given off an odor through the woman's mouth: if it has, she will become pregnant, but otherwise not.[458]

---

456 Hippocrates, *Aphorisms* 5:59. Translation by Francis Adams. Slightly modified.
457 Hippocrates, *Nature of Woman*, §96. Translation by Paul Potter. *Hippocrates Vol. X* (Cambridge, MA: Harvard University Press, 2012), 303.
458 Hippocrates *On Barrenness*, §214. Translation by Paul Potter. *Hippocrates Vol. X*, 339–40.

In each of these iterations of the test a strongly smelling substance is inserted into the woman's vagina. If the odor penetrates from the woman's vagina up through her mouth it means that she can indeed conceive, and therefore she should not be blamed for a couple's lack of conception. Moreover, another Hippocratic treatise, *Superfetation*, describing a rather different version of the test, mentions that if one were to administer it to a currently pregnant woman the smell would not penetrate.[459]

Very similar tests can also be found in two, much older, Egyptian medical papyri. Nearly a century ago Erik Iversen identified the similarities between the Hippocratic passages and the Carlsberg VIII papyrus (likely dating from the 13th century B.C. but possibly reflecting a 19th-century B.C. text) and the Kahun medical papyrus #28 (dating from c. 1800 B.C.). Iversen viewed them as evidence of the direct influence of Egyptian medicine on Greek medicine. The Egyptian texts read:

> To determine who will <bear children> and who will not <bear children>, you should then cause the bulb of an onion to spend the night in her flesh until dawn. If the odor appears in her mouth, she will bear <children>. If <it does not>, she will never <bear children> . . . [460]
>
> Another method. Leave overnight a clove of garlic moistened (with . . .) in the body (i.e. in the vagina). If you smell garlic on her breath, she will give birth (normally). If you cannot smell it, she will not give birth normally, and this will always be the case.[461]

The two tests described in the Egyptian texts are indeed similar to each other and to the Hippocratic ones – a clove of onion or garlic is placed in the woman's vagina, she sleeps on it overnight, and the next day she is inspected to see if the smell is exhaled from her mouth – but the condition being tested in the second instance is somewhat ambiguous. It may be a form of fertility test[462] or it may be, as Jacques Jouanna understands it, a test to predict whether a currently existing pregnancy will eventually be followed with healthy birth.[463] If it is a test of the

---

459 Hippocrates, *Superfetation* §25.

460 Papyrus Carlsberg 8. 4 = Kahun Medical Papyrus 28. Quoted in Totelin, *Hippocratic Recipes*, 181. Iversen's transcription of the papyrus appears in E. Iversen, "Papyrus Carlsberg VIII with some remarks on the Egyptian origin of some popular birth prognoses," *Det. Kgl. Danske Videnskabernes Selskab. Historisk-filologiske Meddelelser* XXVI (1939), 21–22.

461 J. Jouanna, *Greek Medicine from Hippocrates to Galen* (Leiden: Brill, 2012), 5.

462 Strouhal, Evžen, Břetislav Vachala, and Hana Vymazalová. *The Medicine of the Ancient Egyptians.* 1, *Surgery, Gynecology, Obstetrics, and Pediatrics.* 162 Strouhal, Evžen, Břetislav Vachala, and Hana Vymazalová. *The Medicine of the Ancient Egyptians.* Vol. 1, *Surgery, Gynecology, Obstetrics, and Pediatrics* (Cairo: American University in Cairo Press, 2014) 162

463 He concludes, *contra* Iversen, "Thus it is difficult to speak of direct influence." Ibid., 5–6.

health of a pregnancy, then it reflects an understanding of female anatomy that is somewhat at odds with the one found in the Hippocratic gynecological text *Superfetation*, which claims that a pregnant woman should not be permeable to smells from substances inserted into the vagina. However, in both the Egyptian and Greek version of the garlic test, an unblocked passage is a desirable finding indicating the fertility of the woman or the health of her current pregnancy, while obstruction is indicative of ill-health.

Between the Hippocratic period and the dawn of Islam, the procedure continued to be described in medical literature as a fertility test. In his *Gynecology*, Soranus attests that it was used by his predecessors Diocles, Euenor, and Euryphon, though he himself does not subscribe to the underlying physiology behind the test since he believes that that it can provide a false negative test for infertility.[464] (These misgivings are suppressed in later texts that claim Soranus as an authority. For example, the 6th-century Byzantine physician Aetius of Amida appears to suggest that Soranus subscribes to the efficacy of the test.[465]) Galen, unlike Soranus, does not directly challenge the reliability of the garlic test. Instead, in his commentary on *Aphorisms* 5.59, he overlays the test with a humoral significance.[466] According to Galen, if the odor does not permeate up to the woman's mouth it means that the womb and the pathways in the body are clogged, and they are clogged due to an excess of cold or moisture. This clogged state can be rectified by introducing hot, cold, moist, or dry substances to change the humoral balance, thereby restoring fertility. Galen thereby maintains the test but offers a modified interpretation as to how it works. The same is true of Stephanus of Athens's (fl. late-6th/early-7th-century) line of reasoning in his lectures on *Aphorisms*. Stephanus seems to only half-heartedly subscribe to the science underlying the test. He does not refer to a single physical channel which must remain unblocked but rather to a more generalized sense of healthy sympathy and communication by means of "the veins, arteries and nerves." Nonetheless, he understands the test to be meaningful.[467]

Despite these differences in explaining why the test works, until the 3rd/9th century there does not seem to be any substantial change in the understanding of what the garlic test demonstrates: the transfer of the smell of garlic from

464 Soranus, *Gynecology*, 33–4.
465 Aetius of Amida, *The Gynaecology and Obstetrics of the VIth century*, tr. James Ricci (Philadelphia: Blakiston, 1950), 19.
466 Galen, and K.G. Kühn. *Clavdii Galeni Opera Omnia*. (Lipsiae: prostat in officina libraria C. Cnoblochii, 1821–1833), 17: 857.
467 Stephanus, and Leendert Gerrit Westerink, *Commentary On Hippocrates' Aphorisms* (Berlin: Akademie-Verlag, 1985) 160–161.

the vagina to the mouth indicates that a woman will be able to conceive. (There is one possible exception, mentioned in two places in the Talmud, which will be addressed below.[468]) This changes with the medieval iterations of the garlic test.

In the *Firdaws al-ḥikma*, al-Ṭabarī extensively and accurately quotes the Hippocratic texts up until he reaches the garlic test:

> [Hippocrates] also said, "If you want to know if a woman will conceive or not, then sit her on a pierced chair, cover her with a robe, and fumigate her from beneath with costus or sandarac, or aloeswood, and if you find the smell[469] of the incense [emerging] from her nostrils, then she will conceive. If not, then she will not conceive.[470] The reason for [Hippocrates'] statement is that if the smell does not emerge from the nose, that is indicative that the body's passages and the uterus are damaged.
>
> He also said that if a woman drinks mixed honey [hydromel] before sleeping not having eaten, and then she experiences colic around her middle, then she is pregnant.[471] And if not, then she is not. The reason for this statement of his is that the uterus, if it is occupied with a seed, is closed up. Mixed honey provokes bloating and if the womb is closed up, the passage for the wind is narrowed, and this bloating is retained in the [womb] thereby provoking colic. Another person said a woman should place garlic in her vagina and sleep on it, and if the next day there is a smell of garlic then she is pregnant. And if not, then there is no pregnancy in her.[472]

Most of this passage is taken almost verbatim from Hippocratic texts and Galen's commentary on the *Aphorisms*. However, in the last sentence, there is a significant departure from the older texts. In the *Firdaws al-ḥikma*, the incense-based

---

468 See Talmud Bavli *Ketubot* 10b and Talmud Bavli, *Yevamot* 60b.

469 Alternatively: "if the smell is found."

470 Cf. Hippocrates' *Aphorisms* 5:59: "If a woman does not conceive and wishes to ascertain whether she can conceive, having wrapped her up in blankets, fumigate below and, if it appears that the scent passes through the body to the nostrils and mouth, know that of herself she is not unfruitful." Translation by Francis Adams.

471 Cf. Hippocrates' *Aphorisms* 5:41: "If you wish to ascertain if a woman be with child, give her mixed honey to drink when she is going to sleep, and has not taken supper, and if she be seized with colic in the belly, she is with child, but otherwise she is not pregnant." Translation, slightly modified, from Francis Adams. Cf. al-Rāzī, *al-Ḥāwī fī al-ṭibb*, vol. 3, bk 9:50.

472 al-Ṭabarī, *Firdaws al-ḥikma fī al-ṭibb*, 37–38. Siggel translates this into German as "so kann sie empfangen . . . so kann sie nicht empfangen," i. e., she *can* conceive. Given the context of the paragraph, and the grammar of the sentence, I do not think an unmodified reading of the Arabic supports this interpretation. From the context, it appears that this is a test of pregnancy, not a test of potential fertility. See A. Siggel, "Gynäkologie, Embryologie und Frauenhygiene aus dem Paradies der Weisheit über die Medizin des Abū al-Ḥasan 'Alī b. Sahl Rabbān at-Ṭabarī," *Quellen und Studien zur Geschichte Naturwissenschaften und der Medizin* 8 (1941), 238. Weisser appears to read al-Ṭabarī's sentence as I do, see Weisser, *Zeugung, Vererbung, und pränatale Entwicklung*, 159.

version of the procedure diagnoses fertility, but that is not the case when the test is done with garlic. Instead, al-Ṭabarī describes it as a test of whether or not conception has occurred. It is a pregnancy test. Al-Ṭabarī does not seem to feel the need to explain why the emergence of the garlic smell from the mouth of a woman is evidence of her pregnancy. It does not necessarily follow from the initial concept (which he has not discarded) of fertility being dependent on unblocked passages. It does, however, accord with ancient Egyptian texts, and it makes sense if we understand his logic to be that the smell of the garlic on her breath constitutes a desirable outcome irrespective of whether one is testing for fertility or pregnancy.

In Arabic medical texts dating from the next three centuries, we continue to find this procedure described as a test either for fertility or for pregnancy or both, with three different interpretations of what the outcome of the test means. These interpretations are (1) the presence of the scent in her mouth is indicative of fertility, (2) it is indicative of pregnancy, or (3) it is indicative of lack of current pregnancy. In the 4th/10th century, the garlic-as-fertility-test is mentioned by al-Rāzī[473] in Iraq in his *al-Ḥāwī fī al-ṭibb*, and by Aḥmad al-Baladī in Egypt in his obstetrical text.[474] By contrast, an obstetrical text produced in Spain during the same period by ʿArīb b. Saʿīd al-Qurṭubī describes the garlic-based version of the procedure as a pregnancy test and the incense-based version as a fertility test, just as al-Ṭabarī does. Al-Qurṭubī writes, "if the next day the scent of the garlic emerges from the nose, it is a sign of conception. If it does not do so, then she is not pregnant."[475] This is particularly curious because, in the paragraph immediately preceding this one, al-Qurṭubī says that a sign of pregnancy is that the mouth of the uterus is closed over. In theory, such a closing of the cervix would interrupt the passage between the vagina and the mouth. One would thus expect that the transfer of the garlic odor from vagina to mouth would be an indication that the cervix was still open and that pregnancy had not occurred. However, al-Qurṭubī does not appear to be consistent in this regard.

Ibn Sīnā's *Qānūn* describes the garlic test twice, once as a test for fertility or lack thereof, and once as a test for pregnancy or lack thereof but, unlike al-Ṭabarī and al-Qurṭubī, his anatomical theory remains consistent and accords more closely with Hippocratic thought. In his section on the signs of infertility Ibn Sīnā, like the Hippocratics, writes that the presence of the smell indicates

---

473 Cf. Al-Rāzī, *al-Ḥāwī fī al-ṭibb*, vol. 3, book 9:52.

474 Al-Baladī, *Tadbīr al-ḥabālā'*, 18.

475 ʿArīb ibn Saʿīd al-Qurṭubī, *Kitāb khalq al-janīn wa-tadbīr al-ḥabālā wa'l-mawlūdīn* = *La livre de la génération du foetus et le traitement des femmes enceintes et des nouveau-nés* (Algiers: Librairie Ferraris, 1956), 28.

an unobstructed path and hence a prospect of fertility.[476] The test then appears three pages later as a pregnancy test, but the pregnancy is proven absent by the smell of garlic in a woman's mouth. He writes:

> Conception can be diagnosed through tests. Among them is having the woman drink two *waqītas* of Sara-check before sleep, or similarly mixed rainwater, and then seeing whether there is colic or not, because in conjunction these cause retention and bloating in the intestines. Physicians are convinced by this, and it is a positive test, except for those women who are already accustomed to drinking this. Another [test]: she should submit to a fast for a day and then in the evening be wrapped in robes and fumigate herself on a pierced chair with a cone of incense. If the fumes and smell emerge from her mouth and nose, then there is no conception in her. A similar negative test is taking garlic, sleeping on it, and [seeing] if the smell and taste of it is in her mouth or not.[477]

Here the anatomical premise is maintained, i.e. the premise that normally the path from the vagina to the uterus to the mouth is unobstructed, and the existence of an obstruction indicates that either the cervix has closed, as occurs during pregnancy, or there is something in the uterus causing a blockage, i.e. a fetus. What has changed is that finding the path to be unobstructed is no longer necessarily a desirable outcome. The presence of garlic in the mouth is an indication that pregnancy has failed to be achieved.

In slave-buying guides, the procedure appears as a pregnancy test, but with two opposing interpretations. In the *Risāla fī shirā al-raqīq wa-taqlīb al-ʿabīd* by the 5th/11th-century Baghdadi Christian physician Ibn Buṭlān, the author writes about women being sold as slaves. The slave dealer attempts to conceal the fact that they are pregnant by displaying fake menstrual blood.

> What conceals pregnancy: the slaver provides the slave woman with fake blood to display, made from resin and dragon's blood[478] – if she cannot obtain the blood of animals.
>
> To verify the existence of a pregnancy and its health: This knowledge can be obtained by placing beneath the woman incense such as ambergris, and preventing [the smell] from exiting from the sides or openings in her robes. If the smell issues from her mouth, then she is not pregnant. And the opposite [is true too].[479]

---

476 Ibn Sīnā, *Qānūn fī al-ṭibb* 2:564 = *kitāb* III: *fann* 21: *maqāla* 1: *faṣl fī al-ʿalāmāt* [*ʿalāmāt al-ʿuqr*].

477 Ibn Sīnā, *Qānūn fī al-ṭibb* 2:567 = *kitāb* III: *fann* 21: *maqāla* 1: *faṣl fī ʿalāmāt al-ḥabl wa-aḥkāmihi.*

478 I.e. a red dye made from plant resin or cinnabar.

479 Ibn Buṭlān, *Risāla fī shirā al-raqīq wa-taqlīb al-ʿabīd*, 383. I am grateful to Dr. Hannah Barker for drawing my attention to this passage and the subsequent one.

This accords with Ibn Sīnā's view. More than a century later and on a different continent, Ibn Buṭlān's advice appears again, in al-Andalus, in a market-inspector's manual by al-Saqatī from c. 606/1210. Much of al-Saqatī's advice in the surrounding passages is a precis of Ibn Buṭlān's advice, except for his interpretation of this test: he understands it as having the opposite meaning from the one attributed to it by his source.

> They [masculine plural] conceal pregnancy by displaying fake blood, manufactured from resin and dragon's blood, if no animal blood is obtainable. One can become informed [male singular] about the pregnancy of a woman by placing below her incense or ambergris and preventing it from exiting via her sleeves or garments. If the smell issues from her mouth, then she is pregnant. And if it does not, then she is not pregnant.[480]

It is noteworthy that the two Andalusians, al-Saqatī (the 6th/12th-century author of the market inspector's manual) and al-Qurṭubī (the 4th/10th-century author of the obstetrical treatise) interpret the test in the same way, i.e. that the permeation of the smell is a positive sign of pregnancy.

By the 7th/13th-century, we encounter a new iteration of the test with another set of permutations about its interpretation. In his *Kitāb ʻajā'ib al-makhlūqāt wa'l-ḥayawānāt wa-gharā'ib al-mawjūdāt* (Book of The Wonders of Creation and the Peculiarities of Beings) the Persian cosmographer al-Qazwīnī (d. 682/1283) explains the test as follows. "If you want to know whether a woman is a virgin or a non-virgin then mix thinly sliced garlic with honey and tell her to carry it [in her vagina], and then wait two hours. If the odor of the garlic can be smelled from her mouth then she is a virgin, if not then she is a non-virgin."[481] Here once again the permeation of the smell is positive sign, but now it does not indicate fertility, or pregnancy, but rather *virginity.*

Such an interpretation might seem counterintuitive, given that discussions of female virginity tend to presuppose the existence of a physical barrier in the form of a hymen. We might assume that the garlic test could more logically test for virginity by determining hymenal intactness. Under such circumstances, a finding of a garlic smell in a woman's mouth ought to be indicative of the loss of virginity, whereas the lack of smell would indicate that the hymenal obstruction is still in place. Indeed, that is precisely what we find in an Egyptian encyclopedia produced one generation later. The author, Shihāb al-Dīn Ahmad al-Nu-

---

480 Al-Saqatī, *Fī adāb al-ḥisba = Un manuel hispanique de Hisba*, 52.

481 Al-Qazwīnī, *ʻAjā'ib al-makhlūqāt wa-al-ḥayawānāt wa-gharā'ib al-mawjūdāt* (Beirut: Mu'assasat al-Aʻlamī li'l-Maṭbūʻāt, 2000), 231.

wayrī (d. 733/1333) writes that the procedure can be used as a virginity test, as a pregnancy test, and as a fertility test.

> Ḥunayn ibn Isḥāq said[482]: If you want to know if a woman is a virgin or non-virgin have her take peeled garlic and insert it and carry it in her vagina overnight. When she wakes up let her breath out, *and if the smell of the garlic is in her mouth then she is a non-virgin. But if [the smell] is not present in her mouth then she is a virgin.*
>
> So too one may recognize her pregnancy: if the smell of garlic is present then she is not pregnant, and if it is not present then she is pregnant.
>
> If you want to find out the state of woman, whether she may yet become pregnant or not, then have her take rolled birthwort and crush it with the gall of a cow, then have her keep it in overnight. *If the next morning its smell is found in her mouth, then she may become pregnant. And if not, then she is infertile.*[483]

Thus, according to al-Nuwayrī, an obstruction indicates either virginity or pregnancy or sterility, whereas the presence of a smell indicates sexual experience, lack of pregnancy, or fertility. The same virginity test, in slightly different words and without the attribution to Ibn Isḥāq is also found in the therapeutic work *Kanz al-ikhtiṣāṣ* by ʿIzz al-Dīn ibn Aydamar al-Jaldakī, an 8th/14th-century Persian alchemist and physician who traveled as far as Yemen and North Africa. This same passage (without the attribution to Ḥunayn ibn Isḥāq) is also quoted in *Raḥma fī al-ṭibb wa'l-ḥikma*, by the famed Islamic scholar Jalāl al-Dīn al-Suyūṭī (d. 911/1505), in the context of a chapter on restoring virginity to the non-virgin. The description of the garlic test is immediately followed by several recipes for pessaries that restore virginity.[484]

Such formulations, in which both virginity and pregnancy are proven by a lack of smell, continued to be repeated in later Middle Eastern literature. But this is not to suggest that the older interpretations of the garlic test were abandoned. The famous book of erotic medicine by Ibn Kamal Pasha (d. 941/1534) *Rujūʿ al-shaykh ila ṣibāh* (The Return of the Old Man to His Youth) describes the garlic-based version of the test as a means of establishing pregnancy and recommends the incense version of the test to establish fertility and infertility. Ibn Kamal Pasha's interpretation of the garlic test is similar to that of al-Ṭabarī, al-Qurṭubī, and al-Saqatī: if the scent of garlic permeates to her mouth then she is pregnant.

482 I have been unable to locate this quotation in the works of Ḥunayn ibn Isḥāq.
483 al-Nuwayrī, *Nihāyat al-arab fī funūn al-adab* (Beirut: Dār al-Kutub al-ʿIlmiyya, 2004), 12:129. Italics are mine.
484 Jalāl al-Dīn al-Suyūṭī, *Kitāb al-Raḥma fī al- ṭibb wa'l-ḥikma* (Beirut: Dār al-Arqam, 2011), 182 (chapter 136).

Beyond the Islamic world too, the garlic test was the subject of these permutations, with new ones introduced. A particularly interesting version can be found in a 13th-century Hebrew gynecological text from southern Europe called *Sefer ahavat nashim* (The Book of Women's Love). The book recommends fumigating the uterus and, "if the smoke reaches her mouth and is bitter, she is not a virgin; if it does not, she is a virgin. You could do the same to a barren woman: if the smoke goes up to her mouth and is bitter, you will know that she is barren; if not, she is closed and not barren."[485] This too is immediately followed by virginity-restoration recipes. At this point, it seems that the communication of smells from the vagina up to the mouth has become attached to undesirable results, i.e. lack of virginity, and so, by association, it becomes attached to another undesirable outcome, i.e. infertility. So, in this case, the test has the exact opposite diagnostic value of the one articulated in the Hippocratic texts, despite sharing the same gynecological premises.

The history of the garlic test has much to teach us about the nature of medieval learned gynecology. First, the garlic test is an example of an idea whose origins are ambiguous. Its medieval versions clearly reference Greek formulations, but the underlying concept may also be indigenous to parts of the Middle East, present before the translation movement of the early ʿAbbasid period. After all, the garlic test is found even in ancient Egypt, where it was connected with pregnancy rather than fertility. Second, the garlic test suggests some degree of correlation between "book medicine" and medical practice. The very fact that the uses attributed to the garlic test vary, but do so all within one specific theoretical framework, suggests that the garlic test was an actual procedure, not merely an intellectual exercise. By contrast, unvaried and non-specific descriptions of procedures are indicative of their having never been actually implemented, as Emilie Savage-Smith has argued in reference to other medical procedures.[486]

The garlic test also serves to remind us of the basic problems and solutions available to the would-be medieval gynecologist. The basic problem was that women's genitals were internal and hidden, and thus it was difficult to know whether all was well or if something was wrong with respect to fertility, pregnancy, or virginity. One solution to this problem was to posit that one can discover what is happening inside the body by supposing that the internal organs are

485 Caballero-Navas, *Book of Women's Love*, 142. On the history and derivation of medieval Jewish gynecological texts see R. Barkaï, *Les infortunes de Dinah, le livre de la génération: La gynécologie juive au Moyen âge* (Paris: Cerf, 1991).

486 Emilie Savage-Smith, "The Practice of Surgery in Islamic Lands: Myth and Reality," *Social History of Medicine* 13 (2000), 307–321.

connected to the outside, visible world and by mapping what is happening at the entries and exits of the body. The garlic test, and the fumigations too, thus function like an x-ray or sonogram. The modern physician learns about that which is in the body by bombarding the body with electro-magnetic radiation or sound-waves and creates a picture based upon what penetrates the body and what does not. The medieval physician did so using scents.

The garlic test is also significant because it highlights the connections between the diagnosis of women's bodies, blame, and social control. The test invites us to think about certain gynecological practices as not merely medical diagnostic tools but rather as women's rituals. The garlic test is a performance, or ordeal, whose specific meaning is subject to interpretive variation, but whose purpose remains constant. In all its permutations it has a consistent goal: to scientifically uncover the "facts" about a woman's sexual past or her reproductive future, facts which in the present are always in doubt. The test is predicated on the notion that her unknown past and future are possible to discover because they leave a tangible mark on her present body. We might therefore be inclined to view infertility testing, like virginity testing, as a tool of patriarchal intimidation. It threatens women by perpetuating the notion that their bodies can be checked to if they are fit or defective. However, there is another way of interpreting such tests.

In some of the Hebrew and Arabic versions of the procedure as virginity test, the procedure is immediately followed by advice about how to restore or fake virginity. In these contexts, therefore, the garlic test is one of a set of tools to be utilized by a woman to avert blame from herself.

The utility of such a test as a means of defending a woman and restoring her to her husband's good graces is illustrated dramatically in a version found in Babylonian Talmud, from a passage likely originating in the 3rd-century. This version uses not garlic, or incense, but the fumes from a barrel of wine. The test appears in a one of a series of anecdotes, in each of which a groom after the wedding comes before a rabbi and voices his suspicions that his bride was not a virgin. In each case the rabbi to whom the groom brings his concern provides either a theoretical explanation or an empirical test which would account for the lack of appearance of virginity despite the bride being a virgin at the time of consummation. Each anecdote concludes with a recommendation to the groom that he consider himself fortunate and "go enjoy she whom you have acquired."

> A man came before Rabban Gamliel the son of Rabbi [Yehudah Ha-Nasi] and said to him: My master, I engaged in intercourse and did not find blood. She [the bride] said to him: My master, I am still a virgin.

> [Rabban Gamliel] said to them: Bring me two maidservants, one a virgin and one a non-virgin. They brought them to him and he seated them on the opening of a cask of wine. The scent of the [wine] wafted through the non-virgin but the scent of it did not waft through the virgin. He then seated the [wife] on the cask, and the scent of it did not waft through. [Rabban Gamliel] said to the [husband]: Go enjoy she whom you have acquired.
>
> Why did [Rabban Gamliel] not just initially examine [the bride] by this [method]? Because he had heard of [the theory] but had never seen it in practice. And he thought that perhaps it is not certain, and it is not proper to subject Jewish women to indignities needlessly.[487]

This story depicts the test as undignified but ultimately useful in supporting the woman's claims. In the *Aphorisms* too, the fertility test is depicted as a means of proving that a couple's childlessness is not the woman's fault, and Stephanus of Athens suggests that its purpose is to coerce the husband rather than the wife. In other words, the test might not have been wielded primarily as a weapon against women. Rather it might have been a defensive tool, by means of which a woman could attempt to exonerate herself from accusations of fault, and blunt the force of a man's distrust, by "scientifically" assuaging his doubts. The garlic test, like virginity restoration, might well have offered women a shield to fend off patriarchal judgement and condemnation.

487 Talmud Bavli *Ketubot* 10b.

5 Physicians, Midwives, and Female Patients

When drawing on Arabic medical texts in an attempt to shed light on how women experienced infertility, we must ask the question: did the ideas articulated in these texts ever have a practical impact on the way medieval infertile women were treated or how they perceived their infertility? After all, what we have are theories and practices described in books, in a world in which the vast majority of women were not taught to read. While some biographical dictionaries include accounts of individual women who did master a particular body of oral or written texts (such as *ḥadīth* literature, or poetry), we have no such account in the realm of medicine. Therefore, Arabo-Galenic gynecology could have practical implications only if male participants in this literate medical culture shared this culture with female medical practitioners or communicated their ideas directly to female patients. One might well assume, as Manfred Ullmann does, that neither of these things could occur, on the grounds that women would have lacked interest in male opinions about female bodies, or on the grounds that modesty concerns made such interactions taboo. The extant sources, however, do not buttress such assumptions, and instead point at a very different state of affairs.

As a caveat to her own scholarship on ancient gynecological theories, Monica Green writes:

> [T]he transmission of ancient traditions must be understood as a primarily intellectual and literary phenomenon. In all of the cultures discussed . . . literacy levels were so low that a textual medium of knowledge would ipso facto have been inaccessible to the vast majority of people. Hence the reader should not assume (nor have I meant to imply) that the medical practices described here were necessarily those most regularly performed when a woman complained of any illness. Nor, additionally, can we always be sure that the theories expounded in medical literature reflect the attitudes of the contemporary society at large.[488]

The same caveats may be applied to the communities under discussion in this study. When it comes to medieval Middle Eastern societies, we currently have no way of objectively assessing the relative frequency of women receiving gynecological care that was influenced by the Arabo-Galenic literary tradition, as opposed to care guided by familial or local medical lore, or care predicated on religious intervention or the manipulation of supernatural forces. (The intellectual ramifications of these forms of healing are explored from the perspective of certain Islamic jurists in the next chapter.) What we do have, instead, are many tan-

488 Green, "The Transmission of Ancient Theories of Female Physiology," 7.

https://doi.org/10.1515/9783110596588-010

talizing remarks that shed light on the *feasibility* of women receiving gynecological care in the Arabo-Galenic medical tradition.

In the regions and time-period from which there is extant literature (which may well not be representative of the majority of communities), that literature depicts environments in which male physicians interact with female patients, though women appear in only a relatively small percentage of the individual cases mentioned.[489] Literary works, books of medical ethics, biographical dictionaries detailing the exploits of physicians, guides to inspectors policing the marketplace, and works of religious preaching and public morality describe a variety of professional interactions between male physicians and female patients. They refer to medical consultations and to women submitting their urine to male physicians for uroscopy, just as their male counterparts do.[490] Male phlebotomists are depicted as bleeding women. Male physicians examine women in the course of making house calls, take their pulse,[491] and at times engage in

489 E.g., Abū Bakr Muḥammad ibn Zakarīyā al-Rāzī, *Kitāb al-tajārib: maʿa dirāsa fī manhaj al-baḥth al-ʿilmī ʿinda al-Rāzī* (Alexandria: Dār al-Wafā' li-Dunyā al-Ṭibāʿa wa'l-Nashr, 2006), 247–252. The other two known clinical experience casebooks are *al-Majālis fī al-ṭibb* by Abū Jaʿfar Aḥmad b. ʿĪsā al-Hāshimī (fl. 5th/11th-century) and *Kitāb al-Mujarrabāt* by Ibn Zuhr, both from Spain.

490 In Ibn al-Ruhāwī's *Adab al-ṭabīb* there are several anecdotes about women submitting their urine for uroscopy, particularly in order to determine pregnancy and fetal sex. See M. Levey, "Medical Ethics of Medieval Islam with Special Reference to Al-Ruhāwī's 'Practical Ethics of the Physician," 74–75.

491 Consider this anecdote from al-Ghazālī's *Iḥyā ʿulūm al-dīn:* "Someone complained to a physician about his wife being infertile and not bearing any children. The physician felt her pulse and said: 'No need to worry about infertility treatment, for you are going to die in forty days, as is indicated by your pulse.' The woman was overcome with fear and lost all appetite for life; she took out her money, divided it and bequeathed it. She remained without eating and drinking, but the [allotted] time passed without her dying. The husband went to the physician and said: 'She did not die.' He replied: 'I know that. Have sex with her now, and she will give birth.' The husband retorted: 'How so?' The physician explained: 'I saw that she was overweight, and that fat had collected at the orifice of the womb. Moreover, I knew that she would only lose weight if she were afraid of dying, so I put this fear into her. Thus she lost weight, and the obstacle against conception has disappeared.'" Translation (modified) from Peter Pormann's text study handout, "Female Patients, Patrons and Practitioners in 10th and 11th-Century Baghdad: An Unheard Voice?" Institute of Islamic Studies at McGill University, Montreal, May 4, 2007. In another text from the same period called *Daʿwat al-aṭibbā'*, the Christian physician Ibn Butlān complains that people have absurd and scientifically impossible expectations of physicians, and he lists as an example of such expections, the notion that a physician should be able to distinguish a barren from a fruitful woman by feeling her pulse. See. F. Rosenthal, "The Defense of Medicine In The Medieval Muslim World," *Bulletin of the History of Medicine* 43 (1969):529.

more intimate forms of touch. Medical texts also recommend surgeries to be conducted on women, including on their genitals and in obstetrical situations. As for the role occupied by female medical providers in the ecosystem of learned gynecology, the situation is remarkably ambiguous, not only when comparing across communities, but even when considering the writings of individual authors.

Non-gynecological interactions between male medical professionals and female patients

Descriptions of market activity from 6th–7th/12th–13th-century Islamic Spain, Egypt, and Syria portray physicians, pharmacists, surgeons, bonesetters and assorted other medical personnel having storefronts in the market or in similar settings in which women were present.[492] At least some of the medical care provided in these settings clearly reflects the Arabo-Galenic medical tradition. These descriptions come from books of *ḥisba*, guides for market inspectors whose job it was to prevent fraud and physical and moral pollution in the market and other public places. Concerns about the potential for sexual exploitation of women, and scandalous behavior on the part of women, feature prominently in this genre of literature. However, medical practitioners are not particularly scrutinized in this regard.

Ḥisba manuals indicate that, at least in some communities, it was acceptable for male medical practitioners to touch female clients. For example, according to a 6th/13th-century Syrian *ḥisba* manual by al-Shayzarī, male phlebotomists perform cupping on women's thighs to bring down the menses, a practice which is also recommended in the theoretical medical literature.[493] Similarly, a manual by Ibn al-Ukhuwwa, written in 7th/14th Mamluk Egypt, describes male phlebotomists bleeding women, with no mention of modesty-based concerns in doing so. This is the case despite the fact that the author mentions regulations based on

492 See S. Hamarneh, "Origin and Functions of the Ḥisbah System in Islam and Its Impact on the Health Professions," *Sudhoffs Archiv für Geschichte der Medizin und der Naturwissenschaften* 48 (1964), 157–63 and M. Meyerhof, "La surveillance des professions médicales et paramédicales chez les Arabes," *Bulletin de l'Institut d'Égypte* 26 (1944), 119–34. Chipman, *The World of Pharmacy and Pharmacists in Mamlūk Cairo*, 70. See Abū'l-Munā al-Mūhīn al-'Aṭṭār, *Minhāj al-dukkān wa-dustūr al-ayān* (Beirut: Dār al-Manāhil, 1992), 16; Ibn al-Ukhūwwa, *The Ma'ālim al-qurba fī aḥkām al-ḥisba*, 54–59; 'Ibn 'Abdūn al-Tujibī and E. Lévi-Provençal, *Séville Musulmane Au Début Du XIIe Siècle: Le Traité D'ibn Abdun Sur La Vie Urbaine Et Les Corps De Métiers* (Paris: G. P. Maisonneuve, 1947), § 139–40.

493 al-Shayzarī, *Kitāb Nihāyat al-rutba fī ṭalab al-ḥisba*, 96. See Ibn Sīnā, *Qānūn fī al-ṭibb* 2:589 = *Kitāb* 3: *fann* 21: *maqāla* 3: *faṣl fī al-mu'ālajāt.*

modesty concerns in other, non-medical situations. Moreover, when addressing phlebotomists, Ibn al-Ukhuwwa mentions other caveats, but none of these reflect concerns about modesty or sexual taboos.

> No slave must be bled without the owner's permission, nor a minor without that of his guardian, nor a pregnant woman, nor one menstruating. Bleeding must not be performed except in a public place, nor with any but a sharp instrument, nor when he [the operator] is in a state of mental agitation. The *muḥtasib* must exact a promise and a bond from them that in ten specified cases they will not bleed except after consultation with physicians . . .[494]

Here we see menstruation and pregnancy treated as counterindications for bleeding, not as taboo subjects thwarting male medical inquiry and involvement. Indeed, Ibn al-Ukhuwwa later specifically mentions the usefulness of bleeding the saphenous vein to provoke menstruation. (He also mentions counter-indications with respect to male reproduction. He prohibits phlebotomists from cutting or bleeding the veins behind the ears, for fear that it will induce male sterility. Al-Shayzarī includes a slightly longer discussion of this notion, which also appears in the Hippocratic treatise *Airs, Waters, Places.*[495])

Ibn al-Ukhuwwa also instructs the inspector to ensure that the phlebotomist is prepared to conduct circumcisions, on both males and females.

> The phlebotomist should carry with him instruments for circumcision (consisting of a razor and scissors), for it is a duty incumbent upon both men and women. To this the generality of men of learning agree. Abū Ḥanīfa called it a recommended practice, but not a compulsory duty. For the male, it consists in abscission of the prepuce hiding the glans penis, for the female in cutting the skin over the vagina and above the urethra. It is a practice compulsory upon men and women, who must carry it out on themselves and on their children. If it is neglected, the imam must enforce its being carried out.[496]

That phlebotomists were tasked with circumcision can be attributed to their having the requisite sharp tools in their possession. A 13th-century Egyptian shadow play titled, *al-Ṣāni'a*, "The Female Practitioner," features a woman, probably a gypsy, as the titular character, and she is depicted bearing a satchel, lances, cupping glasses, and needles with which she fulfills her roles as phlebotomist, tattooer, circumciser, and fortune-teller.[497] While female phlebotomists are not

---

494 Ibn al-Ukhūwwa, *The Ma'ālim al-qurba fī aḥkām al-ḥisba*, 54. Levy's translation.
495 Al-Shayzarī, *Kitāb Nihāyat al-rutba fī ṭalab al-ḥisba*, 92
496 Ibn al-Ukhuwwa, *The Ma'ālim al-qurba fī aḥkām al-ḥisba*, 56. Levy's translation.
497 P. E. Kahle, "A Gypsy Woman in Egypt in the Thirteenth Century A.D." *Journal of the Gypsy Lore Society*, third series, 29 (1950):11–15.

mentioned in Ibn al-Ukhuwwa's text, they were often involved in female circumcisions in Egypt.[498] Furthermore, in legal literature there is a history jurists encouraging physicians to teach women to perform circumcisions and other medical procedures in order to avoid subjecting women to a male gaze.[499] However, in Ibn al-Ukhuwwa's manual, the description of how to conduct female circumcisions uses masculine grammatical forms for the practitioner.[500]

In addition to *hisba* manuals, medical texts too also give the impression that male practitioners perform circumcisions and genital excisions on women. The 4th/10th-century physicians Ibn Sīnā and al-Zahrāwī, both writing in contexts where female circumcision was not a common practice (in Iraq and Spain respectively) describe in their medical texts how a male physician should go about performing clitorectomies when the clitoris is abnormally large. Ibn Sīnā, for his part, expresses some skepticism regarding whether such a condition actually exists and, if it does, whether it cannot be better managed without surgery.[501] Al-Zahrāwī does not mention such doubts but, following quite closely Paul of Aegina's description of the procedure in his book on surgery, writes "You [masculine] must grasp the clitoris with your hand or with a hook and cut it off. Do not cut too deeply . . . and as for a fleshy growth growing in the cervix and filling it . . . you should cut this too, just as you cut off the clitoris."[502] Al-Zahrāwī is quite clear that it is a male physician performing the operation, and that the surgery entails touching the genitals. One could make the argument that al-Zahrāwī does not consider the clitoris to be female genitalia, and that the medical scenario is thus not considered gynecological or sexually fraught. (He refers to the operation as cutting a clitoris which is so large as to look "deformed" and "erect like a man's" penis). His chapter describing the procedure (chapter 71) precedes the chapters on gynecological surgery but immediately follows the chapter on treating hermaphrodites (chapter 70) and on the mechanics of male castration (chapter 69), which in turn is preceded by chapters on male genitalia. This sort of organization may imply a view that the uncircumcised girl constitutes a stage on a masculine-to-feminine continuum, which moves from males, to castrated men, to hermaphrodites, to uncircumcised girls, to

498 Berkey, "Circumcision Circumscribed: Female Excision and Cultural Accommodation in the Medieval Near East," 20.

499 Ibn ʿĀbidīn, *Ḥāshiyat Radd al-muḥtār*, 9:533.

500 Ibn al-Ukhuwwa, *The Maʿālim al-qurba fī aḥkām al-ḥisba*, 164 in the Arabic.

501 Ibn Sīnā, *Qānūn fī al-ṭibb*, 2:603 = *kitāb* III: *fann* 22: *maqāla* 1, *faṣl fī al-laḥm al-zāʾid wa-ṭūl il-baẓr.*

502 al-Zahrāwī, *Albucasis on Surgery and Instruments*, 457. Cf. Paul of Aegina and Francis Adams, *The Seven Books of Paulus Ægineta* (London: Sydenham Society, 1844), 2:381.

full-fledged women. The chapter in question is taken verbatim from Paul of Aegina's book on surgery, which maintains the same chapter order.[503]

It could perhaps be argued that phlebotomists and surgeons are distinct from physicians, and thus are not elite enough to be considered a threat to sexual respectability nor sufficiently theoretically trained as to be able to communicate Arabo-Galenic medical theory and practice to their patients. However, we also hear of physicians treating women and conversing with them about both medical and non-medical topics. This appears to be the case both in the households of the nobility, where modesty constraints were usually greatest, as well as in less elite households in a variety of places and periods. Numerous tales recounted by Ibn Abī Uṣaybiʿa in his biographical dictionary of physicians, *Kitāb 'Uyūn al-anbā' fī ṭabaqāt al-aṭibbā'*, reference relationships and alliances between male physicians and female patients in the royal household. Some of these relationships are described as occurring at a distance and through intermediaries, such as the one between Khayzurān, the mother of the famed ʿAbbasid caliphs al-Hādī and Hārūn al-Rashīd, and the physician Abū Quraysh. But there are also numerous mentions of physicians visiting the women's quarters. For example, the Samaritan physician and vizier to the Ayyubids Muhadhdhab al-Dīn Yūsuf ibn Abī Saʿīd (d. 624/1227), served as the personal physician to both the male and female members of the royal household. In one story about him a friend of his, a judge, fell out of favor at court and asked Muhadhdhab al-Dīn to advocate for him. In an effort to help, the physician turned to his allies in the harem:

> Seriat al-Malik al-ʿAdil, the mother of al-Malik al-Sālih ibn al-Malik, was unwell at that time. She was of Turkish origin, an intelligent, pious and good woman, very kind and generous. When the Doctor Muhadhdhab al-Dīn came to see her in the harem, he acquainted her with the case of the judge, his troubles and the unjust treatment meted out to him . . . The chief eunuch supported Muhadhdhab's request. But Seriat said: "How can I do anything for the judge, or even mention him to the Sultan? I cannot, because he will ask: 'What makes you speak about the judge, and how is it that you know him?' If he were, say, a doctor who visits us from time to time, or a merchant who sells us cloth, it would be possible for me to talk and intervene; but as it is, I can do nothing."[504]

503 Paul of Aegina and Francis Adams, *The Seven Books of Paulus Ægineta* (London: Sydenham Society, 1844), 2:381. Cf. Ibn Sīnā, *Qānūn fī al-ṭibb*, 2:603 = *kitāb* III: *fann* 22: *maqāla* 1, *faṣl fī al-laḥm al-zā'id wa-ṭūl il-baẓr* in which Ibn Sīnā describes the same surgery, but says there is disagreement as to whether this condition even exists and whether or not it can be managed without surgery.

504 Translation from L. Kopf, *Lives of the Physicians* http://www.tertullian.org/fathers/ibn_abi_usaibia_03.htm, p. 905. Ibn Abī Uṣaybiʿa, *'Uyūn al-anbā' fī ṭabaqāt al-aṭibbā'* (Beirut: Dār Maktaba al-Ḥayāt, 1965), 730.

The woman and the physician then concoct a scheme which ultimately succeeds. From this passage, it is evident that not only does the physician visit the noblewomen, but that he occupies one of the few professions that are perceived as having legitimate business in the harem. The noblewoman says it would seem suspicious for her to be aware of the political fortunes of a judge and to intervene on his behalf, but it would not be inappropriate for her to be seen to do so on behalf of a physician or cloth merchant. The story indicates that in this noblewoman's particular community there are opportunities for educated physicians to converse with women without violating social norms.

Other anecdotes recounted by Ibn Abī Uṣaybīʻa suggest that physicians who personally attended the women of noble households may have been in highly sensitive positions that occasioned some awkwardness, but such obstacles were not insurmountable. The story is told of Saʻīd ibn Tufīl (d. 279/892), an Egyptian physician to the famed founder of the Tulunid dynasty Aḥmad ibn Ṭūlūn, and his accidental protegee in the medical arts, Hāshim.

> When Saʻīd ibn Tufīl first associated with Aḥmad, he had a hireling of ugly appearance, called Hāshim, who, together with his father, worked with flax. He tended Saʻīd's mule and kept watch on it when Saʻīd entered the house of Aḥmad ibn Tūlūn. Saʻīd occasionally had him pound drugs at his house when he took him home with him, and blow upon the fire over the concoctions. Saʻīd ibn Tufīl had a son of handsome appearance, endowed with intelligence and a sound knowledge of medicine. At the beginning of their acquaintanceship, Aḥmad ibn Tūlūn instructed Saʻīd to find a physician for his womenfolk, who would reside at the court during Saʻīd's absence. Said Saʻīd: 'I have a son whom I have taught and made proficient.' Said Aḥmad: 'Present him to me.' When he was introduced, Aḥmad, seeing a handsome youth, possessed of all good qualities, commented to Saʻīd: 'He is not suitable to serve the women; for them I need a person of great knowledge, but ugly appearance.' Saʻīd was reluctant to have a stranger attend the women, for fear that he might disagree and clash with him. He therefore took Hāshim, provided him with a dira'a [a loose outer garment] and slippers and appointed him to the women . . .
>
> 'Umar asked Saʻīd: 'In what position did you install Hāshim?' Saʻīd replied: 'In the service of the women, for the Emir wanted a person of unprepossessing appearance.' Said 'Umar: 'An ugly person with a sound education, fitting the post, could surely have been found among the sons of physicians. You have disgraced the profession . . .'

From this account it would seem that, in the Tulunid court, women were seen by trained male physicians, but it was a position appropriate to a junior person, though still a person old enough to be potentially sexually appealing. The ideal physician under such a circumstance was someone well-educated but not physically attractive. The story continues with Hāshim's great success among the noblewomen, who then personally make the introductions between their trusted physician and the sultan himself.

> Hāshim acquired such high prestige among the women that they preferred him even to Saʿīd, for he prepared medicines which had a beneficial effect on them as regards fatness, pregnancy, the complexion and the growth of hair. When Aḥmad ibn Ṭūlūn's ailment became very severe and the physicians assembled in his presence every morning, Mi'at Alī, the mother of Abū'l-Ashā'ir, said: "A large crowd of physicians has assembled, but Hāshim is not among them. By Allāh, O my Lord, none of them is his equal." Aḥmad said to her: "Have him come to me secretly, so that I may talk to him." She secretly brought him to Ahmad after encouraging him to speak.[505]

As the narrator tells it, the women in this case are happy to draw on the expertise of the male physician, even when it comes to feminine matters such as fertility.

There are many such accounts in Ibn Abī Uṣaybīʿa's work, including mentions of private meetings between physician and female patient.[506] Rarely are modesty measures mentioned in these circumstances. An interesting exception to this rule can be seen in Ibn Abī Uṣaybīʿa's anecdote about the 7th/13th-century court physician in Cairo, Rashīd al-Dīn Abū Ḥulayqa. Ibn Abī Uṣaybīʿa recounts a story about Rashīd al-Dīn's skill. In the story, the physician engages in taking the pulses of all the sick women in the sultan's household, whom he cannot see because they are hidden behind a screen. The sultan himself decides to hide behind the screen together with the women and extends his own arm out in turn. The physician recognizes, by the precise measure of the pulse, that it is in fact that of the ruler, and not of anyone else.[507] The story is interesting because, in mentioning the screen, it suggests that a physician might interact with and even touch a patient without being able to physically see her. However, such measures are not mentioned anywhere else in the biographical dictionary, despite many stories of interactions with female patients. It could well be that the screen is a mere literary device, meant to show off (as it clearly does) the physician's prowess, or else it represents a particular stringency unique to the female members of the royal household in that particular era.[508]

Other genres of literature, less focused on enhancing the reputations of individual physicians, also mention male physicians treating female patients and otherwise interacting with women of the household. A fascinating, if problemat-

---

505 Translation from Kopf, *Lives of the Physicians*, 688. Ibn Abī Uṣaybiʿa, *ʿUyūn al-anbāʾ fī ṭabaqāt al-aṭibbāʾ*, 543.

506 Ibn Abī Uṣaybiʿa, *ʿUyūn al-anbāʾ fī ṭabaqāt al-aṭibbāʾ*, 637.

507 Ibn Abī Uṣaybiʿa, *ʿUyūn al-anbāʾ fī ṭabaqāt al-aṭibbāʾ*, 592.

508 In her discussion of Ottoman medicine, Miri Shefer-Mossensohn explores how women of the highest rank had more limited access to medical care than those of less exalted social position, as a result of the demands of modesty. M. Shefer-Mossensohn, *Ottoman Medicine: Healing and Medical Institutions, 1500–1700* (Albany: SUNY Press, 2009), 130–1.

ic, source of medical practice is a treatise written by the Cairene jurist Ibn al-Ḥājj al-ʿAbdarī (d. 737/1336), in which he castigates his own community for what he believes are the many moral degradations of his age. (This treatise will be examined in more detail in the subsequent chapters.) Among the many reprehensible behaviors he condemns is his fellow Egyptian Muslims' choices when seeking medical care. He is particularly upset with Muslims who summon non-Muslim physicians instead of Muslim ones to tend to members of their household. In his treatise, he lays out many reasons why such conduct is unseemly, one of which focuses on women:

> Even if nothing happens except that the infidel describes a Muslim's wife or daughter to someone else . . . it would be too much for Islamic protective jealousy (*al-ghayra al-islāmiyya*), even if it were not forbidden in the noble Law,[509] God forbid. If someone were to say: 'But the jurists have permitted uncovering nakedness before a physician whether the patient is a man or a woman!' the response is that this is the case only when there is a necessity, and there is no necessity that calls for inviting an infidel when there exists a Muslim physician.[510]

The central argument in this passage is an attack on medical interactions that cross the religious divide, not ones that cross the gender divide. However, the argument implies that both Ibn al-Ḥājj and his hypothetical interlocutor assume that a male physician is expected to see female patients. Moreover, from the interlocutor's statement "but the jurists have permitted uncovering nakedness before a physician whether the patient is a man or a woman," we can infer that this environment is one in which a significant portion of the population assumes that, in a medical context, female nudity is unproblematic. Indeed, the religiously zealous Ibn al-Ḥājj does not dispute this point, rather he argues that such mixed-gender interactions are only permitted if it is a matter of necessity, and there are no medical occasions which require an interaction that crosses the boundaries of both gender and faith.[511] The former is admittedly necessary and acceptable; the latter, he argues, should not be.

---

509 I.e. Even if the reader were to deny his previous stated arguments showing that choosing non-Muslim physicians contravenes the *sharia*, a Muslim man should still disdain such behavior on the grounds of *ghayra*, appropriate sexual possessiveness.
510 Ibn al-Ḥājj, *al-Madkhal*. 3/4:318.
511 There is a great deal of both primary sources and scholarly literature about interreligious medical mixing in the Mediterranean, from the late antique era through the end of the middle ages and beyond. It is not uncommon to find Jewish, Christian, and Islamic texts that condemn such mixing while at the same time confirming its prevalence. See chapter 6.

Evidence of the communication of medical knowledge across the gender divide can be found in a variety of texts that express concern that physicians or pharmacists (both are mentioned) may teach women which drugs are abortifacients, or may furnish women with the drugs. The concern is either that women may in turn use them on themselves or surreptitiously poison another woman out of spite. Some books, including *ḥisba* manuals, specifically tie this concern to the need to uphold the Hippocratic Oath.[512] A detailed warning about such communications can be found in a medical ethics treatise by the 3rd/9th-century Baghdadi Christian physician Isḥāq b. ʿAlī al-Ruhāwī:

> If you are understanding, O friend, you have the advice of the great Hippocrates. He said that you must not mind the impatience of a woman whom you see distressed and afflicted due to her gestation, and not pity her or give her a remedy to make her fetus fall. Whoever does so has no fear of God. There is no reason to kill the fetus. On the contrary, it is necessary to raise it for this brings with it a worthy remuneration.
>
> As to a bad mother, do not show any compassion for her, so that her shame will cause the improvement of many other women. Beware of giving things [i.e. abortifacients] like these; they are prescribed only if you fear the death of the pregnant woman or the fetus. There is no difference whether you administer the drug or you sell it. Before deciding on the drug treatment, it is essential that you read the book of Hippocrates in regard to his oaths to carry out his word. You must adhere to his oaths and go along with his beliefs from which the oaths are derived since these belong to the art of medicine. These must be observed under all conditions.[513]
>
> . . . Together with being concerned about the sellers and storekeepers of the remedies which we have presented, the physician must warn the drug merchant not to give women drugs which make the fetus fall and menstruation flow without his permission.[514]

These exhortations against providing abortifacients indicate that physicians communicated directly with women about matters related to pregnancy. One could possibly read these texts about avoiding abortifacients as simply repeating traditional wisdom, rather than reflecting actual medical practice but, at least in al-Ruhāwī's case, the details suggest a substantial degree of immediacy. He cautions the physician that his "pity" and "compassion" when he sees a "distressed," "afflicted," and "shamed" pregnant woman should not move him to help her procure an abortion. This, in my view, suggests that al-Ruhāwī is speaking from experience, either his own or that of his fellow physicians.

---

512 Al-Shayzarī, 98. *The Maʿālim al-qurba fī aḥkām al-ḥisba*, 167 in Arabic text. Also in Ibn Bassām, *Nihāya al-rutba fī ṭalab al-ḥisba* (Beirut: Dār al-Kutub al-ʿIlmiyya, 2003), 340.
513 Translation in Martin Levey, "Medical Ethics," 56.
514 Ibid., 62. Levey's translation with some significant emendation.

To be sure, depictions of charlatans, mountebanks, and disreputable physicians describe them as being on even more familiar terms with women than is proper. Thus Saladin's physician Ibn Jumay‘ complains that deceptive physicians reach clientele by "gaining the favor of their wives through suitable and alluring drugs, like aphrodisiacs, medicaments for conceiving, fattening and hair-growing by making common cause with the female bath-attendants, hairdressers and midwives, in order that they should talk about them and praise their wonderful medical skill."[515] Here the charge against charlatans is not so much immodesty as playing to the female crowd and consummate networking by means of cultivating relationships with women who are in para-medical professions. This brings us to the question: what sort of relationship did male physicians have with midwives, and did men play a gynecological role with or without midwives as intermediaries?

Gynecological care and interactions between male physicians, female patients, and female intermediaries

In spite of the above-mentioned references to interactions between male physicians and female patients, there is much evidence to suggest that, in the societies from which our texts derive, it was taboo for male physicians to view or touch women's genitals, or at least some women considered the matter in that light. We see this primarily in literary anecdotes. In Ibn Abī Uṣaybī‘a's biographical dictionary, the story is told of Jibrā'īl ibn Bukhtīshū' ibn Jūrjīs, who cures a woman of paralysis during an examination simply by bending his head down and extending his hand toward her skirt as though he intended to lift it, thereby awakening the woman's self-protective instincts.[516] In *al-Faraj ba‘d al-shidda*, al-Tanūkhī tells the story of a wealthy young woman in the countryside who attempts to conceal a terrible pain and discharge in her vagina. Her father, upon finally discovering that she is sick and on death's door, sends for medical care.

> I sent for Yazīd the Urinanalyst and consulted him.
>
> "Would you forgive me," Yazīd asked, "if I make a suggestion? I can issue no prescription unless I am allowed to see the site of the complaint and palpate it with my own hands, and ask the woman questions as to how the disorder may have arisen." Her condition was

---

515 Ibn Jumay‘, *al-Maqāla as-Ṣalāḥiya = Treatise to Ṣalāḥ ad-Dīn on the revival of the art of medicine by Ibn Jumay‘: edited and translated by Hartmut Fähndrich* (Marburg: Kommissionsverlag F. Steiner, 1983).

516 Ibn Abī Uṣaybi‘a, *‘Uyūn al-anbā’ fī ṭabaqāt al-aṭibbā’*, 188.

> now so serious, indeed desperate, that I consented; but after he had examined her externally and found the site of the pain, his questions went on for so long and had so little to do with her illness that I felt tempted to lay violent hands on him. However, I reminded myself of the good character that he bore, and contained myself with difficulty.

The father's impatience with Yazīd, and his need to calm himself by reminding himself of Yazīd's good character, does not appear to stem from his concern that the man is touching his daughter, but rather that the man is asking her seemingly pointless questions instead of helping her.

> At last he said:
> 'Have someone hold the girl down.'
> I gave the order; he thrust his hand into her vagina; she screamed, then fainted; blood spurted out, and he withdrew his hand, displaying a creature smaller than a dung-beetle, which he tossed aside. The girl immediately sat up, crying: 'Papa! You must send this man out of my room, for I am well again.'[517]

The story goes on to explain that the source of the trouble was a tick, contracted while tending cattle. Both stories, about the paralysis and the tick, suggest that modest female patients might be reluctant to have male physicians see or touch their genitals, but that doctors themselves do not have compunctions in this regard. Illness, where it is present, suspends the dictates of modesty. The restoration of such dictates, and deference to women's preferences, is the marker that the medical emergency is over, having been resolved through the cleverness of the physician.

A less celebratory and more mundane expression of women refusing to seek out treatment offered by male physicians can be seen in the famous Sevillian physician Ibn Zuhr's account of having in his youth once come across a woman with a prolapsed uterus, who had not sought male medical care for it. He laments:

> Know that when I was a youth I saw a woman to whom this had happened, and her uterus was like a bracelet which was showing through her vagina. It had been that way for a long time. I do not know what happened to her. Had this been recent, the physician would have been able to undo the injury, God permitting."[518]

517 al-Tanūkhī, *Faraj ba'd al-shidda* (Beirut: Dār Sādir, 1978), 4:215. Translation in Julia Bray, *Writing and Representation in Medieval Islam* (London: Routledge, 2006), 225.
518 Abū Marwān 'Abd al-Malik ibn Zuhr, *Kitāb al-taysīr fī al-mudāwāh wa'l-tadbīr* (Damascus: Dār al-Fikr, 1983), 308–309.

The most explicit description of how sexual propriety factors into medical care appears at the beginning of a chapter in the *Surgery* of al-Zahrāwī, who practiced in Cordoba in the 4th/10th-century. The chapter describes an operation to remove bladder stones. The operation required a medical practitioner to insert his finger either into the anus (if the patient was a male or a virgin female), or into the vagina, to feel for the stone and, using both the inserted finger and an external hand to press down on the bladder, to manipulate the stone to a location near the groin. The practitioner would then make an incision to surgically cut the stone out. He writes:

> It is uncommon for a woman to have a stone. But if it should happen to a woman the treatment is indeed difficult and hindered by a number of things. One is that the woman may be a virgin. Another is that you will not find a woman who will expose herself to a (male) doctor if she is chaste or has close male relatives (*lā tujid imra'a tubīḥ nafsahā lil-ṭabīb idhā kānat 'afīfa aw dhawāt al-maḥārim*).[519] A third is that you will not find a woman competent in this art, particularly not in surgery. Then a fourth is that the place for cutting upon the stone in a woman is a long way from where the stone lies, so the incision has to be deep, which is dangerous. If necessity compels you to this kind of case, you should take with you a competent woman doctor (*imra'a ṭabība muḥsina*). As these are very uncommon, if you are without one then seek chaste/eunuch doctor as a colleague (*fa-uṭlub ṭabīban 'afīfan rafīqan*),[520] or bring a midwife experienced in women's ailments or a woman to whom you may give some instruction in this art (*imra'a tushīr fī hādhihi al-ṣinā'a ba'ḍ al-ishāra*). Have her with you and bid her do all that you enjoin; first of all, in searching for the stone. If she perceives that the woman is a virgin she should pass her finger into the anus and palpate for the stone. If she finds it and keeps her finger on it, then bid her cut down upon it. But if the patient be not a virgin bid the midwife pass her finger into the vulva and palpate for the stone, after she has placed her left hand upon the bladder and applied a good pressure. If she finds the stone she should gradually push it down from the outlet of the bladder as far as she can until it reaches the bottom of the pelvis. Then she should cut down upon it from about the middle of the pudenda near the root of the hip on whichever side she can conveniently feel it; she must keep her finger on the stone, pressing from below. The incision should start by being small; then let her introduce a sound into the small incision, and when she finds the stone then she will enlarge the incision until she knows that it is big enough for the exit of the stone.

519 Spink and Lewis translate "*dhawāt al-maḥārim*" as "married" rather than "having close male relatives."

520 The Arabic word describing this doctor is "*'afīf*" i.e. "chaste," which is not the usual term for a eunuch, though 'Afīf seems to have been commonly used as a personal name given to eunuchs. However, given the context, I think Lewis and Spink's interpretation of *'afīf* as eunuch is plausible.

> . . . If you are hindered by a hemorrhage . . . after some days, when the acute hemorrhage has subsided and suppuration has set in, return to your operating until you get the stone out.[521]

From this description, which is the clearest one we have, it seems that al-Zahrāwī would ideally team up with specially trained eunuchs and women and direct them as they performed examinations and surgeries on women. It should be noted here that while most of the content of this chapter is taken verbatim from the Byzantine physician Aetius of Amida's encyclopedia,[522] all of the passages about midwives, eunuchs, assistants, virgins and chastity seem to be original to al-Zahrāwī.[523] This suggests that these original additions reflect al-Zahrāwī's own place and time. (I have been unable to find any other mention of eunuch physicians in medieval Arabic literary or documentary sources, however they are known to have attended nuns in Byzantium.[524]) Interestingly, he admits that there are few opportunities for a physician to practice this particular surgery. Such admissions are not present in most of his other descriptions of performing operations on women, which would imply that he views those other operations as practical, rather than rare-to-the-point-of-being-theoretical. He connects the rarity of bladder-stone removal surgery specifically to the sensibilities of respectable women, rather than to any reluctance on the part of the physician, or to external policing. Furthermore, his mention of the possibility of teaming up with women doctors as well as midwives and the physician's own female trainees, suggests that he views it as not impossible for a woman to receive some degree of instruction, such that she is conversant with the medical worldview of male practitioners of Arabo-Galenic medicine, even if such a woman is a rarity. By comparison, writing in the same century but on the other side of the Muslim world, Ibn Sīnā discusses the same operation, but makes no mention of a female practitioner or of particular modesty concerns, de-

---

521 al-Zahrāwī, *Albucasis on Surgery and Instruments*, M. S. Spink and G. L. Lewis (Berkeley: University of California Press, 1973), Book 30, Chapter 61, 420 – 423. The translation is a modified version of Spink and Lewis's.

522 Spink and Lewis note the correspondence between the two works, but not the discrepancies. Otherwise, they uncharacteristically choose to not comment on the chapter at all, on the grounds that it "needs no note." Ibid., 420.

523 Cf. Aetius of Amida, *The Gynaecology and Obstetrics of the VI Century*, chapter XCIX, 105.

524 Kathryn M. Ringrose, *The Perfect Servant: Eunuchs and the Social Construction of Gender in Byzantium* (Chicago: University of Chicago Press, 2003), 83.

spite his detailed explanations and warnings about the operation and its permutations.[525]

Another description of the same procedure, from $7^{th}/13^{th}$-century Syria, provides us with a similar account of women's reluctance to undergo bladder-stone removal surgery but seems to take it as a given that the surgery would have to be performed by a woman. The physician Ibn al-Quff writes:

> When stones occur in the bladder of women, their treatment is complicated by five factors: one of them is that the woman might be a virgin, and so there is no path for inserting the finger in the vagina so as to find the stone. Second: few women come forward to undergo said treatment, due to the pain of the incision. Third, we do not find a woman who will permit herself such surgical treatment because they are overcome by bashfulness. Fourth: because the location of the stone is further in them and requires a deeper incision, and that is dangerous. Fifth, she may be pregnant there is a concern that the incision will injure the fetus . . . But, if you want [or: she wants[526]] to attempt to remove it, then seek an expert, intelligent midwife, and order her to do everything that you say . . .[527]

He does not imply that such "expert, intelligent" midwives are rare, as al-Zahrāwī does, nor that it is acceptable for a man to engage in the surgery, as Ibn Sīnā does. We thus see a diversity of attitudes toward the proper division of labor between male and female practitioners with respect to this procedure. It is not clear why this procedure in particular should serve as the context for Ibn al-Quff's elaborations on women's "bashfulness" and al-Zahrāwī's elaborations on allaying modesty concerns. The most likely explanation seems to be that – since there was a long history of offering different methods for removing stones based upon whether the patient was a man, virgin woman, or non-virgin woman – it may have seemed particularly appropriate to build off of that discussion to tangentially address how patients' social identities affect their medical care.

We have remarkably few references to either the existence of or the training of the "competent woman doctor" whom al-Zahrāwī mentions as being so rare. Certainly, the feminine noun "*ṭabība*" i.e. "doctoress" exists, but in the pre-Ottoman period it does not seem to refer to a woman trained in Arabo-Galenic med-

---

525 Ibn Sīnā, *Qānūn fī al-ṭibb*, 2:510 = *kitāb* III: *fann* 19: *maqāla* 1: *faṣl fī al-tadbīr* [re: *ḥiṣāt al-muthāna*].

526 The verb used here is ambiguous and can be read as a second-person masculine or third-person feminine form.

527 Abū al-Faraj ibn Yaʿqūb Ibn al-Quff, *Kitāb al-ʿUmda fī al-jirāḥa* (Hyderabad: Majlis Dā'irat al-Maʿārif al-ʿUthmāniyya, 1937) 2:210 – 11.

icine.[528] More common are references to women ophthalmologists. The most expansive account of women receiving training from a physician in the Arabo-Galenic tradition can be found in Ibn Abī Uṣaybiʿa's description of the multiple generations of the Ibn Zuhr physician-dynasty that flourished in Spain. He writes that the sister and niece of al-Ḥafīd Abū Bakr ibn Zuhr (d. 596/1199) "were knowledgeable in the art of medicine and treatment, and they had much experience in matters pertaining to the treatment of women. And the two of them would attend the women of al-Manṣūr and no one would deliver the children of al-Manṣūr and his household except for al-Ḥafīd's sister Rufayda, or her daughter when her mother died."[529] Ibn Abī Uṣaybiʿa also claims that the caliph's vizier had both Ibn Zuhr and his niece assassinated, an indication that both occupied positions of power. We know little else about these female physicians, not even the name of the assassinated woman. It is reasonable to surmise that the phenomenon of female relatives of physicians practicing gynecological and obstetrical medicine themselves occurred with some frequency, but there are few extant references to such individuals.[530] This is not to suggest that women who provided care were a rarity. There is little reason to doubt that women in general, as part of their role as mothers, wives, sisters, daughters, cooks, and producers and consumers of local knowledge of plants, stones, and magic provided much of the day-to-day care for sick people in both the Middle East and in Europe up until the modern period.[531] However, there is no extant record of female medical providers studying medical books or being trained in the Arabo-Galenic medical tradition.[532]

528 S. D. Goitein writes that the word *ṭabība* occurs several times in the documents of the Cairo Geniza, but he believes these refer to women from lower strata of society, not classically trained physicians. See Goitein, *Mediterranean Society,* I:127–8.

529 Translation from Kopf, *Lives of the Physicians*, 664. Ibn Abī Uṣaybiʿa, *ʿUyūn al-anbāʾ fī ṭabaqāt al-aṭibbāʾ*, 524.

530 These few are identified in Giladi, *Muslim Midwives*, 70–71. The biographical details are quite scant. In the Ottoman period we hear of an unnamed daughter of the chief physician of the Manṣūrī hospital in Cairo, who herself inherited his position after his death in 1036/1626.

531 Savage-Smith and Pormann, *Medieval Islamic Medicine*, 103.

532 Muḥammad b. Ibrāhīm al-Jazarī's (d. 738/1338) biographical dictionary includes a reference to a Cairene woman named Umm Khayr Khadīja bint al-imām Fakhr al-Dīn al-Nawzari (d. 733/1333) who both knew how to write and, in her old age, served as a midwife to the sultan's wife. However, her writing seems to be connected to her religious scholarship, not to any medical knowledge she might have. Apart from her serving as a midwife, there is no indication that she has access to any sort of medical scholarship. Al-Jazarī, *Ta'rīkh ḥawādith al-zamān wa-anbā'ihi wa-wafayaāt al-akābir wa'l-a'yān min abnā'ihi* (Beirut: al-Maktaba al-ʿAṣriyya, 1998) 3:701.

Although the "competent woman doctor" is so rarely mentioned in medical literature, the figure of the midwife appears much more frequently, sometimes as a subordinate and informant, and sometimes more as a colleague. Descriptions of the extent of physicians' dependency upon midwives vary considerably in the medical literature. While there are many references to cooperation between midwives and physicians in the medical compendia, it is just as common for texts not to indicate the presence of an intermediary at all, even in gynecological situations. It should be noted here that it is often difficult to discern which tasks are performed by the male physician, which by female attendant(s) or midwives, and which by the patient herself. In part this is due to the frequent use of passive verb forms in these texts. The matter is further complicated by the fact that it is often grammatically unclear whether the active indicative verbs in Arabic medical manuals are intended to be read as second-person masculine forms or third-person feminine forms.[533] Imperative verb forms, however, make the gender of the practitioner somewhat clearer.

Unsurprisingly, interactions between midwives and physicians frequently appear in discussions of childbirth complications. Once again, the most detailed description of such cooperation is found in al-Zahrāwī's text, in his chapter on handling difficult childbirth. The chapter seems to indicate that the male physician has visual access to the laboring woman. However, the physical interventions in the delivery are conducted by the midwife.

> The midwife must have wisdom and dexterity and be skilled in all these cases and beware of failures and mistakes. I shall explain the technique in these modes of delivery so that she [*or:* you masculine] may be instructed and may be acquainted with them all.
>
> When the fetus comes out by the vertex in the normal manner and yet the delivery is with great difficulty for the woman and you see that her strength is exhausted, then make her sit on a seat and order the women to take hold of her and foment her womb in a decoction of fenugreek in bland oils. Then the midwife should take between two fingers a little scalpel and make an incision in the fetal membrane or open it with the finger nail, to allow the contained waters to flow out; and put pressure upon the woman's abdomen until the fetus comes down . . .[534]

As the chapter continues, however, in addition to using gender-ambiguous verbs al-Zahrāwī also begins using masculine imperatives for actions that require intimate contact with the woman in labor, such as "place [*ḍaʿ* = masculine imper-

533 Weisser makes this same point, see *Zeugung, Vererbung, und pränatale Entwicklung*, 56 – 59.
534 al-Zahrāwī, *Albucasis on Surgery and Instruments*, 468 – 471. The translation is that of Spink with some additions to show grammar. More substantial emendation occurs in the second paragraph.

ative] the woman upon a platform . . . and shake [masculine imperative] the platform." If the baby emerges feet first, he writes "return [masculine imperative] the fetus bit by bit [into the uterus] until you have placed it in a natural position." He suggests that, if all else fails, the physician should make a compound and "anoint [masculine imperative] with it the vagina of the woman and her lower abdomen" and later "press [masculine imperative] gently upon her abdomen."[535] The chapter thus leaves the reader with an image of both male and female practitioners engaged in gynecological practice, at least during medical emergencies.[536]

In another, remarkable depiction of cooperation during an emergency obstetrical operation, al-Zahrāwī explains how to make and use a speculum for opening the womb to extract a stillborn fetus.[537] He then writes:

> When you wish to open the womb with this [speculum], make the woman sit on a couch with her legs hanging down, parted; then introduce the two projections [of the speculum] into the orifice of the womb while you hold [masculine] the end of the instrument lower down between her thighs; then open your hand in the same way as you would with forceps, to the extent to which you wish to open the womb, so as to allow the midwife to see what she desires.[538]

Interestingly, this depiction of the interaction between the physician and midwife does not make clear the hierarchy of roles. One could well read this as the male medical practitioner supporting the more expert midwife.

The division of labor and extent of cooperation between midwives and male physicians is more ambiguous in Ibn Sīnā's *Qānūn*. Ibn Sīnā mentions the role of midwives as informants quite often, both in emergency and in non-emergency situations. For example, he mentions soliciting information from a midwife in the case of an abnormally positioned uterus.

---

535 Ibid., 471.

536 This can also be seen in Hippocratic and other Greek texts. As Leslie Dean-Jones notes, "there is a division of labor within a single case." Dean-Jones, "Autopsia, Historia, and What Women Know: The Authority of Women in Hippocratic Gynecology," in *Knowledge and the Scholarly Medical Traditions*, ed. Donald George Bates (Cambridge: Cambridge University Press, 1995), 55.

537 For a fascinating discussion of how fetal-extraction procedures in medieval Arabic texts were understood and reinterpreted by early-modern European physicians in light of their own innovations in forceps-assisted delivery see H. King, *Midwifery, Obstetrics and the Rise of Gynaecology: The Uses of a Sixteenth-Century Compendium* (London: Routledge, 2017), 142.

538 al-Zahrāwī, *Albucasis on Surgery and Instruments*, 486–9. Spink's translation with my clarifications in brackets.

> Chapter on the declination and distortion of the womb: it is possible for the uterus to incline towards one of the woman's sides, such that the mouth of the uterus is no longer aligned with the path through which the semen flows to it . . . The midwives know the direction of the inclination by feeling with their fingers, and they will know whether it is due to rigidity or laxness . . .[539]

Even as he describes midwives taking the role of genital touching, Ibn Sīnā claims that he is directly involved in patient care, and that he is giving instructions to the midwife and patient.

In other places, Ibn Sīnā gives the impression that the male physician personally oversees and administers gynecological treatment without the mediation of another woman. For example, as part of his description of a method for extracting the placenta after birth, when it has not already emerged, he instructs the physician: "Use substances to induce sneezing . . . once the mouth of the womb dilates, then you insert your hand and extract" the placenta.[540] The instructions in this sentence are grammatically unambiguous, addressing a male in the second person, and directing him to introduce his hand into the birthing woman's uterus.

Ibn Sīnā similarly depicts the male physician as directly involved in the delivery process in his description of abortion procedures and the extraction of a stillborn baby after an arduous labor.

> The management of miscarriage and expelling the dead fetus: At certain times, abortion may be necessary, among them: when the pregnant woman is a small girl whom one fears will die from childbirth. Also when there is a lesion within the womb and extra flesh which makes the exit too small for the baby and it is killed. Also when the fetus has died within the womb of the pregnant woman. Know that if the woman has experienced four days of difficult labor, then the fetus is already dead, so busy yourself [masculine] with the life the mother, and do not busy yourself with the life of the fetus, rather strive [masculine] to expel it. [This] abortion is brought about by means of movements or by means of drugs. The drugs can do so either by killing the fetus, or by forcefully bringing down menstruation . . .[541]

From this description, it seems as though Ibn Sīnā expects the physician to be personally ministering to the laboring woman and extracting the deceased baby himself. There is no mention of a midwife throughout this passage.

---

539 See Ibn Sīnā, *Qānūn fī al-ṭibb*, 2:596= *kitāb* III: *fann* 21: *maqāla* 4: *faṣl fī mīlān al-rahīm.*
540 Ibn Sīnā, *Qānūn fī al-ṭibb*, 2:580 = *kitāb* III: *fann* 21: *maqāla* 2: *fī ikhrāj al-mashīma*
541 Ibn Sīnā, *Qānūn fī al-ṭibb*, 2:578 = *kitāb* III: *fann* 21: *maqāla* 2: *tadbīr al-isqāṭ wa-ikhrāj al-janīn al-mayit.*

Compare Ibn Sīnā's discussion of a difficult labor above with another surgical passage about expelling a dead fetus, for which he assigns a much larger role to intermediaries. He describes the midwife as engaged in the grizzly business of drawing out the fetus by means of hooks poked into its body. He attributes this technique to "the ancients," thereby implying that such a procedure was in his own time a theoretical one, rather than one commonly practiced.

> The [pregnant] woman must lay on the bed on her back, with her head tilted downward and her thighs raised. Then women, or a servant, grasp her on either side. If these [people] are not present, then tie [masculine] her chest to the bed with knots so that her body will not be pulled down when it is stretched. Then the midwife opens that which is covering the neck of the uterus, anoints her left hand with oil, brings her fingers together lengthwise, and inserts them into the mouth of the uterus and dilates it with them. More oil is added, and she ascertains whether it is necessary to insert hooks with which the fetus may be drawn out, and the places which are best for inserting the hooks. These places, in a fetus which is presenting head-first, are the eyes, the mouth, the nape . . .[542]

He goes on to describe the piercing process, and then how to modify that process when the fetus presents feet first, an operation which involves not one hook but two. What is odd about the descriptions of these two procedures for dealing with abortion and obstructed labor is that the first one, featuring a male physician giving his patient expulsive drugs, is quite feasible in terms of medieval medical technique, but the presence of a male medical practitioner does not conform to our expectations of medieval births. By contrast, the second procedure features a female medical practitioner practicing obstetrics, which seems more true-to-life, but it also describes a surgical technique which most likely was never implemented.[543] This discrepancy suggests that we should not view the presence of a midwife in a medical text as correlated with the sensitivity of a particular medical problem or as correlated with the feasibility of a particular form of treatment.

Midwives are also depicted as working in conjunction with male physicians in non-emergency situations which require inserting fingers into the patient's body. Ibn al-Jazzār, writing in 4th/10th-century Qayrawān, deals extensively with gynecology, explaining diagnostic measures and offering a variety of pessaries, pills, and fumigation techniques for treating women's genitals. In those chapters, he mentions the presence of a midwife only twice, once in connection with the treatment of hysterical suffocation, and the other time when discussing the diag-

542 Ibn Sīnā, *Qānūn fī al-ṭibb*, 2:576 = *kitāb* III: *fann* 21: *maqāla* 2: *faṣl fī tadbīr li-ba'ḍ al-qudamā' fī ikhrāj al-janīn al-mayit.*

543 Savage-Smith, "The Practice of Surgery in Islamic Lands," 315.

nosis of uterine tumors. In both cases he indicates that he is "instructing" the midwife.

> We should tell the midwife to rub gently the orifice of the uterus from the inside and outside with one of the oils we have mentioned.[544]

To diagnose the presence of a tumor, he writes:

> If the tumor occurs in the front part of the uterus, it is followed by a heavy pain in the vagina with retention of urine, and if it occurs in the orifice of the uterus, it is followed by pain in the navel and stomach, and if the midwife inserts her finger, she finds the orifice of the uterus closed and hard.[545]

Elsewhere in the same text, Ibn al-Jazzār describes treating a prolapsed uterus with poultices, but he does not mention a midwife. However, the verbs are ambiguous, and can be read as either referring to a male physician binding the groin in a poultice or as a poultice being bound around the site of the injury, with the gender of the practitioner unstated.[546]

In al-Majūsī's *al-Kāmil al-ṣināʿa fī al-ṭibb*, 110 chapters of which are devoted to surgery, he explicitly states that it is the midwife who performs surgeries to treat *rutqa* (the condition mentioned in the previous chapter in which the vagina is too narrow or obstructed). She is also the practitioner who excises obstructions in the uterus arising from previous ulceration.[547]

Sometimes different works by the same author offer conflicting understandings of standard practice. This can be seen in al-Rāzī's works. Some of them contain references to dependence on midwives as intermediaries, while other books covering the same material have no such references. The following gynecological passages in al-Rāzī's *Ḥāwī*, for example, imply direct contact between male physicians and female patients. The verbs directed at the physician here are all masculine singular imperatives.

> The placenta: if you want to expel the placenta, dose her with a sternutatory drug then hold [sing. masc. imperative] her nostrils and mouth, for in such a situation the belly will stretch and tighten, which facilitates the expulsion [of the placenta].[548]

---

544 Ibn al-Jazzār, *Ibn al-Jazzār on Sexual Diseases and Their Treatment*, 275.
545 Ibid., 277.
546 Ibid., 179.
547 al-Majūsī, *al-Kāmil*, 488.
548 For more on the role of sneezing in expelling the fetus see Batten, "The Arabic Commentaries On The Hippocratic Aphorisms," 140 – 178.

> On fibroids: He said: Place [masculine imperative] a mirror under the woman so that you may see the thing as it really is. If there is intense pain present, have [masculine imperative] her sit on a laxative concoction . . . [549]

> To treat *rutqa*, whether it is congenital or as a result of a healed-over wound: Open [masculine imperative] the vagina of the woman and you shall find that the opening of the vagina is covered by something resembling a muscle. This is if the flesh is in the vagina. (If it is in the cervix, then there is nothing to worry about until the girl reaches [the onset of] menstruation, but then [menstruation] might be retained and not flow, and she will as a result experience intense pain and quickly die if she is not treated; and this is because all the blood returns to her body and rots and suffocates it) . . . but this flesh, when it grows in the opening of the vagina, makes it impossible for a man to have intercourse with her, and she cannot menstruate either and she cannot conceive. If it is in the cervix then she can have intercourse but she will not conceive. It may be that this flesh entirely blocks the [entrance to womb] and it may be that there is a small opening from which menses may exit, and it may be that such a [patient] does conceive but both she and the fetus die when there is no way for it to come out.

Other passages describe the physician relaying to the midwife that he needs certain information:

> If you see retention of the menses . . . tell the midwife to touch the cervix and if it is closed without being rigid it is a sign of pregnancy.[550]
>
> The signs of pregnancy: the closing up of the mouth of the uterus. The mouth of the uterus closes when it is occupied and when there are tumors in it. The difference between them is that the tumor is accompanied by stiffness while the closing [of the uterus] due to its being occupied is not accompanied by stiffness, but rather it is in a natural state. The midwife should insert her finger to ascertain it. This is one of greatest signs from the uterus when it is shut.[551]

The *Ḥāwī* consists of a great number of quotations from other writers which have not been edited and synthesized, and so it is entirely possible that none of the above passages reflects common practice in al-Rāzī's own society.

Other works by al-Rāzī more clearly reflect a unified authorial voice, and we might turn to these to learn about the gendered division of labor in gynecological care. In al-Rāzī's *Man lā yahḍuruhu al-ṭabīb* he does not mention midwives at all. As for al-Rāzī's *Manṣūrī fī al-ṭibb*, the modern editor of the only twentieth-century printed edition writes in a footnote that he has chosen to emend the text to limit cross-gender interaction:

549 Al-Rāzī, *al-Ḥāwī*, 15.
550 Al-Rāzī, *al-Ḥāwī*, 9:49. Cf. Al-Baladī, *Tadbīr al-ḥabālā'*, 33.
551 Ibid. 51.

> [glossing the phrase "he gives to the (female) patient"] "It is so in all versions.[552] In these chapters which address women and those diseases of the menses and of the uterus which befall them, the author writes as though speaking about a male [practitioner]. Hence "he gives to the patient," "he administers," "he inserts," "he feeds," etc. We have tried to correct all of the words without pointing out every mistake in the footnotes.[553]

In other words, the modern editor chose to emend the text by changing the active masculine verbs, originally attributed to male physicians, to passive or feminine forms, some of which imply that the patient performs these actions on her own, and others implying the presence of a second woman acting as a medical intermediary. In this footnote, the editor notes that because there were so many such "problematic" references to the male practitioner, he felt it too cumbersome to draw attention to them all. The editor clearly doubts that the medical care mentioned by al-Rāzī could have been provided by a man.

The omissions of references to female intermediaries and practitioners where we might expect to find them has been catalogued by Avner Giladi, in his book, *Muslim Midwives*. He notes that "the midwife is altogether – or almost totally – ignored" in the major works by Thābit b. Qurra, al-Ṭabarī, al-Majūsī, Ibn Zuhr, and Ibn al-Nafīs.[554] In omitting them, the authors instead appear to be addressing, at least grammatically, male practitioners.

Regardless of whether authors of medicals works include references to midwives or not, they all depict a landscape in which male physicians interact with female patients, including those with gynecological problems. They expect male physicians to be in a position to communicate with their female patients about drugs and sell them directly to them. They indicate that male physicians are present in the same room as their female patients and clients, able to speak to them, to look at and touch their patients' bodies to the extent that they could feel the pulse, assess the visual appearance of the patient, hold the patient's nose and mouth, and set up fumigations.

The respectability of genital touching is less clear. There are several references to the notion that women were reluctant to have male physicians see or touch their genitals. However, all of the references to this reluctance suggest that it stems from patient preference rather than medical ethics. Al-Zahrāwī and Ibn Sīnā refer to male involvement during emergency obstetric situations, involvement which appears to include manipulating the emerging baby, while other passages from the same works assign those tasks to the midwife.

552 I.e. All manuscripts use a masculine verb.

553 al-Rāzī, *al-Manṣūrī fī al-ṭibb*, 448..

554 Giladi, *Muslim Midwives*, 73–4.

Both theoretical medical compendia and *ḥisba* manuals corroborate one another in providing the impression that male medical professionals sometimes provide clitorectomies, and male phlebotomists bleed women, and yet we do not see a code of professional ethics attached to those practices. These texts provide no guidance about how to touch patients while avoiding accusations of impropriety. One could well take this data point to mean that such touching rarely happened in actual daily experience. (It could, perhaps, be argued that such tasks are considered menial ones in some societies, and so are unlikely to be performed by men with extensive medical educations and less likely to receive the attention of ethicists.) If we were to argue, however, that these services were rarely offered by men of any class, and that in reality these services were segregated by gender, then we would be forced to argue against the extant textual record. In other words, while we do not have *all* the textual evidence we would expect from a society in which male practitioners frequently treat female patients in ways that involve touching, nonetheless we have too much evidence to be ignored that such interactions were common, and we have very little evidence to the contrary.

As for the extent to which midwives served as intermediaries, multiple sources depict physicians in non-emergency situations asking midwives to conduct examinations and relay information to them about how the cervix feels. The implication is that midwives are working in the capacity of assistants and informants to the physician. Whether it was standard procedure in any particular community for male physicians to have formal professional relationships with midwives is difficult to say. *Ḥisba* manuals and medical ethics treatises do not mention them. However, the reference to charlatans cultivating relationships with midwives suggests that perhaps midwives referred their patients to physicians or otherwise engaged male physicians as consultants. Moreover, one could argue that, just as midwives were known to serve as medical informants for the court system, they could have just as easily served as informants for physicians. From this evidence, it appears that at least some male physicians were working in close enough proximity with midwives and female patients to be able to share medical knowledge.

Theory, practice, and women's access to Arabo-Galenic medical knowledge

The portions of Arabo-Galenic texts pertaining to the treatment of women frequently provide detailed instructions to male physicians and are written as though such men are directly and physically involved in gynecological and obstetrical care. Does this mean that many medieval women likely were taught the Arabo-Galenic system for understanding infertility and participated in that understanding, or was their intellectual experience likely uninformed by such theories? There are three possible interpretations of the practical significance of Arabo-Galenic gynecological writings. (1) The purpose of the texts is to pass along entirely theoretical medical knowledge to physicians. The authors are not concerned about the practice and implementation of these instructions, rather this information exists only because of the medieval propensity toward theoretical thoroughness in encyclopedias. (2) These texts' instructions were intended to have practical value and to be implemented by female medical practitioners. The authors believed their instructions would be read by or otherwise orally conveyed to women who would implement them in gender-segregated settings. Where masculine language is used to describe practitioners, it is merely a grammatical or literary convention and is irrelevant to the meaning of the text. Or (3) the texts' instructions have practical value and were intended to be implemented by male physicians with the help of female assistants or informants. Each of these explanations is plausible but problematic.[555]

One could indeed make the argument that the instructions in these texts were never intended to be applied to the care of patients, and so Arabo-Galenic medical writings can tell us nothing about the kind of medical advice and treatment infertile women received. If so, this would not be unique to infertile women; much of medieval medical writing is thought to bear little relation to the practice of medicine. This seems to be particularly true of surgical medicine.[556] Cesarean sections (including post-mortem ones) are the classic example of a procedure which is repeatedly discussed in medieval Arabic literature but which is not believed to have actually been attempted. The descriptions are too inaccurate and vague and the illustrations reflect hagiographic literary topoi – they are not medical diagrams. Emilie Savage-Smith quotes the 8th/14th-century Egyptian oculist al-Shādhilī in support of this argument.

> We possess written accounts of various procedures which cannot be performed nowadays because there is no one who has actually seen them performed; an example is the instrument designed to cut up a dead fetus in the womb in order to save the mother's life. There are many such procedures: they are described in books, but in our own time [i.e. the four-

555 For an exploration of these issues in the medieval European context see, M. Green, *Making Women's Medicine Masculine: the Rise of Male Authority in Pre-Modern Gynaecology* (Oxford: Oxford University Press, 2008).
556 Savage-Smith, "The Practice of Surgery in Islamic Lands," 307–321.

> teenth century] we have never seen anyone perform them because the practical knowledge has been lost, and nothing remains but the written accounts.[557]

Al-Shādhilī appears to be referring to the procedures Ibn Sīnā mentioned, which called for physician-midwife cooperation.

Other surgical and cauterization procedures for removing bladder stones and tumors and treating hemorrhoids were indeed implemented, according to Savage-Smith. This conclusion is based on the fact that the instruments and instructions provided in the medieval literature were both technically possible to implement and were likely effective. Both medical texts and *ḥisba* manuals suggest that, at least in some places and periods, such surgeries were performed on women as well as men. This is not to say that no women would have compunctions about undergoing such procedures, but rather that such a degree of interaction between the genders was not unthinkable.

Descriptions of medieval Arabic non-surgical treatments of gynecological problems, and particularly of infertility due to amenorrhea, are dynamic, extensive, and detailed. There are literally dozens of recipes for oral pills, pessaries, and incense intended to draw down the menses and restart the reproductive cycle. This is also true of treatments intended to restore humoral balance to the uterus. Occasionally, the author will conclude a recipe with the claim that he has tested it and can confirm its effectiveness. Some of these recipes which appear in medical compendia also appear in pharmacy books such as the *Minhāj al-dukkān*. Taken together, such evidence indicates that authors did not view this part of their texts as unrelated to the practice of medicine.

A few trace references within these recipes indicate that the author thinks women might have access not only to male physicians, but to his text itself. These references all occur in recipes for contraceptives and abortifacients. Ibn al-Jazzār writes: "When I was reading the works of the ancient [physicians] who speak about the forces and helpful and harmful effects of the simple drugs, I found that they mention drugs which corrupt the sperm in the uterus and prevent conception, and drugs which kill the fetus and expel it from the womb. I therefore decided to mention the case of these drugs in this chapter,

---

557 Ibid., 315. Cf. Chapter 66 of al-Zahrāwī's surgery, in which he describes how to operate on "flatulent hernia," also known as pneumatocele. He writes, "I have not seen anyone pluck up enough courage to attempt the operative treatment of this kind of rupture, though the ancients said it ought to be done in the same way as hernia with varicocele, namely . . ." al-Zahrāwī, *Albucasis on Surgery and Instruments*, 447.

so that they will be known and so that women would beware of using them."[558] In his *Kāmil al-ṣināʿa al-ṭibbiyya*, al-Majūsī writes:

> As to medicines which prevent conception, although they should not be mentioned to prevent their use by women in whom there is no good, it is necessary sometimes to prescribe them to those women who have a small uterus, or those who have a disease which, in the case of pregnancy, may cause the woman death in childbirth. Except for women in such predicaments, the physicians should not prescribe [these] medicines. Also, he should not prescribe medicines which cause the menses to flow, or medicines which expel the dead fetus, except to women he can trust, because all these medicines kill the fetus and expel it.[559]

Ibn al-Jazzār's statement implies that what he writes eventually reaches women. Al-Majūsī's statement is somewhat more ambiguous. His phrase "they should not be mentioned" could mean that although it is safe to write about abortifacients for a (male) readership, the drugs should not be spoken of lest it reach the ears of women. Nevertheless, the participation of at least some women in the authors' community of knowledge is assumed.

As to whether women shared the physicians' understanding of humoral medicine – and their beliefs about the role of heat, cold, moisture, and dryness – it seems that that was in and of itself a matter of debate, at least in some locations. Ibn Abī ʿUṣaybīʿa writes:

> I have it on the authority of the sage Rashīd al-Dīn Abū Saʿīd ibn Yaʿqūb the Christian that Abū al-Hasan Saʿīd ibn Hibat Allāh was in charge of treating the sick at the hospital. One day, when in the lunatic ward in order to inspect and treat the inmates, a woman approached him and asked his advice concerning the treatment of her son. When he replied: "You should urge him to take cooling and moistening foods," one of the inmates of the lunatic ward mocked him, saying: "You had better give that prescription to one of your pupils, who has had some experience of medicine and knows some of its rules. As to this woman, what does she know about cooling and moistening things? You should have recommended her something specific that she might readily use."[560]

This story, which is set in 5th/10th-century Baghdad, highlights the opinion that women could not participate in medical discourse in even the most basic way. Women could not even be expected to know what constitutes a "cooling" or "moistening" food. From the inmate's point of view, women might accept particular prescriptions offered by physicians, but they have no notion of how such

558 Translation from G. Bos in Ibn al-Jazzār, *Ibn al-Jazzār on Sexual Diseases*, 290.

559 Translation from B. Musallam, *Sex and Society in Islam*, 70.

560 Translation from Kopf, *Lives of the Physicians*, 480. Ibn Abī Uṣaybiʿa, *ʿUyūn al-anbāʾ fī ṭabaqāt al-aṭibbāʾ*, 342–3.

prescriptions are arrived at. Al-Ruhāwī too, writing in the previous century, claims that among the common people there is disagreement even about the axioms upon which all Galenic fertility medicine is based. He complains "There is also a widespread stupidity among the people that in certain illnesses they may be their own physicians. They believe . . . that women are hotter than men . . ."[561]

Such statements indicate that there were alternative systems available to women for understanding physiology. Indeed, there is a great deal of medical writing in which male physicians complain that they do not command the respect from patients which they deserve, that the masses are ignorant of what decent medicine looks like, and that they are taken in by pseudo-doctors who do not understand basic science. Chapter 6 will explore this topic further. However, it would be a mistake to conclude that either the gender divide or the existence of popular alternatives to the Galenic medical system precluded the gynecological portions of Arabo-Galenic texts from having an audience or an impact on women's medical care.

561 Translation in Martin Levey, "Medical Ethics," 97.

Conclusion to Part II: Medicine and Sexism

For the optimistic student of history, the study of gynecology appears to offer insights into the social construction of gender. That is to say, theories of the health and illness of women's reproductive organs often correspond to socially encouraged and discouraged behavior, as we have seen in the Hippocratic depiction of menstrual retention and the wandering womb. Physicians' descriptions of women's bodies explicitly or implicitly trace the boundaries of women's lives and buttress the confines placed on them, often justifying women's inferior and dependent social positions. Medicine is therefore a mirror for much deeper social constructs, or so a historian might hope. Unfortunately, however, medieval Arabic gynecology flies in the face of this hope and defies any such attempts to torture it into such theoretically neat paradigms.

In many ways, the Arabic side of the Greco-Arabic gynecological tradition appears to be remarkably egalitarian. The theories it articulates with regard to anatomy, sexual lust, conception theory, embryology, hysterical suffocation, and obstetrical care are no more, and often much less, socially coercive in their implications for women than are the theories articulated by its classical predecessors. We also see this in the increased attention paid to male infertility. In part, the medical tradition is egalitarian precisely because it focuses on deriving information about hidden female anatomy and physiology by extending to it conclusions extrapolated from male anatomy and physiology.

Contra Kueny's thesis, the approach to fertility and pregnancy found in medieval Arabic medical literature does not attempt to minimize women's confidence in their bodies. Rather it attempts to make their bodies comprehensible and more predictable through the use of analogies, correspondences, diagnostic rituals, and rational deductions. Extant evidence suggests that medieval women were eager for interventions to improve the likelihood of producing children, and for predictive information. We see this in the truly remarkable number of gynecological recipes available, from Hippocratic times through the middle ages; and, as mentioned in the introduction, even in modern Egypt about half of all visits by women to medical professionals are occasioned by concerns about fertility.

Obviously, from a biomedical perspective, many of the assumptions medieval physicians made about women's physiology and the causes of infertility were incorrect. It is also true that many of these assumptions could flourish due to the social fact that women's genitals were difficult to view as a result of cultural mores, religiously derived or otherwise. However, it is also the case that lack of knowledge about women's reproductive organs was due to a biological, objec-

https://doi.org/10.1515/9783110596588-011

tive fact: that women's genitals and gametes were difficult to view by virtue of being internal. While a pious medieval scholar might view this happy convergence as evidence of God's intelligent design, the modern scholar must be wary, lest it lead us into the temptation to over-interpret physicians' writings as motivated by cultural malevolence rather than by the scientific desire to supplement incomplete data with logical inferences.

Part III: **Healing and Religious Vulnerability**

Introduction to Part III

Illness and medical treatment presented patients with choices and trade-offs that had social and theological significance. A sick person could potentially interact with many varieties of practitioners and healing systems, especially if they lived in one of the urban settings from which most of our sources derive, and if theirs was a long-term condition such as infertility. They could turn to physicians whose concepts of illness and healing derived from academic medicine, or to those offering remedies based upon local knowledge, or to those offering "Prophetic medicine" based upon the medical statements contained in the *ḥadīth*. They could direct prayers for healing toward God, or they could request intervention from saints and holy people, or they could turn to practitioners offering healing through the invocation and manipulation of spirits and demonic forces. They could try all these methods in combination or serially. Alternatively, they could resign themselves to the dictates of Divine Providence and choose non-intervention. In the eyes of many religious thinkers, all of these interventions involved entrusting oneself to a practitioner. It meant sharing experiences with, and being guided by, a particular authority figure, one who thereby exercised a certain degree of influence over the patient. It also entailed some degree of intellectual submission, or leap of faith, or even an open-minded flirtation with a particular epistemological system.

There is a long history of jurists engaging in discussions about the relationship between medical teachings and revealed religion. Some jurists, particularly (but not exclusively) those operating in Mamluk-era Egypt and Syria voiced strong opinions about the religious implications of the pursuit of healing among such varied offerings. These jurists depicted medical treatment as religiously fraught because it could lead to a Muslim putting trust in an authority outside of Islamic authorities, or attributing power to forces other than God and trying to command those forces. The solution, proposed by those who saw this as problem, was to Islamicize aspects of medical knowledge and treatment as much as possible.

When the patient was not only a Muslim, but also a woman, particularly a Muslim woman with reproductive needs, the value of Islamicizing the culture surrounding medicine presented a potential conflict with the value placed on avoiding improper interactions between men and women. The conflict was multi-layered. One layer concerned the general premise found in legal handbooks that it is best to minimize medical interactions between those who are of different religions and different genders. This, of course, led to the question: is it better for a female Muslim patient to receive treatment from a male Muslim

https://doi.org/10.1515/9783110596588-012

medical practitioner or from a female non-Muslim practitioner? The former has the advantage of being Muslim, but the latter has the advantage of being of the same sex. What matters more? A second layer of concern was the potential affinity between Muslim and non-Muslim women, particularly in obstetrical settings. If a non-Muslim woman could be admitted into the presence of a Muslim woman who was not fully clothed, wouldn't that imply that the non-Muslim woman was part of her intimate circle, like a family-member or like her fellow Muslim women? And what if the non-Muslim woman conveyed information about her Muslim patient to non-Muslim men? What if the non-Muslim woman conveyed heretical ideas from the non-Islamic community to her Muslim patient? A third layer of concern had to do with the specter of groups of Muslim women transmitting amongst themselves beliefs and practices that contravened the teachings promulgated by male authoritative interpreters of Islam, i.e. the jurists. What if women – who had fewer opportunities than did men to interact with and receive guidance from male Islamic authorities – instead turned to each other for instruction and guidance when dealing with issues of birth, life, and death? What would their religious experience look like? What effect would it have on the religion of their male family members?

These concerns about the confluence of medicine, religion, and gender surface in a variety of literature produced by the *'ulamā'*, the scholars of Islamic law. In legal compendia and in *ḥadīth* and *ḥadīth* commentaries they appear in chapters devoted to theology, the practice of visiting graves, forms of medical treatment, the propriety of visiting public baths, rules of modesty, interactions with non-Muslims, the trustworthiness of witnesses, and marital rights pertaining to a wife's desire to maintain contact with her birth family and pertaining to a husband's responsibility to provide appropriate lodging and good treatment. Religio-medical concerns also appear in books of *ḥisba*, i.e. market inspectors' manuals, a genre mentioned in chapter 5. These issues are also discussed in books of religious guidance pertaining to women, which consist largely of *ḥadīths* and anecdotes about prominent figures in Islamic history, as well as statements of legal principles. Examples of this genre include Ibn Ḥabīb's (d. 238/852) *Adab al-nisā'*, the volume devoted to women and marriage in al-Ghazālī's (d. 505/1111) *Iḥyā 'ulūm al-dīn*, and books written by Ibn Ḥanbal (d. 241/855), Ibn al-Jawzī (d. 597/1201), and Ibn al-'Aṭṭār (d. 724/1324) which are all titled *Aḥkām al-nisā'*. Religious reflections on medicine also appear in books of "Prophetic medicine" i.e. medical advice treatises based primarily on *ḥadīth*s containing medicinal recommendations, such as al-Tīfāshī's (d. 561/1253), *al-Shifā fī al-ṭibb al-musnad 'an al-sayyid al-Muṣṭafā*, Ibn Qayyim al-Jawziyya's (d. 751/

1350) *al-Ṭibb al-nabawī*,[563] al-Dhahabī's (d. 748/1348) book by the same name, Shams al-Dīn ibn Ṭūlūn's (d. 953/1546) *al-Manhal al-rawī fī al-ṭibb al-nabawī*, and the extensive portion of Ibn Mufliḥ's (d. 763/1361) *al-Ādāb al-shar'iyya* that is devoted to health. Ibn Mufliḥ's book also falls into another category of juristic literature which covers medicine and women's issues extensively: anti-*bid'a* literature. This is a genre characterized by denunciations of "innovation" (*bid'a*), i.e. practices which the author believes depart from "pure Islam." Much of this literature describes, to use a modern phrase, how contemporary society is going to hell in a handbasket. Ibn al-Ḥājj al-'Abdarī's (d. 737/1336) *Madkhal* is a prime example of this sort of literature, as is Ibn Taymiyya's (d. 728/1328) *Iqtiḍā' al-ṣirāṭ al-mustaqīm.*

Although some of this literature is written in a more personal and dramatic style than is typical of *faṭwā*s or legal compendia, the legal upshot of the jurists' arguments in these texts usually does reflect the same judgments that are found in their legal schools' more authoritative and influential books. The authors encourage and discourage the same behavior which their *madhhab* encourages and discourages, and rarely do they forbid that which their *madhhab* discourages or permits (with some exceptions that will be discussed below). However, in comparison to most canonically authoritative manuals of law, some examples of this literature articulate in more detail the authors' own views of the social settings and intellectual underpinnings of the legal rulings found in the canon, i.e. their personal understanding of the motivations and anxieties that underlie common legal positions.

The jurists who advocate for the Islamicization of the medical experience indicate that they feel embattled. The tone of much of their writings is overtly preachy and exhortative in style; it is the voice of dissent rather than of coercive power. Even as anti-*bid'a* texts, treatises about women, and market-inspector manuals promulgate a rather restrictive notion of what should be considered religiously and socially acceptable, they testify to the widespread practice of the very activities which they condemn.[564]

This literature depicts the quest for healing as a form of exploration, for both men and women. When a woman explored the avenues available to help her overcome infertility, the intellectual territory she had to negotiate in the course of her exploration was contoured not only by attitudes toward sexual propriety, but also by concerns about heterodoxy. Such concerns about heterodoxy are im-

---

563 The book is an excerpt from Ibn Qayyim al-Jawziyya's *Zād al-ma'ād*.
564 H. Lutfi, "Manners and Customs of Fourteenth-Century Cairene Women: Female Anarchy versus Male Shar'i Order in Muslim Prescriptive Treatises," in *Women in Middle Eastern History*, ed. Nikki Keddie and Beth Baron (New Haven: Yale University Press, 1993), 102.

portant for understanding the jurists' attitudes not just toward women's gynecological activities, but also toward women's other gatherings connected with the life cycle. These attitudes and legal positions were not marginal even if, when it comes to women's conduct, in some places and times they might have been "more honored in the breach than in the observance." After all, calls for restrictions on women's religious excursions and public presence occasionally resulted in the enforcement of highly restrictive public policies,[565] especially during stressful periods such as times of plague.[566] Furthermore, even when dramatic "crackdowns" were not in force, theoretical articulations of religious ideals still exerted power. As Ahmed Ragab puts it:

> The degree of the commitment to the canonical text or its canonized interpretations varied greatly through history. However, the religious ideal was never seen as an unattainable model but rather a possible alternative and a desirable goal. Muslims were demanded to seek closeness to these traditions, which covered much of the daily life. They were in constant internal socio-cognitive debate between the desired and the lived or between the ideal and the daily. Although it is naive to take these views and commandments as indicators of how people lived their lives, it is equally naive to discredit them as important sources for understanding the daily life of the inhabitants of the medieval Middle East and their social and intellectual constructs.[567]

"The religious ideal" constructed in these texts potentially intersected at several different points with an infertile Muslim woman's search for healing. First, at the nexus between medical science and theology, magic, and prayer; second, where medical need conflicted with religious modesty regulations; and third, at the point where the jurists regulated (or tried to regulate) a woman's social network, the network from which she derived her worldview, including her beliefs and knowledge about the causes of her infertility and her options for reversing it.

---

565 For example, in Mamlūk Cairo, we know of at least six separate occasions when the government issued proclamations just before the 'īd holidays prohibiting women from vising holy tombs at Qarāfa and Ṣaḥrā'. Evidently whatever success the proclamations enjoyed were short-lived. See T. Ohtoshi, "The Manners, Customs, and Mentality of Pilgrims to the Egyptian City of the Dead: 1100–1500 A. D." *Orient* 29 (1993), 30.
566 Lutfi, "Manners and Customs of Fourteenth-Century Cairene Women," 101.
567 A. Ragab, "Epistemic Authority of Women in the Medieval Middle East," *HAWWA* 8 (2010), 183.

6 Religiously Classifying the Medical Marketplace of Ideas

Intellectual eclecticism and the pursuit of medical knowledge

Writing in the 8th/14th-century, the Syrian Ḥanbalī jurist Ibn Mufliḥ differentiated between the pious and impious patient as follows:

> If a person engages in medical treatment with the intention of following *sunna*-approved treatments and cares for his body which God has bestowed upon him with the best care – that constitutes faith and prosperity. But if he fears in his heart – if Satan whispers to him that if he does not receive treatment then he may perish, and Satan deludes him into believing that without him he would die, and with such a motivation he engages in medical treatment – then he is an infidel.[568]

In Ibn Mufliḥ's analysis, impiety in medicine is a manifestation of fear: fear that adhering to God's dictates will not lead to the desired outcome and that health can only be obtained by cultivating relations with an external power. That external power is characterized as Satanic. It is this reliance upon an external power that transforms treatment from an act of faith into an act of infidelity.

Juristic discussions about the status of medicine in Islam developed around a small set of *ḥadīth*s attributed to the Prophet. Among the most frequently mentioned is the Prophetic statement that "God did not send down any disease without also sending down its cure."[569] This was interpreted to mean that the *sharī'a* either permits or recommends engaging in medical intervention. Another frequently cited *ḥadīth* refers to the Prophet's treatment of his own health.

> 'Ā'isha said: "When the Prophet of God's illnesses became great, both Arab and non-Arab physicians would give him prescriptions and we would treat him."[570]

This report was cited as proof that there is nothing impious about treating illnesses. Another version of the same report has 'Ā'isha explaining that she herself acquired her knowledge of medicine from these physicians in the process of

568 Ibn Mufliḥ, *Ādāb*, 2:335.
569 Al-Bukhārī, *Ṣaḥīḥ al-Bukhārī*, 76 (*ṭibb*):1, no. 5378.
570 Aḥmad ibn Ḥanbal (d. 241/855), *Musnad Ibn Ḥanbal* (Cairo: Dār al-Ma'ārif, 1951), 6:67. Muḥammad b. Aḥmad al-Dhahabī (d. 748/1348), *al-Ṭibb al-nabawī* (Beirut: Dār Iḥyā al-'Ulūm, 1990), 224. Muḥammad ibn Mufliḥ (d. 763/1361), *al-Ādāb al-shar'iyya* (Beirut: Mu'assasat al-Risāla, 1996), 2:335. Aḥmad ibn Yūsuf al-Tīfāshī (d. 561/1253), *al-Shifā fī al-ṭibb al-musnad 'an al-sayyid al-Muṣṭafā* (Beirut: Dār al-Ma'rifa, 1988), 203.

https://doi.org/10.1515/9783110596588-013

caring for her husband. The "non-Arab" physicians with whom Muḥammad consulted seem to have been understood as specifically non-Muslim physicians, as this *ḥadīth* was often followed immediately by a statement that a Muslim may indeed consult a *dhimmī* physician, but he should exercise caution when doing so.[571] For example, in his *al-Ṭibb al-nabawī* al-Dhahabī quotes this fragment of the *ḥadīth* and then glosses it using statements by Ibn Ḥanbal about heeding the advice of *dhimmī* physicians.

> "When the Prophet of God's illnesses became great, both Arab and non-Arab physicians." Aḥmad [ibn Ḥanbal] said: it is permissible to defer to a physician from the *ahl al-dhimma* when he prescribes permitted treatments. But his directives must not be listened to when he prescribes forbidden treatments, such as alcohol, etc. Similarly, his directives are not listened to with regard to breaking fast instead of fasting, praying while sitting [instead of prostrating] etc. Regarding such directives, they are not to be accepted unless received from physicians who are pious Muslims. Aḥmad is also quoted as disliking mixed or concocted medicines produced by the *ahl al-dhimma*. He said, according to the recension of Aḥmad b. al-Ḥasan, "It is disliked to drink a polytheist's medicines." Al-Marūzī said, "Aḥmad commanded me not to buy for him prescriptions from a Christian. He said it was because [the Christian] could not be trusted not to mix into it something forbidden, such as poisons or ritual impurities, while maintaining it to be healthful."[572]

Thus, drawing on this precedent set by the Prophet Muḥammad, the *'ulamā'* formed a consensus that seeking medical treatment was permissible, but they also understood the same *ḥadīth* as depicting a fraught social reality: illness compels people to put themselves in the hands of diverse, even non-Muslim, practitioners.

Some *ḥadīth*s attributed to the Prophet were interpreted as highlighting the negative aspects of medical intervention:

> 70,000 of my people will enter paradise without a reckoning: those who did not have themselves charmed (*lā yastarqūn*), did not consult auguries, did not have themselves cauterized, and who entrusted themselves to God.[573]

This *ḥadīth* was understood as implying the preferability of trusting in God's providence to medical intervention generally, not just with respect to these

---

571 The explicit identification of the non-Arabs with infidels appears in 'Abd al-Ḥayy ibn 'Abd al-Kabīr al-Kattānī's, *Niẓām al-ḥukūma al-nabawiyya al-musamma al-tarātīb al-idāriyya* (Beirut: Dār al-Arqam, 1996), 353. This, of course, makes historical sense as well, given that there were very few non-Arab Muslims during the lifetime of the Prophet.

572 al-Dhahabī, *al-Ṭibb al-nabawī*, 2:224

573 Muslim, *Ṣaḥīḥ Muslim*, 1:198, no. 218. Cf. al-Bukhārī, *Ṣaḥīḥ al-Bukhārī*, 76 (*ṭibb*):17, no. 5705.

three specific activities. A commonly quoted anecdote has Aḥmad ibn Ḥanbal reciting this *ḥadīth* when praising sick people who choose not to inform a physician about their illness and instead decide to forgo treatment.[574] However even Ibn Ḥanbal is depicted as viewing treatment is legitimate, saying "healing is a concession [*rukhṣa*], and refraining from it is on a higher level."[575] Other jurists portray medical intervention in a more positive light. Both the Shāfiʿī and Ḥanafī legal schools view medical treatment as preferable to non-treatment, as does the influential Ḥanbalī jurist Ibn al-Jawzī. Mālik is said to have taken the position that "engaging in [medical treatment] and refraining from it are equal . . . there is nothing wrong with engaging in medical treatment and there is nothing wrong in refraining from it."[576]

Even those jurists who were wary of medicine, such as Ibn Ḥanbal, did not condemn medicine as necessarily sinful, only potentially so. There were, indeed, people who argued that medicine is inherently impious as it betrays a desire to thwart God's designs, but in juristic literature we most often hear of the existence of this view from those who consider it to be pernicious and feel obliged to refute it. For example, in his 8th/14th-century *ḥisba* manual from Egypt, Ibn al-Ukhuwwa argues in favor of raising the profile of medicine as a necessary and noble profession. As part of that argument he quotes a *ḥadīth:*

> Abū Hurayra said: One day, one of the men of the Anṣār, a companion of the Prophet, was wounded. The Prophet summoned two physicians who were in Medina and instructed them to treat him. The two said, "O Messenger of God, we used to treat and thwart [bodily harm] during the *jāhiliyya*. But then Islam came, and isn't Islam *tawakkul* [entrusting oneself to God]?" He said, "treat him, for He who sent down diseases also sent down their treatments." Then the two attending him treated him, and he recovered.[577]

---

574 Ibn Mufliḥ, *Ādāb*, 2:333, al-Dhahabī, *al-Ṭibb al-nabawī*, 2:221. Cyril Elgood, "Tibb-ul-Nabbi or Medicine of the Prophet, Being a Translation of Two Works of the Same Name. I: The Ṭibb-ul-Nabbi of al-Suyūṭī. II: The Ṭibb-ul-Nabbi of Mahmud bin Mohamed al-Chaghayni, together with Introduction, Notes and a Glossary" *Osiris* 14 (1962), 125. Elgood ascribes this anonymous treatise to the 9th/15th-century Shafiʿī scholar al-Suyūṭī, but due to the fact that one manuscript of it includes an owner's date from 783/1391, and another manuscript found in the Bodleian library lists the author as al-Dhahabī, the current scholarly consensus is that the treatise is likely al-Dhahabī's. See, Emilie Savage-Smith, "Islamic Medical Medical Manuscripts at the National Library of Medicine," Nlm.nih.gov. https://www.nlm.nih.gov/hmd/arabic/prophetic_med2.html (accessed August 21, 2018).

575 Ibn Mufliḥ, *Ādāb*, 2:333.

576 Ibn Mufliḥ, *Ādāb*, 2:334.

577 Ibn al-Ukhuwwa, *The Maʿālim al-qurba fī aḥkām al-ḥisba*, 166–7 in Arabic.

The notion that undergoing medical treatment reveals a lack of *tawakkul*, trust in God, seems to have been a feature of some Sufi thought.[578] This sort of argument is raised and denounced in several different medical texts. The Persian physician Ibn Abū al-Faraj ibn Hindū, writing in the early 5th/11th-century, articulates a common counter-argument:

> Those who fear that acknowledging the existence of medicine means infringing upon God's determination of man's fate (*qadā'*) ought to stop eating when they are hungry and drinking when they are thirsty. God may very well have destined them to perish from hunger and thirst. Thus, if they eat and drink, they infringe upon God's determination of fate. They end up by substituting their wish for His wish.[579]

Several belle-lettrist texts also feature debates along similar lines for and against the use of medicine, some of whose arguments are obviously facetious and exaggerated.[580]

The jurists do not tend to object to medical interference per se. Rather, some jurists, particularly the ones writing in the Fatimid and Mamluk eras, make the claim that the religious identity of practitioners, the medical theory underlying treatment, and the ingredients used in treatment, all have religious consequences. For this reason, such jurists are interested in categorizing medical intervention according to source of illness, type of treatment, practitioner of treatment, and the spiritual state of the patient. They frequently use terminology which distinguishes between "natural" (*ṭabīʿī*) and "magical" (*siḥrī*) sources of illness,[581] contrasts "physical" (*ṭabīʿī* or "pertaining to the *abdān*") and "spiritual" (*ilāhī* or "pertaining to *dīn*") treatments,[582] and they compare "the medicine of the physicians" to "the medicine of the Prophet" and to "the medicine of itinerants and old women." These jurists claim that the patient's attribution of the source of their illness, their choice of cure, and their choice of medical practitioner reflects upon their religious status, which in turn influences the outcome of their treatment.

---

578 N. Fancy, *Science and Religion in Mamluk Egypt: Ibn al-Nafīs, Pulmonary Transit, and Bodily Resurrection* (London: Routledge, 2013), 68. On this topic see B. Reinert, *Die Lehre vom tawakkul in der klassischen Sufik* (Berlin: de Gruyter, 1968).
579 F. Rosenthal, "The Defense of Medicine In The Medieval Muslim World," 523.
580 Ibid.
581 Shams al-Dīn ibn Ṭūlūn (d. 953/1546), *al-Manhal al-rawī fī al-ṭibb al-nabawī* (Hyderabad: Anwār al-Maʿārif, 1987), 352.
582 Ibn Qayyim al-Jawziyya, *al-Ṭibb al-nabawī* (Beirut: Dār al-Fikr = Dār Iḥyā al-Kutub al-ʿArabiyya, 1957), 17.

Lack of classification of medicine in the *ḥadīth* collections

Two categories of physical illnesses are recognized in *ḥadīth* literature: (1) those caused by humans utilizing occult practices, which include sorcery (*siḥr*) and the evil eye (*al-'ayn*),[583] and (2) those caused by Divine will and nature. A large variety of treatments are recognized as potentially effective though not all are permitted or recommended. These treatments include the intervention of physicians, sorcerers, astrologers, and prophets; the use of foodstuffs, bloodletting, cupping, cauterization, drugs, alchemy, clysters, individual prayer, ablutions, bathing, incantations using the Qur'ān (*ruqya*),[584] amulets (*tamā'im*),[585] soothsaying, and other forms of magic. The chapters on medicine in the *ḥadīth* collections do not provide a rigid methodology for thinking about the etiology of illness or what constitutes medical attention. Rather the *ḥadīth*s provide an eclectic catalog of "things that might help" people, with hygiene, diet, and particular foodstuffs extolled above all others. The *ḥadīth*s also comment on therapies, indicating that the Prophet praised cupping and disliked cauterization.[586] The disapproval of cauterization does not seem to be based on any particular theological concern, rather it is depicted as a treatment of last resort.[587] Many *ḥadīth*s depict the prophylactic usefulness of reciting specific Qur'ānic verses. The Prophet recited some of these together with blowing, spitting or hand-motions, and he praised his companions when they used Qur'ānic verses to perform healing incantations.[588] Other *ḥadīth*s condemn resorting to incantations, auguries, and astrology, or say that it would be best not to use them.[589] These condemnations, however, do not tend to dismiss these actions as useless, nor do they demonstrate a clear-cut differentiation between different spheres of medical knowledge, i.e. in the *ḥadīth* collections there is no "high medicine" or "low medicine" clearly defined along the lines of etiology, source, or the social class of its practitioners. There is no sense that illnesses of natural origin ought to be treated by "natural" medicine, or that supernatural illnesses must be fought by occult means. Incantations are effective against scorpions, scabs,

---

583 E.g. *Ṣaḥīḥ al-Ṭirmidhī*, 2:27.
584 E.g. *Musnad ibn Hanbal*, 3:421. *Ṣaḥīḥ Muslim* 2:223.
585 See Ibn Mufliḥ, *Ādāb*, 3:64–69
586 al-Bukhārī, *Ṣaḥīḥ al-Bukhārī*, 76 (*ṭibb*):4, no. 5683.
587 Ibn Mufliḥ, *Ādāb*, 2:334; Elgood, "Tibb-ul-Nabbi or Medicine of the Prophet," *Osiris* 14 (1962), 144.
588 Ibn Qayyim al-Jawziyya, *al-Ṭibb al-Nabawī*, 144; al-Bukhārī, *Ṣaḥīḥ al-Bukhārī*, 76 (*ṭibb*):32, no. 5735.
589 Ibn al-Jawzī, *Aḥkām al-nisā'* (Kuwait: Maktabat dār Ibn Qutayba, 1989), 97–100.

and ulcers.[590] Breakfasting on seven dates shields one from the effects of both poisons and witchcraft for the rest of the day.[591]

The roots *ṭ-b-b* and *ʿ-l-j*, "treat" are both used in the *ḥadīth* in describe healing a patient either by means of natural medicine or through magic or incantations. Both are also used to describe a patient physically affected by malicious sorcery. We see *ṭ-b-b* used as a synonym for *s-ḥ-r*, "bewitchment" in the following *ḥadīth* from *Ṣaḥīḥ al-Bukhārī*.

> ʿĀʾisha said: The Messenger of God had been bewitched (*suḥira*) such that he thought he had had sexual relations with his wives, but he had not done so. Sufyān said: this is a most severe form of sorcery, if that is so. Then [The Prophet] said: 'ʿĀʾisha, know that God has informed me about what I inquired of Him. Two men came to me, and one of them sat by my head and the other by my feet. The one at my head said to the other, what ails this man? He said, he is bewitched (*maṭbūb*). [The first] said, "who bewitched him (*man ṭabbahu*)?"[592]

Another *ḥadīth* uses *ʿ-l-j* in reference to some sort of taboo magic to arouse a husband's ardor.

> From Khālid b. Maʿdān: a woman came to the Messenger of God and said, 'O Messenger of God, do you look well upon my producing something to make [my husband] love me?' He said, 'Fie upon you, fie upon you! What you have said is heinous!' Then he had her expelled and ordered water and spilled it on the spot where she had been. Later the Messenger of God learned that the woman had become devout and her situation had improved.
>
> From Ibn Masʿūd: He said, I visited ʿĀʾisha, mother of the faithful, with my mother and she had women who were coming to her with questions. A woman came to her and said, "O mother of the faithful, may a woman pitch her tent?" She said, "There is nothing wrong in it." Then the woman left, and the women said to [ʿĀʾisha], "Do you know what she wanted, O mother of the faithful?" She said, "What do you mean?" They said, "She wanted to treat (*tuʿālija*) her husband! ʿĀʾisha said, "Bring her back to me." So they brought her back and she said to her, "Fie upon you" and she forbade her. Then she said, "Salt in fire, salt in fire, expel her from me and wash her traces with water and lotus leaves."[593]

---

590 Cyril Elgood, "Tibb-ul-Nabbi or Medicine of the Prophet," 154.
591 Cyril Elgood, "Tibb-ul-Nabbi or Medicine of the Prophet," 138.
592 Al-Bukhārī, *Ṣaḥīḥ al-Bukhārī*, 76 (*ṭibb*):49 no. #5765. Al-Khaṭṭābī comments, "*Maṭbūb* means bewitched (*masḥūr*) and *ṭibb* means sorcery (*saḥr*)." Al-Khaṭṭābī, *Aʿlām al-Ḥadīth fī sharḥ Ṣaḥīḥ al-Bukhārī* (Mecca: Jāmiʿat Umm al-Qurā, Maʿhad al-Buḥūth al-ʿIlmīyah wa-Iḥyāʾ al-Turāth al-Islāmī, Markaz Iḥyāʾ al-Turāth al-Islāmī, 1988), 1499. Cf. Ibn Mufliḥ, Ādāb, 3:84 on the various meaning of *ṭibb*.
593 Ibn Habīb, *Kitāb adab al-nisāʾ*, 230–32.

In both of these cases, terms which have medical significance are used to refer not just to magic, but to "offensive" magic rather than "defensive" magic. The root *'-l-j* in particular seems to have used in connection with a wife's interference with her husband's natural affections and libido. Thus, there does not seem to be an entirely separate vocabulary to distinguish between providing medical care, healing potions, and offensive sorcery.

The word *ṭabīb* however, may refer exclusively to a practitioner of medicine. For while the root *ṭ-b-b* is used with regard to magic, the word *ṭabīb* does not seem to be so utilized. The historian of Islamic medicine Lawrence Conrad writes that this is itself a marker of the Islamic era.

> "Should one go the doctor (*ṭabīb*)?", one saying of the Prophet has a man ask Muḥammad; and the answer is that he should, for "God sends down no malady without also sending down with it a cure". In this account, transmitted in many variant forms and one of the most widespread of medical sayings from the Prophet, a sharp distinction was now drawn between the old-style *ṭabīb*, the master of spells and charms, and a different kind of *ṭabīb* who searches out the cures provided by God, the giver of all things.[594]

Medieval jurist Ibn Qayyim al-Jawziyya notes that while the root *ṭ-b-b* can refer to magic in some literature, it does not when used in legal contexts.[595]

Jurists on the "medicine of the physicians"

The lack of systematic differentiation in the *ḥadīth* collections does not carry over into the works on medicine produced by the 'ulamā', that is to say, the books of Prophetic medicine, the chapters on medicine in legal manuals, and the legal *adab* treatises, even though all of these draw heavily on the *ḥadīth*s. Rather, the literature produced by the jurists, like the medical literature produced by the doctors in the Arabo-Galenic tradition, depicts medical practice as bifurcated between high medicine as practiced by the physicians, and low medicine as practiced by ignoramuses, charlatans, and old women.

The jurists consistently use the term *ṭabīb* as an umbrella term for a variety of medical professionals, none of whom are associated with the occult. As Ibn Qayyim al-Jawziyya explains, in interpreting *ḥadīth*s about a *ṭabīb*, one must understand the term to apply to:

---

594 L. Conrad, The Western Medical Tradition:800 BC to AD 1800 (New York: Cambridge University Press, 1995), 98.

595 Ibn Qayyim al-Jawziyya, *al-Ṭibb al-nabawī*, 107–9.

> . . . all those who carry out treatment either through general prescriptions or the practice of a specialized method of healers. If he uses a koḥl stick he is an oculist; if a scalpel and ointments, he is a surgeon; if a knife, a circumciser; an incising instrument, a phlebotomist; cupping glasses and a sharp knife, a cupper. He is known by his bonesetting equipment and his bandages if a bonesetter; by his irons and fire if a cauteriser; by his waterskin-bag if one who administers clysters.[596]

The one professional who is not mentioned in this list is the pharmacist. However, the physicians' pharmacological activities greatly concern the jurists and so it seems that we should understand the term *ṭabīb* as also referring to pharmacists when used in the texts produced by the ʻulamāʼ.

This literature depicts physicians as a class which shares a body of intellectual precepts: they venerate Galen, they do not believe in any form of treatment other than "natural" medicine;[597] however, they do believe that *khawāṣṣ* exert real impact. The term *khawāṣṣ* (literally: special properties) is used generally in Arabic literature to refer to a variety of beliefs about the healing powers of stones, metals, bones, and even letters and numbers.[598] However, when the jurists write about the physicians' use of *khawāṣṣ*, they seem to be referring to the use of stones or metals which can cause physical effects, even from a distance, by means of magnetism or "sympathy." Their effects are not supernatural, but they cannot be explained by means of logic.[599] Their properties and uses are known through empirical experience. The existence of this category of treatment in the high medical tradition becomes important to those jurists seeking to situate Prophetic medicine within that tradition.

In polemical literature by the proponents of the Prophet medical tradition, the proponents of "physicians' medicine" are accused of attacking Islam and Prophetic medicine on the grounds that (a) Islam has no medical teaching, (b) to the extent that Islam has a medical teaching it is derivative from, and subject to, Greek medicine, and (c) Prophetic medicine is wrong in ascribing to the evil eye and sorcery the power to cause physical damage and in attributing real curative power to incantations.

The jurists do not reject the "medicine of the physicians" as untrue, or in and of itself religiously suspect. Indeed, the Greek medical heritage is frequently

---

596 Ibn Qayyim al-Jawziyya, *al-Ṭibb al-Nabawī*, 112. Translation from Penelope Johnstone, *Medicine of the Prophet* (Cambridge: Islamic Texts Society, 1998), 107.
597 Ibn Ṭūlūn, *al-Manhal al-rawī*, 352.
598 Ibn Qayyim al-Jawziyya says that the number seven possesses special healing properties but that Hippocrates and Galen and the other physicians are unaware of them. Ibn Qayyim al-Jawziyya, *al-Ṭibb*, 79.
599 Ibn Qayyim al-Jawziyya, *al-Ṭibb*, 134.

quoted and implicitly referenced in all of the books of Prophetic medicine which include the authors' own voices, such as those by Ibn Qayyim al-Jawziyya, al-Dhahabī, Ibn Ṭūlūn, and al-Suyūṭī, and they frequently mention physicians in the Arabo-Galenic tradition. However, these authors are concerned about the relationship of medical science to religious science. This is both a theoretical question about the categories of knowledge and epistemology, and a practical question about whether one must entrust one's bodily well-being and one's spiritual well-being to the same authorities or to different ones.

It is common in the texts written by the jurists about medicine to cite al-Shāfiʿī as saying: "Knowledge is of two kinds: the knowledge of religions (*adyān*) is jurisprudence and the knowledge of bodies (*abdān*) is medicine."[600] The implication is that religious knowledge and medical knowledge are separate, that medical knowledge is not a subset of religious knowledge, and that it is incumbent on the Muslim community to produce experts in both sciences. Nonetheless, it is important to at least some of the ʿulamā' to establish that Islam itself provides both kinds of knowledge. An oft-quoted story has a Christian physician remarking that Islam has no medical teaching. The Muslim respondent cites Qur'ān 7:31 "eat and drink and do not be extravagant; Truly, He loves not the extravagant"[601] and comments, "God has combined all of medicine into half of a verse of our book." The Christian is suitably impressed and replies: "Your scripture and your prophet have left no medicine for Galen," i.e. there is nothing more for Galen to add to Islamic medical knowledge.[602] The jurists are under no illusions about the shortcomings of such a retort. Rather they make several separate and sometimes competing arguments about the existence and relevance of Islam's contribution to medical knowledge.

One argument is that while Islam does not provide its own medical theory, it does provide knowledge of specific cures based on the empirical evidence of experience (*tajārib*). Moreover, this specific knowledge is not simply acquired through happenstance, but rather is derived from the Prophet Muḥammad's per-

600 Al-Bayhaqī, *Manāqib al-Shāfiʿī* (Cairo: Maktabat Dār al-Turāth, 1971) 2:114. Ibn Mufliḥ, *al-Ādāb al-sharʿiyya* (Beirut: Mu'assasat al-Risāla, 1996), 2:335. In the *Biḥār al-anwār*, this statement is attributed to the Prophet Muḥammad. Al-Majlisī, *Biḥār al-anwār* (Beirut: Mu'assasat al-Wafā', 1983) 1:220.

601 Translation from Alan Jones, *The Qur'ān* (Exeter: E. J. W. Gibb Memorial Trust, 2007), 150.

602 Ibn Mufliḥ, *Ādāb*, 2:340; Ibn al-Ḥājj, *al-Madkhal*, 3/4:324 and Ibn al-Jawzī, *Zād al-masīr fī ʿilm al-tafsīr* (Beirut: Dār al-Fikr, 1987) 3:128; Jamāl al-Dīn al-Surramurrī, (d. 776/1374) *Shifā' al-ālām fī ṭibb ahl al-Islām*. See Bürgel, "Secular and Religious Features of Medieval Arabic Medicine," 57.

fect knowledge. Ibn Ṭūlūn (d. 953/1546) quotes Abū Sulayman al-Khaṭṭābī (d. c. 388/998) as making this point:

> Know that medicine is of two kinds: rational medicine (*al-ṭibb al-qiyāsī*) which is Greek and which people use in most lands, and the medicine of the Arabs and the Indians, which is empirical medicine (*ṭibb al-tajārib*). Most of what the Prophet established is in accordance with what the Arabs established, except that which he specified as deriving from prophetic knowledge by means of revelation and that transcends everything which physicians understand and the doctors know. Everything which he did or said is on the highest level of correctness, for God kept him from saying anything but truth and from doing anything but rightly.[603]

The jurists seek to bolster the argument that Muḥammad was medically knowledgeable by showing where *ḥadīth*s correspond to specific Arabo-Galenic principles and to so-called "Greek" pharmacological knowledge.[604] They are, however, aware that this too presents a logical and theological pitfall. The Egyptian Mālikī scholar Ibn al-Ḥājj addresses this issue with regard to the Prophetic statement that "the black seed (*al-ḥabba al-sawdā'*) is a cure for all things except death."[605]

> One of the 'ulamā' said that the physicians say the black seed is beneficial for treating only seventeen diseases. He [the *'alim*] claimed that this *ḥadīth* is subject to that. [i.e. The *ḥadīth*'s claim that the black seed is a cure-all is true only to the extent that it overlaps with the findings of the physicians.] He [the *'alim*] said: "And so, anyone who wants to use it should ask the physicians about it and if they inform him that it is beneficial for that particular disease he uses it, and if not he does not, or however [the physician] says."
>
> But Abū Muḥammad[606] [one of Ibn al-Ḥājj's teachers] rejected that saying: "God forbid that I should in so doing say 'the possessor of perfect light reported something, but we will subject it to the opinion of the possessors of shadows.'"

---

603 Ibn Ṭūlūn, *al-Manhal al-rawī*, 10. The quotation appears in Al-Khaṭṭābī, *A'lām al-ḥadīth fī sharḥ Ṣaḥīḥ al-Bukhārī*, 2107–8.

604 In Elgood's translation of al-Dhahabī, this occurs on pages 54, 55 and 66 (in which two *ḥadīths* are compared with the Hippocratic Oath), 61, 71 76, 78, 79, 83, 86, 92, 95, 97–8, 98, 103, 108, 109, 112, 114–5, 136, 138, 139, 166 and 171 (in which Prophetic embryology is compared to Hippocratic embryology). Although much of Near Eastern pharmacological knowledge came from farther East, in the *Ṭibb al-nabawī* books, only sources such as Hippocrates, Galen, Dioscorides, and Ibn Sīnā are cited.

605 This *ḥadīth*, although widely cited, is problematic because the spice in question required 'translation' into medieval parlance. There is a debate as to whether the black seed refers to coriander or cumin. Al-Dhahabī offers both translations and prefers the first. Ibn al-Ḥājj says it is the second, see Ibn al-Ḥājj, *al-Madkhal*, 3/4:322.

606 This is Abū Muhammad 'Abdallāh ibn Sa'd ibn Abī Jamra al-Andalūsī (d. 675 / 1300), who is cited repeatedly in the *Madkhal* and was one of Ibn al-Ḥājj's teachers. Like Ibn al-Ḥājj, he migrated from the Maghrib /Andalus region to Egypt.

> It was said to [Abū Muḥammad]: "So what then is the connection between what the Prophet reported and what the physicians say?" He said, "The answer is two-fold. First: the black seed is beneficial for all diseases, as the Prophet reported, for he saw with the perfect light which God had granted him and bestowed upon him, and he saw that it is beneficial for all diseases. The people of medicine saw in the shadows their own thoughts and did not know more than seventeen. Alternatively: indeed, the black seed was beneficial for seventeen diseases as the physicians said, but then God made it beneficial for this People (*umma*) for all of the diseases, just as [this *umma*] has been distinguished with special qualities from other peoples in being honored with the Prophet."
>
> This statement of his is clearly evident. But it all goes back to the intention (*niyya*) of the sick person in dealing with this. For the principle is that everything which proceeds from the Lawgiver is tied to the acceptance [of it] and the strength of faith. Therefore, the endeavor will succeed in proportion to the intention, and the possessor of [the intention] will triumph in his objective.[607]

Abū Muḥammad rejects the notion that, in order to make practical use of Prophetic medicine, it needs to be evaluated on the basis of whether it accords with physicians' medicine. Instead he offers two contradictory alternatives for understanding the relationship between the two forms of medical advice. Either there is one medical truth to which the Prophet has full access and the physicians have limited access, or there are two different medical truths, one which is true for Muslims and one which is true for all others. Ibn al-Ḥājj's comment ("the endeavor will succeed in proportion to the intention") further elaborates upon the second concept: the more pious one is, the "more Muslim" one is, the more one is subject to the rules of one medical reality over another.

This concept of multiple medical realities appears often, particularly in Ibn al-Qayyim's *al-Ṭibb al-nabawī*.

> When the heart turns toward the Lord of the Worlds, the Creator of both illness and medicine, the One who regulates nature and disposes of it as He wishes, [the patient] responds to other medicines, different from those which pertain to one whose heart is turned away and far from Him.[608]

Similarly, he writes:

> This [particular practice] is something which the physician's treatments do not include, nor can anyone benefit from it who denies it, or ridicules it, or doubts it, or who carries it out as an experiment without believing that it will benefit him. If there exist in nature *khawāṣṣ* – whose causes the physicians cannot explain to us, but which they consider to have special

607 Ibn al-Ḥājj, *al-Madkhal*, 3/4:323.

608 Ibn Qayyim al-Jawziyya, *al-Ṭibb*, 7. Translation from Penelope Johnstone, *Medicine of the Prophet*, 9. Translation slightly modified.

> qualities which render them exceptions to natural rules – so what if their heresy and ignorance makes them deny *al-khawāṣṣ al-shar'iyya?*[609]

The claim in these statements is that the choice of treatment which a person makes, and the degree of enthusiasm about that treatment, is a reflection upon that person's level of faith. Moreover, that person's level of faith influences the degree to which a treatment can be effective. The implication of such a view is that when a patient chooses a physician she puts faith in that physician and becomes affiliated with the worldview he offers. If she is cured by him it is, at least in part, a testament to her conviction. Conversely, if she chooses an alternative healing system, and fails to be healed, that too reflects upon her faith.

This conception of healing makes "the medicine of the physicians" religiously problematic for another reason: the physicians are stereotypically associated with Christian-Jewish-Hellenic impiety. The jurists are deeply concerned about, but paradoxically perpetuate, the perception that non-Muslims constitute either the majority of physicians, or the most popular physicians among Muslim patients. Often the jurists attribute this to Muslims having ceded the domain of medicine to non-Muslims. This stereotype is promulgated in several different genres, over a long period of time, in a variety of regions. For example, in books of Prophetic medicine al-Shāfi'ī (who lived in the 2nd/8th century) is cited as being "grieved to see how much Muslims had lost of this science. Often he used to say: They have lost one third of human knowledge and have allowed themselves to be replaced by Jews and Christians. He also used to say: Verily the People of the Book have now conquered and surpassed us in this sublime Art."[610] Similarly, centuries later in his *ḥisba* manual Ibn al-Ukhuwwa claims:

> [The practice of medicine] is a communal obligation, and yet among Muslims no one fulfills it. Many a town has no physician except a member of the people of *dhimma*, whose legal testimony with regard to matters pertaining to physicians or medical science cannot be legally accepted. We see no [Muslim] occupying himself with it; and instead everyone flocks to the study of *fiqh*, and more particularly that portion of it given over to disputes and litigiousness . . . How could religion permit a person to occupy himself with a communal obligation that the community is already fulfilling, and to neglect an obligation that no one is fulfilling? Isn't this due only to medicine not being directly conducive to obtaining positions as judges and in government, through which a person can promote himself over his peers

609 Ibn Qayyim al-Jawziyya, *al-Ṭibb*, 134.
610 Elgood, "Tibb-ul-Nabbi," 128. Cf. Ibn Ṭūlūn, *al-Manhal al-rawī*, 6: "Al-Shāfi'ī used to lament the medicine which the Muslims have lost, saying: 'They have lost a third of knowledge and consigned it the Jews and Christians." Al-Dhahabī, *al-Ṭibb al-nabawī*, 228.

> and rule over his enemies? But alas, knowledge of religion has been obliterated. God is the only help and upon Him we must depend to rescue us from this madness which infuriates the Merciful One and amuses Satan.[611]

Ibn al-Ukhuwwa blames the supposed preponderance of *dhimmis* among physicians on the supposedly neglectful attitude of learned Muslims. In another *ḥisba* manual, from the 6th/12th century, the Sevillian jurist Ibn ʿAbdūn articulates a different permutation of al-Shāfiʿī's fear of the loss of what was originally "Muslim" medical knowledge. He writes:

> Scientific books should not be sold to Jews or Christians, except those pertaining to their own religion. For they translate books of science and attribute them to their coreligionists and bishops, when the books are authored by Muslims. And it is best not to permit a Jewish or Christian physician to attend and treat Muslims, for they do not bear Muslims goodwill. They may treat only their coreligionists; for if a person does not bear Muslims goodwill, how can he be entrusted with their lives?[612]

Here non-Muslims are also associated with medicine, but not due to Muslim neglect of the science but rather due to non-Muslims translating books authored by Muslims, thereby acquiring an undeserved reputation for scientific achievement.

Even outside of legal literature, Muslim physicians are also depicted as having trouble competing for patients, or at least such is the stereotype. In his *Kitāb al-bukhalāʾ*, al-Jāḥiẓ (d. 255/869) famously depicts a miserly Muslim physician pleading that business is bad for him, even during a period of plague, due to his difficulty in attracting patients. The physician says:

> For one thing, they know I happen to be a Muslim and folk held the belief before I began to practice medicine, no indeed even before I was born, that Muslims are not successful in medicine. Then my name is Asad and it ought to have been Ṣalīb, Jibrāʾīl, Yuḥannā and Bīrā. My surname is Abūʾl-Ḥārith and it ought to have been Abū ʿĪsā, Abū Zakariyyā and Abū Ibrāhīm. I wear a shoulder mantle of white cotton and my shoulder mantle ought to be black silk. My pronunciation is an Arab pronunciation and my dialect ought to have that of the people of Jundī Sābār.[613]

---

611 Ibn al-Ukhuwwa, *The Maʿālim al-qurba fī aḥkām al-ḥisba,* 166 in Arabic.
612 al-Tujibī and E. Lévi-Provençal, *Séville Musulmane Au Début Du XIIe Siècle: Le Traité D'ibn Abdun Sur La Vie Urbaine Et Les Corps De Métiers,* 57 in Arabic. Cf. al-Saffārīnī, *Ghidhāʾ al-albāb li-sharḥ Manẓūmat al-ādāb* (Beirut: Dār al-Kutub al-ʿIlmiyya, 1996), 2:12.
613 Translated by R. B. Serjeant, *The Book of Misers* (London: Garnet & Ithaca Press, 2000), 86. He means that if had a traditionally Christian name or Persian appearance, rather than a Muslim or Arab appearance, he would attract more patients.

Kitāb al-bukhalā' is a book of satire, ridiculing this fictional Arab Muslim physician for coming up with unconvincing excuses for his miserliness. So we might guess that in fact people were assumed not to care about the Christian and non-Arab traits which the miser claims patients value. But jurists writing in a variety of periods and contexts also allege in all seriousness that there is a preference for *dhimmī* doctors among some Muslims.[614] Ibn al-Ḥājj, writing in early 8th/14th-century Cairo, gives several reasons for this. First, the *dhimmī*s have a reputation for being more knowledgeable and have better medical *ijāza*s (certifications). As a result, according to Ibn al-Ḥājj, even those Muslims who mistrust *dhimmī*s sometimes choose to deal with their ambivalent attitude towards them by consulting first a *dhimmī* and then double-checking with a Muslim physician.

> Some people are on their guard regarding what I have said [about the malevolence of the non-Muslim doctor] and they retain a Muslim doctor and a Christian or a Jewish doctor and relay what the infidel recommended to the Muslim.[615] This too is unseemly.[616]

There is some indication that one of the reasons a Muslim might turn to a non-Muslim physician is that there are distinct disadvantages to being treated by someone from one's own community. Ibn al-Ḥājj urges Muslim doctors to make themselves attractive to Muslim patients by keeping the private information they learn from patients visiting their house out of circulation in the mosque. He also tells them a Muslim physician must be especially compassionate with patients while at the same time forcefully reminding them that they must not consult anyone less pious than he.

> When a physician wishes to leave his home for the mosque, he must make the intentions (*niyyāt*) that were previously mentioned [in the chapter on] the behavior of an *'ālim* when he leaves his house for the mosque. For knowledge (*'ilm*) is in fact of two kinds: the knowledge of religions and the knowledge of bodies. Each of them, if performed with the correct intention, is among the greatest acts of worship, and God enters into its practice and there is no substitute for it in the world. [The physician] should intend in doing so to embody the pure *sunna* in his doctoring, and to promote that which provides assistance to his Muslim brothers, removes distress from them, and supports them in the face of calamities and misfortunes. He should make the intention of hiding the nakedness of his Muslim brothers and not disclose anything except that which the law demands to be disclosed. For this reason

---

614 Moshe Perlmann, "The Position of Jewish Physicians in Medieval Muslim Countries," *Israel Oriental Studies* 2 (1972), 315–19.

615 However, Ibn Mufliḥ mentions two Ḥanbalīs who do just that and he does not reprove them, see Ibn Mufliḥ, *Ādāb al-shar'iyya*, 2:428.

616 Ibn al-Ḥājj, *al-Madkhal*, 3/4:318.

> the sick person, and whoever is responsible for him, are commanded not to resort to anyone except someone who embodies these characteristics. [The physician] must intend to be compassionate toward them . . . and he should urge upon the sick person and his guardian that they should not resort to any doctor except one who may be described as religious, upright, and trustworthy.[617]

This is followed by descriptions of the elaborate pains that a Muslim doctor must take to avoid exposing his patients' secrets either when his patients are visiting him in his house or when he sees them on non-medical occasions, such as in the mosque: "For the patient might have illnesses which he does not want to expose to anyone, especially the 'ulamā'."[618] At the same time, Ibn al-Ḥājj reminds the physician that he must himself investigate the intimate details of a patient's family life in order to provide the patient with the best treatment, even when such details reveal unseemly behavior.[619]

Such instructions suggest that some Muslim patients might have deliberately avoided Muslim physicians precisely because seeing a doctor within their own community might increase the risk of exposure and embarrassment. These risks were probably all the weightier since many maladies were thought to result from specific misbehavior.[620] Moreover, Muslim medical practitioners could be called upon to provide legal testimony, while non-Muslim practitioners could not. Furthermore, there is some evidence from biographical dictionaries of the Mamluk period that the 7th/13th-century witnessed a "decline of the philosopher-physician and the rise of the *faqīh*-physician" in the Mamluk world.[621] Perhaps this too was a source of concern for potential Muslim patients. If the Muslim physician and the *'ālim* were one and the same, and a patient wanted to keep embarrassing information from the *'ālim*, it would provide an incentive to the patient to seek medical care from a non-Muslim.

---

617 Ibn al-Ḥājj, *Madkhal*, 3/4:335.

618 Ibn al-Ḥājj, *Madkhal*, 3/4:336.

619 Ibn al-Ḥājj approvingly quotes a case where an astute doctor suspects that his patient's father was not his actual one. He summons the patient's mother for a private meaning "with no third person present" and tells her that the only way to save her son's life is to reveal to the physician the identity of the true father. The mother says she was impregnated by a passing Bedouin man. The physician is then able to cure the son using Bedouin medicine. Ibn al-Ḥājj, *Madkhal*, 3/4:339.

620 For example, it was commonly thought that birth defects were a result of aberrant sexual positions. Kathryn Kueny, "The Birth of Cain: Reproduction, Maternal Responsibility, and Moral Character in Early Islamic Exegesis," *History of Religions* 48 (2008), 121.

621 Leigh Chipman, *The World of Pharmacy and Pharmacists in Mamlūk Cairo* (Boston: Brill Academic Publishers, 2009), 127.

Perhaps unsurprisingly, medieval Christian and Jewish authorities sometimes expressed a similar fear that the faithful prefer to turn to outsiders for medical attention. Some Jewish authors claimed that their co-religionist consider Muslims and Christians to have a better medical tradition and condemned this practice by invoking a Talmudic statement saying that Jews may entrust their wealth to a non-Jew, but not their bodies.[622] Meanwhile church authorities in Crusader kingdoms promulgated decrees banning Latin Christians from consulting with physicians from other religions. They expressed concern that Latin Christians denigrate the medical authorities from their own religious community and prefer Muslim, Jewish, Samaritan, and Syrian Christian practitioners.[623]

When jurists argued against such cross-confessional treatment, what were they afraid would happen? Ibn al-Ḥājj lists many negative consequences to patronizing non-Muslim doctors:[624] it takes work away from Muslims, it puts Muslims at physical risk from the malevolence of Jewish doctors,[625] and it normalizes relationships with Jews and Christians which should not be normalized and may result in proselytizing.

The notion that cross-confessional medicine either serves as a testament of normalization, or causes normalization, of cross-confessional relationships and trust is supported not only by literary condemnations of such activities, but also in documentary evidence. For example, in the Cairo Geniza we find a letter of recommendation, from 7th/13th-century Cairo and written in Arabic script, testifying to the competence and good character of a Jewish physician named Abū al-Ḥasan ibn Abū Sahl ibn Ibrāhīm. The letter is written in the name of witnesses who identify themselves as "free, honourable and good Muslim men." The letter explains that "since someone has requested them, they have responded by registering their testimony to what they know of his trustworthiness, reliability, probity, expertise, uprightness and knowledge." They testify that the physician "is a man of honor . . . trustworthy in the profession that he practices, reliable, on account to his devotion to his religion . . . in holding session in street stalls and in having freedom of access to the houses of people and the dwellings of those

622 G. Bos, "On Editing and Translating Medieval Hebrew Medical Texts," *Jewish Quarterly Review* 89 (1998), 102–103.

623 B. Kedar, "Jews and Samaritans in the Crusading Kingdom of Jerusalem," *Tarbiz* 53 (1984), 397, 404.

624 Ibn al-Ḥājj, *Madkhal*, 3/4:316–21.

625 Ibn al-Ḥājj, *Madkhal*, 3/4:318. In this rather colorful section, Ibn al-Ḥājj describes the disgruntled mindset and plotting of the Jewish doctor and does not mention Christians. Cf. Perlmann, "The Position of Jewish Physicians in Medieval Muslim Countries," 317.

whom he treats. They have not known him to exhibit anything but charity, probity, trustworthiness, reliability and integrity."[626]

Those who objected to Muslims frequenting non-Muslim medical practitioners had additional concerns beyond social issues. The inability of non-Muslims to offer medical testimony in court was also a source of anxiety. But the most tangible problem posed by cross-confessional medicine, and the one which is most frequently cited in Prophetic medicine treatises as well as books of religious preaching such as those by Ibn Mufliḥ and Ibn al-Ḥājj, is that non-Muslim doctors might recommend treatments which are at odds with Islamic law, such as sitting instead of prostrating oneself in prayer and not participating in Ramaḍān fasts.[627] Another commonly mentioned concern is that a non-Muslim physician might offer a medicine which includes impure substances which are either ritually unclean (i. e. *najāsāt*) or deliberately poisonous.[628] For this reason jurists who dealt with the issue of non-Muslim physicians treating Muslim patients wrote that it is either forbidden or disliked to ingest a compound drug given by a non-Muslim physician, unless a Muslim has verified its individual components. Even more worrisome was the possibility that a non-Muslim doctor might be quick to recommend ingesting alcohol. While the utility and legality of the use of alcohol in medicine was a matter of some dispute,[629] the Prophetic medical literature adamantly forbids it. However, al-Dhahabī's extensive protestations against therapeutic alcohol strongly suggest that many Muslims thought it proper to view medical situations as an exception to the general prohibition:

---

626 Cairo Geniza document T-S NS 305.115, edited and translated by Geoffrey Khan. G. Khan, *Arabic Legal and Administrative Documents in the Cambridge Genizah Collections* (Cambridge: Cambridge University Press, 1993), 247–50.
627 Elgood, "Tibb-ul-Nabbi," 126.
628 Usually, concern about *najāsāt* is associated with Christian physicians and malevolence with Jewish ones. Aḥmad ibn Ḥanbal is quoted as associating both with Christians, and his opinion is cited in Ibn Mufliḥ, *Ādāb*, 2:428 and al-Dhahabī in Elgood, "Tibb-ul-Nabbi," 127. Cf. al-Dhahabī, *Ṭibb*, 224, where the focus is also on Christians. In contrast, Ibn al-Ḥājj focuses on Jewish physicians, claiming that Jews, by monopolizing the professions of physician, oculist, and accountant, attempt to master Muslims' bodies and worldly goods. Ibn al-Ḥājj, *Madkhal*, 3/4:320. A view that does not distinguish between Christians and Jews is found in Muḥammad b. Aḥmad b. Sālim al-Saffārīnī al-Ḥanbalī's (d. 1188/1774) statement is his book of *adab:* "It is reprehensible for us to entrust one of (the *ahl al-kitāb*) with preserving our bodies by means of medicine because they are our enemies. How can we entrust someone who is our enemy with our souls?" al-Saffārīnī, *Ghidhā' al-albāb li-sharḥ Manẓūmat al-ādāb* (Beirut: Dār al-Kutub al-'Ilmiyya, 1996), 2:12.
629 For a summary of the controversy, see *al-Mawsū'a al-fiqhiyya* (Kuwait: Wizārat al-Awqāf wa'l-Shu'ūn al-Islāmiyya, 2004), 5:27–8.

> Another tradition says that the Prophet was asked about wine, whether it could be used as a medicine. And he replied: Wine is not a medicine. This is a tradition related by Abū Dāwūd and al-Tirmidhī . . .
>
> Ṭāriq ibn Suwayd relates: I said to the Prophet that we grew grapes and pressed out the juice and drank it. And he said: Do not do so. So I went back to him and said: I cure the sick with it. And he replied: Verily that is not healing: it is producing a disease. This saying is related by Muslim, Abū Dāwūd, and al-Tirmidhī and it is a reliable and accurate tradition.
>
> Said al-Khaṭṭābī: Call it a disease, for in the drinking of the juice of the grape there is somewhat of sin. And indeed it is quite true that there is no advantage to be gained from wine. The enquirer when he enquired already knew that it contained sin. But he was enquiring about its natural advantages. But the Prophet disclaimed them and rejected these too. And God knoweth all things.
>
> It is evident that wine is a remedy for some diseases. Yet the Prophet transferred it from the boundaries of this World to the boundaries of the Next World and from a consideration of the natural to a consideration of the lawful. Some one else has remarked that God in His glory deprived wine of all its uses when He disallowed it. And God is all-knowing. [630]

Despite the diversity of opinions found in other books written by the 'ulamā' about medical uses of alcohol, the proponents of Prophetic medicine stake out the position that although alcohol may indeed have healing properties, nevertheless those properties should not be taken into consideration.

Proponents of Prophetic medicine, despite their protests against some aspects of the culture of "the physicians," tend to portray Prophetic medicine, not as a set of stringencies or restrictions, but rather as a source of additional and better alternatives to Arabo-Galenic medicine. They appeal directly to the instinct toward medical experimentation, urging Muslim patients to experiment with Islam and to give it a chance to help them meet their medical needs. Ibn Qayyim al-Jawziyya in particular makes this appeal repeatedly. For example, he quotes a *ḥadīth* in which the Prophet uses qusṭ (costus) to cure pleurisy. In exasperation the jurist writes:

> Its benefit for one who has pleurisy is hidden from ignorant physicians, so they deny it. But if that ignorant one heard that this statement comes from Galen, he would accord it the status of a [holy] text . . . Now we have already said that the medicine of the physicians, relative to the medicine of the prophets, is more lacking than the medicine of itinerants and old women relative to the medicine of the physicians;[631] and that there is a greater gap between what has been encountered through revelation and what has been encoun-

630 Elgood, "Tibb-ul-Nabbi," 80.

631 A similar phrase can be found in Jamāl al-Dīn al-Surramurrī's (d. 776/1374) *Shifā' al-ālām fī ṭibb ahl al-Islām.* p.2 of manuscript.

tered through empiricism and logic, than between the dimwit and the keen man. But if those ignorant ones were to find a drug written down by one of the Jewish, Christian, or polytheistic physicians, they would receive it welcomingly and warmly, and would not hesitate to try it.[632]

Ibn al-Qayyim argues that physicians place so much trust in the authority of Galen that they receive his opinions as holy writ. Similarly, he complains that when a non-Muslim physician makes a recommendation people are willing to try it. But since the Prophet made the recommendation, the physicians and the people dismiss it.

Ibn al-Qayyim's exasperation with the unwillingness of some people to recognize " true" medical knowledge mirrors the tone of the medical writings of the physicians themselves, who also complain that potential patients are likely to solicit help from the wrong sort of authorities. The physician al-Rāzī produced two treatises on this topic, one titled, *Epistle on the Reason Why the Ignorant Physicians, the Common People, and the Women in the Cities Are More Successful than Men of Learning in Treating certain Diseases and the Physician's Excuse for This* and the other titled, *On the Causes Why Most People Turn away From Excellent Physicians towards the Worst Ones.*[633] The Christian physician Ṣā'id ibn al-Ḥasan (d. after 464/1072) wrote:

How amazing is this [that patients are cured at all], considering that they hand over their lives to senile old women![634] For most people, at the onset of illness, use as their physicians either their wives, mothers or aunts, or some [other] member of their family or one of their neighbors. He [the patient] acquiesces to whatever extravagant measure she might order,

632 Ibn Qayyim al-Jawziyya, *al-Ṭibb al-nabawī*, 274.

633 Pormann and Savage-Smith, *Medieval Islamic Medicine*, 90. Neither work is extant in Arabic. However, the second one exists in medieval Hebrew translation. M. Steinschneider, "Wissenschaft und Charlatanerie unter den Arabern im neunten Jahrhundert," *Virchows Archiv* (1866) 36:570–86 and 37:560–65; reprinted in *Beiträge zur Geschichte der arabisch-islamischen Medizin* (Frankfurt: Institut für Geschichte der arabisch-islamischen Wissenschaften, 1987), 2:39–61.

634 The image of the "old woman" dispenser of medical knowledge in medieval Arabo-Islamic medical and religious literature is not quite equivalent to the one found in the literature of medieval Christian Europe. The latter seems to invest her with more demonic power, more "savage" piety, and more ignorance. See Jole Agrimi and Chiara Crisciani, "Savoir médical et anthropologie religieuse: Les représentations et les fonctions de la vetula (XIIIe-XVe siècle)," *Annales. Économies, Sociétés, Civilisations* 48 (1993), 1292. A comparative study of the depiction of the "active" old woman in medieval Middle Eastern and European literature would be a welcome addition to the field of women's history. See, for example, the first chapter of Shihāb al-Dīn Aḥmad al-Tīfāshī's depictions of old women in *Nuzhat al-albāb fī-mā lā yūjad fī kitāb.*

> consumes whatever she prepares for him, and listens to what she says and obeys her commands more than he obeys the physician.[635]

The physicians who write about the medicine of "the ignorant," "the common people," and "old women" appear to be referring what we would call "folk medicine." In spite of its lowly associations, folk medicine also receives the attention of the jurists, just as "high medicine" does.

Jurists on resorting to folk medicine

Both the jurists and the physicians indicate that it is quite common for a patient to seek treatment in their own home, often from the women of the household. Peter Pormann suggests that "women probably provided much medical care for members of both sexes, even if the elite male physicians took a dim view about their activities."[636] Rarely are such activities described with any detail, and it is difficult to determine the full scope of the activities Ibn al-Qayyim refers to when writing disparagingly about the "medicine of itinerants and old women" and setting it in contrast to the "medicine of the physicians." Ibn al-Ḥājj, a contemporary of Ibn al-Qayyim, offers some unusually detailed descriptions. He claims that women practitioners view the inversion of aspects of correct behavior as a form of treatment.[637] For example midwives make use of reviled substances for the purposes of easing difficult labor and protecting the newborn.

635 Translation by Peter Pormann in Pormann, "The Art of Medicine: Female Patients and Practitioners in Medieval Islam," 1598–99. Ṣā'id ibn al-Ḥasan, *At-Tašwīq aṭ-ṭibbī des Ṣā'id ibn al-Ḥasan*, ed. Otto Spies (Bonn: Selbstverlag des Orientalischen Seminars der Universitat Bonn, 1968), fol. 27b.

636 Pormann, "The Art of Medicine," 1599.

637 The performance of prohibited and unnatural acts is thought to aid in gaining control over demons. Ibn al-Nadīm writes that this is particularly true in Egypt, which he calls "the Babylon of the magicians." Dols, *Majnūn: the Madman in Medieval Islamic Society*, 265. There are many references to such beliefs in modern ethnographies as well, especially in Edward Westermarck's descriptions of early twentieth-century Morocco. For example, he describes how infertile women in several different tribes eat the flesh or drink the urine of male puppies to become pregnant with male offspring. Westermarck, *Ritual and Belief in Morocco* (London: Macmillan, 1926), 1:585. He also describes how "the *jnūn* help people to practice witchcraft . . . A person who for this purpose wants to summon a Jewish *jinn* does all sorts of disgusting and forbidden things. He eats his own excrements, and dirties his clothes with them; drinks his own urine if thirsty, and sprinkles his clothes with it; puts his right slipper on his left foot and his left slipper on his right foot, and wears all his clothes with the inside out; makes an ablution with urine, and prays with his face turned in the wrong direction, that is, not toward Mecca. He writes

> For the midwives in our time are rarely careful about avoiding impurities. The midwife comes in contact with the parturition blood and other impurities and then touches the newborn and his clothes – all without washing off the impurities with pure water. This is not permitted, yet some of the midwives let the newborn suck on their [the midwives'] fingers which have been in contact with impurities and claim that it is healthy for this and that, but this is all a lie and falsehood and contrary to the pure *sunna* . . . Some of them, when childbirth is difficult for the woman, take out the center of a loaf of bread and put mouse-dung inside it and they have her eat it until it is all gone. They explain this with the claim that this will ease the birth for her. This is without a doubt stupidity, for [the Prophet] is known to have said: God, Great and Sublime, does not grant healing by means of something which is forbidden.[638]

Other jurists, when describing the care of children and the care of women in the midst of childbirth, caution against the folk-practice of manipulating objects and texts to uncover information or to bend supernatural powers to the will of the practitioner in order to effect healing.[639]

The jurists also describe women turning to the services of men who heal bodily injuries, or possibly inflict them, by means of the written word. For example, Ibn al-Ukhuwwa (a contemporary of Ibn al-Qayyim and Ibn al-Ḥājj) writes in his *ḥisba* manual about the services offered by astrologers and letter-writers. Among the services they provide, in addition to reading horoscopes and writing correspondence, is magical control over sickness:

> They must be constrained from engaging in sorcery. They must not write for any person any spirit-magic such as love-sickness, agitation, hemorrhage, ophthalmia, tongue-tie, etc. For doing witchcraft is forbidden, and when a person is found to be doing it, rebuke him so as to deter others . . . When one of them is found violating these restrictions and writing what is forbidden, the *muḥtasib* must remove him and chastise him, and if he returns, rebuke him again.[640]

Ibn al-Ukhuwwa further says that "most of those who frequent them are women." For this reason, rather than marginalizing the presence of these practitioners, Ibn al-Ukhuwwa instructs the market inspector to insist that astrologers

---

on a paper the name of the *jinn* he wants to summon inside a *jedwal*, in accordance with the instructions he gets from a book on a subject; burns the paper together with some coriander seed, and in burning it recites the name of the *jinn* and some passages from the Koran with the word Allāh and other holy words exchanged for *šitan*; and continues this recitation until the *jinn* comes." Ibid., 1:360.

638 Ibn al-Ḥājj, *al-Madkhal*, 3/4:221.

639 E.g. al-Saffārīnī, *Ghidhā' al-albāb*, 22; Ibn Mufliḥ, *Ādāb*, 3:66; and Ibn al-Jawzī, *Aḥkām al-nisā'*, 99.

640 Ibn al-Ukhuwwa, *The Ma'ālim al-qurba fī aḥkām al-ḥisba*, 183–84 in Arabic.

and letter-writers sit in the middle of the highway, rather than in isolated alleys or indoors. The public placement of the letter-writers makes it easier to monitor those men who loiter near them for the purpose of making contact with members of the opposite sex.

In spite of its supposed prevalence, the 'ulamā' do not accord folk medicine the same respect that they accord the medicine of the physicians, and so they have less need to define its precise relationship to the Islamic system of knowledge. In high medicine, the great physicians such as Galen represent an alternative source of authority to the Prophet Muḥammad. This is not the case with folk medicine. Yet folk medicine presents a challenge of its own to Islam. Instead of representing an alternative to Muḥammad's therapeutic knowledge, it represents an alternative to God's power over the world itself and an alternative to the notion that Islamic ritual as propounded by the 'ulamā' is the best way to defend oneself from the dangers posed by the world.

The problem with the use of sorcery and the eating of unclean foods is explained by Ibn Mufliḥ. People "believe that these are modes of treatment and healing, when in fact they result in polytheism (*shirk*), because people attempt to repel the fates which have been set down for them, and they request [beings] other than God to repel the suffering which He himself ordained."[641] One modern scholar, in characterizing the views of Ibn Qayyim al-Jawziyya, frames the theological problem thus: "[Ibn Qayyim al-Jawziyya views] the occultic sciences as so many pantheistic demons eating away at Islam's spiritual innards, where God's undivided omnipotence was parceled out to stars and birds, and elemental nature was charged with a transmutational potency that appeared to be self-sustained."[642]

In the face of this *shirk*, the jurists have two options: either to ban all magical practices or to find a means of accommodating them in an Islamic framework. The problem with banning them is that much of the *ḥadīth* literature supports the idea that supernatural forces influence health and that the Prophet's companions made use of incantations and talismans and other elements found in folk medicine.[643] Therefore almost all jurists instead find ways of Islamicizing the magical impetus. Texts and images that are not in Arabic, or are not understood, are prohibited, as is the invocation of beings other than God.[644] But it is

641 Ibn Mufliḥ, *Ādāb*, 3:66, citing the opinion of Ibn al-Athīr from the *Nihāya*.
642 John W. Livingston, "Science and the Occult in the Thinking of Ibn Qayyim al-Jawziyya" *Journal of the American Oriental Society* 112 (1992), 600.
643 For some examples, see Ibn Qayyim al-Jawziyya, *Ṭibb*, 127–46, 276–79 and al-Dhahabī's *al-Ṭibb al-nabawī*, 276–7.
644 Ibn Mufliḥ, *al-Ādāb al-shar'iyya*, 2:334.

acceptable and encouraged to recite Qur'ānic verses, to write them down on bowls and paper in mystical patterns, and to perform rituals with such objects for medicinal or prophylactic purposes. Some authorities even instruct non-Muslim medical practitioners (who treat Muslims) to recite Qur'ānic verses in their healing rituals, despite the general opposition to non-Islamic use of the Qur'ān.[645] For example, in the *Muwaṭṭa*, Mālik b. Anas reports an interaction between the first caliph, Abū Bakr, and his daughter 'Ā'isha, the Prophet's widow. "Abū Bakr al-Ṣiddīq visited 'Ā'isha while she had a [health] complaint and a Jewish woman was reciting an incantation over her. Abū Bakr said, 'Recite an incantation over her using the Book of God.'" On the basis of this report al-Shāfi'ī rules that non-Muslims can use Qur'ānic-based incantations when treating a Muslim.[646]

Several examples of Islamicized incantations and talismans for childbirth purposes can be found in Prophetic medicine books and other literature produced by jurists. Muḥammad ibn Aḥmad al-Saffārīnī's (d. 1188/1774) descriptions list previously known talismans[647] but also include the occasional diagram[648]:

> Imām Aḥmad said: For a woman experiencing difficult childbirth one writes on a bowl or something clean, "In the name of God the Benevolent the Merciful, there is no god but God, the Compassionate the Noble, the Sublime God, the Master of the Throne, the Great, praise be to God the Master of the Worlds: 'On the day they see it, it will be as if they had tarried only for an evening or its forenoon.' (Qur'ān 79:46[649]) 'On the day when they see what they have been promised, it will seem to them as they had lingered for only an hour of a single day. A proclamation.' (Qur'ān 46:35)". Then she should drink from it and anoint her bosom with what remains.
>
> Aḥmad, may God be pleased with him, reported: These words come from Ibn 'Abbās, may God be pleased with them both, and Ibn al-Sunnī cited it in *'Amal al-yawm wa'l-layla.*[650]
>
> And from al-Dīnawarī's *Kitāb al-Mujālasa* . . . "Jesus son of Mary encountered a cow whose child was stuck in her belly. She said: 'O word of God, call upon God to deliver me.'

---

645 A.S. Tritton, *Caliphs and their Non-Muslim Subjects* (London: F. Cass, 1970), 8.

646 Malik b. Anas, *al-Muwaṭṭa*, 50 (*al-'ayn*):4 no. 11. Al-Shāfi'ī, *Kitāb al-umm*, 7:241.

647 These two prescriptions are identical to the ones found in Ibn Qayyim al-Jawziyya, *Ṭibb*, 277. A recipe fragment from thirteenth-century Quṣayr also uses Qur'ān 84, see Li Guo, *Commerce, Culture, and Community in a Red Sea Port in the Thirteenth Century* (Leiden: Brill, 2004), 311. The fragment says: "For a woman who wants to [. . .] a child." Guo understands this recipe to be a fertility charm, but it seems more likely to me that it is a charm to be used during labor.

648 al-Saffārīnī, *Ghidhā' al-albāb*, 2:23.

649 Translations of the Qur'ānic passages are from Alan Jones, *The Qur'ān*, 556.

650 Abū Bakr Aḥmad ibn Muḥammad al-Dīnawarī, known as Ibn al-Sunnī (d. 364/974), *Kitāb 'amal al-yawm wa'l-layla* (Beirut: Mu'assasat al-Kutub al-Thaqāfiyya, 1988).

He said: 'O You who creates soul from soul and brings out soul from soul, deliver her.' And she cast out what was in her belly.'" When the woman's childbirth is difficult, this should be written for her.[651]

Al-Tatā'ī al-Mālikī mentions the following in his commentary on the preface of the *Mukhtaṣar:*[652] One of the people of knowledge who wrote this verse and tied it to a woman experiencing difficult childbirth set it in this form. I have seen in one collection that it is supposed to be tied to her left thigh and this is the diagram of the placement of the verse.[653]

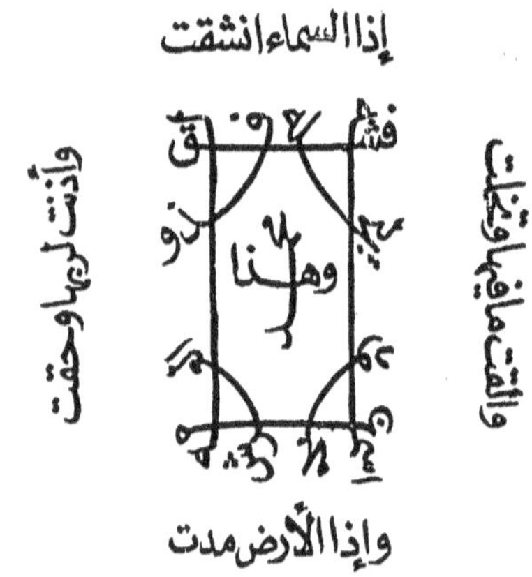

When the heaven is split asunder
And listens to her Lord as she must
When the earth is spread out
And casts out what is in her and is empty (Q 84:1–4)

He derived for him,
in order to honor him,
part of His name.
Thus the Lord of the Throne is called
Maḥmūd, and this one Muḥammad
(*Ḥassān ibn Thābit)

It is easy to appreciate the aptness of the Qur'ānic verse used in this talisman. Its description of the physical contortions of heaven and earth on judgment day is readily applicable to the contortions of childbirth, and the feminine language applied to the heavens is easily transferable to the laboring woman. The purpose of the poetic verse by Ḥassān ibn Thābit praising the Prophet Muḥammad is somewhat less clear. One possibility, however, is that the poem at the center of the talisman is there to replace a picture of a supernatural being. Thus a textual invocation of Muḥammad substitutes for a physical depiction and invocation of a spirit.

651 Abū Bakr al-Dīnawarī (d. 333/944), *al-Mujālasa wa-jawāhir al-'ilm* (Frankfurt am Main: Veröffentlichungen des Institutes für Geschichte der arabisch-islamischen Wissenschaften, 1986), no. 1996.

652 Muḥammad b. Ibrāhīm b. Khalīl al-Tatā'ī al-Mālikī (d. 942/1535).

653 The translation of the poetic verse by Ḥassān ibn Thābit is from Annemarie Schimmel, *And Muhammad is His Messenger: the veneration of the Prophet in Islamic piety* (Chapel Hill: University of North Carolina Press, 1985), 106.

There is a general consensus among the jurists that the use of texts in amulets and healing rituals is acceptable, so long as the texts are derived from Islamic scripture. Ibn al-Ḥājj, however, encourages people to recite elaborate prayers in conjunction with the use of Qur'ānic verses, prayers which explicitly distance magical rituals from the trappings of polytheism. Here is one such prayer:

> Write, "O God, You are the giver of life and death, You are the Creator and you are the Maker, and You send tribulation and You give dispensation, and You are the Healer . . . O God, I ask You with Your beautiful names and Your supreme attributes, O You in whose hands lie tribulation and dispensation and healing and treatment, I ask You with the miraculous [verses] of Your Prophet Muḥammad . . . there is no harm except Your harm and no benefit except Your benefit . . . and no wrongdoing committed by man can get past You, and no jinn can be fortified with a charm by means of Your perfect speech which they cannot get past, nor can any sin by man or jinn. I ask You . . . to heal him and to pardon him and to rebound what afflicts him upon his enemies." The way to use [this prayer] is to write it in saffron on a clean vessel or paper, then to wash the bowl in water or dissolve the paper in water, and then to drink the water completely. Then he should place his hands in the remaining moisture in the bowl and use them to wipe as much of his body as he can.[654]

The actions prescribed by Ibn al-Ḥājj in this passage have all the hallmarks of magical healing. The incantation is written on a medicine bowl using a specific ink and the patient ingests and anoints himself with the "substance" of the text. The purpose of ingesting a substance and anointing the body with it is to change something about the body in order to heal it. The purpose of performing an incantation is to exert control over a supernatural being and to compel it to act in one's favor. However, this prayer is a theological declaration which subverts the implied meaning of the ritual. It denies that people can change and heal their own bodies[655] and it denies that God can be compelled to do the bidding of the one performing the enchantment. In this way Ibn al-Ḥājj preserves the physical content of magical medicine while Islamicizing its verbal content.

When the jurists consider the question of how a Muslim ought to go about obtaining medical treatment, they evaluate medical options in relative terms. Few things are absolutely forbidden or commanded, but they urge Muslim patients to choose between better and worse options. What makes a particular treatment better or worse is not just the objective practice of the treatment, but rather which authorities and epistemological systems the patient acknowl-

654 Ibn al-Ḥājj, *al-Madkhal*, 3/4:327–8.
655 This language closely resembles the language by certain *mutakallimūn* in subordinating medicine to Divine will and occasionalism. See, for example, 'Abd al-Jabbār al-Hamadhānī's *Tathbīt dalā'il al-nubūwa* (Cairo: Dār al-Muṣṭafā, 2006) 2:615–16.

edges in choosing that treatment. What is important to the jurists is that medical knowledge is acquired, and medical treatment is practiced, through an Islamic conduit. However, when the patient is a Muslim woman, the concern to Islamicize the culture surrounding medicine runs up against the value placed on gender separation. This creates a conflict of values for the jurists.

7 Heterodoxy and Healthcare Among Women

The jurists who viewed the choice of medical practitioner as religiously and socially fraught did not seek to ban religiously problematic practitioners. When seeking medical assistance they gave preference to medical practitioners from some demographics over others, but they valued the preservation of life and health more. Indeed, it was precisely because life and health were so valued that there was a high degree of tolerance for inter-cultural interactions in medical situations, and so there was also increased opportunity for problematic interactions. We have seen evidence of such tolerance in practice in *ḥisba* manuals, belles-lettres, and documents from the Cairo Geniza. And we have seen theoretical tolerance in the example of the Prophet Muḥammad and his companions turning to both Arab and non-Arab doctors, and Muslim and non-Muslim practitioners, during their illness.

Respect for medical skill did not, however, preclude jurists from considering better and worse identities for medical care providers. Rather, they discussed and calculated whom it was more or less preferable for a patient to turn to for medical attention. For female patients, this calculation came with added complications, and the treatment of infertile women came with even more. Modesty-based restrictions were most easily relaxed in cases of life-threatening emergency and old age – two situations which did not usually apply to women battling infertility. Infertility involved neither extreme pain nor imminent death and thus did not constitute an obvious medical emergency according to Islamic law.[656]

---

656 These are the standards used by the Ḥanafī school to determine if there is a medical necessity which makes it permissible for Muslims to have their sexual organs examined by members of the opposite sex. See Ibn ʿĀbidīn (d. 1252/1836), *Ḥāshiyat Radd al-muḥtār* (Cairo: al-Bābī al-Ḥalabī, 1966), 6:371. The Ḥanafī jurist ʿAbd Allāh b. Maḥmūd al-Mawṣilī (d. 683/1284) says that the same circumstances which permit a Muslim to drink wine and eat the flesh of pigs also apply in judging when it is permissible for a woman to be examined by a male physician. al-Mawṣilī, *al-Ikhtiyār li-taʿlīl al-Mukhtār* (Beirut: Dār al-Risāla al-ʿĀlamiyya, 2009), 4:108. I have found no specific medieval reference to infertility as an emergency, but a prominent modern Shāfiʿī jurist, Nūḥ ʿAlī Salmān al-Quḍāh (d. 2010) the former Grand Mufti of Jordan, has said that infertility does indeed constitute an extenuating medical circumstance and writes, "Necessary treatment . . . includes gynecological examinations for women with fertility problems, which are permissible." N. Keller, *The Reliance of the Traveller: a Classic Manual of Islamic Sacred Law* (Chicago: Sunna Books, 1991), 514. By contrast a Saudi *muftī*, Shaykh ʿAbd Allāh al-Jibrīn, specifically says that infertility is not a medical emergency and hence requires the assistance of a female physician. See *al-Muslimūn* (March 1, 1991), 8, referred to in Vardit Rispler-Chaim, *Islamic Medical Ethics in the Twentieth Century* (Leiden: Brill, 1993), 63. In a similar *fatwā*, al-Jibrīn advises a husband that it is impermissible for him

https://doi.org/10.1515/9783110596588-014

Moreover, more often than not, infertility must have been a long-term problem in a way that a life-threatening disease was not. If an initial attempt at a cure proved unsuccessful, an infertile patient would have had the time and motivation to look further afield and seek another practitioner or system of healing for a more effective treatment. Lastly, midwifery and medicine pertaining to the genitals was subject to special religious restrictions on interactions between Muslim women and non-Muslim women.

In determining who should theoretically be the person to provide medical attention to a female patient, the jurists placed a value both on maintaining boundaries between members of the opposite sex and in promoting Muslim practitioners. As is true of the discussion about medicine generally (described in chapter 6) texts about women's medical care speak less of commanded and forbidden medical practitioners and more about preferable and undesirable options. Most often, juristic preference for medical practitioners was expressed in terms of general dicta: "a Muslim before a non-Muslim" and "a woman before a man" should examine a female Muslim patient.[657] I.e. a female Muslim practitioner was the most favored healthcare provider for a Muslim woman, and a male non-Muslim was the most unfavorable provider. But what did the jurists want to happen when the choice was less clear-cut?

The Shāfiʿī jurists in particular are interested in teasing out the relative weight of the various factors that go into choosing a practitioner, doing so in their commentaries on al-Nawawī's (d. 676/1278) *Minhāj al-ṭālibīn*, which states that men can treat women, and women can treat men, "provided that there is no woman to treat the woman or man to treat the man. And there should be no *dhimmī* while a Muslim is available."[658] The Syrian Shāfiʿī jurist Shihāb al-Dīn al-Adhraʿī (d. 783/1381) for example, teaches that an infidel woman is preferable to a Muslim man and that under most circumstances she is preferable to a kinsman (*maḥram*) when it comes to viewing a Muslim woman's body. However, in cases where the practitioner must examine the woman's genitals, rather than a non-Muslim female practitioner, al-Adhraʿī gives preference to any kind of "quasi-kin" (*naḥw maḥram*), a term which appears to refer to slaves, eunuchs,

---

to present his wife to a male physician for the purposes of diagnosing and relieving female infertility. ʿAbd al-ʿAzīz Ibn Bāz et al., *Fatāwā Islamiyya* (Riyadh: Darussalam, 2001), 140.

657 al-Shirbīnī, *Mughnī al-muḥtāj*, 3:133. ʿAbd al-Hamīd al-Shirwānī, *Ḥawāshī al-Shirwānī wa-Ibn Qāsim al-ʿAbbādī ʿalā Tuḥfat al-muḥtāj bi-sharḥ al-Minhāj li-Ibn Ḥajar al-Haytamī* (Beirut: Dār al-Kutub al-ʿIlmiyya, 1996), 9:39 – 40.

658 Jalāl al-Dīn ibn Aḥmad al-Maḥallī (d. 864/1459), *Kanz al-rāghibīn sharḥ Minhāj al-ṭālibīn*.

and young boys who are not yet pubescent.[659] He further designates a eunuch as preferable to a pubescent boy (*murāhiq*), who in Shāfiʿī jurisprudence is described as an older boy who is still a minor although developed enough to be capable of narrating to others what he sees.[660] However al-Adhraʿī concludes that he prefers "the most skilled person – even if he is of the opposite gender and religion" to other practitioners.[661] Al-Adhraʿī's final conclusion favors skill above all but still takes into consideration gender, religion, and kinship. He also differentiates between general medical care and care involving viewing the genitals. In the latter case he claims that a non-Muslim woman providing genital-related care is more problematic than having certain males provide medical care.

Al-Adhraʿī's system has some gaps; he does not explain precisely how he situates non-Muslim kinsmen and male quasi-kin in this system. The Shāfiʿī jurist al-Bulqīnī (d. 805/1403) describes more clearly the following order of preference in seeking out medical care for a female Muslim patient:

> A female Muslim, then a Muslim boy who is not pubescent (*ghayr murāhiq*), then one who is pubescent (*murāhiq*), then an infidel non-pubescent boy, then a pubescent one, then an infidel woman, then a Muslim *maḥram* (kinsman), then an infidel *maḥram*, then a non-kin Muslim man, then an infidel one.[662]

The jurist Shihāb al-Dīn al-Qalyūbī's (d. 1079/1659) order of preference adds another layer, taking into account the notion of kinswomen, and differentiating between them and a female practitioner who is not closely related to the patient. Al-Qalyūbī writes:

> For a Muslim woman (patient) a Muslim female kinswoman (*maḥram*) takes precedence, then a Muslim female non-*maḥram*, then a Muslim boy who is not pubescent, then a *dhimmī* non-pubescent boy, then an adult male Muslim *maḥram*, then an adult male infidel *maḥram*, then a Muslim eunuch, then an infidel eunuch, then a *dhimmī* female *maḥram*, then a *dhimmī* female non-*maḥram*, then a Muslim pubescent boy, then a non-Muslim pubescent boy, then an adult non-maḥram Muslim, then an adult non-maḥram infidel. The goal is to give precedence to members of the same gender over others, and to *maḥrams*

---

659 ʿAbd al-Hamīd al-Shirwānī, *Ḥawāshī al-Shirwānī wa-Ibn Qāsim al-ʿAbbādī ʿalā Tuḥfat al-muḥtāj bi-sharḥ al-Minhāj li-Ibn Ḥajar al-Haytamī* (Beirut: Dār al-Kutub al-ʿIlmiyya, 1996), 9:40.
660 E. Alschech, "Out of Sight and Therefore Out of Mind: Early Sunnī Islamic Modesty Regulations and the Creation of Spheres of Privacy," *Journal of Near Eastern Studies* 66 (2007):282.
661 al-Adhraʿī's opinion appears in Ibn Ḥajar al-Haytamī's (d. 973/1567) commentary on al-Nawawī's *Minhāj al-ṭālibīn* known as *Tuḥfat al-muḥtāj bi-sharḥ al-Minhāj*. See al-Shirwānī, *Ḥawāshī al-Shirwānī*, 9:40
662 al-Shirwānī, *Ḥawāshī al-Shirwānī*, 9:40.

> over others, and to those who have rights to see more over others. [And of these criteria] one who possesses the same gender takes precedence, then *maḥram* status, and then the same religion.[663]

The modern commentator ʿAbd al-Ḥamīd al-Shirwānī analyzes al-Bulqīnī's list with some concern and surprise, since some of it clashes with general modesty regulations.

> [In al-Bulqīnī's list] the Muslim pubescent boy takes precedence over the infidel non-pubescent boy, despite the former being like a non-kinsman[664] compared to the latter, since a [non-pubescent boy] is usually treated as a *maḥram*[665] or like an *ʿadim* (mental deficient)! [I.e. al-Shirwānī finds it odd that a male older boy, who is usually treated as a foreign male when it comes to nudity, is preferable to an infidel younger boy who is usually treated as not possessing sexual awareness.] As for the infidel pubescent boy taking precedence to the infidel woman: what he has chosen follows the ruling in the *Minhāj*. [I.e. al-Shirwānī identifies this as in keeping with the legal tradition.] He discriminates between the Muslim and the infidel *maḥram* even though they are equal in terms of viewing [a kinswoman]. And he considers a pubescent boy, whether Muslim or infidel, to take precedence over a *maḥram*, whether Muslim or infidel, even though the former is like a non-kinsman . . . Wouldn't the infidel woman take precedence over the pubescent boy, be he a Muslim or an infidel? For a pubescent boy is like an adult when it comes to [the legality of his] gaze, while an infidel woman has [the legal right] to gaze upon what is exposed in the course of daily life . . .[666]

Below is a visual representation of al-Bulqīnī's and al-Qalyūbī's lists, with the parenthetical information based on al-Shirwānī's comments.

---

663 Shihāb al-Dīn al-Qalyūbī, *Hāshiyatā al-Imāmayn al-muḥaqqiqayn al-mudaqqiqayn al-Shaykh Shihāb al-Dīn al-Qalyūbī wa'l-Shaykh ʿUmayra ʿalā sharḥ Jalāl al-Dīn al-Mahallī ʿalā Minhāj al-ṭālibīn* (Beirut: Dār al-Kutub al-ʿIlmiyya), 3:322.

664 There are two views within the Shāfiʿī school about the status of a *murāhiq:* one is that in his presence a woman should cover herself to the same extent as she would in the presence of a kinsman. The other, which al-Nawawī prefers, is that he is to be considered like an adult non-kinsman, and she must cover herself accordingly, see al-Nawawī, *Rawḍat al-ṭālibīn*, 7:22. and al-Shirwānī, *Ḥawāshī al-Shirwānī*, 9:30.

665 *al-Mawsūʿa al-fiqhiyya*, 31:52.

666 Al-Shirwānī, *Ḥawāshī al-Shirwānī*, 9:40.

Al-Bulqīnī's order of preference	Female	Kin	Muslim
1. Muslim **woman**	**Yes**	Either	Yes
2. Muslim young boy	n/a	(Yes)	Yes
3. Muslim older boy	(No)	No	Yes
4. Non-Muslim young boy	n/a	(Yes)	No
5. Non-Muslim older boy	(No)	No	No
6. Non-Muslim **woman**	**Yes**	No	No
7. Muslim kinsman	No	Yes	Yes
8. Non-Muslim kinsman	No	Yes	No
9. Muslim non-kinsman	No	No	Yes
10. Non-Muslim non-kinsman	No	No	No

al-Qalyūbī's order of preference	Female	Kin	Muslim
1. Muslim **kinswoman**	**Yes**	Yes	Yes
2. Muslim non-**kinswoman**	**Yes**	No	Yes
3. Muslim younger boy	n/a	Quasi	Yes
4. Non-Muslim younger boy	n/a	Quasi	No
5. Muslim adult kinsman	No	Yes	Yes
6. Non-Muslim adult kinsman	No	Yes	No
7. Muslim eunuch	Ambiguous	Quasi	Yes
8. Non-Muslim eunuch	Ambiguous	Quasi	No
9. Non-Muslim **kinswoman**	**Yes**	Yes	No
10. Non-Muslim non-**kinswoman**	**Yes**	No	No
11. Muslim older boy	(No)	No	Yes
12. Non-Muslim older boy	(No)	No	No
13. Muslim adult non-kinsman	No	No	Yes
14. Non-Muslim adult non-kinsman	No	No	No

Many aspects of these orders of preference may at first seem counterintuitive. Both jurists prefer that a non-Muslim male child or a non-Muslim eunuch serve in a gynecological capacity rather than a non-Muslim woman. Al-Qalyubī even prefers that a non-Muslim adult kinsman serve rather than a non-Muslim woman, meaning that even though neither are Muslim, the male relative is preferable to the non-related woman!

In these lists neither gender, nor kinship, nor religious status take absolute precedence in determining the most appropriate medical support for a Muslim woman. It is clear that a male, non-Muslim, non-kinsman is the least appropriate person for a Muslim woman to interact with. But once that case is excluded, we have examples of gender trumping kinship (a Muslim non-kinswoman is preferable to a male kinsman), but also of kinship trumping gender (al-Qalyūbī prefers a kinsman to a non-Muslim woman, and both jurists prefer a young boy – who is a quasi-kin – to a non-Muslim woman). Usually gender trumps religion (a non-Muslim woman is preferable to an adult Muslim non-kinsman), but sometimes religion trumps gender (al-Bulqīnī prefers a Muslim older boy to a non-Muslim woman). Kinship can trump religion (a non-Muslim kinsman is preferable to Muslim non-kinsman), and sometimes religion trumps kinship (for al-Bulqīnī a Muslim older boy – who usually has the status of a non-kinsman when it comes to issues of nudity – is preferable to a non-Muslim young boy – whose status is usually that of someone who triggers few or no nudity restrictions at all). Most interestingly, both jurists are less inclined to resort to non-Muslim women than to non-Muslim boys and eunuchs.[667]

What accounts for these complicated orders of preference and what do they mean? In making these lists, the Shāfi'ī jurists are engaging in a theoretical intellectual exercise of limited influence. But this exercise does not exist in a vacuum, rather it draws on a wide-ranging and much-quoted body of texts and discussions about Muslim women's medical and intellectual interactions with men, with non-Muslim women, and with their fellow Muslim women. Such discussions are the topic of this chapter.

Muslim female patients, male practitioners and the preservation of sexual boundaries

The Shāfi'ī, Ḥanafī,[668] and Ḥanbalī[669] schools of law all permit a male physician to view and touch a woman's genitals if there are no alternative medical practitioners available. By comparison, the Mālikī school uniformly prohibits male physicians from doing so.[670] Non-Mālikī discussions about who ought to attend

---

667 I have been unable to find references to eunuch physicians. However, an Arabic Cairo Geniza document from the 6–7th / 12–13th centuries contains a question to a *mufti* about the appropriateness of having a trusted Jewish eye-doctor "who has no beard" visiting the household of Muslims, specifically the *ḥaram*. It is possible that the physician's beardlessness is mentioned to signify that he is not quite a man, and is perhaps a youth. Cairo Geniza document Or. 1080.15.62 in Khan, *Arabic Legal and Administrative Documents in the Cambridge Genizah Collections*, 296.
668 *Fatāwā al-hindiyya* (Būlāq: al-Maṭba'a al-Kubrā al-Amīriyya, 1892), 5:330.
669 Ibn Qudāma (d. 620/1223), *al-Mughnī* (Cairo: Maktabat al-Qāhira, 1968), 7:101 and Abū Ya'lā ibn al-Farrā' (d. 458/1066), *al-Jāmi' al-ṣaghīr* (Riyadh: Dār Aṭlas, 2000), 398. In the *Kashshāf al-qinā'*: "A doctor may view and touch whatever it is necessary for him to view and touch, even her genitals and inside her, because this is a matter of obvious need, even if he is a non-Muslim." Manṣūr ibn Yūnus ibn Idrīs al-Buhūtī, *Kashshāf al-qinā'* (Beirut: Dār al-Fikr, 1982), 5:13.
670 Aḥmad Muḥammad Kan'ān, *al-Mawsū'a al-ṭibbiyya al-fiqhiyya* (Beirut: Dār al-Nafā'is, 2000), 748. The Mālikī jurist al-Nafrāwī (d. 1125/1714), writes that it is preferable for a male doctor

a sick woman speak of an order of preference or precedence given which medical practitioners are immediately available. These texts presume a pressing medical necessity or emergency, or else a legal need to establish female virginity or pubescence.[671] One exception is al-Nawawī (d. 676/1278) who explicitly allows male practitioners to view the bodies of female patients under non-emergency circumstances, such as for the purposes of medical education. He writes, "where it is forbidden to look it is also forbidden to touch, but both are permitted for bleeding, cupping and treating. I say, looking is also permitted for teaching and for testifying."[672] Otherwise, a medical necessity which would theoretically allow a male physician to view the genitals of a female patient is usually defined as having the same high bar that would permit a Muslim to drink wine or eat the flesh of pigs, or it is defined as occurring when a person is in extreme physical pain or in mortal danger.[673]

Even as most jurists permit male practitioners to treat female patients in medical situations where such interaction is a "necessity," they still describe male practitioners attending female patients as an unfortunate, necessary evil. They express a concern about the sexual invasiveness of a man's gaze, describing it as weighing more heavily on a female patient than a female practitioner's gaze does.[674] The possibility of the development of an illicit sexual relationship is not generally mentioned as a concern, since it is understood that a family member will also be present in the room, rather it is the gaze that constitutes a form of harm in and of itself.

---

to operate by having a woman look at the genitals and describe them to him, since "I think no one says that a man's viewing a woman's genitals is permissible . . . If that which is witnessed is... in the area of her back or belly or somewhere else outside of her genitals, no one but women may witness it, and for a man to view it is not permissible even if the woman wishes it. But if it is in her genitals and the woman is sure that there is an injury, there should be women to look at her genitals and their testimony is accepted. He [the doctor] should follow Khalīl's direction and come with two women to witness for him from two viewpoints." Aḥmad b. Ghunaym al-Nafrāwī, *al-Fawākih al-dawānī* (Cairo: Muṣṭafā al-Bābī al-Ḥalabī, 1955), 2:367.

671 Muṣṭafā al-Suyūṭī (d. 1243/1827), the Ḥanbalī, also mentions in this context that a hand-amputator may also view the body of his "patient." al-Suyūṭī, *Maṭālib ūlī al-nuhā fī sharḥ ghāyat al-muntahā* (Damascus: al-Maktab al-Islāmī, 1961), 5:15.

672 Al-Nawawī, *Minhāj al-ṭalibīn* in al-Shirbīnī (d. 977/1570), *Mughnī al-muḥtāj ilā maʿrifat maʿānī alfāẓ al-Minhāj* (Cairo: Maṭbaʿat Muṣṭafā al-Bābī al-Ḥalabī, 1958), 3:132.

673 ʿAbd Allāh b. Maḥmūd al-Mawṣilī (d. 683/1284), a Ḥanafī, says the necessity in this case is the same as the necessities which make it permissible to drink wine and eat the flesh of pigs (al-Mawṣilī, *Al-Ikhtiyār li-taʿlīl al-Mukhtār*, 4:108). Ibn ʿĀbidīn says the school agrees that a male physician can treat a female patient's genitalia only if she is in unbearable pain or might die. Ibn ʿĀbidīn, *Ḥāshiyat Radd al-muḥtār*, 9:533. Cf. *Fatāwā al-Hindiyya*, 5:330.

674 al-Shirbīnī, *Mughnī al-muḥtāj*, 3:133.

The jurists also worry that an inappropriate medical practitioner might compromise his or her patient's modesty by describing her body to a third party. Such a possibility is mentioned particularly with regard to non-Muslim practitioners, both men and women, who are not *sharīʿa*-bound to guard the privacy of their patients. We have already seen an impassioned declaration of this concern in a passage by Ibn al-Ḥājj:

> The sixth reason [why it is unacceptable for a non-Muslim doctor to treat a Muslim even if a Muslim doctor serves as a second physician] is that it is detestable and abominable if the patient is a Muslim woman, because the infidel is the enemy of God, and he would enjoy viewing her and palpating her. It has already been said that a Muslim woman is not permitted to reveal any part of her body to a Christian woman or Jewish woman. If this is true regarding a woman, how much more so regarding a man? For a Muslim woman would need to reveal some of her body so that [the physician] could see the part that hurts, and this would be welcomed by an enemy of God and an enemy of his Prophet . . . Even if nothing happens except that the infidel describes to someone a Muslim's wife or daughter or [demonstrates] some other kind of their many reprehensible tendencies, it would be too much for Islamic protective jealousy (*ghayra*), even if it were not forbidden in the noble Law, God forbid. If someone were to say: "But the 'ulamā' have permitted uncovering nakedness before a physician whether the patient is a man or a woman!" the response is that this is the case when there is a necessity, and there is no necessity that calls for inviting an infidel when there exists a Muslim physician.[675]

Ibn al-Ḥājj makes a number of arguments in this passage. The first is that a non-Muslim male physician constitutes a risk because he may take sexual pleasure in viewing and touching a Muslim woman. However, even if a non-Muslim physician does not himself directly engage in this behavior, there is a fear he will describe his patient to someone else, which would be intolerable. He also claims that a Muslim woman is forbidden from revealing any part of her body to even a non-Muslim woman, a train of thought that will be discussed below. The central argument in this passage is thus an attack on Muslim/non-Muslim medical interaction, not on male/female interaction. It is precisely because male doctors are assumed to treat women that Ibn al-Ḥājj sees it as important that those doctors be Muslim. Ibn al-Ḥājj is not suggesting that most of his fellow Muslim Cairenes see the world as he does, or practice as he would wish them to. Indeed, Ibn al-Ḥājj himself admits that many of his fellow Muslims see it as perfectly Islamically justifiable for both non-Muslim male physicians and female practitioners to view and treat female Muslim patients. Rather, he argues against his fellow Muslims who view illness as an occasion which makes it acceptable to cross the boundaries of both confession and gender.

675 Ibn al-Ḥājj, *al-Madkhal*, 3/4:318.

Ibn al-Ḥājj is not, however, a lone voice operating on the margins of Islamic thought. In chapter 6 we discussed others who held similar views regarding non-Muslim physicians, i.e. male practitioners. The legal position of the non-Muslim female medical practitioner who treats Muslim female patients is more complex. Three different legal factors come into play, and it is this complexity that accounts for the odd orders of preference articulated by al-Qalyubī and others. The first legal factor relates to nudity, specifically to rules about the extent to which Muslim women must cover themselves in the presence of non-Muslim women. The second factor is the general legal principle that "necessity makes permitted" the setting aside of nudity prohibitions. Childbirth is considered to be such a necessity. The third legal factor is one we have not yet examined, and that is the tradition established by the companions of the Prophet that specifically prohibits a Muslim woman from allowing a non-Muslim woman to see her genitals and serve as her midwife during childbirth.[676] As we shall see, in the interplay of these three factors, modesty restrictions based on sexual threats are intertwined with modesty restrictions based on cultural threats.

Muslim female patients, non-Muslim female practitioners, and the preservation of sexual and intellectual boundaries

The extent to which a Muslim woman should be willing to expose herself to the gaze of a non-Muslim woman is a matter of some debate among the medieval jurists. While Islamic jurisprudence regarding nudity and modesty does not differentiate between Muslim and non-Muslim male viewers with regard to the male Muslim body, nudity and modesty between women is another matter. Juristic debates about Muslim women's modesty with respect to non-Muslim women take as their starting point varying interpretations of Qur'ān 24:31.

> Say to the believing women, that they cast down their eyes and guard their private parts, and reveal not their adornment . . . save to their husbands, or their fathers, or their husbands' fathers, or their sons, or their husbands' sons, or their brothers, or their brothers' sons, or their sisters' sons, *or their women*, or what their right hands own, or such men as attend them, not having sexual desire, or children who have not yet attained knowledge of women's private parts . . .[677]

676 Ibn Kathīr, *Tafsīr al-Qur'ān al-'aẓīm* (Riyadh: Dār Ṭayba lil-Nashr wa'l-Tawzī', 1997), 6:48.
677 Q. 24:31. Translation from A. J. Arberry, *The Koran Interpreted* (London: Allen & Unwin, 1955). The italics are mine.

The phrase "or their women" is interpreted in two ways by the medieval jurists. One interpretation deemphasizes the possessive "their" and understands the verse to mean that a Muslim woman is exempted from covering herself in the presence of women in general, just as she is exempt from covering herself in the presence of male family and household members. In accordance with this interpretation, some jurists permit a non-Muslim woman to view the same parts of the body that a Muslim woman may view. The other interpretation understands "their" (which is grammatically a third person plural feminine possessive adjective) as meaning "those affiliated with" a Muslim woman. Among proponents of this interpretation, the phrase "their women" refers to Muslim women's female co-religionists, since it would be wrong to suggest affiliation with non-Muslim women. Thus women who are non-Muslims are refused admission into a Muslim woman's sphere of intimates.

Both interpretations of the verse can be found among Ḥanbalīs, beginning with Ibn Ḥanbal himself. Both are attributed to him in the *Aḥkām al-nisā'*.

> Muḥammad b. 'Alī told me that al-Athram told him that Abū 'Abdallāh [Ibn Ḥanbal] said: Some people are of the opinion that she should not remove her head cover (*khimār*) in the presence of a Jewish or Christian woman, for [the non-Muslim woman] is not one of "their women." But I am of the opinion only that neither a Jewish woman nor a Christian woman, nor anyone else who is not her fellow [Muslim] woman may view her genitals, nor may they be a midwife to her when she gives birth. But as to viewing [just] her hair, it is not a problem.
>
> Muḥammad b. Abī Hārūn narrated from Isḥāq bin Ibrāhīm who said: I asked Abū 'Abdallāh [ibn Ḥanbal] if a Muslim woman may expose her head in the presence of *dhimmī* women. He said, "She is not permitted to expose her head to *dhimmī* women, because God said 'or their women.'" [Isḥāq bin Ibrāhīm] also said: I heard Abū Abdallāh, when asked about this verse "or their women" say, "The women of the People of the Book – whether Jewish or Christian – may not be midwives for a Muslim woman and may not view her."[678]

According to al-Athram, Ibn Ḥanbal does not, in general, object to non-Muslim women viewing a Muslim woman. However, midwifery and viewing the genitals represent an exception and an extra stringency. According to Isḥāq b. Ibrāhīm, Ibn Ḥanbal objects to non-Muslim women viewing even a Muslim woman's hair, and of course they cannot serve as midwives to her.

In the *Mughnī*, Ibn Qudāma (d. 620/1223) continues to articulate both positions, ascribing them both to Ibn Ḥanbal, but advocates for the less restrictive

678 Ibn Ḥanbal, *Aḥkām al-nisā' 'an al-imām Abī 'Abdallāh Aḥmad ibn Muḥammad ibn Ḥanbal, riwāya Abī Bakr al-Khilāl* (Beirut: Mu'assasat al-Rayyān lil-Ṭibā'a wa'l-Nashr, 2002), 38.

view, meaning that a Muslim woman need not cover herself in the presence of women generally, whether Muslim or non-Muslim. However, even where Ibn Ḥanbal and Ibn Qudāma take the less restrictive position and say that with regard to nudity and sexuality there is no difference between Muslims and non-Muslims, they make an exception with regard to a non-Muslim woman viewing a Muslim woman's genitals, particularly in the context of serving as a midwife during a birth.[679]

> The rule of a woman with a woman is the same as a man with a man. There is no difference between two Muslim women and a Muslim woman with a *dhimmī* woman, just as there is no difference between two Muslim men and a Muslim man with a *dhimmī* man concerning viewing. Aḥmad [ibn Ḥanbal] said "some people rule that [a Muslim woman] may not remove her clothing in the presence of a Jewish or Christian woman, but I rule that [a non-Muslim woman] only cannot look at her genitals and cannot serve as her midwife when she gives birth." However, Aḥmad also has another view: that a Muslim woman cannot remove her head-cover (*khimār*) in the presence of a *dhimmī* woman and cannot enter a bathhouse together with her. And that is the position of Makḥūl and Sulaymān b. Mūsā on His statement "or their women." The first position stems from [the fact] that Jewish and other female infidels would visit with the Prophet's wives and they did not cover themselves, and he did not command them to cover themselves . . . For veiling between men and women happens for a reason that is not present between a Muslim and a non-Muslim woman. So it is not necessary to impose veiling between them, just like between a Muslim and a *dhimmī* man, for veiling is made necessary where there are explicit texts or analogy, and neither of these are present. As regards His statement, "or their women" the likely intention is "all women."[680]

Among medieval jurists, the Ḥanbalīs generally take the position that a non-Muslim woman is no different from a Muslim woman with respect to nudity, i.e. the laws are parallel to those pertaining to nudity and modesty between men, meaning that only the area of the body between the navel and knees must be concealed.[681] By contrast, most Mālikīs[682] and Shāfiʿīs (with the promi-

---

679 However, one nineteenth-century Ḥanbalī source does say that, if necessary (not explained), a non-Muslim midwife is permitted to deliver a child. al-Suyūṭī, *Maṭālib ūlī al-nuhā*, 5:15.

680 Ibn Qudāma, *al-Mughnī*, 7:105–106.

681 E.g. Ibn Qudāma, Ibn Munjī, and Ibn Taymiyya. The influential theologians al-Ghazālī (Shāfiʿī) and Ibn ʿArabī (Malikī) hold the same view. Alshech, "Notions of Privacy in Classical Sunni Islamic Thought," 164.

682 Al-Khurashi, *Ḥāshiyat al-Khurashī ʿalā' Mukhtaṣar Khalīl* (Dār al-Kutub al-ʿIlmīyah, 2015) 1:46. Al-Dasūqī (d. 1230/1815), *Ḥāshiyat al-Dasūqī ʿalā al-Sharḥ al-kabīr* (Cairo: Dār al-Iḥyā' al-Kutub al-ʿArabiyya, n.d.), 1:344. However, Ibn ʿArabī (d. 543/1148) cites both opinions in his com-

nent exception of al-Ghazālī[683]), and some Ḥanafīs[684] require a Muslim woman in the presence of a non-Muslim woman to cover herself to much the same extent that she would in front of a strange man, with the possible exception that she can reveal whatever is necessary to go about her daily business. In this view, while a Muslim woman may reveal everything that is not between her knees and navel to other Muslim women, she may reveal only her face and palms to non-Muslim women. Other Ḥanafīs take a position midway between these two poles by placing non-Muslim female viewers in the same category as kinsmen, rather than the same category as foreign men, with the result that a Muslim woman may reveal more of her body in their presence. However, midwifery and similar situations in which another person must look at a Muslim woman's genitals represent a special case according to medieval jurists from across the legal schools.

One of the reasons articulated for being wary of non-Muslim women viewing Muslim ones is the fear that they might describe Muslim women to their husbands. This explanation is usually ascribed to 'Abdallāh Ibn 'Abbās (d. 68/687) and is presented in its fullest form in Ibn Kathīr's (d. 774/1373) commentary on the above-mentioned Qur'ānic verse.

> His statement "or their women" means she may display her ornaments to Muslim women as well, but not to the women of the *dhimma*, lest they describe them to their husbands. This is a concern with regard to all women, but more so with regard to *dhimmī* women because no restriction stops them from doing so, while a Muslim woman is taught that this is forbidden and she is kept from doing so. For the Messenger of God said, "a woman should not touch a woman and describe her to her husband as though he himself could see her" . . . Ḥārith b. Qays reported, "The Commander of the Faithful 'Umar b. al-Khaṭṭāb wrote to Abū 'Ubayda, 'It has been brought to my attention that some Muslim women are frequenting bathhouses together with polytheistic women. Now, it is not permitted for a woman who believes in God and the Last Day to have her nakedness seen by anyone but her co-religionists'" . . . Ibn 'Abbās said, "'Or their women' refers to Muslim women, and she must not show the Jewish or Christian woman her throat, earring, or sash, or that which only a *maḥram* may see" . . . Mujāhid said, "A Muslim woman should not remove her head-covering while with a polytheistic woman" . . . Both Makḥūl and 'Ubāda b. Nusayy disliked having Christian, Jewish, or Magian women serve as midwives to a Muslim woman . . . Ibn 'Aṭā' narrated from his

mentary on Qur'ān 24:31 and prefers the reading that all women are the same in this regard. Ibn al-'Arabī, *Aḥkām al-Qur'ān* (Beirut: Dār al-Kutub al-'Ilmiyya, 1991), 3:385.

683 Al-Ghazālī, *al-Wasīṭ fī al-madhhab* (Cairo: Dār al-Salām, 1997), 5:30. Referred to in E. Alshech, "Notions of Privacy in Classical Sunni Islamic Thought" (Ph.D. Dissertation: Princeton University, 2004), 164.

684 Al-Ḥaṣkafī (d. 1088/1677) in Ibn 'Ābīdīn, *Ḥāshiyat Radd al-muḥtār 'alā al-Durr al-mukhtār* (Beirut: Dār al-Fikr, 1992), 6:371.

> father.[685] "When the companions of the Prophet first came to Jerusalem, Jewish and Christian women would serve as midwives to their wives. And this, if true, was due to the exigencies of the circumstance, or it was a tribulation."[686]

Ibn Kathīr interprets the phrase "or their women" to mean that non-Muslim women are excluded from intimate access to Muslim women, and initially he claims that the purpose of such exclusion is not to preserve Muslim women from the gaze of non-Muslim women themselves, but rather from men's "vicarious" gazes. However, the early Islamic authorities he cites to show that Muslim women should not fraternize with non-Muslim women do not mention fear of male gazes. Rather he cites a series of prohibitions which purport to date to the time of the Islamic conquest of Jerusalem under 'Umar,[687] which was not the first time when Muslim women encountered non-Muslim ones, but was the first time when they did so while outnumbered and residing in a foreign environment. These prohibitions restricted Muslim women from frequenting bathhouses with non-Muslim women, exposing their bodies to them, and receiving gynecological services from them. The underlying motive is not articulated as part of the narrative about the choice to prohibit such contact.

The fear that a non-Muslim woman (who lacks proper Islamic instruction) would describe a Muslim woman to her husband does not sufficiently explain why this prohibition is attributed to the period of the conquests rather than to the lifetime of the Prophet. Nor does it explain why the early Islamic authorities and all of the schools of law designate childbirth as creating a special impediment to non-Muslim women interacting with Muslim ones. After all, medical need usually occasions waiving modesty restrictions, rather than imposing more confining ones. If non-Muslim and Muslim women are essentially equal vis-à-vis nudity, as the Ḥanbalīs claim, why does childbirth make it licit for a Muslim woman to view her fellow woman's genitals but illicit for a non-Muslim to do so? If, as the Shāfi'īs (and the Mālikīs and Ḥanafīs) say, a non-Muslim woman is a risk because she might describe a Muslim woman, why then does al-Bulqīnī's order of precedence give preference to both Muslim and non-Muslim male children, whether younger or older, over a non-Muslim woman? After all, when it comes to legal discussions of nakedness, the defining characteristic of

---

685 Also in Ibn Abī Ḥātim al-Rāzī (d. 327/938), *Tafsīr al-Qur'ān al-'aẓim li-Ibn Abī Ḥātim* (Mecca: Maktabat Nizār Muṣṭafā al-Bāz, 1997), 8:2577.

686 Ibn Kathīr, *Tafsīr al-Qur'ān al-'aẓīm*, 6:47–48.

687 One version of this report says that the 'Umar in question is the caliph 'Umar II, that is, 'Umar b. 'Abd al-'Azīz, and the person he tasks with the enforcement of this law is Abū Bakr b. 'Amr b. Ḥazm. Ibn al-Jawzī, *Aḥkām al-nisā'*, 30.

children is that they are able, and have a tendency, to describe what they see.[688] Indeed, if they could not describe what they see they could not possibly be old enough to provide emergency medical attention. Moreover if the concern is that a non-Muslim woman might describe a Muslim woman, why does al-Bulqīnī rule that it is preferable to employ an infidel pubescent boy who is as able to engage in descriptions as a woman is, who similarly has no Islamic-based compunctions about doing so, and who is himself considered to possess a form of sexual desire?[689] These seeming inconsistencies suggest that the fear that a man might vicariously experience a Muslim woman's exposed body is not the central issue, or at least not the only concern, governing either early prohibitions on non-Muslim midwifery or later Shāfiʿī jurists' orders of preference for medical care.

Instead, it makes sense to view restrictions on Muslim women being attended by non-Muslim midwives and frequenting bathhouses with them not as a product of concerns about privacy and sexual violation, but rather as an expression of concerns about the intellectual intimacy occasioned by bathhouse attendance and midwifery itself. These two activities have more in common than just the element of nudity. When a woman visited the bathhouse, it was likely that she was in a state that had religious, biological, and social significance. The same is true of the occasions when a woman required a midwife. A birthing room served as the locus for the woman's transition to motherhood, the baby's entrance into the world and, often enough, the departure of either mother or baby from this world to the next. A bathhouse served as the locus for an unwed woman's transition into marriage, a wife's transition into motherhood, and a menstruating woman's transition from an impure to a pure state. Thus both the bathhouse and the birthing room were places associated with liminality. These states of liminality were thought to be dangerous and to render women especially vulnerable to attacks by demons and the evil eye, as well as the physical dangers posed by childbirth.[690] A woman did not deal with these dangers

688 See Eli Alshech, "Notions of Privacy," 162–63.

689 This seems to have confused later Shāfiʿī jurists as well, hence al-Qalyūbī does not give preference to the pubescent boy over the non-Muslim woman. However, he still gives preferences to the non-Muslim eunuch over a non-Muslim female *maḥram*, even though Shāfiʿī jurists do believe that eunuchs experience lust and engage in a form of sexual relations. Alshech, "Notions of Privacy," 168.

690 Works written by medieval men say that women went to the bathhouse in connection with life-cycle events, and both documentary and literary evidence demonstrate a widely held belief that women were vulnerable at these times. These works do not explain precisely what medieval women said or did to protect or heal themselves. However, there are many descriptions by modern anthropologists of contemporary women's cultures and their concepts of magic and liminality with the bathhouse as the locus and the midwife as the authority for the transmission and

alone, rather she was coached through them by friends, older women, and others who were thought to have knowledge and expertise. Bathhouses and birthing rooms were thus places where women dealt with anxieties about vital aspects of their lives. Therefore, the bathhouse and the birthing room were prime loci for the transmission of inherited culture and knowledge, and the expression of authoritative wisdom and power. It makes sense then that the jurists sought to restrict interactions between Muslim and non-Muslim women in such contexts for fear that non-Muslim women would propagate culture and knowledge that ran counter to the teachings of Islam.[691]

---

performance of that culture. See A. Cuffel, "Polemicizing Women's Bathing among Medieval and Early Modern Muslims and Christians, *The Nature and Function of Water, Baths, Bathing, and Hygiene from Antiquity through the Renaissance*, ed. C. Kosso and A. Scott (Leiden: Brill, 2009). C. M. Obermeyer, "Pluralism and Pragmatism: Knowledge and Practice of Birth in Morocco," *Medical Anthropology Quarterly* 14 (2000), 186–87 and E. S. Drower, "Women and Taboo in Iraq," *Iraq* 5 (1938), 116–17. On the significance of liminal rites and the linguistic connections between women's life-cycle events, see R. Natvig, "Liminal Rites and Female Symbolism in the Egyptian Zar Possession Cult," *Numen* 35 (1988), 64–66.

691 One Moroccan anthropologist compares the role of the bathhouse to mobile-phones, in terms of their importance as the main source of communication and information for women, especially ones who otherwise do not leave their homes. S. Graiouid, "Communication and the Social Production of Space: the Hammam, the Public Sphere and Moroccan Women," *Journal of North African Studies* 9 (2004), 1, 105 and 107. Erika Friedl, writing about Iran, notes that bathhouse is where women "exchanged news, discussed problems, and politicked. This was also where the most private of all entities, the body, was revealed to public scrutiny: pregnancies invariably were first noted here, and if a woman could conceal elsewhere that she had been beaten, in the bath her bruises told the tale and her condition became public." E. Friedl, "The Dynamics of Women's Spheres of Action in Rural Iran," in *Women in Middle Eastern History*, 214. Another anthropologist, writing about Morocco, describes the bathhouse in a similar way: "It is one of the rare places where [women] meet women who do not belong to their *qurāb* or 'close ones', that is, the circle of friends, relatives, and neighbours with whom they interact on a daily basis. Here a woman is likely to pick up news that would not have reached her ears within the close surroundings of her '*dār wa darb*', the house and the alley where she lives. In the public bath she has the opportunity to extend her personal network beyond the women in her immediate surroundings. The scars and tattoos on the nearly naked bodies of the bathing women tell details of their personal histories without words. This creates an atmosphere of temporary intimacy that may encourage a woman to pour out her heart to any woman who happens to sit next to her. Sharing personal problems with a stranger who has no access to her own social network has the additional advantage that she does not have to be afraid that her confidentialities will leak out to her 'close ones' in the form of gossip that could have repercussions on her reputation. In this way, the weekly visit to the public bath serves as an 'escape' from the family privacy that envelopes women most of the other days in the week." Marjo Buitelaar, "Public Baths as Private Places," in *Women and Islamization*, ed. Karin Ask and Marit Tjomsland (Oxford: Berg, 1998), 114.

Shielding Muslim women from heterodox gynosocial contexts

The argument that medieval Islamic jurists feared that Muslim women would learn false beliefs through their contacts with non-Muslims is not a new one.[692] However, it seems to go unnoticed that the anxiety expressed by some 'ulamā' about Muslim women meeting with non-Muslim women also extends to occasions where Muslim women meet with each other, particularly in the context of life-cycle marking occasions. These occasions include wedding feasts, funerals and mourning ceremonies, and sickbed visits, as well as public bathhouse attendance.

There are numerous examples in *ḥadīth*s and juristic literature of these activities being considered as a set and strongly condemned. Many of these condemnations are voiced in a curious way: it is not only Muslim women who engage in these activities against their husbands' will who are disparaged, but rather men who permit their wives to engage in these activities are condemned as well. For example, a *ḥadīth* attributed to 'Alī in the Shī'ite legal compendium *Da'ā'im al-Islām* by Qāḍī Nu'mān (d. 363/974) quotes him as saying:

> "He who complies with the wishes of his wife in four things, God will hurl him into the Fire." He was asked, "What is this compliance, O Commander of the Faithful?" 'Alī said, "The demand to attend marriage feasts (*'urusāt*), to join mourning sessions (*niyāḥāt*), to go visiting the sick (*'iyādāt*) and to visit bathhouses (*ḥammāmāt*)."[693]

Similar statements can be found in Sunnī religious guidance about women.[694] Ibn Ḥabīb's (d. 238/853) *Adab al-nisā'* attributes the following statement to the Prophet, in which the husband is blamed for not preventing his wife from engaging in these activities.

---

692 Alexandra Cuffel writes about this issue in two of her articles: "Polemicizing Women's Bathing among Medieval and Early Modern Muslims and Christians," cited above, and "From Practice to Polemic: Shared Saints and Festivals as 'Women's Religion' in the Medieval Mediterranean," *BSOAS* 68 (2005), 401–19.

693 Translation by Asaf A. A. Fyzee, *Pillars of Islam* (New York: Oxford University Press, 2004), 2:201. Slightly modified.

694 Cf. Birgivi (d. 981/1573) who writes that a woman "should not be sent to be with non-relatives . . . nor to their houses or weddings, nor to the public bath, nor to visit the sick if they are not intimate relatives." M. Zilfi, *Women and Slavery in the Late Ottoman Empire: The Design of Difference* (New York: Cambridge University Press, 2010), 56. See also Cuno, *Modernizing Marriage: Family, Ideology, and Law in Nineteenth- and Early Twentieth-Century Egypt*, 91.

> [The Prophet Muḥammad] said: There are four things for which, if he complies with his wife in them, God throws a man into the Fire: thin clothing, bathhouses, mourning sessions, and weddings.[695]

Ibn al-Jawzī's (d. 597/1201) *Aḥkām al-nisā'* also condemns women for visiting the sick and attending funerals, claiming that even if her family does not recognize these as problematic, Satan certainly does.

> 'Abdallāh [b. Mas'ūd] said: Women are nakedness, so keep them at home. When a woman goes out into the street her family says to her, "Where are you going?" She responds, "I am visiting the sick" and "I am following a funeral procession." But Satan never lets up on her . . . and a woman can never supplicate before God as well as she could by staying in her house and worshipping God there.[696]

In the Ḥanafī manual of law, *al-Baḥr al-rā'iq,* Ibn Nujaym (d. 969/1561) differentiates between excursions outside the home that a wife has a right to make regardless of her husband's wishes, excursions a wife can make so long as she has her husband's permission, and excursions she may not make even if her husband does permit them and for which both are considered blameworthy.

> [A Muslim wife] can go out to visit her parents and *maḥārim*, and it is right for her to go out to her parents every week with or without [her husband's] permission, and to visit her *maḥārim* once each year with or without his permission. As for going out to visit family beyond this, she can do so with his permission . . . He may permit her to go out to visit her parents and to pay condolence and sick calls to them, and to visit her *maḥārim* and to mourn them.
>
> As for other occasions, there are seven circumstances under which a man is allowed to permit her to go out: [1] to visit her parents, [2] to pay sick calls to them, and [3] to mourn them or either one of them; [4] to visit *maḥārim*, [5] if she is a midwife or [6] a washer or [7] has some other legitimate reason to go out with or without his permission, and *ḥajj* is one of these. But excluding these, he should not permit her to visit outsiders, pay them sick calls, and attend wedding celebrations, and she should not go out. If he does permit it and she goes out, they both are at fault. She should also be prevented from going to the bathhouse.[697]

All of these statements about bathhouses, weddings, sick visits, and mourning observances suggest that these are activities to which a husband or other family member might well have no objection. The activities do not appear to be neces-

695 Ibn Ḥabīb, *Kitāb adab al-nisā'*, 295

696 Ibn al-Jawzī, *Aḥkām al-nisā'*, 54.

697 Zayn al-Dīn b. Ibrāhīm Ibn Nujaym al-Miṣrī (d. 970/1563), *Baḥr al-rā'iq sharḥ kanz al-daqā'iq* (Quetta: al-Maktaba al-Mājidiyya, 1983), 3:195.

sarily associated with female licentiousness. Ibn al-Jawzī indicates that when a women wants a persuasive excuse to go out she says, "I am visiting the sick, I am following a funeral procession," showing that not only do male family members tend to condone such behavior, but they view it as the best reason for a woman to be out of the house. Similarly, the threat of hellfire leveled against husbands who do not curb their wives' participation in such excursions suggests that these are not activities that a husband would necessarily view as indecent or infringing upon his rights or interests. If they were, there would be less of a need to threaten husbands and disallow them from exercising their own discretion on this matter, because their own self-interest would be enough.

What then makes these activities objectionable, in the eyes of the jurists? Why would husbands be depicted as not necessarily sharing the same concerns as the jurists, and why would women engage in such activities anyway? Before offering my own answer to these questions, it is worth exploring two explanations that I believe are insufficient in answering them. The first insufficient explanation is that the condemnation of bathhouses, sick visits, mourning rites, and weddings has little to do with the activities themselves but rather has more to do with upholding husbands' rights to keep their wives at home where they are sexually accessible. The second insufficient explanation is that participation in the above-mentioned events is condemned only because these events provide cover for mixed-gender interactions and lascivious behavior. Both of these explanations consider the condemned activities with a focus only on men's access to women for the purposes of sex, male sexual jealousy, and the desire to control or regulate women's bodies. In contrast to these explanations, I would argue that juristic concern regarding these activities are about women's access to their fellow women for the purposes of conversation, orthodox theological "jealousy," and the desire to control or regulate women's intellectual experiences.

It is true that legal treatment of women's *khurūj*, i.e. exits or excursions from the home, in general is predicated on notions of husbands' sexual rights. Among the contractual prerogatives and responsibilities between husband and wife in Islamic thought is the husband's right to initiate sexual intercourse whenever he wishes (under most circumstances) and for that reason he has a right to control his wife's mobility outside the home, lest her excursions make her sexually unavailable.[698] (She in turn has the right to demand he provide a proper home.) Thus, one important topic of legal discussions about women's excursions is the mediation between the opposing preferences of a husband and a wife when the

698 Ali, "Marriage in Classical Islamic Jurisprudence," 12.

latter wishes to leave and the former wishes for her to remain. The jurists identify which excursions a wife has a right to insist upon despite his objections, and which excursions a husband has a right to curtail if he so desires. For example, in the passage just quoted from *al-Baḥr al-rāʾiq*, Ibn Nujaym writes that a wife has a right to see her parents at least once weekly, and her other relatives at least once every year, regardless of the preferences of her husband. Beyond that, a husband can determine whether to allow the parents into his home and whether to permit or forbid more frequent contact, on the grounds that he has both a right to determine who enters his home and has the right to insist his wife remain at home where she will be available to him. In adjudicating such instances, the jurists consider the clash between the desires of the two opposite parties, the husband and the wife, with the husband most often empowered to make the choice about whether to retain or forgo his wife's presence. However, as we have seen, with regard to certain types of activities, i.e. bathhouse attendance, weddings, mourning rituals, and sick visits, the husband's prerogatives are not at issue and he is condemned if he permits his wife to leave for such purposes.

Ibn Nujaym does not say explicitly *why* a husband is not permitted to allow his wife to leave the house to participate in burials, go to bathhouses, etc. It is true that there are many customs associated with these activities which the jurists condemn, such as inappropriately excessive mourning rituals, the playing of musical instruments, and gender mixing. But, when husbands are instructed not to permit their wives to attend weddings and other social occasions, often there is no claim that it is only particular secondary circumstances which make it impermissible for women to attend such functions. For example, regarding funeral processions, the Andalusian Mālikī jurist, ʿAbd al-Malik ibn Ḥabīb writes explicitly, "Women are not permitted to follow funerals even if there are no wailers."[699] A similar statement from another of Ibn Ḥabīb's writings, *Kitāb al-wāḍiḥa min al-sunan w'al-fiqh* is quoted in the 4th/10th-century *ḥisba* manual of Ibn Abd al-Raʿūf, who depicts it as applicable law. "Women are forbidden to assemble to mourn the dead, whether in secret or in public, even when the mourning is not accompanied at all by funereal songs."[700] By stating that even private (rather than public) mourning assemblies are forbidden for women, and even ones that do not involve singing, the author makes explicit

699 Ibn Ḥabīb, *Kitāb adab al-nisāʾ*, 238.

700 E. Lévi-Provençal, *Trois Traités Hispaniques De Hisba: Texte Arabe* (Cairo: Publications De L'institut Français D'archéologie Orientale Du Caire, 1955), 77. See. R. Arié, "Traduction annotée et commentée des traités de ḥisba d'Ibn ʿAbd Al-Raʾūf et de ʿUmar al-Garsīfī," *Hespéris Tamuda* 1 (1960), 24.

that his objections to such activities are not based solely on ancillary concerns, such as the potential for women to make a spectacle of themselves in public.

Regarding the drawbacks of bathhouse attendance, the most obvious objection is to the ancillary nudity involved. But this does not fully account for the negative attitude toward women's bathhouse use. There is even a weak *ḥadīth* which claims that were one to remove nudity altogether from the bathhouse experience, one could still not make it acceptable for women:

> It is reported that ʿĀ'isha asked the Messenger of God about the bathhouse and he said, "Far be it from me [to go to] bathhouses. And there is nothing good in bathhouses for women." She said, "O Messenger of God, they enter it wearing a loincloth." He said, "No, not even if they were to enter it wearing a loincloth and a sleeved shirt and a head-covering. For no woman removes her head-covering anywhere other than her husband's house without removing the curtain between herself and her God."[701]

Many *ḥadīth*s, more commonly accepted as authentic by medieval scholars, permit men to use public baths, so long as they wear a loincloth, but still forbid women altogether from frequenting them.[702] Others *ḥadīth*s forbid women from attending bathhouses unless they are sick and need to enter for birth or post-partum purposes.[703]

The extensive record of authorities condemning these activities is matched by an equally extensive record of women insisting on engaging in them and finding them meaningful. For example, al-Wansharīsī's *al-Mi'yār al-Muʿrib* contains the following query addressed to a 3rd/9th-century Cordoban jurist, depicting women's devotion to mourning rituals.

> Yaḥyā[704] was asked: What if a man dies, and his mother or his sister or his wife go out to the grave, and with them are women who are their neighbors? What about a woman whose husband or child has died, and some of her relatives make a habit of visiting his grave every Friday or so? What if she weeps loudly, or the women join her in loud cries?
>
> Should they be forced back and forbidden to go out? And if they are forbidden, but then go back to doing it, should [the men] beat them? . . .

---

701 "This was reported by al-Ṭabarānī in the *al-Awsaṭ* as one of ʿAbd Allāh b. Lahīʿa's reports." Al-Haytamī, *Majmaʿ al-Zawā'id*,1:278. Cf. al-Ṭabarānī (d.360/971), *al-Muʿjam al-awsaṭ* (Cairo: Dār al-Ḥaramayn, 1995) 3:321. It so happens that there are several reports from Ibn Lahīʿa which are especially restrictive with regard to women, and al-Ṭabarānī does not consider him to be fully trustworthy,

702 Ibn Mājah, *Sunan*, 33 (adab):94 = no. 3749.

703 Ibn Mājah, *Sunan*, 33 (adab):93 = no. 3748.

704 I.e. Yaḥyā b. Yaḥyā al-Laythī (d. 234/848).

He said: Women should not go to graves to seek mercy for their children or husbands at all.[705]

From the question, we can see that the women are assumed to be going to the cemetery for actual death rituals, rather than using the cemetery as a pretext for a more frivolous outing. We can see also that this is a women's communal activity. It takes place among female relatives and neighbors, and it does not seem to be a venue where men suspect sexually compromising behavior is likely to occur. It is the actual ritual content being performed by groups of women that concerns the men. Moreover, we see that the men think that these rituals and communal outings are so important to women, that they will risk male wrath in order to engage in them.

The bathhouse was similarly important for women. While for men it served as a venue for physical cleaning and routine physical maintenance – bathhouses retained male barber-surgeons, cuppers, phlebotomists, and masseurs for the use of their male patrons but not their female ones[706] – for women they were also strongly associated with physical and spiritual cleansing from the impurities associated with menstruation, defloration, birth, and postpartum healing and with the lifecycle events surrounding these changes. Modern ethnographies and the fragmentary evidence we have from medieval sources suggest that the bathhouse was also the site for pre-nuptial instruction, fertility rites, and gynecological treatment. This was true for Christians and Jews, as well as Muslims.

Muslim (as well as Christian[707]) religious figures decried women attending the bathhouse but felt the need to make an exception for women experiencing illness, pregnancy and post-partum recovery. Many *ḥadīth*s to this effect are quoted in Ibn Ḥabīb's *Adab al-nisāʾ*:

From ʿAbd Allāh b. ʿAmr b. al-ʿĀṣ regarding the Messenger of God: He said, "You will conquer the land of the foreigners and in it you will find buildings called bathhouses. Men should not enter them except with a loincloth, and prohibit your women from them except those who are post-partum or who are sick."

From Umm Kalthūm who said, "I visited the bathhouse with ʿĀʾisha and said to her, 'Didn't you used to despise the bathhouse?' She said, 'I am sick, and it is permitted to a sick

705 Al-Wansharīsī, *al-Miʿyār al-Muʿrib* 6:419 – 20

706 J. Sourdel-Thomine, "Ḥammām," in *Encyclopaedia of Islam*, 2nd ed., ed. P. Bearman et al. (Leiden: Brill, 1960), 3:139 – 44.

707 A. Cuffel, "Polemicizing Women's Bathing among Medieval and Early Modern Muslims and Christians, *The Nature and Function of Water, Baths, Bathing, and Hygiene from Antiquity through the Renaissance*, ed. Cynthia Kosso and Anne Scott (Leiden: Brill, 2009), 174 n.10.

woman.' That was when she was suffering from skin disease, so I covered her in henna from head to toe."[708]

Bathhouse attendance, henna applications, marital and fertility rites and instruction, and midwifery went hand in hand. Brides used to visit the bathhouse twice, in preparation for marriage and immediately following the consummation of marriage.[709] The second visit immediately preceded "the night of henna." Some late legal works mention in passing that on these occasions the bride would be accompanied by a midwife. For example, Ibn 'Ābidīn (d. 1252/1836) writes:

> It is understood among the people in our time that a virgin receives extra things in addition to the *mahr* (dower). Among them are things to be given before consummation such as money for the *naqsh*[710] and the bathhouse, for a garment called the "*lifāfat al-kitāb*," and for other garments which the husband gives to her and which the bride's family gives the midwife and the bathhouse attendant and other such women. Also among them are things to be paid after consummation, like the wrap and the slippers and the checkered cloth, and the bath clothes. These are customary and understood and fall in the category of customary law.[711]

Modern anthropological texts about bathhouse use among 20th-century Muslim communities in the Maghreb, Egypt, and Iraq describe how, even when women visit the bathhouse without a professional midwife in attendance, they often have a designated companion who is entrusted with performing healing and prophylactic rites.[712] They also show that the bride's attendant(s) who bathe and cover her with henna are the women who instruct her about consummating her marriage.[713]

---

708 Ibn Ḥabīb, *Kitāb adab al-nisā'*, 234–35.

709 Sourdel-Thomine, "Ḥammām."

710 Literally: Inscribing (with black ink) usually applied to the skin but sometimes to eggs as well. The *naqsh* ceremony is currently most commonly associated with wedding ritual in Morocco and Yemen. Ibn 'Ābidīn lived primarily in Damascus.

711 E.g., Ibn 'Ābidīn, *Ḥāshiyat Radd al-Muḥtār*, 4:272.

712 R. Natvig, "Liminal Rites and Female Symbolism," 64. For an Iraqi example see E. S. Drower, "Woman and Taboo in Iraq," 106.

713 In one description of a wedding in Giza, Egypt in the 1920s, the author (a teacher in a reformatory school) translates the term *balāna* as village midwife. She describes how the bathhouse attendant/midwife on the wedding night "mocked [the bridegroom] loudly for not being a man, seized his hand and, wrapping a large piece of stiffly starched butter-muslin round his first and second finger, dragged him towards the bride . . . the bridegroom then, with the assistance of the *belana*, proceeded to break the hymen with his two fingers." E. E. Perkins, "Marriage Ceremony in Lower Egypt," *Man* 32 (1932), 64. E. W. Lane describes the midwife

The significant religious role and religio-medical role attached to the other women accompanying a woman to the bathhouse is also alluded to in medieval Jewish texts. In 12th-century Egypt, Maimonides and nine of his Rabbanite colleagues publish an edict condemning "the majority" of Egyptian Jewish women for what the Rabbanite authorities consider to be a heretical Karaite practice: when the menstruating woman (*niddah*) goes to the ritual bath (*mikveh*) to purify herself, instead of submerging herself in the water by herself, she seeks purification from other women.

> [M]ost of the women rely on complete heresy, a matter not spoken by God, and it is this: the *niddah* takes a woman who is not a *niddah* to sprinkle her with water that she supposes is pure; the *niddah* thinks that if she should sprinkle herself, she will not be purified and will not be permissible to her husband. This activity is called by them [the women] "sprinkling."[714]

In other words, women in an impure state go to the ritual bath with other women and insist the water purifies by virtue of being sprinkled by a religiously pure, fellow woman. That not only invests women with religious importance but also means that women must go to the bathhouse even when they are not impure, in order to provide this religious service for each other. Jewish sources from other communities also attest to women being accompanied to the mikveh regularly by midwives prior to pregnancy so as to promote fertility. Some medieval Jewish texts describe it as a matter of course that midwives accompany Jewish women to ritual baths on a monthly basis, although the evidence of this comes from European Jewish communities.[715]

---

and bathhouse attendant as two separate individuals who both have paid roles in the marriage ceremony. The bathhouse attendant participates in the wedding night, see Lane, *An Account of the Manners and Customs of the Modern Egyptians* (New York: The American University of Cairo Press, 2003), 163 and 171. In a passage which Lane wrote in Latin but which was expurgated, he describes the same breaking-of-the-hymen ceremony, see Jason Thompson, "Small Latin and Less Greek: Expurgated Passages from Edward William Lane's *An Account of the Manners and Customs of the Modern Egyptians*," *Quaderni di Studi Arabi* 1 (2006), 13.

714 Translation by Shaye Cohen. S. Cohen, "Purity, Piety, and Polemic: Medieval Rabbinic Denunciations of 'Incorrect' Purification Practices," in R. Wasserfall, ed. *Women and Water: Menstruation In Jewish Life and Law.*(Hanover, NH: University Press of New England [for] Brandeis University Press, 1999) 91.

715 For example, in Jewish communities in medieval Europe, "midwives accompanied women on their monthly visits to the ritual bath and were expected to help promote fertility." E. Baumgarten, *Mothers and Children: Jewish Family Life in Medieval Europe* (Princeton: Princeton University Press, 2004), 31. A 12th-century Ashkenazi Jewish text translated by Baumgarten assumes that universally women perform their monthly ablutions accompanied by another woman who is

Bathhouses, cemeteries, sickbeds, and weddings were thus sites of intellectual, religious activity for women. One of the most dramatic portrayals of Muslim women's hunger for these communal religious occasions can be found in Ibn Ḥabīb's *Adab al-nisā*, in a remarkable dialogue imagined to have taken place between the Prophet Muḥammad and Asmā' bint Yazīd, a companion of the Prophet famous for her initiative, piety, transmission of *ḥadīth*, and participation in battles.

> The Messenger of God was sitting with a crowd of his companions when he encountered a woman of the Anṣār named Asmā'. She greeted him and then said, "O Messenger of God, I am the messenger of those who are behind me – a group of Muslim women – all of whom speak with my voice and are of my opinion! God sent you to all people, to men and to women, and we trusted you and followed you and we believed what was revealed to you!
>
> Then God favored you – the community of men – over women, with manifold advantages, and bestowed upon you Friday communal prayer and the acts of congregating, visiting the sick, following funeral processions, the *ḥajj*, and *'umra* after the *ḥajj*. And He singled you out for greater favors than this – with frontier mobilization (*ribāṭ*) and *jihād* in the path of God. But what about us – the community of women? We are confined and curtained off, the fosters of your offspring, the climax of your desire, and the foundations of your homes. We raise your children for you. We weave your clothing for you, and we let no one else but you into your beds. Is there no reward for us, O Messenger of God?"
>
> The Prophet turned to his companions and said, "Have you ever heard anything like this woman's speech?' They said, 'No! By the One who sent you with prophecy, O Messenger of God. We have not seen among women one with so far-reaching a mind and such a deep question as this."
>
> Then he faced her and said to her, "O woman, go and be instructed and instruct the women of your quarter, and all those women, Anṣār and Muhājirīn, that you encounter, and all Muslim women: if one of you is a good spouse to her husband, and he is pleased with you for one hour of the day, it is equal to *jīhād* and *ribāṭ* and *ḥajj* and *'umra* and following a funeral and visiting the sick, and communal prayer – that is the meritorious deed of a woman."[716]

In this text, it is men who attain religious merit through communal prayer, pilgrimage, visiting the sick, burying the dead, and fighting together on behalf of Islam. Women are imagined to envy men not for their social power or dominance, but rather because they have religious duties which require congregation,

---

there to promote her fertility. The text says that in a town where women are particularly fertile, it is because the midwives who accompany them to the ritual bath are benevolent, whereas in a town where there are few successful births, it is because the midwives who accompany women to the bath are not enhancing fertility but rather spreading infertility through witchcraft. Ibid., 47.

716 Ibn Ḥabīb, *Kitāb adab al-nisā*, 264–5.

and the activities they do in community with one another are religiously valued. Such communal, religiously-valuable activities, in Ibn Ḥabīb's telling, is what Muslim women want for themselves.

That other male authorities too recognize this desire among Muslim women, and recognize the fulfillment offered by the activities they are trying to steer women away from, is also suggested by the fact that often their condemnations of these excursions are immediately followed in legal texts by a suggestion that husbands provide women with a means of attaining religious learning from men. Consider the continuation of the above-quoted passage in *al-Baḥr al-rā'iq.*

> . . . he should not permit her to visit outsiders, pay them sick calls, and attend wedding celebrations, and she should not go out. But if he does permit it and she goes out, they both are at fault. She should be prevented from going to the bathhouse.
>
> If she wishes to go out to attend a learning session without her husband's approval, she cannot do so. If she [has a legal issue], and her husband asks the *'ālim* on her behalf and conveys [the information] to her, she is not allowed to go out; however if he is not in a position to go ask himself, she is allowed [to go ask the *'ālim*] even without her husband's approval. If she does not have any particular [legal] concern but she wants to go out to the learning circle to learn about issues having to do with ablutions and prayer, if the husband can memorize the issues and recount them to her, he can prevent her [from attending herself]. If he cannot memorize them, it preferable for him to allow her [to attend] sometimes; although if he does not allow it, there is nothing to be done and she is not permitted to go out so long as she has no particular [legal] concern.[717]

Compare this passage to a *ḥadīth* in which 'Ā'isha urges women to refrain from going to the bathhouses in separate but complementary appeals to husbands and wives. She concludes with a command to men: "O you men, whoever among you believes in God and the Last Day will never send [his wife] to the bathhouse. Men are in charge of (*qawwamūn 'alā*) women (Qur'ān 4:34), so guard your women and do not bring blame upon yourself, and teach them the Qur'ān and command them to exalt God all day long, and do not invite them to leave their houses."[718]

It seems from the formulation in this *ḥadīth* and in the *Baḥr al-rā'iq* that the authorities in these texts are proposing that wives, instead of attending bathhouses, weddings, funerals, and sick beds, ought to learn Islam from their husbands or, failing that, from the *'ulamā'* themselves. In other words, they think that the two activities are both means of fulfilling the same need, and one

717 Ibn Nujaym, *Baḥr al-rā'iq sharḥ kanz al-daqā'iq*, 3:195. Cf. Abū Yaḥyā Zakariyya al-Anṣārī (d 926/1520), *Asnā' al-maṭālib* (Beirut: Dār al-Kutub al-'Ilmiyya, 2001), 7:469–70.
718 Ibn Ḥabīb, *Kitāb adab al-nisā'*, 235.

means is impious whereas the other is pious. The correlation between the two kinds of activities is rarely explained explicitly. Here the 8th/14th-century Cairene jurist Ibn al-Ḥājj is the welcome exception.

Ibn al-Ḥājj on women's networks of knowledge

Ibn al-Ḥājj famously[719] writes in his *Madkhal*, "A woman should take [but] three excursions out in her lifetime: out to the house of her husband when she is given to him, out when her parents die, and out to her own grave."[720] However, in the same book he writes, "If a woman has a husband he is required to teach her, if she is ignorant of the law. If he does not, she should ask him to do so. If he does not do so, she should ask to leave [the house] to acquire knowledge. If he does not permit her to leave, she should do so without his permission."[721] He explicitly says that "an *ʿālim* must prevent his family [i. e. wives] from female socializing."[722] Immediately following this statement, however, he makes an exception. He says that it is right for a woman who has been taught law by her husband to meet with groups of women who have no access to knowledge from men in their own household and to teach them Islamic law which pertains to them. He writes that at such an assembly one must be wary lest the gathering becomes a forum for

> . . . any corrupt practices which women do when they gather together. Since most of their gatherings are not without talk of those deplorable practices with which they have grown up and which have found a place in their hearts as though they were religious rites . . .
>
> The practices which some of them hold to – which have become deeply ingrained in their hearts, and which have become so through women's talk and through talk with those men who indulge women (for anyone who witnesses and is silent is like one who participates) – include the deplorable practice of designating some of the days of the year and days of the week, such that every day has its particular activities which cannot be done on any other day. They regard anyone who disagrees with them [fem.] on this matter as portending evil and they attribute to him ignorance (*jahl*) and lack of knowledge.[723]

Ibn al-Ḥājj claims that women's gatherings are sites for the promulgation of a female religious culture, complete with "religious rites" and their own evaluations

719 See Huda Lutfi, "Manners and Customs of Fourteenth-Century Cairene Women," 99–121.
720 Ibn al-Ḥājj, *al-Madkhal*, 1/2:177.
721 Ibid., 1/2:199.
722 Ibid., 1/2:198.
723 Ibid., 1/2:199–200.

of knowledge and ignorance. In other places in the *Madkhal*, Ibn al-Ḥājj claims that women have their own parallel religious system. He refers to *khilāf* (differences of opinion) among women about how to calculate the duration of menstruation and how to purify oneself, and he claims that all their opinions are contrary to the laws of the *sharīʿa*, which they would know if they learned from men instead of from each other.[724] He says Muslim women have elaborate rules for observing the Sabbath (on Fridays, Saturdays, and Sundays) and annual holiday rituals to bring good luck for the following year.[725] They also have a slew of rituals surrounding childbirth. It is in the context of his description of midwifery and the culture surrounding childbirth that Ibn al-Ḥājj makes the remarkable observation that this impious female religion is the natural result of gender segregation.

> Men have more direct contact with the ʿulamāʾ than women do, for women are secluded (*muḥtajibāt*) and as a result they generally grow up in ignorance (*jahl*). Because of their remoteness from knowledge and from knowledgeable people, they generally take up many deplorable practices and rarely do they avoid that which the pure *sharīʿa* opposes.[726]

He spells out the problem: the ideal of *ḥijāb* isolates women from men, as it should. However men, in the form of the ʿulamāʾ and their students, are the transmitters of "pure" Islam, as are the books of the ʿulamāʾ.[727] As a result of their isolation from both the society of men and from Islamic religious knowledge, women turn to the company of other women and to the knowledge they have to offer. Thus women's *jahl* (ignorance) is the direct consequence of *ḥijāb*. Ibn al-Ḥājj's solution for fixing this deplorable state of affairs is to discourage each woman from the company and religion of her fellow women, and to replace this with greater access to one man, i.e. her husband, and to her husband's correct religious culture.

Ibn al-Ḥājj repeatedly describes women as engaging in innovation and syncretism but, rather than connecting it to intrinsic intellectual and moral weakness on their part,[728] he usually attributes it to lack of male interest in sharing *ʿilm* (knowledge) with women and with conversing with them generally.

---

724 Ibid., 1/2:154–5.
725 Ibid., 1/2:201–2.
726 Ibid., 3/4:220.
727 Ibid., 1/2:155. Cf. Katz, *Women in the Mosque: A History of Legal Thought and Social Practice*, 5.
728 On the attribution of intellectual weakness to women, see Karen Bauer, "'Traditional' Exegesis of Q 4:34," *Comparative Islamic Studies* 2 (2006), 129–142. Huda Lutfi, in a previously cited article, notes that Ibn al-Ḥājj also mentions the infamous *ḥadīth* stating that "women are lacking

> It is disgusting in a would-be-*'ālim* or an *'ālim*, whose wife is asked about something religious which women need, for her not to have knowledge of it, while he is supposed to be responsible for her. This is one of the most disgusting things, and it is most contemptible when he is supposed to be an example to be followed.[729]
>
> It is incumbent upon him to make a great effort to teach his family [i.e. wives] . . . for women generally will learn the laws which apply to them. So if they are ignorant about something which is required of them, then that is due to the concealment of knowledge.[730]

He writes humorously that if a man is so devoted to his own acquisition of religious knowledge that he cannot make time to communicate knowledge to his wife, then the honest thing for him to do is to not interact with his wife in any way whatsoever.

> He devotes himself to learning and leaves no room for anything else – and good for him – so he busies himself with what is in front of him and does not become sidetracked. It is said about the qāḍī 'Abd al-Wahhāb: when he came to Cairo he got married and lived with his wife for years and then he died. Her family wanted to marry her off, and she said to them "marry me off as a virgin." They said to her, "How? You lived for years with him." She said, "The first night he came to me and prayed two *rak'as* and then sat and looked in his books and did not raise his head. And he did that for several days. So one day I got up and got dressed and adorned myself and flirted before him. Then he raised his head, looked, smiled, and then took the pen which was in his hand and drew it across my face, and so destroyed my adornment. Then he bent his head down in his book and never again lifted it again until he went to join his Lord." So anyone who has such sublime determination, let him proceed in his footsteps.
>
> The 'ulamā' say, "One who seeks knowledge needs six things which he cannot do without, and if he lacks any one of them his knowledge is commensurately lacking. They are: eager determination, piercing intellect, patience, sustenance, a guiding shaykh, and long life." So if he wishes to relax, how can he make the intention of doing so while exemplifying the *sunna*, as [the Prophet] said, "Relax your hearts from time to time?" He intended by this that one should introduce gaiety to one's family [i.e. wives] by attending to them [fem. pl.] and talking with them [fem. pl]. It is incumbent upon

---

in intelligence and religion." Ibn al-Ḥājj invokes the *ḥadīth* three times. In the first instance, he explains that although women are permitted to wear silk, men are not. The reason for this is that women are deficient and men are perfect, so what need have men to add to their own perfection. In the other two instances, he argues that men have allowed women to determine the laws pertaining to themselves and have accepted women's authority with regard to law, even though women make up the laws themselves rather than rely on the norms expounded by the jurists. He reminds husbands that male religion is correct and female faux-religion is incorrect, so husbands should evangelize women. Ibn al-Ḥājj, *al-Madkhal*, 1/2:107, 174, and 3/4:312–3.

729 Ibid., 1/2:356.

730 Ibid., 1/2:358.

> him to be with his family and his children as one of them and not above them. I mean by this that he should be friendly and agreeable with them.[731]

He then goes on to describe how Muḥammad socialized with and taught his wives. He emphasizes communication both in the sense of the Prophet and his family enjoying each other's conversation, and in the sense of the Prophet taking an interest in molding his wives' beliefs and teaching his wives how to go about their activities.

The communication of learning from husband to wife is not necessarily as pleasant as his descriptions of the Prophet's household suggests. Elsewhere Ibn al-Ḥājj cites approvingly the example of his teacher's attitude toward his own wife.

> I heard my master Abū Muḥammad say, "When I got married I told my wife: do not move and do not speak a word in my absence, rather set it aside until I come back, for I am responsible for your behavior in its entirety. I was responsible for myself alone, but now I am responsible for myself and for you, and so I must fulfill ten prayers [i.e. the five daily prayers required of two people] and similarly for all of the obligations and so too for every virtue which I am accountable for," etc., such that he exaggerated to her saying, "if you move the jug from one place to another, inform me of it." He said, "[I did] that for fear that she would do something thinking that no religious law applied to it when in fact there was one that did, and she continued to inform me about everything she did."[732]

Ibn al-Ḥājj urges husbands to be extremely controlling over their wives' domestic activities – a wife should not even move a jar in her home without her husband's input. But this control has a purpose beyond the mere display of power and submissiveness. Its purpose is to create a situation where a wife asks her husband for religious instruction and he supplies it to her. This situation is the pious alternative to a woman seeking guidance from her fellow women, as Ibn al-Ḥājj indicates in his discussion of washing (*ghusl*).

> He should instruct [his wife] also about what happens if the [menstrual] blood persists and continues beyond its usual course and then stops. The laws of this are discussed in the books of jurisprudence. Also, if it persists and does not stop, then she is a *mustaḥāḍa* and he must instruct her regarding [i.e. warn her against] what some [women] do: when one of them stops menstruating, she goes out to the bathhouse and washes there, not knowing the laws of washing and what they require of her and instead she just cleans her body and nothing more. Now, if she prays having washed in this manner, her prayers are not correct. And it is not permitted for her husband to have intercourse with her if she

731 Ibid., 1/2:358–59.
732 Ibid., 1/2:152.

> does not, after menstruating, wash herself with a *ghusl al-shar'ī* (religiously correct washing), because there is no intention (*niyya*) present in [her actions]. So it is obligatory for him to teach her the laws of this. If she does formulate the intention, her washing is correct and so prayer, intercourse, and everything which was forbidden to her during her state of menstruation becomes lawful to her, irrespective of whether this was before the filth ceased or after, contrary to what some [women] do – in [thinking] that the washing consists of going into the bath and cleaning oneself there, without an intention – due to their ignorance of the laws in this regard.
>
> He should also instruct them regarding this innovation (*bid'a*) which some women do in declaring things unlawful, in that they believe that a woman is not purified until she puts her hand in her vagina and cleans inside it, and that if she does not do this she is not considered to have washed . . . and the cause of this is lack of learning and lack of understanding of the *ḥadīth*s of the Messenger of God.[733]

Ibn al-Ḥājj repeatedly, throughout the *Madkhal* encourages husbands to communicate with their wives, to become more involved in women's rituals, and to offer a substitute for the advice of other women. He is so insistent that men involve themselves and even direct traditionally female spheres of activity that he tells husbands (and, to a lesser extent, other responsible males if no husband is present) to involve themselves in midwives' traditional domains. He even goes so far as to instruct husbands to converse with midwives (who are presumably unrelated to them) so that midwives can receive male, Islamic instruction:

> It is incumbent upon the guardian [of the newborn], and certainly within his rights, to ask the midwife how she receives the newborn. For the midwives in our time are rarely careful about avoiding impurities, and the midwife comes in contact with the parturition blood and other impurities and then touches the newborn and his clothes – all without washing off the impurities with pure water. This is not permitted, still some of the midwives let the newborn suck on their [the midwives'] fingers which have been in contact with impurities and claim that it is healthy for this and that. But this is all utterly false and contrary to the pure *sunna* . . .
>
> But if the guardian were to ask about these things, such corrupt practices would be discontinued, then he could instruct her as to what precautions against impurities she must take for her part and for the newborn's. If she is already knowledgeable about this, well and good. If she is not knowledgeable, then she will learn the laws of this as a result of his questioning of her about them. Even so, most [midwives] have grown up practicing abominable customs which lead to the altogether forbidden practices previously mentioned.[734]

In spite of his claim that midwives will welcome such instruction and adopt masculine, "Islamic" childbirth practices in place of their own customs, Ibn al-Ḥājj is

733 Ibid., 1/2:155.
734 Ibid., 3/4:221.

not impervious to other ways women may view such interference. He prefaces his demand that husbands involve themselves in events leading up to and following childbirth with the warning: "It is incumbent on the guardian of the newborn not to defer to [midwives], neither to their opinions nor to their practices, even if they become angry or disdainful, or his interference with them leads to them quitting and going away."[735]

Ibn al-Ḥajj comes to the conclusion that husbands need to oversee and instruct midwives because it is the logical endpoint to his claim that husbands should be the primary providers of knowledge and social context to their wives. He claims this role for husbands because the alternatives to it are for women to acquire information and culture either by violating the rules of gender segregation and interacting with non-kinsmen, which is abhorrent because of the sexual indecency of such behavior, or by turning to other women, which is abhorrent because these other women promulgate their own culture which he believes consists of a thin veneer of misunderstood Islamic practices which are undergirded by Christian / Jewish / pre-Islamic beliefs.[736] The reason that women's culture is so un-Islamic, he says, is that women are kept from Islamic knowledge and ritual practice by virtue of the dictates of gender segregation (which he approves of whole-heartedly) and because of male Muslims' neglect

735 Ibid., 3/4: 220.

736 For a brief overview of these practices, see the above-mentioned article by Huda Lutfi. In at least one passage, Ibn al-Ḥājj may actually be conflating Muslim women with non-Muslim women. He writes, "He must not allow his wife to enter the bathhouse, since nowadays it consists of corrupt religion and deplorable practices. For our *'ulamā'* disagreed regarding a woman with a woman: is it categorized like the law of a man with a man? *Or like the law of a man with a non-kinswoman?* Or like a man with a *maḥram* woman? But they (fem.) have dispensed with all of this and have violated general consensus by entering bathhouses stark naked. Even if we grant that a woman may [choose to] conceal what is between her navel and her knees, they (fem.) reprove her, saying things they must not, until she removes her covering. Then this is compounded with another forbidden thing, and that is a Jewish or Christian woman, who is not permitted to see the body of a free Muslim woman. But in the bathhouse, Muslim, Christian, and Jewish women get together, exposed to each other's nakedness. So how can one allow his wife to enter it?" Ibn al-Ḥājj, *al-Madkhal*, 1/2:352. What is remarkable about this passage is that he claims that some *'ulamā'* argued that two Muslim women are allowed to see no more of each other than an unrelated man and woman. I am not sure that any jurist formally argues this with respect to Muslim women. Rather, some argue this with respect to a Muslim woman being viewed by a non-Muslim woman. It is almost a consensus among the jurists that the laws regarding viewing nakedness are for "a (Muslim) woman with a (Muslim) woman" like "a man with a man." See *al-Mawsū'a al-fiqhiyya*, 40:359–60.

and lack of interest in the intellectual lives of their womenfolk, for which he castigates them repeatedly.[737]

When Ibn al-Ḥājj expresses an anxiety that women are turning to other women in times that are pregnant with religious significance, and so are placing their trust in Muslim women and learning from them rather than from the 'ulamā', are his views representative of other jurists? We cannot know for certain, since other jurists do not explain their motivations so explicitly. However, Ibn al-Ḥājj's formal legal recommendations, which are based upon this anxiety, are indeed widespread in juristic literature. The *Madkhal* is typical in exhorting husbands to limit their wives' participation in the gatherings surrounding birth, sickness, marriage, and death, even when men are not particularly bothered by their wives' activities and even when women are quite insistent on engaging in such activities. The *Madkhal* is also in keeping with other traditions of encouraging men to provide their wives with some sort of access to Islam as interpreted by the 'ulamā'.

Heterodoxy and women's medicine

In summary, there is a strain of medieval juristic thought that seeks to regulate who Muslim women entrust their bodies to, who may be counted among their intimates, and who may be permitted to take on authority roles in moments of existential significance. This regulation is not aimed just at preserving modesty and avoiding sexual violation, as has sometimes been assumed. Rather, such regulation reflects concerns about intellectual influence and susceptibility. These concerns parallel the jurists' anxieties about male Muslim medical patients seeking healing. As we saw in the previous chapter, even for male Muslim patients there was a concern that the pursuit of health could be religiously compromising, since it meant entrusting oneself to potentially non-Islamic authori-

---

737 In an article about a twentieth-century Palestinian bedouin tribe, Lila Abu-Lughod describes how the facts of male-female social segregation in that particular tribe create a situation where there is an autonomous female society, whose conversations men are not privy to, and which considers itself authoritative and responsible for bringing up young women and inculcating them with culture and knowledge. When men involve themselves, or women involve men, in the women's sphere they are resented for doing so. In this society, husbands may have little conversation with their own wives. Abu-Lughod reports, "even when they are not working, men and women rarely socialize together. Indeed, my host's senior wife confessed to me that before I had come to live with them and to spend time chatting with my host in her room, she had never spent an entire evening in his company." Abu-Lughod, "A Community of Secrets: The Separate World of Bedouin Women," *Signs* 10 (1985), 640.

ties and epistemologies precisely when health concerns could make people fearful and thus intellectually vulnerable.

The jurists were indeed concerned about women patients' modesty with respect to male physicians, but they were also concerned about non-Muslim female medical practitioners, and even about Muslim female ones. Just as some jurists did not want Muslim men developing an intimacy with non-Muslim physicians for fear that it would normalize relations with non-Muslims, subvert trust in God and in revelation, and lead to the patient ingesting forbidden substances and being lax in their religious obligations, so too those same jurists did not want Muslim women developing an intimacy with non-Muslim women such that they consider them to be among "their" women, did not want them engaging in "innovation," and did not want them ingesting forbidden substances and being lax about impurity. In my opinion, it is this concern that motivates the Shāfiʿī jurists' preference to have boys provide medical care, even non-Muslim ones, rather than women: women are more likely to be intimate with other women and thus susceptible to imbibing a worldview from them. Women in gynecological and obstetrical situations are less likely to identify with boys in this way. Hence the objections to a non-Muslim midwife are not based solely on fears of sexual access and the dangers of male-female contact. Rather, they are also based on concerns regarding intellectual access and the dangers of female-female contact. The non-Muslim midwife is problematic because she communicates an un-Islamic culture in a moment of spiritual significance and intellectual vulnerability.

This is not a problem associated strictly with non-Muslim practitioners. Some jurists are also concerned about the potential for Muslim women to have an "un-Islamic" influence upon each other, due to the gulf between Muslim women's culture and the male, Islamic culture propagated by the jurists themselves. The jurists routinely, though with very little explanation, encourage husbands to restrict their wives from interacting with other women, both Muslim and non-Muslim, in a variety of important venues for the communication of culture, communal knowledge, and healing rituals. Interestingly, in the same contexts where they curtail wives' access to the main forums for exchanges between women, the jurists encourage husbands to talk to their wives and to expose them to the Islamic culture promulgated by the ʿulamāʾ, ideally by teaching their wives their own knowledge or by relaying to them the ʿulamāʾs answers to particular questions or discourses from the *majālis al-ʿilm* (learning circles) or, failing that, by allowing their wives to ask questions and to attend the *majālis al-ʿilm* themselves.

Ibn al-Ḥājj al-ʿAbdarī, exceptionally, provides a motivation for such legal guidelines. He says that due to gender segregation and male lack of interest,

Muslim women have little access to male ʿulamāʾ and consequently have little access to authentic Islam, and so they instead perpetuate ignorance and polytheism amongst themselves. Therefore, says Ibn al-Ḥājj, husbands are encouraged to limit the transmission of women's (non-Islamic) culture and to instead promote an Islamic culture where the husband serves as the conduit for orthodox, male knowledge and instruction. Ibn al-Ḥājj then takes this to the logical conclusion: since medicine ought to be Islamicized, and even Muslim women are perpetuators of non-Islamic culture, then husbands too should be involved in obstetrical care.

Conclusion to Part III: A Tafsīr about the First Woman's Fertility and Theological Vulnerability

Treating illness was, for the most part, deemed compatible with Islamic theological orthodoxy. But the desperation brought on by illness, the lack of consensus about how to understand illness, the frequent failure of medical treatments, and the "faith" and power dynamics implied in the relationship between patient and practitioner invested sickness and healing with theological repercussions which potentially skewed toward heterodoxy in one form or another. Women, who were physically separated from the authorized interpreters of Islam, and who were deemed by some to be mentally deficient in religious matters, were depicted as in even greater danger in this regard. The jurists' interpretation of the field of medicine, when augmented with concerns about the religious ignorance and heterodoxy of Muslim women, and coupled with concerns about the physically intimate nature of medical intervention, could put Muslim women seeking gynecological care in a particularly uncomfortable position. Moreover, for young women who were mothers and aspiring mothers, it might have been even more difficult to make a distinction between medical and religious practice and authority, since medical care focusing on fertility and menstruation was intertwined with women's social roles and their ritual purity. Physical robustness, sickness, and death, i.e. "medical issues" were likely to have been a constant concern in their religious lives – in the form of menstruation, pregnancy, miscarriage, birth, stillbirth, breastfeeding and infant mortality.

All of these themes are encapsulated in a story told about the first woman, Eve, and her involvement with the Devil, Iblīs. The story appears in many different iterations.[738] The following are the versions recounted in al-Ṭabarī's (d. 310/923) history:

> (1) According to . . . Samura b. Jundab: None of Eve's children survived. Therefore, she vowed that if one of her children were to survive, she would call him 'Abd al-Ḥārith [al-Ḥārith being one of Satan's names.] When a child of hers survived, she called him 'Abd al-Ḥārith. That was due to Satan's inspiration.
>
> (2) According to . . . Ibn 'Abbās: Eve would give birth to Adam's children and make them worship God, calling them 'Abdallāh, 'Ubaydallāh, and the like. But then they would

738 These sources are referred to in an article by D. A. Spellberg, although she interprets the implications of the story differently. Spellberg, "Writing the Unwritten Life of the Islamic Eve: Menstruation and the Demonization of Motherhood," *International Journal of Middle Eastern Studies* 28 (1996), 305–24.

https://doi.org/10.1515/9783110596588-015

die. Now Iblīs came to her and to Adam and said: Were you to give them other names, they would survive. So, when she gave birth to a male child for Adam, they called him 'Abd al-Ḥārith. In this context, God revealed His word (Q. 7:190) from "It is He Who created you from a single soul" until "the two set up for Him associates in connection with what He had given them" to the end of the verse.

(3) According to . . . Sa'īd b. Jubayr: When Eve became heavy with her first pregnancy, Satan came to her before she gave birth, and said: Eve, what is that in your womb? She said: I do not know. He asked: Where will it come out, from your nose, your eye, or your ear? She again replied: I do not know. He said: Don't you think, if it comes out healthy, you should obey me in whatever I command you? When she said: Yes, he said: Call him 'Abd al-Ḥārith! Iblīs – May God curse him! – was called al-Ḥārith. She agreed. Afterwards, she said to Adam: Someone came to me in my sleep and told me such and such. Adam said: That is Satan. Beware of him, for he is our enemy who drove us out of Paradise. Then Iblīs – May God curse him! – came to her again and repeated what he had said before, and she agreed. When she gave birth to the child, God brought him out healthy. Yet, she called him 'Abd al-Ḥārith. This is [meant by] God's word: "They set up for Him associates in connection with what he had given them" to "And God is above your associating [others with him]."

(4) When [Sa'īd b. Jubayr] was asked whether Adam associated [others with God], he replied: God forbid that I should assume Adam did that! However, when Eve was heavy with child, Iblīs came and said to her: Where will this one come out, from your nose, your eye, or your mouth? He thereby caused her to despair [because she did not know and was afraid of what was going to happen]. Then he said: Don't you think that, when it comes out perfectly formed – Ibn Wakī' said that Ibn Fuḍayl added: without harming or killing you – you should obey me? When she agreed, he said: Call him 'Abd al-Ḥārith, and she did. Jarīr added: So Adam's associating [others with God] was only in the name.

(5) So she – meaning Eve – gave birth to a boy. Iblīs came to her and said: Call (plural) him my servant (*'abdī*)! If you don't, I shall kill him. Adam said to him: I obeyed you [once before], and you caused me to be driven out of Paradise. So he refused to obey him and called the child 'Abd al-Raḥman "Servant of the Merciful One." Satan – May God curse him! – gained power over the boy and killed him. Eve bore another child, and when she gave birth to it, Satan said: Call him my servant! If you don't, I shall kill him. Adam said to him [again]: I obeyed you [once before], and you caused me to be driven out of Paradise. So he refused to obey him and called the boy Ṣāliḥ, and Satan killed him. The third time around, Iblīs said to Adam and Eve: If you (pl.) want to overcome me, call him 'Abd al-Ḥārith. Iblīs's name was al-Ḥārith. He was called Iblīs when he was bedeviled (*ublisa*) – became confused. This [is meant by God's word] where He says: "They set up for him associates in connection with what He had given them" – meaning in connection with the names."[739]

739 Franz Rosenthal, *History of al-Ṭabarī: General Introduction and From the Creation to the Flood* (Albany: SUNY Press, 1989), 320 – 2. Arabic: al-Ṭabarī, *Tārīkh al-rusul wa'l-mulūk* (Leiden: Brill, 1879), 1:149 – 51.

Eve is quite literally hell-bent on producing a viable son. In versions (1), (2), and (5), her desperation stems from the fact that she has already experienced either pregnancy loss or infant death,[740] despite the fact that (in versions 2 and 5) she had shown her devotion to the true God by naming her children as His servants. In versions (3) and (4) her desperation stems from her fears, prior to her first birth, about how childbirth works. Any audience of the story would recognize the fear that the thing in her body might emerge from her facial orifices as extremely naïve, although some might empathize with her ignorance about the physiology of birth and her inability to know what precisely is inhabiting her body.[741] To a medieval audience, however, her fear that either her child or she herself might not survive the ordeal is perfectly sensible. In these respects, Eve's concern to ensure her own in health, the health of her child, and her success in giving "birth to a male child for Adam," is reflective of the concerns of medieval wives generally.

In versions (2) and (5), Adam and Eve find that their choice to name their child "the Servant of God," i.e. to show their dedication to true religion, does not result in health – their children die anyway. In response, either Eve or both parents call their child "the Servant of the Devil." This proves to be an effective course of action, for their children are healthy. The texts are of two opinions as to why this happened. In versions (1) and (2), the children dedicated to God die for no apparent reason. No foul play is mentioned but God simply does not choose to keep them alive. So Eve shops around for another source of health and settles on invoking Satan. In version (3), the child dedicated to Satan survives due to God's efforts, not Satan's, although Eve gives credit to Satan. In version (4) too, Eve gives credit to Satan, but it is unclear whether this is deserved or not. In version (5), the children dedicated to God are killed by Satan, while the one dedicated to Satan lives on. The children's ill-health is thus not a result of nature or Divine negligence, as Satan himself provides the disease. Adam and Eve are perfectly aware that Satan is the cause of their troubles, yet they choose to throw in their lot with him because he is ultimately more effective than God is

740 It is not clear from al-Ṭabarī's account when the death takes place. In Ibn Ḥanbal's account, which he traces to Samura ibn Jundab, Satan seems to kill the fetus in utero. Aḥmad ibn Ḥanbal, *Musnad* (Cairo: n.p., 1895), 5:11.

741 In Ibn Sa'd's version of the story, Satan appears in disguise to Eve during one of her later pregnancies and tells her that unlike in her previous (successful pregnancies), this fetus is misformed like an animal, and she panics. He says he will heal the fetus if the child is named for him. Ibn Sa'd, *Ṭabaqāt*, 1:14. A medieval audience, living in a period when endogamy and malnutrition were common, may have been particularly receptive to Eve's terror about her fetus' birth-defects.

when it comes to securing their child's health. Remarkably, in all versions of the anecdote the decision to dedicate the child to Satan is depicted as a perfectly logical and effective course of action, if birthing successfully is the ultimate goal.[742]

In this story Satan is a figure who has the power to protect, who can understand things which Eve is at a loss to explain, who poses a threat which necessitates propitiation, and who offers a plausible alternative after a first attempt proves to be ineffective. In these respects, Satan is similar to both the "high" physicians and the "low" medical practitioners, and to their respective medical systems, as depicted by those jurists who consider them a threat. The jurists warn that these medical practitioners and systems may indeed be effective, and they may indeed offer knowledge which Islam seemingly lacks. The jurists also warn that sometimes malicious physicians in fact cause the illnesses which they purport to cure. And they recognize that Muslims turn to non-Islamic medicine because when people are sick they will turn to anyone and everyone. Even the Prophet, when he was sick, turned to both Muslims and non-Muslims for help.

In the story of Eve and her quest for healthy children, turning to Satan to keep her child healthy is one and the same thing as dedicating her child to Satan. There is no ultimate difference between the realm of *abdān* (bodies) and the realm of *dīn* (religion), except that God is seemingly less effective in the former than in the latter. It is not entirely clear whether Eve is aware that the individual she ultimately entrusts her health to is Satan. In version (5), she definitely is aware, but in versions (1), (2) and (4), Eve is "inspired" or instructed by someone whom she may or may not recognize, to change her child's name to 'Abd al-Ḥārith, but it is not at all clear that Eve is aware that al-Ḥārith is Satan's name.[743] In version (3), Eve seems to be unaware until Adam explains that al-Ḥārith refers to the Devil. However, even with this information in hand she dedicates her son to al-Ḥārith thinking that it was he who caused her to give birth to a healthy child. In this respect too, Eve's relationship with Satan reflects the jurists' concerns about patient-provider relations. Patients may not realize that what they are doing constitutes *shirk*, and even once they do realize it they may no longer be concerned. In Eve's case, in version (3), she is rendered especially vulnerable because she, unlike her husband Adam, does not have direct knowledge about Satan's identity and about who does and does not constitute "the enemy." This too reflects the view held by jurists such as Ibn al-Ḥājj

742 The one exception is Ibn Sa'd's version in which 'Abd al-Ḥārith dies.

743 In Ibn Sa'd's version, it is explicitly stated that Satan cleverly refers to himself as al-Ḥārith so that Eve will not recognize him.

that a woman, unlike her husband, does not have direct knowledge about what constitutes correct religious practice and hence has trouble identifying its opposite.

Denise Spellberg understands the above story as promoting "the demonization of motherhood." This is a plausible interpretation but, if so, the story does so in a very strange manner. Whereas Eve's other sin, the eating of the fruit of the forbidden tree and the "cutting" of the tree, is characterized as resulting from stupidity, appetite, or the desire to violate the divine order by acquiring immortality, this sin is characterized as the result of Eve's desire to achieve what is not only possible but also desirable for her as a wife – she would like to produce children for her husband. The story thus does not demonize motherhood so much as it depicts the ferociousness of mothers' dedication to their own fertility. They will turn to God to produce children but, if that fails, they will turn elsewhere too.

Epilogue: Infertility and the Study of Women's History

To study barrenness is to study the history of women's struggles in a distilled form. Infertile women encountered the same expectations, were subject to the same restrictions, looked to the same forms of support, and engaged in the same religious practices as did fertile women; but the constraints and opportunities that accompanied womanhood had repercussions that were potentially more weighty for them. By studying the factors which particularly informed the lives of barren women, we also illuminate important swaths of women's experiences more generally. The purpose of this book, therefore, has been to establish a framework for inquiry into medieval barren women's experiences, one that can help orient us as we try to identify what was at stake for these women, what possibilities were available to them, and how women invested their energies.

This book has examined three bodies of evidence which can inform us about the experience of female infertility: Islamic legal discussions pertaining to women's reproductive capacities, Arabo-Galenic medical texts, and religious works preaching about medical practitioners and healing practices. These three foci reflect the aspects of women's infertility which had the most to do with men and, more specifically, the aspects of women's infertility which were most subject to the influence exerted by exclusively male institutions. The choice to attempt to understand women's experiences through such masculine lenses might have initially struck readers of this study as odd, even frustrating. This methodology, however, has its strengths.

Among my primary reasons for studying women's history in this way is my desire to answer questions that are important to my own 21st-century community without mischaracterizing what was important to the older communities I study. I have attempted to produce an analysis which speaks to issues of patriarchy, the construction of gender, feminine ritual, and women's empowerment, and to shed light on these concerns in a way which respects and preserves the modes of thought, the genre expectations, and the authorial intent behind these medieval texts. Of all the sources we have available, the books produced by the jurists and the physicians are best-suited to this task because these genres are better understood by historians than are other written sources (for the moment at least), and because they exist in great abundance and have attracted a great deal of scholarly attention. My hope is that by rooting my exploration in these texts, the medieval people who are at the center of this endeavor would recognize the individual topics of discussion in this book as familiar ones, though they might be

https://doi.org/10.1515/9783110596588-016

surprised by the juxtaposition of those individual topics or the weight attributed to them.

This study deals in generalizations and possibilities. I hope some students of women's history will find the generalizations useful for alerting them to phenomena they would have otherwise failed to notice and for helping them to make sense of their own explorations into the lives of individuals and individual communities. I hope still others will come forward with counter-examples to my arguments, and with modifications and improvements upon my theories. The study of women's social history in the medieval Middle East is still at its early stages, and we have a great deal of work to do to begin to do justice to the experiences of those women.

Infertility and family law

Certain underappreciated aspects of marital law and social practice had a disparate impact on barren women. For example, we have seen that first marriages for medieval women frequently took place at an age when women were likely to have been developmentally sub-fecund. This has consequences for understanding infertility, but it also has consequences for understanding women's history more broadly. With regard to infertility, the implications of early marriages are, first, that women may well have come to be viewed as infertile much earlier in their lifetimes than they would today, and consequently would have experienced the pressure to find a cure early on. Such cures could themselves exacerbate fertility problems or create ones where none existed. A second implication of early marriage is that, in the worst circumstances, coitus could itself result in damage to a girl's reproductive organs. Such situations are mentioned in Islamic legal manuals and some *fatwā* collections, though I surmise that they were rare. However, even when early marriage did not have these severe medical consequences, the phenomenon may inform our understanding of certain marriage dynamics. If many women did not complete the puberty process until they were in their early 20s, then wives in their mid-teens likely appeared to be physically more child-like than they do today, and thus more likely to be viewed as in need of protection, tutelage, and supervision. It is perhaps then no wonder that, for first marriages, brides were given little autonomy,[744] and their preferences commanded relatively little respect; but, when they became matrons, moth-

744 See K. Ali, *Marriage and Slavery in Islam*, 33.

ers-in-law, widows, or divorcées, they seem to have acquired much more authority.[745]

With regard to Islamic law, infertility highlights medieval ambivalence toward the institutions of divorce and polygamy. In some instances, divorce seems to have been viewed as running counter to the barren wife's interests, and this made the option of accepting polygamy as a means of avoiding divorce sometimes palatable. Sometimes infertile women who were subject to the threat of divorce would attempt to shield themselves from its effects by insisting that they were in fact pregnant, or had not menstruated, and thus they could continue to be attached to their former husband for an extended period of time. On the other hand, we also hear of women attempting to hasten divorce proceedings so that they could find new husbands, and sometimes having trouble doing so because they were not menstruating regularly.

While menstrual irregularity and unusual claims of pregnancy had special implications for infertile women, they also have much to teach us about women's experiences more broadly. Uncertainty surrounding menstruation and conception highlights the extent in which women had some degree of privacy and ability to choose how to present their bodies. We have seen that, in biological matters which were legally significant for marriage and divorce, women in a range of societies seem to have been in a position to conceal, reveal, or define their own status before society at large and before their husbands. We have encountered newlywed husbands who seem to be surprised to find that their wives are younger than expected or are not menstruating regularly. We have seen husbands and wives resorting to the competing testimonies of midwives to establish the wife's level of maturation or pregnancy status. We have seen wives and midwives expediently changing their testimony about pregnancy status. Women themselves testify about whether or not they have menstruated or felt signs of pregnancy. They even testify as to whether the father of their fetus is a long dead husband rather than a living one. This has implications for our understanding of how women managed the intrusion of society at large into intimate matters that were considered to be of public religious and legal concern, such as the preservation of clear-cut lines of paternity. The dependence upon women's testimony suggests that, despite the scrutiny and restrictions attached to women's reproductive roles, in many communities women did have opportunities for privacy. This

745 Cf. Goitein, *Mediterranean Society*, 3:162–4. For an illuminating anthropological discussion of how assessments of a woman's competence change over the course of her lifetime within a rural Egyptian village see Morsey, *Gender, Sickness, and Healing in Rural Egypt: Ethnography in Historical Context*, 52–4.

means that women could sometimes not only fashion their own responses to external pressures on them, but could also exert a practical pressure of their own. We see this, for example, with the woman who claimed to be carrying her long dead husband's child, even when she remarried.[746] Due to her testimony, her deceased husband's relatives consider her child to be one of their own kin. In this way, women were sometimes invested with a certain trust and a capacity for defining their own public status.

The study of childlessness also highlights conflicting attitudes towards women's inheritance rights and, more fundamentally, toward their familial affiliation. A married woman was part of two families, the one she was born into and the one she married into, and she transferred wealth between them.[747] She received wealth from her birth family via her dowry and through her inheritance. If she had children at the time of her death and she predeceased her other heirs, her father and her mother would inherit one sixth each, and the rest would be inherited by her husband and children. Thus, two thirds would be lost to the birth family. If she had no children, her birth family would lose half, and that would include half of her trousseau, items which had sentimental as well as monetary value, and which would pass into the hands of the husband and his family. If, on the other hand, a woman was predeceased by her husband, then she would inherit from him an eighth of his wealth if he had a child, and a quarter of his wealth if they were childless, thereby depriving the other heirs from his family of it. In theory, such laws meant that married women always represented the removal of a significant amount of wealth from one of their two families, but childless married women represented an often greater loss with fewer tangible benefits. We see that when married childless women predeceased their husbands, the women's birth families pursued aggressive legal measures to prevent such losses. Meanwhile, childless widows were at risk of being disinherited in favor of their husbands' blood relatives.[748]

---

746 al-Wansharīsī, *al-Mi'yār al-Mu'rib*, 4:54–5.

747 By contrast, her husband belonged to the family in which he was born, and their son would be part of his father's family too. This form of association is visible in a variety of settings, but it is most easily seen in the Islamic inheritance laws pertaining to grandchildren. The son of a son belonged to his father's and paternal grandfather's lineage, and he could potentially inherit from his paternal grandfather and paternal uncles. But the son of a daughter did not belong to his maternal grandfather's lineage, and could not inherit from any of his maternal relatives other than from his mother herself.

748 E.g. The story of Khātūn and Dalīla in *Alif Layla or Book of the Thousand Nights and One Night*, W. H. Macnaghten (Calcutta, 1839), 3:418.

Medieval gynecology and its significance

Medieval Arabo-Galenic gynecology highlights the complicated relationship between scientific and religious understandings of anatomy and reproduction. Some of the theories put forth in medical books matched religious beliefs and correlated with legal and practical norms. For example, as Basim Musallam has shown, the two-seed understanding of conception was a scientific theory particularly favored by Ibn Sīnā and his physician-jurist successors such as Ibn Qayyim al-Jawziyya. It also matched up with a particular *ḥadīth* ascribed to the Prophet Muḥammad, and correlated with a legal and practical willingness to make use of contraception.[749] Similarly, the notion that breastmilk was made from menstrual blood accorded well with Islamic notions of kinship via breastmilk. This concept was retained even as a competing notion that milk was a product of semen was also widely believed.[750]

Not all biological ideas that had religious importance were echoed in Arabo-Galenic gynecological literature, however. And not all gynecological knowledge had an impact on religious thought. The concept of the "sleeping fetus" was not integrated into Arabo-Galenic gynecology. Nor, for that matter, was religious interest in virginity. In the opposite direction, scientific tests of fertility were never integrated into Islamic legal thought.

Similarly, medical theorization about gender differences did not necessarily mirror social attitudes towards gender relations. Sherry Sayed Gadelrab, for example, published a substantial article on medical depictions of the anatomical differences between the genders.[751] Gadelrab's article takes up the question of whether the physicians of the medieval Islamic world viewed women's anatomies and hence qualities as essentially defective versions of men's bodies and qualities, or whether (to borrow a slightly more modern turn of phrase, which is not Gadelrab's) "men are from Mars and women are from Venus," i. e. two opposite species.[752] When analyzing Ibn Sīnā's work, she noted that in his *Qānūn*, a work focused on medical treatment, he depicts male and female genitalia as

---

749 A. Giladi, *Infants, Parents and Wet Nurses: Medieval Islamic Views on Breastfeeding and Their Social Implications*, 60.

750 Ibid. 21, 26, 80.

751 S. Gadelrab, "Discourses on Sex Differences in Medieval Scholarly Islamic Thought," *Journal of the History of Medicine and Allied Sciences* 66 (2011), 40–81. Cf. A. Ragab, "One, Two, or Many Sexes: Sex Differentiation in Medieval Islamicate Medical Thought" *Journal of the History of Sexuality*, 24(2015), 428–454.

752 The question relates to the thesis articulated in Thomas Laqueur's *Making Sex: Body and Gender from the Greeks to Freud* (Cambridge: Harvard University Press, 1990).

near equivalents, which were to be treated based on shared premises about bodily health, from the point of view of the physician. However, in his book on nature, the *Kitāb al-ḥayawān*, Ibn Sīnā depicted masculine and feminine nature as "more divergent behaviorally in human beings than in any other animal, as has been noticed by the natural philosophers."[753] Thus, Ibn Sīnā could hold the view that men and women are completely different and unequal (with women comparing unfavorably to men) and could identify that inequality as rooted in anatomy and physiology, while simultaneously arguing that, anatomically, men's and women's reproductive organs were largely equivalents. In other words, even among people who held "chauvinistic" views of women, that chauvinism did not extend into every scientific area involving gender, and even among people who held egalitarian views regarding men and women's reproductive organs, that did not translate into a social egalitarianism.

The quest for conception: women's access to medical practitioners

In a reassessment of Ullmann's claim that there were no opportunities for theoretically trained physicians to apply their gynecological knowledge due to gender segregation, this book has argued that the preponderance of the evidence available to us suggests otherwise. Medical works, *ḥisba* manuals, literary anecdotes, and anti-*bid'a* literature all indicate that trained male practitioners did treat women in a variety of medical situations, including intimate ones which involved direct observation of the patient, taking her pulse, bleeding and cupping her, discussing contraceptives and abortifacients, and operating in the area of the groin. There is little reason to doubt that such interactions were commonplace in many parts of the Middle East. As for the propriety of medical situations which involved viewing and touching women's genitals and performing surgery on them, the textual evidence is more varied. Such interactions are described in medical manuals, sometimes with a midwife taking on an explicitly-defined role as intermediary and sometimes not. Midwives seem to be particularly likely to be mentioned in situations which involved the practitioner introducing a hand or finger into the vagina. However, multiple sources suggest it was thought appropriate for men to engage in clitorectomies,[754] even though in modern contexts the

753 Gadelrab, 26. citing Ibn Sīnā, *Kitāb al-ḥayawān.*
754 Al-Zahrāwī, *Albucasis on Surgery and Instruments*, 457 and Ibn al-Ukhuwwa, *The Ma'ālim al-qurba fī aḥkām al-ḥisba*, 56.

practice is largely associated with female practitioners.[755] Men are also described as working collegially with women practitioners in heroic interventions for obstructed labor and childbirth. Some of the procedures described, however, were likely theoretical possibilities only, rather than practical ones. This is certainly the case with regard to cesarean sections, and probably with regard to perinatal dismemberment, but in other cases the practicability of suggested treatments which involve men in the birthing room is more ambiguous.

Legal and moralistic writings authored by jurists provide a different perspective, one which complements the view we get from medical writings. Their policing of boundaries highlights the prevalence of the opposite phenomenon.

> If someone were to say: "But the 'ulamā' have permitted uncovering nakedness before a physician whether the patient is a man or a woman!" the response is that this is the case when there is a necessity, and there is no necessity that calls for inviting an infidel when there exists a Muslim physician.[756]

In this passage, it is clear that in 8th/14th-century Cairo there is an expectation that the male physician, regardless of religious affiliation, would view and touch his female patient in the course of providing medical attention. It is also clear that there are those in Ibn al-Ḥājj's audience who commonly assert that jurists have no objection to uncovering nakedness (though Ibn al-Ḥājj does not mentioned whether this includes genitals) before a medical practitioner regardless of gender or religion.

Against this backdrop, Ibn al-Ḥājj argues that Muslim women should not be revealing themselves even to non-Muslim women, let alone to non-Muslim men. In response to those who raise the argument that the impropriety associated with nakedness does not pertain to medical situations, he argues that the impropriety is still there if a woman is exposed to a non-Muslim, male or female, when she has the opportunity to be seen by a Muslim practitioner. As we have seen, Ibn al-Ḥājj's legal positions on this matter are not unique to him. There was a long tradition, stemming from certain *ḥadīth*s attributed to the time of 'Umar's conquest of Jerusalem, of forbidding Muslim women from exposing themselves to non-Muslim women. When it came to the practical ranking of preferred medical practitioners, there is a debate among the jurists as to the relative distastefulness of exposing Muslim women to female non-Muslim medical practitioners as opposed to male Muslim ones.

755 Berkey, "Circumcision Circumscribed: Female Excision and Cultural Accommodation in the Medieval Near East," 20.
756 Ibn al-Ḥājj, *al-Madkhal*, 3/4:318.

The objection to non-Muslim practitioners was not based exclusively on concerns of sexual impropriety. (The concerns extended to male non-Muslim practitioners and their male patients, and even to nominally Muslim practitioners who were overly worshipful of the Greek medical tradition and dismissive of the Prophetic pronouncements on medicine.) Rather, in addition to the issue of sexual exposure, the objections were also based on concerns about the intellectual and spiritual influence healers have over their patients. This is not to suggest that there is a concerted trend in *fiqh* itself to legislate restrictions on seeking treatment from those practicing Arabo-Galenic medicine. There is no such legal tradition. But there is a history of such sentiments being expressed in the *adab* literature produced by jurists, who seem to be casting themselves in the role of embattled scolds.

The objections to subjecting oneself to the intellectual and spiritual influence of those who offer a system of belief and a system of authoritativeness outside of the orthodox Islamic one, had particular implications for women. These implications are most clearly articulated by Ibn al-Ḥājj, but Ibn al-Ḥājj is certainly operating within a long-standing strand of religious discourse. Ibn al-Ḥājj argues not only that non-Muslim women pose an intellectual threat to Muslim women and lead them astray (and through them also their husbands and families) by encouraging the adoption of syncretistic practices, but also that Muslim women can pose this threat as well. This is not entirely the fault of Muslim women or a result of their inborn spiritual deficiencies. Rather, Ibn al-Ḥājj argues, because Muslim women are secluded from most Muslim men, they do not have sufficient access to the teachers of orthodox Islam (what he refers to as "the pure Law") who are themselves men. The result, he claims, is that there is a religious vacuum among women, a vacuum which creates a space for women to construct and perpetuate their own religious ritual. This ritual centers upon the life cycles and matters of menstruation, sex, birth, sickness, and death.

Infertility and choice

The legal, biological, scientific, and religious concepts described in this book constitute gravitational poles which exerted sometimes overt and sometimes subtle pressure on the environments in which infertile women found themselves. These forces did not all exert pressure in the same direction. For example, the legal tendency to define the requisites of marriage as based on sexual rights and responsibilities ran afoul of those social pressures which accorded a greater role to the reproductive element of marriage. The desirability of marrying fertile women competed with the desirability of marrying virgins, some of whom were too young to be able to show signs of fertility. In the wake of widowhood or divorce, the pressures to ensure lineage by monitoring women's menstrual cycles were hampered by the biological fact that menstrual cycles are inexact proxies for reproductive status. Moreover, the tendency to seclude women from men, and women from society at large during the *'idda* period, made monitoring menstrual cycles difficult or unfeasible. The pressure exerted by Islamic law to include women as heirs to family property competed with the roles women necessarily played as liaisons to other families. The tendency to concentrate both scientific knowledge and religious authority in the hands of men, and to thereby make women dependent on men for medical and religious guidance, ran up against modesty restrictions, restrictions which pulled women towards turning to other women for medical and religious guidance, much to the chagrin of male authorities.

All this means that there was a range of ways in which a barren woman could experience infertility, and there was a range of ways in which people could choose to treat barren women, in both the medical and social senses of "treat." However, many of those choices would have been fraught and unstable. A couple or a husband could choose to remain childless and monogamous, but in such a situation the inheritance system would create conflicts between the couple and their in-laws, and possibly with their own birth families. A woman could choose to seek treatment for her barrenness at the hands of either Galenic medical practitioners, or practitioners of folk medicine, or of magic, or through the intercessions of holy persons – but none of those options would necessarily come without condemnation on the grounds of either sexual impropriety or heterodoxy. This range of choices, and the instability of those choices, takes on greater dramatic significance when we consider that infertility was often a lifelong condition, the ramifications of which changed as husbands and wives progressed into middle and old age. Those choices once made could be revisited again and again over the course of many years. Thus, the experience of infertility was a dynamic one, subject both to forces beyond anyone's control and subject to the individual choices and maneuverings of women, their husbands, their medical practitioners, and their extended families.

Bibliography

Primary Sources and Translations

'Abd al-Razzāq b. Hammām. *Muṣannaf.* 12 vols. Beirut: *Dār al-Kutub al-'Ilmiyya*, 2000.

Abū Dāwūd Sulaymān Ibn al-Ash'ath. *Sunan.* Riyadh: Maktab al-Ma'ārif lil-Nashr, 1996.

Aetius of Amida. *The Gynaecology and Obstetrics of the VI century*, tr. James Ricci. Philadelphia: Blakiston, 1950.

Alif Layla or Book of the Thousand Nights and One Night, ed. W. H. Macnaghten, 4 vols. Calcutta, 1839. English Translation: Richard Burton. The Book of a Thousand Nights and a Night, 10 vols. Benares: Kamashastra Society, 1885.

al-Anṣārī, Zakarīyā ibn Muḥammad. *Asnā al-maṭālib fī sharḥ Rawḍ al-ṭālib.* 9 vols. Beirut: Dār al-Kutub al-'Ilmiyya, 2000.

Arberry, A. J. *The Koran Interpreted.* London: Allen & Unwin, 1955.

Aristotle. *Generation of Animals.* Tr. A.L. Peck. Cambridge: Loeb Series, Harvard University Press, 1943.

Aristotle. *History of Animals Vol VII-X.* Tr. D. M. Balme. Cambridge: Loeb Series, Harvard University Press, 1991.

al-'Aṭṭār, Abū'l-Munā al-Mūhīn. *Minhāj al-dukkān wa-dustūr al-ayān.* Beirut: Dār al-Manāhil, 1992.

al-'Ayntābī, Maḥmūd b. Aḥmad. *al-Qawl al-sadīd fī ikhtiyār al-imā' wa'l-ābīd.* Beirut: Mu'assasat al-Risāla, 1996.

al-'Aẓīmābādī, Muḥammad Shams al-Ḥaqq. *'Awn al-ma'būd sharḥ Sunan Abī Dāwūd.* 2 vols. Beirut: Dār Ibn Ḥazm, 2005.

al-Baghdādī, 'Abd al-Laṭīf. *Kitāb al-Ifāda wa'l-i'tibār.* London: Allen and Unwin, 1965.

al-Baladī, Abū al-'Abbās Aḥmad ibn Muḥammad. *Tadbīr al-ḥabālā wa'l-aṭfāl wa'l-ṣibyān.* Beirut: Dār al-Kutub al-'Ilmiyya, 2004.

al-Bayhaqī, Aḥmad b. al-Ḥusayn. *al-Sunan al-kubrā.* Beirut: Dār al-Kutub al-'Ilmiyya, 2003.

al-Bayhaqī, Aḥmad b. al-Ḥusayn. *Manāqib al-Shāfi'ī.* 2 vols. Cairo: Maktabat Dār al-Turāth, 1971.

al-Biqā'ī, Burhān al-Dīn Ibrāhīm. *Iẓhār al-'aṣr li-asrār ahl al-'aṣr*, 3 vols. Riyadh: n.p., 1993.

al-Buhūtī, Manṣūr b. Yūnus. *Kashshāf al-qinā'.* 6 vols. Beirut: Dār al-Fikr, 1982.

al-Buhūtī, Manṣūr b. Yūnus. *Sharḥ muntahā al-irādāt.* 3 vols. Beirut: Dār 'ālam al-Kutub, 1993

al-Bukhārī, Muḥammad ibn Ismā'īl. *Ṣaḥīḥ al-Bukhārī.* Vaduz, Liechtenstein: Thesaurus Islamicus Foundation, 2000.

al-Dardīr, Aḥmad ibn Muhammad. *Sharḥ al-kabīr 'alā Mukhtasar Khalīl* in *Ḥāshiyat al-Dasūqī 'alā al-Sharḥ al-kabīr.* 4 vols. Beirut: Dār al-Fikr, n.d.

al-Dasūqī, Muḥammad ibn Aḥmad. *Ḥāshīyat al-Dasūqī 'alā al-Sharḥ al-kabīr.* 4 vols. Beirut: Dār al-fikr, n.d.

al-Dhahabī, Muḥammad b. Aḥmad. *al-Ṭibb al-nabawī.* Beirut: Dār Iḥyā al-'Ulūm, 1990.

al-Dīnawarī, Abū Bakr. *al-Mujālasa wa-jawāhir al-'ilm.* Frankfurt am Main: Veröffentlichungen des Institutes für Geschichte der arabisch-islamischen Wissenschaften, 1986.

Dioscorides and T.A. Osbaldeston. *Dioscorides De Materia Medica: a New English Translation.* Johannesburg: IBIDIS, 2000.

Duran, Shimon b. Tsemah. *Sefer ha-Tashbets.* Lemberg: Uri Ze'ev Salat, 1891.

https://doi.org/10.1515/9783110596588-017

al-Fayyūmī, Aḥmad ibn Muḥammad. *al-Miṣbāḥ al-munīr fī Gharīb al-Sharḥ al-kabīr*. Beirut: Dār al-Kutub al-ʿIlmiyyah, 1978.

Galen. *De Usu Partium*. Translated by Margaret Tallmadge May. *On the Usefulness of the Parts*. 2 vols. Ithaca: Cornell University Press, 1968.

Galen. *On the Anatomy of the Uterus*. Translated by Charles Mayo Goss. "On the Anatomy of the Uterus." The Anatomical Record 144 (1962): 77–83.

Galen. *On Hippocrates' On the Nature of Man*. tr. W. J. Lewis and J.A. Beach. https://www.ucl.ac.uk/~ucgajpd/medicina%20antiqua/tr_GNatHom.html (accessed July 1, 2017.)

al-Ghazālī, Abū Ḥāmid. *Iḥyā ʿulūm al-dīn*. 5 vols. Cairo: Mu'assasat al-Ḥalabī, 1967.

al-Ghazālī, Abū Ḥāmid. *al-Wasīṭ fī al-madhhab*. 7 vols. Cairo: Dār al-Salām, 1997.

al-Hamadhānī, ʿAbd al-Jabbār. *Tathbīt dalā'il al-nubuwwa*. Cairo: Dār al-Muṣṭafā, 2006.

al-Ḥarīrī and F. Steingass. *The Assemblies of al-Ḥarīrī; Student's edition of the Arabic text; with English notes, grammatical, critical, and historical*. London: Sampson Low, Marston & Co. 1897.

al-Ḥaṣkafī, Muḥammad ibn ʿAlī. *Durr al-mukhtār*. In *Hāshiyat Radd al-Muḥtār ʿalā al-Durr al-mukhtār*. 8 vols. Cairo: Muṣṭafa al-Ḥalabī, 1966.

al-Ḥaṭṭāb, Muḥammad b. Muḥammad. *Mawāhib al-jalīl*. 6 vols. Beirut: Dār al-Fikr, 1992.

al-Haythamī, Nūr al-Dīn ʿAlī ibn Abī Bakr. *Majmaʿ al-zawā'id*. 10 vols. Beirut: Dār al-Kutub al-ʿIlmiyya, 2001.

Hippocrates. *De Morbis Mulierum*. Translated by Ann Ellis Hanson. "Hippocrates: 'Diseases of Women 1.'" Signs 1 (1975): 567–584.

Hippocrates. *De Virginum Morbis*. Translated by Ann Ellis Hanson and Rebecca Flemming. "Hippocrates' 'Peri Partheniôn' (Diseases of Young Girls): Text and Translation." Early Science and Medicine 3 (1998): 241–252.

Hippocrates. *Genuine Works of Hippocrates*. Tr. Francis Adams. London: The Sydenham Society, 1849.

Hippocrates. *Hippocrates Vol. X*. Tr. Paul Potter. Cambridge, MA: Harvard University Press, 2012.

Ibn ʿAbd al-Ra'ūf and E. Lévi-Provençal. *Trois Traités Hispaniques De Hisba: Texte Arabe*. Cairo: Publications De L'institut Français D'archéologie Orientale Du Caire, 1955.

Ibn ʿAbd al-Ra'ūf and Rachel Arié. "Traduction annotée et commentée des traités de ḥisba d'Ibn ʿAbd Al-Ra'ūf et de ʿUmar al-Garsīfī." *Hespéris Tamuda* 1 (1960), 5–38.

Ibn ʿAbdūn al-Tujibī and E. Lévi-Provençal, *Séville Musulmane Au Début Du XIIe Siècle: Le Traité D'ibn Abdun Sur La Vie Urbaine Et Les Corps De Métiers*. Paris: G. P. Maisonneuve, 1947.

Ibn ʿĀbidīn, Muḥammad Amīn b. ʿUmar. *Hāshiyat Radd al-Muḥtār ʿalā al-Durr al-mukhtār*. 8 vols. Cairo: Muṣṭafa al-Ḥalabī, 1966. 14 vols. Riyadh: ʿĀlam al-Kutub, 2003.

Ibn Abī Shaybah, Abū Bakr ʿAbdallāh b. Muḥammad. *Muṣannaf fī al-aḥādīth waʾl-āthār*. Jedda: Dār al-Qiblah lil-Nashr waʾl-Tawzīʿ, 2006.

Ibn Abī Uṣaybīʿa, Aḥmad ibn al-Qāsim, *ʿUyūn al-anbāʾ fī ṭabaqāt al-aṭibbāʾ*. Beirut: Dār Maktabat al-Ḥayāt, 1965. Partial English translation available online: L. Kopf. *Lives of the Physicians*. http://www.tertullian.org/fathers/ibn_abi_usaibia_03.htm

Ibn Abī Zayd al-Qayrawānī, Abū Muḥammad ʿAbd Allāh. *al-Nawādir wa'l-ziyādāt ʿalā mā fī al-mudawwanah min ghayrihā min al-ummahāt*, ed. ʿAbd al-Fattāḥ Muḥammad al-Ḥulw. 15 vols. Beirut: Dār al-Gharb al-Islāmī, 1999.

Ibn al-ʿArabī, Muḥammad ibn ʿAbdallāh. *Aḥkām al-Qurʾān*, 2 vols. Beirut: Dār al-Kutub al-ʿIlmiyya, 1991.
Ibn al-ʿAṭṭār, Muḥammad ibn Aḥmad. *Kitāb al-Wathāʾiq waʾl-sijillāt* (Formulario notarial Hispano-Arabe), ed. Ch. Gendrón and F. Corriente. Madrid: Majmaʿ al-Muwaththiqīn al-Majrīṭī, 1983.
Ibn Bābawayh, Muḥammad b. ʿAlī. *Man lā yaḥḍuruhu al-faqīh*. Mashhad: al-Majmaʿ, 1988.
Ibn al-Barrāj, ʿAbd al-ʿAzīz ibn Niḥrīr. *al-Muhadhdhab*, 2 vols. Qom: Mūʾassasat al-Nashr al-Islāmī, 1986.
Ibn Bassām, *Nihāya al-rutba fī ṭalab al-ḥisba*. Beirut: Dār al-kutub al-ʿilmiyya, 2003.
Ibn Bāz, ʿAbd al-ʿAzīz et al. *Fatāwā Islamiyya*. Riyadh: Darussalam, 2001.
Ibn Ezra, Abraham. *Sefer Hanisyonot = The Book of Medical Experiences Attributed to Abraham Ibn Ezra: Medical Theory, Rational and Magical Therapy: A Study In Medievalism*, ed. J. Leibowitz and S. Marcus. Jerusalem: Magnes Press, 1984.
Ibn Ḥabīb, ʿAbd al-Mālik. *Kitāb adab al-nisāʾ al-mawsūm bi-kitāb al-ghāya waʾl-nihāya*. Paris: Dār al-Gharb al-Islāmī, 1992.
Ibn Ḥajar al-Haytamī, Aḥmad ibn Muḥammad. *Tuḥfat al-muḥtāj fī sharḥ al-minhāj in Ḥawāshī al-Sharawānī wa-Ibn-Qāsim al-ʿAbbādī ʿalā tuḥfat al-muḥtāj bi-sharḥ al-minhāj li-Ibn Ḥajar al-Haytamī*. 13 vols. Beirut: Dār Iḥyāʾ al-Turāth al-ʿArabī, 1988.
Ibn al-Ḥājj, Muḥammad b. Muḥammad. *al-Madkhal*. 4 vols. Beirut: Dār al-Kutub al-ʿIlmiyya, 1995.
Ibn Ḥanbal, Aḥmad. *Musnad*. 11 vols. Beirut: ʿĀlam al-Kutub, 1998 and Cairo: Dār al-Maʿārif, 1951.
Ibn Ḥanbal, Aḥmad. Masāʾil al-Imām Aḥmad bin Ḥanbal riwāyat Isḥaq ibn Ibrāhīm ibn Hāniʾ al-Nayṣābūrī. Beirut: al-Maktab al-Islāmī, 1979.
Ibn Ḥanbal, Aḥmad. *Masāʾil al-Imām Aḥmad ibn Ḥanbal wa-Isḥāq ibn Rāhwayh*. 10 vols. Medina: ʿImādat al-Baḥth al-ʿIlmī, 2004.
Ibn Ḥanbal, Aḥmad. *Aḥkām al-nisāʾ ʿan al-imām Abī ʿAbdallāh Aḥmad ibn Muḥammad ibn Ḥanbal, riwāya Abī Bakr al-Khilāl*. Beirut: Muʾassasat al-Rayyān lil-Ṭibāʿa waʾl-Nashr, 2002.
Ibn Ḥazm, ʿAlī ibn Aḥmad. *al-Muḥalla*. 11 vols. Cairo: Idārat al-Ṭibāʿa al-Munīriyya, 1928 and Beirut: Maktab al-tijārī lil-tibāʿa, 1969.
Ibn Ḥibbān, Muḥammad. *al-Majrūḥīn min al-muḥaddithīn*. Aleppo: Dār al-Waʿy, 1975.
Ibn Isḥāq, Ḥunayn. *Kitāb al-mawlūdīn*. Baghdad: Majmaʾ al-Lugha al-Siryāniyya, 1978.
Ibn Isḥāq al-Jundī, Khalīl. *Mukhtaṣar*. Cairo: Dār al-Ḥadīth, 2005.
Ibn al-Jawzī, Abū al-Faraj ʿAbd al-Raḥmān ibn ʿAlī. *Aḥkām al-nisāʾ*. Kuwait: Maktabat Dār Ibn Qutayba, 1989.
Ibn al-Jawzī, Abū al-Faraj ʿAbd al-Raḥmān ibn ʿAlī. *Zād al-masīr fī ʿilm al-tafsīr*. 8 vols. Beirut: Dār al-Fikr, 1987.
Ibn al-Jazzār al-Qayrawānī. *Ṭibb al-fuqarāʾ waʾl-masākīn*. Tehran: Muʾassasah-ʾi Muṭālaʿāt-i Islāmī, Dānishgāh-i Tihrān, 1996.
Ibn al-Jazzār al-Qayrawānī and Gerrit Bos. *Ibn al-Jazzār on Sexual Diseases and Their Treatment: a critical edition, English translation and introduction of Book 6 of Zād al-musāfir wa-qūt al-ḥāḍir*. London, Kegan Paul International, 1997.
Ibn Jumayʿ. *al-Maqāla as-Ṣalāḥiya = Treatise to Ṣalāḥ ad-Dīn on the revival of the art of medicine by Ibn Jumayʿ: edited and translated by Hartmut Fähndrich*. Marburg: Kommissionsverlag F. Steiner, 1983.

Ibn Kathīr, Ismā'īl ibn 'Umar. *Tafsīr al-Qur'ān al-'aẓīm*, 8 vols. Riyadh: Dār Ṭayba lil-nashr wa'l-tawzī', 1997.
Ibn Kathīr, Ismā'īl ibn 'Umar. *Qiṣaṣ al-anbiyā'*. Damascus: Dār Ibn Kathīr, 1992.
Ibn Mājah, Muḥammad ibn Yazīd. *Sunan*. 5 vols. Riyadh: Maktab Ma'ārif lil-Nashr, 1996.
Ibn Manṣūr, Sa'īd. Sunan. 3 vols. Bombay: Dār al-Salafiyya, 1982.
Ibn Mufliḥ, Muḥammad. al-Ādāb al-shar'iyya. 3 vols. Beirut: Mu'assasat al-Risāla, 1996.
Ibn al-Naqīb and Noah Keller, *The Reliance of the Traveller: A Classic Manual of Islamic Sacred Law by Ahmad ibn Naqib al-Misri*. Chicago: Sunna Books, 1991.
Ibn Nujaym, Zayn al-Dīn b. Ibrāhīm. *Baḥr al-rā'iq sharḥ kanz al-daqā'iq*. 9 vols. Quetta: al-Maktaba al-Mājidiyya, 1983.
Ibn al-Quff, Abū al-Faraj ibn Ya'qūb. *Kitāb al-'Umda fī al-jirāḥa*. 2 vols. Hyderabad: Majlis *Dā'irat al-Ma'ārif al-'Uthmāniyya*, 1937.
Ibn Qayyim al-Jawziyya, Muḥammad. *al-Tibyān fī aqsām al-Qur'ān*. Cairo: n.p., 1933.
Ibn Qayyim al-Jawziyya, Muḥammad. *Zād al-ma'ād fī hady khayr al-'ibād*. 6 vols. Beirut: Mu'assasat al-Risāla, 1998.
Ibn Qayyim al-Jawziyya, Muḥammad. *al-Ṭibb al-nabawī*. Beirut: Dār al-Fikr = Dār Iḥyā al-Kutub al-'Arabiyya, 1957. English translation: *Medicine of the Prophet*. tr. Penelope Johnstone. Cambridge: Islamic Texts Society, 1998.
Ibn al-Qiftī, 'Alī ibn Yūsuf. *Inbāh al-ruwāt 'alā anbāh al-nuḥāt*, ed. Muḥammad Ibrāhīm. Cairo: Dār al-Kutub al-Miṣriyya, 1950.
Ibn Qudāma, Muwaffaq al-Dīn 'Abd Allāh ibn Aḥmad. *al-Mughnī*. 10 vols. Cairo: Maktabat al-Qāhira, 1968.
Ibn Rushd, Muḥammad b. Aḥmad (al-jadd). *al-Bayān wa'l-taḥṣīl wa'l-sharḥ wa'l-tawjīh wa'l-ta'līl fī masā'il al-mustakhraja*, ed. Muḥammad Ḥajjī. 20 vols. Beirut: Dār al-Gharb al-Islamī, 1984.
Ibn Rushd, Muḥammad b. Aḥmad (al-jadd). *Fatāwā Ibn Rushd*. 3 vols. Beirut: Dār al-Gharb al-Islāmī, 1987.
Ibn Rushd, Muḥammad b. Aḥmad (Averroes). *Bidāyat al-mujtahid*. 2 vols. Cairo: Dār al-Salām, 1995. English translation: *The Distinguished Jurist's Primer: A Translation of Bidāyat Al-Mujtahid*, tr. Imran Ahsan Khan Nyazee. 2 vols. Reading: Garnet, 2000.
Ibn Rushd, Muḥammad b. Aḥmad (Averroes). *Kulliyāt fī al-ṭibb*. Morocco: Ma'had al-Jinirāl Frankū, Lajnat al-Abḥāth al-'Arabīya al-Isbānīya, 1939.
Ibn Sa'd, Muḥammad. *al-Ṭabaqāt al-kubrā*, 8 vols in 4. Beirut: Dār Iḥya' al-Turāth al-'Arabī, 1996.
Ibn Sahl and Oliver Kahl. *Sābūr Ibn Sahl's Dispensatory in the Recension of the 'Aḍudī Hospital*. Leiden: Brill, 2009.
Ibn Sīnā. *al-Qānūn fī al-ṭibb*. 3 vols. Būlāq: al-Maṭba'a al-Āmira, 1878.
Ibn Sīnā. *al-Shifā'*. 4 vols. Cairo: al-Hay'a al-Miṣrīya al-'Āmma lil-Ta'līf, 1970.
Ibn al-Sunnī, Aḥmad b. Muḥammad. *Kitāb 'amal al-yawm wa'l-layla*. Beirut: Mu'assasat al-Kutub al-Thaqāfiyya, 1988.
Ibn Taymiyya, Taqī al-Dīn, *Fatāwā al-nisā'*. Cairo: Maktabat al-Qur'ān, 1987.
Ibn Taymiyya, Taqī al-Dīn. *Majmū' fatāwā*. 37 vols. Medina: Majma' al-Malik Fahd li-Ṭibā'at al-Muṣḥaf al-Sharīf, 2004.
Ibn al-Ukhuwwa and R. Levy. *The Ma'ālim al-qurba fī aḥkām al-ḥisba of Ḍiyā' al-Dīn M. b. M al-Qurashī al-Shafi'ī known as ibn al-Ukhuwwa*. London: Cambridge University Press, 1938.

Ibn Ṭūlūn, Shams al-Dīn. *al-Manhal al-rawī fī al-ṭibb al-nabawī.* Hyderabad: Anwār al-Ma'ārif, 1987.
Ibn Zuhr, 'Abd al-Malik ibn Abī al-'Alā'. *Kitāb al-taysīr.* Rabat: Akādīmīyat al-Mamlaka al-Maghribiyya, 1991.
Al-Jāḥiẓ. *Kitāb al-Bukhalā'.* English translation: *The Book of Misers*, tr. R. B. Serjeant. London: Garnet & Ithaca Press, 2000.
Al-Jazarī, Muḥammad b. Ibrāhīm. *Ta'rīkh ḥawādith al-zamān wa-anbā'ihi wa-wafayaāt al-akābir wa'l-a'yān min abnā'ihi.* 3 vols. Beirut: al-Maktaba al-'Aṣriyya, 1998.
Jones, Alan. *The Qur'ān.* Exeter: E. J. W. Gibb Memorial Trust, 2007.
al-Kāsānī, Abū Bakr ibn Mas'ūd. *Badā'i' al-ṣanā'i'.* 7 vols. Beirut: Dār al-Kutub al-'Ilmiyya, 1986.
al-Khaṭṭābī, Abū Sulayman. A'lām al-Ḥadīth fī sharḥ Ṣaḥīḥ al-Bukhārī. Mecca: Jāmi'at Umm al-Qurā, Ma'had al-Buḥūth al-'Ilmiyyah wa-Iḥyā' al-Turāth al-Islāmī, Markaz Iḥyā' al-Turāth al-Islāmī, 1988.
Lemay, H. R. *Women's Secrets: A Translation of Pseudo-Albertus Magnus's "De Secretis Mulierum" with Commentaries.* Albany: State University of New York Press, 1992.
Lyons, M. C. and J. N. Mattock. *Kitāb al-ajinna li-Buqrāṭ.* Cambridge: Pembroke Arabic Texts, 1978.
Maimonides, Moses. *Teshuvot ha-Rambam.* 3 vols. Jerusalem: Mikitse Nirdamim, 1957.
al-Majlisī. *Biḥār al-anwār.* 44 vols. Beirut: Mu'assasat al-Wafā', 1983.
al-Majūsī, 'Alī ibn al-'Abbās. *al-Kāmil al-ṣinā'a fī al-ṭibb*, 2 vols. Cairo: al-Maṭba'ah al-Kubrā al-'Āmira, 1877.
Mālik b. Anas. *al-Muwaṭṭa'*, ed. 'Abd al-Majīd Turkī. Beirut: Dār al-Gharb al-Islāmī, 1999.
Mannā, Ḥasan Murad. *Fatāwā wa-tawjīhāt.* Cairo: Dār al-Ṣafwa, 1990.
al-Marghīnānī, Maḥmūd ibn Aḥmad. *Muḥīṭ al-burhānī fī al-fiqh al-Nu'mānī.* 9 vols. Beirut: Dār Iḥyā' al-Turāth al-'Arabī, 2003.
al-Marwarrūdhī, Ḥusayn ibn Muḥammad ibn Aḥmad. *Fatāwā al-qāḍī Ḥusayn ibn Muḥammad al-Marwarrūdhī.* Amman: Dār al-Fatḥ, 2010.
al-Māwardī. *Kitāb al-ḥāwī al-kabīr.* 19 vols. Beirut: Dar al-Kutub al-'Ilmiyya, 1999.
al-Mawṣilī, 'Abdallāh b. Maḥmūd. al-Ikhtiyār li-ta'līl al-Mukhtār. 5 vols. Beirut: Dār al-Risāla al-'Ālamiyya, 2009.
Muslim ibn al-Ḥajjāj. *Ṣaḥīḥ Muslim.* 5 vols. Beirut: Dār Iḥyā' al-Turāth al-'Arabī, 1955.
al-Nafrāwī, Aḥmad b. Ghunaym. *al-Fawākih al-dawānī.* 2 vols. Cairo: Muṣṭafā al-Bābī al-Ḥalabī, 1955.
al-Najafī, Muḥammad Ḥasan ibn Bāqir. *Jawāhir al-kalām fī sharḥ Sharā'i' al-Islām*, 15 vols. Beirut: Mu'assasat al-Murtaḍā al-'Ālamiyya, 1992.
al-Nasā'ī, Aḥmad ibn Shu'ayb. *Sunan.* Riyadh: Maktab al-Ma'ārif lil-Nashr, 1996.
Naṣār, 'Allām. "*Fatwā* – January 19, 1952." In *Fatāwā dār al-iftā' al-miṣriyya.* Cairo: Wizārat al-Awqāf, 1980.
al-Nawawī, Muḥyī al-Dīn. *Minhāj al-ṭālibīn.* Beirut: Dār al-Minhāj, 2005. English translation: *Minhaj et Talibin: A Manual of Muhammadan Law according to the School of Shafii*, tr. E. C. Howard. London: W. Thacker & Co., 1914.
al-Nawawī, Muḥyī al-Dīn. *Rawḍat al-ṭālibīn wa-'umdat al-muftīyīn.* 8 vols. Beirut: al-Maktab al-Islāmī, 1991.
Nu'mān ibn Muḥammad and A. A. Fyzee. *Pillars of Islam*, 2 vols. New York: Oxford University Press, 2004

al-Nuwayrī, Shihāb al-Dīn Aḥmad ibn 'Abd al-Wahhāb. *Nihāyat al-arab fī funūn al-adab.* Beirut: Dār al-kutub al-'ilmiyya, 2004.

Niẓām. *al-Fatāwa al-hindiyya*, 6 vols. Būlāq: al-Maṭba'a al-Kubrā al-Amīriyya, 1892.

Paul of Aegina and Francis Adams. *The Seven Books of Paulus Ægineta.* 3 vols. London: Sydenham Society, 1844.

al-Qalyūbī, Shihāb al-Dīn Aḥmad ibn Aḥmad. *Qalyūbī wa-'Umayrah: hāshiyatā al-imāmayn al-muḥaqqiqayn al-mudaqqiqayn al-Shaykh Shihāb al-Dīn al-Qalyūbī wa'l-Shaykh 'Umayrah 'alá Sharḥ Jalāl al-Dīn al-Maḥallī 'alá Minhāj al-ṭālibīn lil-Shaykh Muḥyī al-Dīn al-Nawawī fī fiqh madhhab al-Imām al-Shāfi'ī.* 4 vols. Cairo: Dār Iḥyā' al-Kutub al-'Arabiyyah, 1960.

al-Qarāfī, Shihāb al-Dīn Aḥmad b. Idrīs. *al-Dhakhīrah.* 15 vols. Beirut: Dār al-Gharb al-Islāmī, 1994.

al-Qazwīnī, Zakarīyā ibn Muḥammad. *'Ajā'ib al-makhlūqāt wa-al-ḥayawānāt wa-gharā'ib al-mawjūdāt.* Beirut: Mu'assasat al-A'lamī lil-Maṭbū'āt, 2000.

al-Qummī, 'Alī ibn Ibrāhīm. *Tafsīr al-Qummī.* 3 vols. Qum: Mu'assasat al-Imām al-Mahdī, 2014.

al-Qurṭubī, 'Arīb ibn Sa'īd. *Kitāb khalq al-janīn wa-tadbīr al-ḥabālā wa'l-mawlūdīn = La livre de la génération du foetus et le traitement des femmes enceintes et des nouveau-nés.* Algiers: Librairie Ferraris, 1956.

al-Rāzī, Muḥammad ibn Zakarīyā. *al-Ḥāwī fī al-ṭibb.* Beirut: Dar al-kutub al-'ilmiyya, 2000.

al-Rāzī, Muḥammad ibn Zakarīyā. *Kitāb Shukūk 'alā Jālīnūs.* Tehran: Mu'assasah-'i Muṭāla'āt-i Islāmī, Dānishgāh-i Tihrān, 1993.

al-Rāzī, Muḥammad ibn Zakarīyā. *Kitāb al-tajārib: ma'a dirāsa fī manhaj al-baḥth al-'ilmī 'inda al-Rāzī.* Alexandria: Dār al-Wafā' li-Dunyā al-Ṭibā'a wa'l-Nashr, 2006.

al-Rāzī, Muḥammad ibn Zakarīyā. *al-Manṣūrī fī al-ṭibb.* Kuwait: Ma'had al-makhṭūṭāt al-'arabīya, 1987.

al-Rāzī, 'Abd al-Raḥmān ibn Abī Ḥātim. *Tafsīr al-Qur'ān al-'aẓim li-ibn abī Ḥātim.* 8 vols. Mecca: Maktabat Nizār Muṣṭafā al-Bāz, 1997.

al-Saffārīnī, Muḥammad b. Aḥmad b. Sālim. *Ghidhā' al-albāb li-sharḥ Manẓūmat al-ādāb.* 2 vols. Beirut: Dār al-Kutub al-'Ilmiyya, 1996.

Ṣā'id ibn al-Ḥasan. *At-Tašwīq aṭ-ṭibbī des Ṣā'id ibn al-Ḥasan*, ed. Otto Spies. Bonn: Selbstverlag des Orientalischen Seminars der Universitat Bonn, 1968.

al-Sarakhsī, Muḥammad ibn Aḥmad. *al-Mabsūṭ.* 30 vols. Beirut: Dār al-Kutub al-'Ilmiyya, 1993.

al-Shāfi'ī, Muḥammad ibn Idrīs. *Kitāb al-umm.* 8 vols. (Beirut: Dār al-Ma'rifa, 1990).

al-Shayzarī, 'Abd al-Raḥmān ibn Naṣr. *Kitāb nihāyat al-rutba fi ṭalab al-ḥisba lil-Shayzarī.* Cairo: Lajnat al-ta'līf wa'l-tarjama wa'l-nashr, 1946.

al-Shirbīnī, Muḥammad b. Aḥmad. *Mughnī al-muḥtāj ilā ma'rifat ma'ānī alfāẓ al-Minhāj.* 6 vols. Cairo: Maṭba'at Muṣṭafā al-Bābī al-Ḥalabī, 1958.

al-Shirwānī, 'Abd al-Ḥamīd. *Ḥawāshī tuḥfat al-muhtāj bī sharḥ al-Minhāj.* 10 vols. Cairo: Maktaba al-tijāriyya al-kubra bi-Miṣr, 1938 and Beirut: Dār al-Kutub al-'Ilmiyya, 1996.

Las Siete Partidas, tr. Samuel Parsons Scott. Chicago: The Comparative Law Bureau of The American Bar Association, 1931.

Soranus, and Oswei Temkin. *Soranus's Gynecology.* Baltimore: Johns Hopkins University Press, 1956.

Stephanus, and Leendert Gerrit Westerink. *Commentary On Hippocrates' Aphorisms*. Berlin: Akademie-Verlag, 1985.
al-Suyūṭī, Jalāl al-Dīn. *Kitāb al-Raḥma fī al-ṭibb wa'l-ḥikma*. Beirut: Dār al-Arqam, 2011.
al-Suyūṭī, Muṣṭafā ibn Sa'd. *Maṭālib ūlī al-nuhā fī sharḥ ghāyat al-muntahā*, 6 vols. Damascus: al-Maktab al-Islāmī, 1961.
al-Ṭabarānī, Aḥmad. *al-Mu'jam al-kabīr*. 25 vols. Cairo: Maktabat Ibn Taymiyya, 1983.
al-Ṭabarānī, Aḥmad. *al-Mu'jam al-awsaṭ*. 10 vols. Cairo: Dār al-Ḥaramayn, 1995.
al-Ṭabarī, Abū Ja'far. *Tārīkh al-rusul wa'l-mulūk*. Leiden: Brill, 1879. English translation: Franz Rosenthal. *History of al-Ṭabarī: General Introduction and From the Creation to the Flood*. Albany: SUNY Press, 1989.
al-Ṭabarī, 'Alī ibn Sahl Rabbān. *Firdaws al-ḥikma fī al-ṭibb*. Berlin: Maṭba'at Āftāb, 1928.
al-Ṭahāwī, Aḥmad b. Muḥammad. *Sharḥ ma'ānī al-āthār*. 4 vols. Beirut: 'Ālam al-Kutub, 1994.
al-Tīfāshī, Aḥmad ibn Yūsuf. *al-Shifā fī al-ṭibb al-musnad 'an al-sayyid al-Muṣṭafā*. Beirut: Dār al-Ma'rifa, 1988.
al-Tirmidhī, Muḥammad b. 'Īsā. *Ṣaḥīḥ al-Tirmidhī*. 13 vols. Cairo: Maṭba'ah al-Miṣriyya bi'l-Azhar, 1934.
al-Ūshī, Sirāj al-Dīn Abū Muḥammad 'Alī ibn 'Uthmān, *al-Fatāwā' al-Sirājiyya*. Lenasia, South Africa: Dār al-'ulūm Zakariyyā, 2011.
al-Wansharīsī, Aḥmad ibn Yaḥyā. *al-Mi'yār al-mu'rib wa'l-jāmi' al-mughrib 'an fatāwā ahl Ifrīqiya wa'l-Andalus wa'l-Maghrib*. 13 vols. Rabat: Wizārat al-Awqāf wa'l-Shu'ūn al-Islāmiyya lil-Mamlaka al-Maghribiyya, 1981.
al-Zahrāwī, Abū al-Qāsim Khalaf ibn 'Abbās and M.S. Spink and G. L. Lewis, *Albucasis on Surgery and Instruments: A Definitive Edition of the Arabic Text with English Translation and Commentary*. Berkeley: University of California Press, 1973.
al-Zurqāni, Muḥammad ibn 'Abd al-Bāqī. *Sharḥ al-Zurqānī 'alá Mukhtaṣar Sayyidī Khalīl*. Beirut: Dār al-Kutub al-'Ilmiyya, 2002.

Secondary Scholarship

Abasiattai, A. M. et al. "Vaginal Injuries During Coitus in Calabar: A 10-year Review." *Nigerian Postgraduate Medical Journal* 12.2 (2005): 140–4.
Abramson, Shraga. "On the Takkanah of Tuletula (Toledo) Regarding the Husband's Inheritance of his Wife's Estate." *Zion* 60 (1995): 201–224.
Abu-Lughod, Lila. "A Community of Secrets: The Separate World of Bedouin Women." *Signs* 10 (1985): 637–659.
Abu-Lughod, Lila. "Feminist Longings and Postcolonial Conditions." In *Remaking Women, Feminism and Modernity in the Middle East*, ed. L. Abu-Lughod, 3–32. Princeton: Princeton University Press, 1988.
Agrimi, Jole and Chiara Crisciani, "Savoir médical et anthropologie religieuse: Les représentations et les fonctions de la vetula (XIIIe-XVe siècle)." *Annales* 48 (1993), 1281–308.
Ali, Kecia. *Marriage and Slavery in Early Islam*. Cambridge: Harvard University Press, 2010.
Ali, Kecia. "Marriage in Classical Islamic Jurisprudence: A Survey of Doctrines." In *The Islamic Marriage Contract*, ed. Frank Vogel and Asifa Quraishi, 23–25. Cambridge: Harvard University Press, 2008.

Ali, Kecia. Sexual Ethics & Islam. Oxford: Oneworld Publications, 2006.

Alsammani, Mohamed Al-Khatim. "Imperforate Hymen Complicated with Genital Mutilation: A Case Report," *Journal of Clinical Case Reports* 2 (2012): 107.

Alshech, Eli. "Notions of Privacy in Classical Sunnī Islamic Thought." Ph.D. Dissertation: Princeton University, 2004.

Alshech, Eli. "Out of Sight and Therefore Out of Mind: Early Sunnī Islamic Modesty Regulations and the Creation of Spheres of Privacy." *Journal of Near Eastern Studies* 66 (2007): 267–90.

ʿAmmār, Ḥāmid. *Growing up in an Egyptian village; Silwa, Province of Aswan.* New York, Octagon Books, 1966.

Amster, Ellen. *Medicine and the Saints.* Austin: University of Texas Press, 2013.

Amundsen, Darrel W. and Carol Jean Diers. "The Age of Menopause in Medieval Europe." *Human Biology* 45 (1973): 605–612.

Anonymous, "Some Facts and Figures About Women's Situation In Pakistan," *Manushi* 12 (1982): 5.

Antoun, Richard. "On the Modesty of Women in Arab Muslim Villages: A Study in the Accommodation of Traditions." *American Anthropologist* 70 (1968): 671–697.

Antoun, Richard. "Social Organization and the Life Cycle in an Arab Village," *Ethnology* 6 (1967): 294–308.

Ashtor, Eliyahu. "The Diet of Salaried Classes in The Medieval Near East." *Journal of Asian History* 4 (1970): 1–24.

Azam, Hina. *Sexual Violation in Islamic Law.* New York: Cambridge University Press, 2015.

Barkaï, Ron. *Les infortunes de Dinah, le livre de la génération: La gynécologie juive au Moyen âge.* Paris: Cerf, 1991.

Baskin, Judith. "Rabbinic Reflections on the Barren Wife." *Harvard Theological Review* 82 (1989): 101–14.

Batten, Rosalind. "The Arabic Commentaries On The Hippocratic Aphorisms: Arabic Learned Medical Discourse On Women's Bodies (9th-15th Cent.)." Ph.D. Dissertation: University of Manchester, 2018.

Bauer, Karen. "'Traditional' Exegesis of Q. 4:34." *Comparative Islamic Studies* 2 (2006): 129–142.

Baumgarten, Elisheva. *Mothers and Children: Jewish Family Life in Medieval Europe.* Princeton: Princeton University Press, 2004.

Bayoumi, Abbas. "Survivances Egyptiennes." *Bulletin de la Société royale de géographie d'É gypte* 19 (1937): 279–287.

Behrend-Martínez, Edward. "Female Sexual Potency in a Spanish Church Court, 1673–1735." *Law and History Review* 24.2 (2006): 297–330.

Behrend-Martínez, Edward. *Unfit for Marriage: Impotent Spouses On Trial In the Basque Region of Spain, 1650–1750.* Reno: University of Nevada Press, 2007.

Berkey, Jonathan. "Circumcision Circumscribed: Female Excision and Cultural Accommodation in the Medieval near East." *International Journal of Middle East Studies* 28.1 (1996): 19–38.

Boddy, Janice. *Wombs and Alien Spirits: Women, Men, and the Zar Cult in Northern Sudan.* Madison: University of Wisconsin Press, 1986.

Bojlén, K. and M.W. Bentzon. "The Influence of Climate and Nutrition on Age at Menarche: A Historical Review and a Modern Hypothesis." *Human Biology* 40 (1968): 69–85.

Bos, Gerrit. “On Editing and Translating Medieval Hebrew Medical Texts.” *Jewish Quarterly Review* 89 (1998): 101–122.
Bouhdiba, Abdelwahab. *La Sexualité en Islam*. Paris: Presses Universitaires de France, 1975. English translation: *Sexuality in Islam*. London: Saqi Books, 2004.
Boylan, Michael. “The Galenic and Hippocratic Challenges to Aristotle’s Conception Theory.” *Journal of the History of Biology* 18 (1984): 83–112.
Boylan, Michael. “Galen’s Conception Theory.” *Journal of the History of Biology* 19 (1986): 62.
Cohen, Shaye J. D. “Purity, Piety, and Polemic: Medieval Rabbinic Denunciations of “Incorrect” Purification Practices.” In *Women and Water: Menstruation in Jewish Life and Law*, ed. R. Wasserfall, 82–100. Hanover, NH: Brandeis University Press, 1999.
Buitelaar, Marjo. “Public Baths as Private Places.” In Karin Ask and Marit Tjomsland, *Women and Islamization*, 103–124. Oxford: Berg, 1998.
Bürgel, Johann Christoph. “Secular and Religious Features of Medieval Arabic Medicine.” In *Asian Medical Systems: A Comparative Study*, ed. Charles Leslie, 44–62. Berkeley: University of California Press, 1976.
Caballero-Navas, Carmen. *The Book of Women’s Love and Jewish Medieval Medical Literature on Women = Sefer Ahavat Nashim*. New York: Kegan Paul, 2004.
Canaan, Taufiq. “Unwritten Laws Affecting the Arab Woman of Palestine.” *Journal of the Palestine Oriental Society* 11 (1931): 172–203.
Carroll, Lucy. “Life Interests and Intergenerational Transfer of Property Avoiding the Law of Succession.” *Islamic Law and Society* 8 (2001): 245–286.
Chaudhry, Ayesha S. “Unlikely Motherhood in the Qur’ān: Oncofertility as Devotion.” In *Oncofertility: Reflections from the Humanities and Social Sciences*, ed. T. K. Woodruff et al., 287–94. New York: Springer, 2010.
Chipman, Leigh. *The World of Pharmacy and Pharmacists in Mamluk Cairo*. Leiden: Brill, 2010.
Colin, Joël. *L’enfant endormi dans le ventre de sa mère: étude ethnolinguistique et juridique d’une croyance au Maghre*b. Perpignan: Centre d’études et de recherches juritiques sur les espaces méditerranéen et africain francophones (CERJEMAF), 1998.
Conrad, Lawrence. *The Western Medical Tradition: 800 BC to AD 1800*. New York: Cambridge University Press, 1995.
Coulson, Noel J. *A History of Islamic Law*. Edinburgh: Edinburgh University Press, 1964.
Cuffel, Alexandra. “From Practice to Polemic: Shared Saints and Festivals as ‘Women’s Religion’ in the Medieval Mediterranean.” *Bulletin of the School of Oriental and African Studies* 68 (2005): 401–19.
Cuffel, Alexandra. “Polemicizing Women’s Bathing among Medieval and Early Modern Muslims and Christians.” In *The Nature and Function of Water, Baths, Bathing, and Hygiene from Antiquity through the Renaissance*, ed. Cynthia Kosso and Anne Scott 171–188. Leiden: Brill, 2009.
Cuno, Kenneth M. *Modernizing Marriage: Family, Ideology, and Law in Nineteenth- and Early Twentieth-Century Egypt*. Syracuse: Syracuse University Press, 2015.
Darmon, Pierre. *Trial by Impotence: Virility and Marriage in Pre-Revolutionary France*. London: Hogarth Press, 1985.
Das, Aileen. “Galen and the Arabic traditions of Plato’s Timaeus.” Ph.D. thesis: University of Warwick, 2013.

Dean-Jones, Leslie. "Menstrual Bleeding according to the Hippocratics and Aristotle." *Transactions of the American Philological Association* 119 (1974): 177–191.

Dean-Jones, Leslie. *Women's Bodies in Classical Greek Science*. Clarendon Press: Oxford, 1994.

Delaney, Carol. *The Seed and the Soil: Gender and Cosmology in Turkish Village Society*. Berkeley: University of California Press, 1991.

Dols, Michael. *Majnūn: the Madman in Medieval Islamic Society*. New York: Oxford University Press, 1992.

Drower, E. S. "Women and Taboo in Iraq." *Iraq* 5 (1938): 105–117.

Edelstein, Ludwig. *Ancient Medicine*. Baltimore: Johns Hopkins Press, 1967.

Effah, Kofi. "A Reformulation of the Polygyny-Fertility Hypothesis." *Journal of Comparative Family Studies* 30 (1999): 381–408.

Elgood, Cyril. "Tibb-ul-Nabbi or Medicine of the Prophet, Being a Translation of Two Works of the Same Name. I: The Ṭibb-ul-Nabbi of al-Suyūṭī. II: The Ṭibb-ul-Nabbi of Mahmud bin Mohamed al-Chaghayni, together with Introduction, Notes and a Glossary." *Osiris* 14 (1962): 33–192.

Fancy, Nahyan. *Science and Religion in Mamluk Egypt: Ibn al-Nafīs, Pulmonary Transit, and Bodily Resurrection*. London: Routledge, 2013.

Fancy, Nahyan. "Womb Heat versus Sperm Heat: Hippocrates against Galen and Ibn Sīnā in Ibn al-Nafīs's Commentaries." *Oriens* 45 (2017): 150–175.

Faraone, Christopher. "Magical and Medical Approaches to the Wandering Womb in the Ancient Greek World." *Classical Antiquity* 30 (2011): 1–32.

Faraone, Christopher. "The Rise of the Demon Womb in Greco-Roman Antiquity." *In Finding Persephone: Women's Rituals in the Ancient Mediterranean*, ed. M. Parca and A. Tzanetou, 224–37. Bloomington: Indiana University Press, 2007.

Fargues, Philippe. "The Stages of the Family Life Cycle in Cairo at the End of the Reign of Muḥammad 'Alī, According to the 1848 Census." *Harvard Middle Eastern and Islamic Review* 5 (2000): 1–39.

Flemming, Rebecca. "The Invention of Infertility in the Classical Greek World: Medicine, Divinity, and Gender." *Bulletin of the History of Medicine* 87 (2013): 565–590.

Flemming, Rebecca. *Medicine and the Making of Roman Women: Gender, Nature, and Authority from Celsus to Galen*. New York: Oxford University Press, 2000.

Friedl, Erika. "The Dynamics of Women's Spheres of Action in Rural Iran." In *Women in Middle Eastern History: Shifting Boundaries in Sex and Gender*, eds N. R. Keddie and B. Baron, 195–214. New Haven: Yale University Press, 1991.

Friedl, Erika. *Women of Deh Koh*. London: Penguin Books, 1991.

Friedman, Mordechai. *Ribui nashim be-Yisrael =Jewish Polygyny in the Middle Ages*. Jerusalem: Mossad Bialik, 1986.

Gadelrab, Sherry Sayed. "Discourses on Sex Differences in Medieval Scholarly Islamic Thought." *Journal of the History of Medicine and Allied Sciences* 66 (2011): 40–81.

Garver, Valerie. "Childbearing and Infancy in the Carolingian World." *Journal of the History of Sexuality* 21 (2012): 208–244.

Giladi, Avner. *Infants, Parents and Wet Nurses: Medieval Islamic Views on Breastfeeding and their Social Implications*. Leiden: Brill, 1999.

Giladi, Avner. *Muslim Midwives: The Craft of Birthing in the Premodern Middle East*. New York: Cambridge University Press, 2015.

Gilchrist, Roberta. *Medieval Life: Archaeology and the Life Course*. Woodbridge: Boydell Press, 2012.
Gilman, Sander et al. *Hysteria Beyond Freud*. Berkeley: University of California Press, 1993.
Goitein, S. D. *Mediterranean Society*. 6 vols. Berkeley: University of California Press, 1999.
Good, Mary-Jo Delvecchio. "Of Blood and Babies: The Relationship of Popular Islamic Physiology to Fertility." *Social Science & Medicine* 14 (1980): 147–156.
Graiouid, Said. "Communication and the Social Production of Space: the Hammam, the Public Sphere and Moroccan Women." *Journal of North African Studies* 9 (2004): 104–130.
Granqvist, Hilma. *Child Problems Among the Arabs*. Helsingfors: Södorström, 1950.
Granqvist, Hilma. *Marriage Conditions in a Palestinian Village*. 2 vols. Helsingfors: Akademische buchhandlung, 1931–1935.
Green, Monica. "The Transmission of Ancient Theories of Female Physiology and Disease Through the Early Middle Ages." Ph.D. Dissertation: Princeton University, 1985.
Green, Monica. *Making Women's Medicine Masculine: The Rise of Male Authority in Pre-Modern Gynaecology*. Oxford: Oxford University Press, 2008.
Green, Monica. "Caring for Gendered Bodies." In *Oxford Handbook of Medieval Women and Gender*, ed. Judith Bennett and Ruth Mazo Karras, 345–61. Oxford: Oxford University Press, 2013.
Guo, Li. *Commerce, Culture, and Community in a Red Sea Port in the Thirteenth Century*. Leiden: Brill, 2004.
Guo, Li. "Tales of a Medieval Cairene Harem: Domestic Life in al-Biqāʿī's Autobiographical Chronicle," *Mamluk Studies Review* 9 (2005): 101–121.
al-Hājirī, Sārah Shāfī. *al-Aḥkām al-muttaṣila bi'l-ʿuqm wa'l-injāb wa-man' al-ḥaml fī al-fiqh al-Islāmī*. Beirut: Dār al-Bashā'ir al-Islāmīya, 2013.
Hamarneh, Sami. "Origin and Functions of the Ḥisbah System in Islam and Its Impact on the Health Professions." *Sudhoffs Archiv für Geschichte der Medizin und der Naturwissenschaften* 48 (1964): 157–173.
Hansen, Nicole Bernadette. "Motherhood in the Mother of the World: Continuity and Change of Reproductive Concepts and Practices in Egypt from Ancient to Modern Times." Ph.D. dissertation: University of Chicago, 2006.
Hanson, Ann Ellis. "Continuity and Change: Three Case Studies in Hippocratic Gynecological Therapy and Theory." In Women's History and Ancient History, ed. S. Pomeroy, 73–110. Chapel Hill: University of North Carolina Press, 1991.
Hennigan, Peter. *The Birth of a Legal Institution: The Formation of the Waqf in Third-Century A.H. Ḥanafī Legal Discourse*. Leiden: Brill, 2004.
Inhorn, Marcia. *Infertility and Patriarchy: The Cultural Politics of Gender and Family Life in Egypt*. Philadelphia: University of Pennsylvania Press, 1996.
Inhorn, Marcia. *Quest for Conception: Gender, Infertility, and Egyptian Medical Traditions*. Philadelphia: University of Pennsylvania Press, 1994.
Iversen, Erik. "Papyrus Carlsberg VIII with some remarks on the Egyptian origin of some popular birth prognoses." *Det. Kongelige. Danske Videnskabernes Selskab. Historisk-filologiske Meddelelser* 26 (1939): 1–31.
Jauanna, Jacques. *Greek Medicine from Hippocrates to Galen*. Leiden: Brill, 2012.
Jaussen, Antonin. *Coutumes des Arabes au pays de Moab*. Paris: V. Lecoffre, 1908.

Jennings, Ronald C. "Women in Early 17th Century Ottoman Judicial Records: The Sharia Court of Anatolian Kayseri." *Journal of the Economic and Social History of the Orient* 18 (1975): 53–114.

Johnston, William. "Sexually Transmitted Diseases and Demographic Change in Early Modern Japan." *East Asian Science, Technology, and Medicine* 30 (2009): 74–92.

Joannides, Dimitri. *Esquisse de la gynécologie et de l'obstétrique chez les égyptiens et les grecs.* Cairo, 1934.

Joannides, Dimitri. *La gynécologie et l'obstétrique chez Avicenne (Ibn Sina) et leurs rapports avec celles des grecs.* Cairo, 1938.

Joannides, Dimitri. *La gynécologie et obstétrique de Paul d'Egine et son influence sur la médecine arabe.* Cairo, 1940.

Joosse, Peter. *The Physician as a Rebellious Intellectual: The Book of the Two Pieces of Advice or Kitāb al-Naṣīḥatayn by 'Abd al-Laṭīf ibn Yūsuf al-Baghdādī.* Frankfurt am Main: Peter Lang Edition, 2014.

Kahle, Paul. "A Gypsy Woman in Egypt in the Thirteenth Century A.D." *Journal of the Gypsy Lore Society*, third series, 29 (1950): 11–15.

Kan'ān, Aḥmad Muḥammad. *al-Mawsū'a al-ṭibbiyya al-fiqhiyya.* Beirut: Dār al-Nafā'is, 2000.

Karras, Ruth Mazo. *Sexuality in Medieval Europe: Doing Unto Others.* New York: Routledge, 2005.

Katz, Marion Holmes. *Body of the Text.* Albany: SUNY Press, 2002.

Katz, Marion Holmes. "Scholarly Authority and Women's Authority in the Islamic Law of Menstrual Purity." In *Gender in Judaism and Islam: Common Lives, Uncommon Heritage, ed.* Firoozeh Kashani-Sabet and Beth S. Wenger, 73–104. New York: NYU Press, 2014.

Katz, Marion Holmes. *Women in the Mosque: A History of Legal Thought and Social Practice.* New York: Columbia University Press, 2014.

Kedar, Benjamin Z. "Jews and Samaritans in the Crusading Kingdom of Jerusalem." *Tarbiz* 53 (1984), 387–408.

Khan, Geoffrey. *Arabic Legal and Administrative Documents in the Cambridge Genizah Collections.* Cambridge: Cambridge University Press, 1993.

Khattab, Hind et al. *Women, Reproduction, and Health in Rural Egypt.* Cairo: American University in Cairo Press, 1999.

King, Helen. *Hippocrates' Woman: Reading the Female Body in Ancient Greece.* London: Routledge, 1998.

King, Helen. "Galen and the widow: towards a history of therapeutic masturbation in ancient gynaecology." *EuGeStA: Journal on Gender Studies in Antiquity* 1 (2011), 205–235.

Krakowski, Eve. *Coming of Age in Medieval Egypt.* Princeton: Princeton University Press, 2018.

Kruk, Remke. "Pregnancy and Its Social Consequences In Mediaeval And Traditional Arab Society." *Quaderni Di Studi Arabi* 5/6 (1987): 418–30.

Kueny, Kathryn. *Conceiving Identities: Maternity in Medieval Discourse and Practice.* Albany: State University of New York Press, 2013.

Kueny, Kathryn. "The Birth of Cain: Reproduction, Maternal Responsibility, and Moral Character in Early Islamic Exegesis." *History of Religions* 48 (2008): 110–129.

Kulin, H. et al. "The Effect of Chronic Childhood Malnutrition on Pubertal Growth and Development." *American Journal of Clinical Nutrition* 36 (1982): 527–36.

Larguèche, Dalenda. *Monogamie en Islam: l'exception kairouanaise. Manouba: Centre de publication universitaire*, 2011.

Lamdan, Ruth. "Child Marriage in Jewish Society in the Eastern Mediterranean during the Sixteenth Century." *Mediterranean Historical Review* 11 (1996): 37–59.

Lane, Edward W. *An Account of the Manners and Customs of the Modern Egyptians*. New York: The American University of Cairo Press, 2003.

Lane, Edward W. *Arabic-English Lexicon*. 8 vols. London: Williams and Norgate, 1893.

Laqueur, Thomas. *Making Sex: Body and Gender from the Greeks to Freud*. Cambridge: Harvard University Press, 1990.

Layish, Aharon. "The Mālikī Family "Waqf" according to Wills and "Waqfiyyāt." *Bulletin of the School of Oriental and African Studies* 46 (1983): 1–32.

Layish, Aharon. *Marriage, Divorce, and Succession in the Druze Family*. Leiden: Brill, 1982.

Legey, Françoise. *The Folklore of Morocco*, tr. Lucy Hotz. London: Unwin, 1935.

Levey, Martin. "Medical Ethics of Medieval Islam with Special Reference to Al-Ruhāwī's 'Practical Ethics of the Physician'." *Transactions of the American Philosophical Society* 57.3 (1967): 1–100.

Lewin, Benjamin. *Otsar ha-ge'onim*. Jerusalem: Hebrew University, 1928.

Lewis, M., F. Shapland and R. Watts. "On the Threshold of Adulthood: A New Approach for the Use of Maturation Indicators to Assess Puberty in Adolescents from Medieval England." *Journal of Human Biology* 28 (2016): 48–56.

Little, Donald P. "A Fourteenth-Century Jerusalem Court Record of a Divorce Hearing: A Case Study." *In Mamluks and Ottomans: Studies in Honour of Michael Winter*, ed. D. J. Wasserstein and A. Ayalon, 66–85. London: Routledge, 2006.

Livingston, John W. "Science and the Occult in the Thinking of Ibn Qayyim al-Jawziyya." Journal of the American Oriental Society 112 (1992): 598–610.

Longombe, Ahuka Ona et al. "Fistula and Traumatic Genital Injury from Sexual Violence in a Conflict Setting in Eastern Congo: Case Studies." *Reproductive Health Matters* 16.31 (2008): 132–141.

Lutfi, Huda. "Manners and Customs of Fourteenth-Century Cairene Women: Female Anarchy versus Male Shar'i Order in Muslim Prescriptive Treatises," 99–121. In *Women in Middle Eastern History*, ed. Nikki Keddie and Beth Baron. New Haven: Yale University Press, 1993.

Lydon, Ghislaine and Bruce S. Hall. "Excavating Arabic Sources for the History of Slavery in Western Africa," 15–49. In *African Voices on Slavery and the Slave Trade*, ed. Alice Bellagamba, Sandra E. Greene, and Martin A. Klein. Cambridge: Cambridge University Press, 2016.

Maher, Vanessa. "Women and Social Change in Morocco." In *Women in the Muslim World*, ed. L. Beck and N. Keddie, 100–123. Cambridge: Harvard University Press, 1978.

Marcus, Abraham. *The Middle East on the Eve of Modernity: Aleppo in the Eighteenth Century*. New York: Columbia University Press, 1989.

Marmon, Shaun. "Domestic Slavery in the Mamluk Empire: a Preliminary Sketch." In *Slavery in the Islamic Middle East*, ed. Shaun Marmon, 1–24. Princeton: Markus Wiener Pub., 1999.

Mathee, Mohamed. "Women's Agency in Muslim Marriage: Fatwās from Timbuktu." *Journal for Islamic Studies* 31 (2011), 75–95.

Meacham, Tirzah. "Marriage of Minor Girls in Jewish Law: A Legal and Historical Overview." *In Jewish Legal Writings by Women*, ed. M. D. Halpern and Ch. Safrai, 23–37. Jerusalem: Urim Publications, 1998.

Meyerhof, Max. "La surveillance des professions médicales et paramédicales chez les Arabes." *Bulletin de l'Institut d'Égypte* 26 (1944): 119–34.

Mirza, Younus. "Remembering the Umm al-Walad." In *Concubines and Courtesans: Women and slavery in Islamic History*, ed. M. Gordon and K.A. Hain, 297–337. Oxford: Oxford University Press, 2017.

Moors, Annaliese. "Inheritance: Contemporary Practice." In *Encyclopedia of Women in the Islamic Cultures*, ed. Suad Joseph, 2: 299–302. Leiden: Brill, 2003–2007.

Morsey, Soheir A. *Gender, Sickness, and Healing in Rural Egypt*. Boulder, CO: Westview Press, 1993.

Morsey, Soheir A. "Sex Differences and Folk Illness." In *Women in the Muslim World*, ed. L. Beck and N. Keddie, 599–616. Cambridge: Harvard University Press, 1978.

Motzki, Harald. "Geschlechtsreife und Legitimation zur Zeugung im frühen Islam." In *Geschlechtsreife und Legitimation zur Zeugung*, ed. Ernst Wilhelm Müller, 479–550. Freiburg/Munich: Karl Alber GmbH, 1985.

Muleta, M. and G. Williams. "Postcoital Injuries Treated at the Addis Ababa Fistula Hospital, 1991–97." *Lancet* 354(1999): 2051–2.

Musallam, Basim. "The Human Embryo in Arabic Scientific and Religious Thought." In *The Human Embryo: Aristotle and the Arabic and European Traditions*, ed. G. R. Dunstan, 32–46. Exeter: University of Exeter Press, 1990.

Musallam, Basim. *Sex and Society in Islam: Birth Control Before the Nineteenth Century*. Cambridge: Cambridge University Press, 1983.

Natvig, Richard. "Liminal Rites and Female Symbolism in the Egyptian Zar Possession Cult," *Numen* 35 (1988): 57–68.

Obermeyer, Carla Makhlouf. "Pluralism and Pragmatism: Knowledge and Practice of Birth in Morocco." *Medical Anthropology Quarterly* 14 (2000): 180–201.

O'Dowd, Michael J. *The History of Medications for Women: Materia Medica Woman*. New York: Parthenon Publishing Group, 2001.

Ohtoshi, Tetsuya. "The manners, customs, and mentality of pilgrims to the Egyptian city of the dead: 1100–1500 AD." *Orient* 29 (1993): 19–44.

Olszowy-Schlanger, Judith. *Karaite Marriage Documents From the Cairo Geniza: Legal Tradition and Community Life In Mediaeval Egypt and Palestine*. Leiden: Brill, 1998.

Omran, Abdel Rahim. *Family Planning in the Legacy of Islam*. Routledge: New York, 1992.

Parent, A. S. et. al. "The timing of normal puberty and the age limits of sexual precocity: variations around the world, secular trends, and changes after migration." *Endocrine Reviews* 24.5 (2003): 668–93.

Patai, Raphael. *Sex and Family in the Bible and the Middle East*. New York: Doubleday, 1959.

Peirce, Leslie. *Morality Tales: Law and Gender in the Ottoman Court of Aintab*. Berkeley: University of California Press, 2003.

Peirce, Leslie. "Seniority, Sexuality, and Social Order: the Vocabulary of Gender in Early Modern Ottoman Society." *In Women in the Ottoman Empire*, ed. Madeline C. Zilfi. Leiden: Brill, 1997.

Perkins, E. E. "Marriage Ceremony in Lower Egypt." *Man* 32 (1932): 63–66.

Perlmann, Moshe. "The Position of Jewish Physicians in Medieval Muslim Countries." *Israel Oriental Studies* 2 (1972), 315–19.
Pinheiro, Cristina Santos. "The Medical Sources in the Chapters about Sterility of Rodrigo de Castro's De universa mulierum medicina." In *The Palgrave Handbook of Infertility In History: Approaches, Contexts and Perspectives*, ed. Gayle Davis and Tracey Loughran. London: Palgrave Macmillan, 2017.
Pormann, Peter. *The Oriental Tradition of Paul of Aegina's Pragmateia*. Leiden: Brill, 2004.
Pormann, Peter. "Female Patients, Patrons and Practitioners in 10th and 11th-Century Baghdad: An Unheard Voice?" Montreal, Institute of Islamic Studies at McGill University, May 4, 2007.
Pormann, Peter. "The Art of Medicine: Female Patients and Practitioners in Medieval Islam," *Lancet* 373 (2009): 1598–9.
Pormann, Peter. "The Hippocratic Aphorisms in the Arabic Medical Tradition." *Aspetar* 2 (2013): 412–415.
Pormann, Peter and Emilie Savage-Smith. *Medieval Islamic Medicine*. Washington, D.C.: Georgetown University Press, 2007.
Porter, Venetia, Liana Saif, and Emilie Savage-Smith, "Amulets, Magic, and Talismans." In *Companion to Islamic Art and Architecture*. Wiley-Blackwell, 2017.
Powers, David. "Women and Divorce in the Islamic West: Three Cases." *Hawwa* 1 (2003): 29–45.
Prentice, S. et al. "Evidence for a Downward Secular Trend in Age of Menarche in a Rural Gambian population." *Annals of Human Biology* 37 (2010): 717–721.
Preus, Anthony. "Biomedical Techniques for Influencing Human Reproduction in the Fourth Century B.C." *Arethusa* 8 (1975): 237–63.
Preus, Anthony. "Galen's Criticism of Aristotle's Conception Theory." *Journal of the History of Biology* 10 (1977): 65–85.
Qarāmī, Amāl. *al-Ikhtilāf fī al-thaqāfa al-ʿarabīya al-islāmīya*. Beirut: Dār al-Madār al-Islāmī, 2007.
Ragab, Ahmed. "Epistemic Authority of Women in the Medieval Middle East." *Hawwa* 8 (2010): 181–216.
Ragab, Ahmed. "One, Two, or Many Sexes: Sex Differentiation in Medieval Islamicate Medical Thought." *Journal of the History of Sexuality* 24 (2015): 428–454.
Rank, Scott. "Polygamy and Religious Polemics in the Late Ottoman Empire: Fatma Âliye and Mahmud Es'ad's Ta'addüd-i Zevcât'a Zeyl." *Cihannüma: Tarih ve Coğrafya Araştırmaları Dergisi* 1/2 (2015): 61–79.
Rapoport, Yossef. "Matrimonial Gifts in Early Islamic Egypt." *Islamic Law and Society* 7.1 (2000): 1–36.
Rapoport, Yossef. *Marriage, Money, and Divorce in Medieval Islamic Society*. Cambridge: Cambridge University Press, 2005.
Rây, P. and H.N. Gupta. Caraka Samhita; A Scientific Synopsis. New Delhi: National Institute of Sciences of India, 196.
Reinert, Benedikt. *Die Lehre vom tawakkul in der klassischen Sufik*. Berlin: de Gruyter, 1968.
Riddle, John. *Contraception and Abortion from the Ancient World to the Renaissance*. Cambridge: Harvard University Press, 1992.
Riddle, John. Goddesses, Elixirs, and Witches: Plants and Sexuality throughout Human History. New York: Palgrave Macmillan, 2010.

Ringrose, Kathryn M. *The Perfect Servant: Eunuchs and the Social Construction of Gender in Byzantium.* Chicago: University of Chicago Press, 2003.
Rispler-Chaim, Vardit. *Islamic Medieval Ethics in the Twentieth Century.* Leiden: Brill, 1993.
Rispler-Chaim, Vardit. "Ḥasan Murād Mannā: Childbearing and the Rights of a Wife." Islamic Law and Society 2 (1995): 92–99.
Rispler-Chaim, Vardit. *Disability in Islamic Law.* Dordrecht: Springer, 2010.
Rosenfeld, H. "Processes of Structural Change within the Arab Village Extended Family." *American Anthropologist* 60 (1958): 1127–1139.
Rosen, Tova and Uriah Kfir. "What Does a Father Want?: An Unpublished Poem and Its Intertexts." In *Studies in Arabic and Hebrew Letters in Honor of Raymond P. Scheindlin*, ed. Jonathan Decter and Michael Rand, 129–53. Piscataway, NJ: Gorgias Press, 2007.
Rosenthal, Franz. "The Defense of Medicine in the Medieval Muslim World." *Bulletin of the History of Medicine* 43 (1969): 519–32.
Sabra, Adam. *Poverty and Charity in Medieval Islam: Mamluk Egypt, 1250–1517.* Cambridge: Cambridge University Press, 2000.
Sadeghi, Behnam. *The Logic of Law-Making in Islam: Women and Prayer in the Legal Tradition.* Cambridge: Cambridge University Press, 2013.
Sait, Siraj and Hilary Lim. *Land, Law and Islam: Property and Human Rights in the Muslim World.* New York: Zed Books, 2006.
al-Sālimī, Nūr al-Dīn 'Abd Allāh ibn Ḥumayyid. *Īḍāḥ al-bayān fī nikāḥ al-ṣibyān: aḥkām tazwīj al-ṣighār.* Beirut: al-Dār al-'Arabiyya lil-'Ulūm, 2006.
Sanders, Paula. "Gendering the Ungendered Body: Hermaphrodites in Medieval Islamic Law." In *Women in Middle Eastern History: Shifting Boundaries in Sex and Gender*, ed. Nikki R. Keddie and Beth Baron, 74–95. New Haven: Yale University Press, 1991.
Savage-Smith, Emilie. "The Practice of Surgery in Islamic Lands: Myth and Reality." *Social History of Medicine* 13 (2000): 307–321.
Savage-Smith, Emilie. "Islamic Medical Medical Manuscripts at the National Library of Medicine," Nlm.nih.gov. https://www.nlm.nih.gov/hmd/arabic/prophetic_med2.html (accessed August 21, 2018).
Sayeed, Asma. *Women and the Transmission of Religious Knowledge in Islam.* Cambridge: Cambridge University Press, 2013.
Schimmel, Annemarie. *And Muhammad is His Messenger: The Veneration of the Prophet in Islamic Piety.* Chapel Hill: University of North Carolina Press, 1985.
Scott, S. and J. Duncan. *Demography and Nutrition: Evidence from Historical and Contemporary Populations.* Oxford: Wilson & Sons, 2008.
Serour, G. I. et al. "Infertility: A Health Problem in the Muslim World." *Population Sciences* 10 (1991): 41–58.
Serrano, Delfina. "Legal Practice in an Andalusī-Maghribī Source from the Twelfth Century CE: The Madhāhib al-ḥukkām fī nawāzil al-aḥkām." *Islamic Law and Society* 7 (2000): 187–234.
Serrano, Delfina. "Rape in Mālikī Legal Doctrine and Practice." *Hawwa* 5 (2007): 166–207
Shaham, Ron. *The Expert Witness in Islamic Courts.* Chicago: University of Chicago Press, 2010.
Shatzmiller, Maya. "Women and Property Rights in Al-Andalus and the Maghrib: Social Patterns and Legal Discourse." *Islamic Law and Society* 2 (1995), 219–57.

Shefer-Mossensohn, Miri. *Ottoman Medicine: Healing and Medical Institutions, 1500–1700.* Albany: SUNY Press, 2009.
Siggel, Alfred. "Gynäkologie, Embryologie und Frauenhygiene aus dem Paradies der Weisheit über die Medizin des Abū al-Ḥasan 'Alī b. Sahl Rabbān at-Ṭabarī." *Quellen und Studien zur Geschichte Naturwissenschaften und der Medizin* 8 (1941): 216–272.
Sohrabvand, Farnaz et al. "Comparison of Hysterosalpingography and Avicenna's Method for Evaluation of Tubal Patency." *Traditional and Integrative Medicine* 1 (2016): 90–95.
Sonbol, Amira El-Azhary. "A History of Marriage Contracts in Egypt." In *The Islamic Marriage Contract*, ed. Frank Vogel and Asifa Quraishi, 87–122. Cambridge: Harvard University Press, 2008.
Sonbol, Amira El-Azhary. "Shari' Court Records And Fiqh As Sources Of Women's History." *Religion & Literature* 42 (2010): 229–246.
Sourdel-Thomine, J. "Ḥammām." In *Encyclopaedia of Islam*, 2nd ed., ed. P. Bearman et al. Leiden: Brill, 1960.
Spectorsky, Susan. *Chapters on Marriage and Divorce.* Austin: University of Texas Press, 1993.
Spellberg, Denise. *Politics, Gender and the Islamic Past.* New York: Columbia University Press, 1994.
Spellberg, Denise. "Writing the Unwritten Life of the Islamic Eve: Menstruation and the Demonization of Motherhood." *International Journal of Middle Eastern Studies* 28 (1996): 305–24.
Sprinkle, Robert. "The Missing Politics and Unsettled Science of the Trend toward Earlier Puberty." *Politics and the Life Sciences* 20.1 (2001): 43–66.
Steinschneider, Moritz. "Wissenschaft und Charlatanerie unter den Arabern im neunten Jahrhundert." *Virchows Archiv* 36 (1866): 570–86 and 37: 560–65.
Tanner, James M. *Fetus Into Man: Physical Growth from Conception to Maturity.* Cambridge: Harvard University Press, 1990.
Thompson, Jason. "Small Latin and Less Greek: Expurgated Passages from Edward William *Lane's An Account of the Manners and Customs of the Modern Egyptians.*" *Quaderni di Studi Arabi* 1 (2006): 7–28.
Thompson, Joseph Parrish. *Photographic Views of Egypt, Past and Present.* Boston: J. P. Jewett, 1856.
Tillier, Mathieu. "Women before the Qāḍī under the Abbasids." *Islamic Law and Society* 16 (2009): 280–301.
Tobi, Yosef. "Inheritance Rights of Jewish Women and Moslem Women in Yemen." *Proceedings of the Seminar for Arabian Studies* 24 (1994): 201–208.
Totelin, Laurence. *Hippocratic Recipes: Oral and Written Transmission of Pharmacological Knowledge in Fifth- and Fourth-century Greece.* Boston: Brill, 2008.
Tritton, A. S. *Caliphs and their Non-Muslim Subjects.* London: F. Cass, 1970.
Tucker, Judith E. "Muftīs and Matrimony: Islamic Law and Gender in Ottoman Syria and Palestine." *Islamic Law and Society* 1.3 (1994): 265–300.
Tucker, Judith E. *In the House of the Law: Gender and Islamic Law in Ottoman Syria and Palestine.* Berkeley: University of California Press, 2003.
Ullmann, Manfred. *Die Medizin im Islam.* Leiden: Brill, 1970.
Ullmann, Manfred. "Zwei spätantike Kommentare zu der hippokratischen Schrift 'De morbis muliebribus.'" *Medizinhistorisches Journal* 12 (1977): 245–262.

Ullmann, Manfred. *Islamic Medicine.* Edinburgh: Edinburgh University Press, 1978.
van de Walle, Etienne et al. *Regulating Menstruation: beliefs, practices, interpretations.* Chicago, University of Chicago Press, 2001.
van der Eijk, Philip J. Diocles of Carystus. Leiden: Brill, 2001.
Verskin, Alan. "A Muslim-Jewish Friendship in the Medieval Mediterranean: ʿAlī Ibn al-Qifṭī's Biography of Rabbi Yūsuf Ibn Shamʿūn." In *The Idea of the Mediterranean*, ed. Mario Mignone, 184–199. Stony Brook: Forum Italicum Publishing, 2017.
Wall, L. L. "Dead Mothers and Injured Wives: The Social Context of Maternal Morbidity and Mortality among the Hausa of Northern Nigeria." *Studies in Family Planning* 29 (1998): 341–59.
Weisser, Ursula. *Zeugung, Vererbung, und pränatale Entwicklung in der arabisch-islamischen Mittelalters.* Erlangen: Hannelore Lüling, 1983.
Vieille, Paul. "Family Alliance and Sexual Politics." In *Women in the Muslim World*, ed. Lois Beck and Nikki Keddie, 451–472. Cambridge, Mass: Harvard University Press, 1978.
Vom Bruck, Gabriele. "Elusive Bodies: The Politics of Aesthetics among Yemeni Elite Women." *Signs* 23 (1997): 175–214.
Weinstein, Roni "Impotence and the Preservation of the Family in the Jewish Community of Italy in the Early Modern Period" (Hebrew). In *Sexuality and the Family in History = Eros, erusin, ve-isurim: miniyut u-mishpachah ba-historiyah*, ed. I. Bartal and I. Gafni Jerusalem: Merkaz Zalman Shazar le-toldot Yisrael, 1998.
Weitz, Lev. "Syriac Christians in the Medieval Islamic World: Law, Family, and Society," Ph.D. Dissertation: Princeton University, 2013.
Westermarck, Edward. *Ritual and Belief in Morocco.* 2 vols. London: Macmillan, 1926.
Westreich, E. "Infertility as Ground for Polygamy in Jewish Law in Italy: Interaction among Legal Traditions at the time of the Renaissance." *Olir – Osservatorio delle libertà ed istituzioni religiose* 2 (2003): 1–28.
Wizārat al-Awqāf wa'l-Shuʾūn al-Islāmiyya, Dawlat al-Kuwayt. *al-Mawsūʿa al-fiqhiyya.* 45 vols. Kuwait: Wizārat al-Awqāf wa'l-Shu'ūn al-Islāmiyya, 2004.
Yazbak, Mahmoud. "Minor Marriages and Khiyār al-Bulūgh in Ottoman Palestine: A Note on Women's Strategies in a Patriarchal Society." *Islamic Law and Society* 9.3 (2002): 386–409.
Zacharias, L. and R. Wurtman. "Age at Menarche: Genetic and Environmental Influences." *New England Journal of Medicine* 280 (1969): 868–75.
Zarinebaf-Shahr, Fariba. "Women, Law, and Imperial Justice in Ottoman Istanbul in the Late Seventeenth Century." In *Women, the Family, and Divorce Laws in Islamic History*, ed. Amira El Azhary Sonbol, 81–95. Syracuse: Syracuse University Press, 1996.
Zaydān, ʿAbd al-Karīm. *al-Mufaṣṣal fī aḥkām al-marʾa wa'l-bayt al-Muslim fī al-sharīʿa al-Islāmiyya.* 11 vols. Beirut: Muʾassasat al-Risāla, 1994.
Zilfi, Madeline C. *Women and Slavery in the Late Ottoman Empire: The Design of Difference.* New York: Cambridge University Press, 2010.

Index

Abdallāh ibn Ḥanbal (d. 290/903) 72
Abortion 4, 7, 20, 31, 68, 140–143, 184, 193f., 200f., 281
Abū Bakr al-Ṣiddīq (d. 13/634) 28, 233
Abū Ḥanīfa (d. 150/767) 42, 74, 178
Abu-Lughod, Lila 14, 268
Adhraʿī (d. 783/1381) 238f.
Aetius of Amida (fl. late 5th/early 6th century A.D.) 60, 124, 134, 157f., 166, 188
ʿĀ'isha bint Abī Bakr (d. 58/678) 13, 25–28, 72, 94, 211, 216, 233, 256f., 261
Alcohol and wine 139, 142, 151, 173, 212, 227f., 237, 243
ʿAlī ibn Abī Ṭalib (d. 40/661) 27, 34, 252
ʿAlqama ibn Qays (d. 62/681) 71f.
Amenorrhea, *see* Menstruation: amenorrhea
Amster, Ellen 83f.
Amulets, *see* Magical healing and the occult *and* curses
Annulment, *see* Divorce: annulment on the basis of physical defects
Arabian Nights, see *Thousand and One Nights, The*
ʿArīb ibn Saʿd, *see* al-Qurṭubī, ʿArīb ibn Saʿīd
Aristotle (d. 322 B.C.) 6, 121, 124f., 127–129, 132–138, 151, 154f., 162
Ashtor, Eliyahu 64
Asmā' bint Yazīd (d. ca. 64/680) 260
Astrology and astronomy 118, 215, 231
ʿazl, *see* Contraception

Baghdādī, ʿAbd al-Laṭīf (d. 629/1231) 126f.
Bathhouses and bathing 13, 17, 88, 185, 208, 215, 247–267
Behrend-Martínez, Edward 53–55
Bidʿa (innovation) 12, 209, 266, 281
Biqāʿī, Burhān al-Dīn Ibrāhīm (d. 885/1480) 84f.
Birth defects 225, 272f.
Bleeding, *see* Cupping and phlebotomy
Bouhdiba, Abdelwahab 3, 33
Breastmilk and breastfeeding 3, 25, 67, 71, 74, 81, 83, 112, 117, 129f., 132, 151, 280
Buhūtī, Manṣūr ibn Yūnus (d. 1051/1641) 38, 42f.
Bulqīnī, Abū Ḥafṣ ʿUmar ibn Raslān (d. 805/1403) 239–242, 249f.
Burial and mourning practices 208, 252–257

Cauterization 200, 212, 215, 218
Cemeteries, *see* Burial and mourning practices
Charlatans 185, 198, 217
Chastity 30, 120, 187, 254
– *see also* Virginity
Child and perinatal mortality 27, 29, 193, 256, 271–275
Childbirth
– dangers and injuries 52, 60, 193, 201, 271–274
– difficult labor 191–194, 231
– health benefits 130
– magical and medical practices 149, 191–194, 231, 233f.
– modesty and social intimacy 245–257, 263, 265–268, 282
Chipman, Leigh 225
Christians and Christianity 9, 15
– as medical authorities 148, 212, 219, 222–227, 229, 244
– dissolution of marriage among 31f., 53–56
– midwifery and bathing 244, 246–248, 257, 267
Circumcision and clitorectomy 48, 50, 178f., 198, 218, 281f.
Coitus interruptus, *see* Contraception
Conception, theories of 6, 10f., 117f., 133f., 136f., 143, 149–152, 203
Contraception 7, 10f., 20, 31, 39f., 45f., 50, 111, 140f., 149, 157, 200, 208, 281
Coulson, Noel 84

https://doi.org/10.1515/9783110596588-018

Cupping and phlebotomy 132, 136, 155, 160, 176–180, 198, 215, 218, 243, 257, 281
Curses 98 f., 216, 231

Dāwūd al-Ẓāhirī (d. 270/884) 42, 84
Death, *see* Burial and mourning practices; Divorce: deathbed; Infant and perinatal mortality; Inheritance
Dhahabī, Muḥammad b. Aḥmad (d. 748/1348) 209, 211–213, 219 f., 222, 227, 232
Dioscorides (d. ca. 90 A.D.) 124, 140, 148 f., 220
Divorce
– among Christians and Jews 31–34, 53–56, 90, 96–100
– annulment on the basis of physical defects 31, 34–36, 38–56
– deathbed 106 f.
– *khul'* (wife-initiated divorce) 36–38, 90 f.
– non-menstruating women 7, 53–56, 58, 67–75, 80–83, 86–88
– *ṭalāq* (husband-initiated repudiation) 3 f., 18, 20, 27, 31–33, 36 f., 44, 56, 75–80, 83, 94 f., 106 f., 113, 162, 278, 284
– *see also 'idda*; Pregnancy: *rāqid*
Diyya (bloodwit) and compensation for injuries 50 f., 105
Dols, Michael 8–10, 14

Egypt, Ancient 131, 168, 172
– *see also* Modern Middle Eastern communities
Embryo 6 f., 117 f., 121, 131–136, 144–147, 150, 203, 220
Eunuchs 180, 187 f., 238–242, 250
Eve (Ḥawwā') 271–275
Examinations (of medical patients) 53–56, 80–82, 84, 89, 118, 131, 139, 164, 174, 176, 185–188, 237 f.

Fargues, Philippe 65
Fasting 47, 85, 151, 169, 212, 227
Fāṭima bint Muḥammad (d. 11/633) 27
Fatwās 12, 25, 37 f., 40, 67–70, 73–80, 83–86, 106–108, 237
Fertility testing (men and women) 34 f., 94, 121, 132, 137 f., 163–174
Fetal sex diagnosis 151 f., 176
Financial concerns, *see* Inheritance; Lawsuits; *Mahr* (dower payment from husband to wife); Trousseaux
Fistula 42, 46, 48–52
Flemming, Rebecca 136 f.
Friedl, Erika 4 f., 93 f., 108, 251

Gadelrab, Sherry Sayed 280 f.
Galen (d. ca. 216 A.D.) 49, 121, 123–128, 131, 134–136, 138, 152, 154–157, 160, 166 f, 218–220, 228 f., 232
Garlic 164–174
Genital defects (legal) 31, 35–56, 89, 111, 142
Geniza (Cairo) 66, 96–100, 190, 226 f., 242
Ghazālī, Abū Ḥāmid (d. 505/1111) 29 f., 176, 208, 247 f.
Giladi, Avner 14–16, 190, 197
God and piety 6, 18, 20 f., 29, 41, 118, 120, 141, 184, 204, 207, 211–214, 217, 219–224, 231–233, 235, 244, 248, 252 f., 260 f., 269, 271–275
Green, Monica 122, 124, 155, 175

Ḥadīth 19, 26–31, 33 f., 38, 50, 94, 111, 150, 175, 207 f., 211–213, 215–217, 220, 228, 232, 252, 256 f., 260 f., 263, 266, 280, 282
Ḥafṣa bint 'Umar (d. 45/665) 27 f, 30
Ḥanafī legal school
– contraception 40, 45
– dissolution of marriage 37, 42, 44–45, 47
– inheritance 104
– marriage and domestic life 50, 52, 253, 255, 261
– medical and modesty matters 213, 237, 243
– menstruation, *'idda*, and pregnancy 70, 72–74, 84, 88
– *see also* Abū Ḥanīfa, Ibn 'Ābidīn; Ibn Nujaym; Kāsānī
Ḥanbalī legal school
– contraception 40
– dissolution of marriage 39, 41–45, 95

- marriage and domestic life 49, 95, 102
- medical and modesty matters 211–213, 224, 227, 242 f., 246 f.
- menstruation, *'idda*, and pregnancy 67, 70–74, 80
- *see also* Ibn Ḥanbal; Ibn al-Jawzī, Ibn Mufliḥ; Ibn Qayyim al-Jawziyya; Ibn Qudāma; Saffārīnī; Ibn Taymiyya

Hansen, Nicole 6, 17
Ḥasan al-Baṣrī (d. 110/728) 39
Ḥassān ibn Thābit (fl. mid-1st/7th century) 234
Ḥaṭṭāb, Muḥammad (d. 954/1547) 33, 47
Henna 258
Hippocrates (d. c. 370 B.C.) and Hippocratic texts
- fertility, infertility, and pregnancy 129–131, 136–143, 147 f., 151, 164–168, 172, 178
- hysterical suffocation 129, 153–155, 158 f., 203
- marriage 121, 129 f., 153, 158 f., 203
- menstruation and retention of menses 128–130, 203
- reproductive theories 132 f., 147
- transmission and reinterpretation 124–126, 132, 136, 164–168, 172, 218, 220

Hippocratic oath 184, 220
Ḥisba manuals for market inspectors 12, 88, 136, 170, 176–179, 184, 198, 200, 208 f., 213, 222 f., 231, 237, 255, 281
Humoral temperaments 35, 123, 128, 133, 135, 137 f., 144 f., 151 f., 156, 161–163, 201
Ḥunayn ibn Isḥāq (d. 260/873) 147, 171
Hysterical suffocation 129, 144, 151, 153–160, 194, 196, 203

Iblīs, *see* Satan
Ibn 'Abbās (d. 68/687) 233, 248, 271
Ibn 'Abdūn, Muḥammad ibn Aḥmad (d. early 6th/12th century) 177, 223
Ibn Abī Ṣādiq al-Nīsābūrī (d. after 462/1068) 127
Ibn Abī Uṣaybī'a (d. 668/1270) 180–182, 185, 190, 201
Ibn Abī Zayd al-Qayrawānī (d. 386/996) 38, 46, 48, 86
Ibn 'Ābidīn, Muḥammad Amīn b. 'Umar (d. 1252/1836) 51, 57, 73, 179, 237, 243, 258
Ibn al-'Aṭṭār, 'Alā' al-Dīn 'Alī ibn Ibrāhīm (d. 724/1324) 208
Ibn al-Ḥājj al-'Abdarī (d. 737/1336) 12 f., 17, 183, 209, 219–221, 224–227, 230 f., 235, 244 f., 262–270, 274, 282
Ibn al-Ḥasan, Ṣā'id (d. after 464/1072) 229 f.
Ibn al-Jawzī (d. 597/1201) 12, 141, 208, 213, 215, 219, 231, 249, 253 f.
Ibn al-Jazzār al-Qayrawānī (d. 369/980) 60, 132, 140, 145–147, 157 f., 160, 194 f., 200 f.
Ibn al-Mawwāz, Muḥammad (d. 281/894) 48, 82
Ibn al-Nafīs (d. 687/1288) 197
Ibn al-Quff (d. 685/1286) 189
Ibn al-Ukhuwwa (d. 729/1329) 177–179, 213, 222 f., 231
Ibn Buṭlān (d. 1066/458) 88, 169 f., 176
Ibn Ḥabīb, 'Abd al-Malik (d. 238/852) 29, 150, 208, 216, 252 f., 255, 257 f., 260 f.
Ibn Ḥanbal, Aḥmad (d. 241/855) 42 f., 70–73, 95, 208, 212 f., 246 f.
Ibn Ḥazm, 'Alī ibn Aḥmad (d. 456/1064) 37, 42
Ibn Hindū, Abū al-Faraj (d. 410/1019) 214
Ibn Jumay' (d. 594/1198) 185
Ibn Kamal Pasha (d. 941/1534) 171
Ibn Kathīr (d. 774/1373) 141, 245, 248 f.
Ibn Mufliḥ, Muḥammad (d. 763/1361) 12, 209, 211, 213, 219, 224, 227, 231 f.
Ibn Nujaym (d. 970/1563) 50, 253, 255, 261
Ibn Qayyim al-Jawziyya (d. 751/1350) 40–42, 70, 208 f., 214 f., 217–219, 221 f., 228–233, 280
Ibn Qudāma (d. 620/1223) 39 f., 42–44, 48–50, 60, 73, 242, 246 f.
Ibn Rushd, Abū al-Walīd Muḥammad (al-Jadd, d. 520/1126) 37, 75, 80–82, 85, 88
Ibn Rushd, Muḥammad (Averroes, d. 595/1198) 38, 84, 134

Ibn Sahl, Abū al-Aṣbagh ʻIsā (d. 486/1093) 89
Ibn Sīnā (d. 427/1037) 49, 60, 119, 134, 136 f., 144, 146, 149 f., 153, 157 – 163, 168 – 170, 177, 179 f., 188 f., 192 – 194, 200, 280 f.
Ibn Taymiyya (d. 728/1328) 38 – 40, 42, 45, 67, 70, 74 f., 80, 102, 209
Ibn Tufīl, Saʻīd (d. 279/892) 181 f.
Ibn Ṭūlūn, Aḥmad (d. 270/884) 181 f.
Ibn Ṭūlūn, Shams al-Dīn (d. 953/1546) 209, 214, 218 – 220, 222
Ibn Zuhr family of physicians 127, 136, 176, 186, 190, 197
ʻidda (waiting period following end of a marriage) 33, 36 f., 41, 56, 67 – 85, 88, 90 f., 112, 284
Impotence 8, 31, 41 f., 44 f., 48, 52 – 56, 89 f., 97, 112, 117, 161
Informants and intermediaries
– legal contexts 57, 75 f., 86, 89 – 91
– medical 148, 180, 185, 191 – 195, 197 – 199, 243, 281
Inheritance 16, 19 f., 68, 71 f., 81 – 83, 87. 100 – 110, 112, 279, 284
Inhorn, Marcia 5 f., 16 f., 105, 161
Injuries to the reproductive organs 35, 46, 49 – 56, 58, 89, 105, 142
Innovation, *see Bidʻa*
Insanity, *see* Madness
Iversen, Erik 165
ʻIyāḍ, Qāḍī (d. 544/1149) 75, 78

Jāḥiẓ (d. 255/869) 223
Jaldakī, ʻIzz al-Dīn ibn Aydamar (d. 743/1342) 171
Jennings, Ronald 109
Jesus 233
Jews and Judaism
– bathing and *mikveh* 246 – 248, 257, 259, 267
– divorce 15, 33 f., 55, 69, 90, 96 – 100
– engaging in *ruqya* (healing using Qurʼānic verses) 233
– inheritance 102
– interactions with Muslim women 244, 246 – 249, 267
– *jinn* 230
– marriage age 50, 66 f.
– medical patients 9, 226
– medical practitioners 164, 222 – 224, 226 f., 229, 242, 244, 247 – 249
– polygamy 34, 96 – 100
– sabbath 13, 98, 263
– virginity tests 172, 174
Jouanna, Jacques 165
Jundīshāpūr 148, 223

Kāsānī, ʻAlāʼ al-Dīn (d. 587/1191) 40, 44 f., 52, 73
Khadīja bint Khuwaylid (d. 619 A.D.) 27
Khaṭṭābī, Abū Sulayman (d. ca. 388/998) 216, 220, 228
Khawāṣṣ (items with special healing properties) 147, 149, 218, 221 f.
Khayzurān, mother of caliphs al-Hādī and Hārūn al-Rashīd 180
Khurūj (excursions) and religious educational opportunities for women 253 – 265
Kueny, Kathryn 1, 11, 112, 120, 146, 203

Legal testimony 55, 60, 76 – 79, 82 – 91, 222, 225 – 227, 243, 278 f.
Lewis, Mary 63
Lim, Hilary 110
Lithotomy 187 – 189, 200

Madness 8 – 10, 38, 41 f., 129, 153, 159
Magical healing and the occult 4 f., 16, 83, 98, 163, 190, 210, 214, 216 f., 230, 250
– amulets 5, 160, 215, 23 – 235
– objections to 216, 232, 235
– *ruqya* 215, 233
– squares 149
– stones 147 – 149, 218
– written word 231, 233, 235
Mahr (dower payment from husband to wife) 33, 36 – 38, 41, 76 f., 96, 98 f., 103, 105 f., 258
Maimonides, Moses (d. 1204 A.D) 97, 127, 259
Majūsī (d. 384/994) 49, 119, 136 f., 144, 149, 159 f., 162 f., 195, 197, 201

Mālik ibn Anas (d. 179/795) 42, 74, 84, 213, 233
Mālikī legal school
- dissolution of marriage 38, 42, 46–48
- marriage and domestic life 86, 255
- medical and modesty matters 48 f., 52, 89, 213, 233 f., 242, 247, 249
- menstruation, *'idda*, and pregnancy 70, 73–75, 78, 80, 82, 84, 107
- *see also* Ibn Abī Zayd al-Qayrawānī; Ibn Ḥabīb; Ibn al-Ḥājj; Ibn al-Mawwāz; Ibn Rushd; Ibn Sahl; 'Iyāḍ, Qāḍī; Mālik ibn Anas ; Saḥnūn; Wansharīsī
Māriyya the Copt (d. 16/637) 27
Markets 87, 136, 170, 177, 209, 231 f.
Marriage 4, 18, 25 f., 31, 35, 37, 41, 53 f., 58, 65–67, 72 f., 77, 85, 88, 95, 102–104, 106 f., 252, 254, 258, 277
- companionship between spouses 12, 107, 264–266
- desirable attributes in a spouse 28–31
- disclosure of prospective harm to the other spouse 31, 39 f., 47
- legal minors and physical maturity 53–56, 58–63, 65–67, 85
- medically recommended 129 f., 153, 158 f.
- remarriage 20, 32, 54, 58, 67, 71–80, 86, 90 f., 107
- *see also* Contraception; Divorce; *'idda*; *Mahr*; Minors
Marwarrūdhī, Ḥusayn ibn Muḥammad (d. 462/1069) 37 f., 85
Māwardī (d. 450/1058) 39, 46, 51
Medicine of the prophet *see* Prophetic medicine
Medicines and pharmacy 139 f., 142 f., 146, 148 f., 169, 212, 224, 227, 231
- *see also* Abortion
Menarche, *see* Menstruation: menarche
Menopause, *see* Menstruation: menopause
Menstruation
- amenorrhea and irregular 8, 25, 57–58, 67–84
- fertility 29, 35, 49, 68, 141
- legal significance 25, 33, 36, 51, 57–58, 66–81, 85 f.
- menarche 53, 57–68, 85 f., 112
- menopause 20, 44, 57, 69–74, 80, 93
- physiology 57, 59, 61–68, 128–131, 153–161
- purification 26, 85, 259, 263, 266
- retention 49, 129, 140 f., 152–161, 196
Midwives
- interactions with male medical practitioners 49, 119, 122, 159 f., 175–200, 281
- practices 231, 258–260, 263, 266 f.
- providing legal testimony 57, 83–91, 278
- non-Muslim 238, 245–252, 269
Minors and youths
- boys 63, 133, 178, 186, 239–242, 250, 269
- girls 26, 50, 53–63, 65–67, 69, 85–87, 96, 98, 102, 123, 125, 129 f., 159, 179, 193, 196, 277
Miscarriage 29, 117, 120, 132, 142, 144, 146–148, 151 f, 193, 271
Modern Middle Eastern communities
- Egyptian 3–6, 16 f., 32, 65, 84, 105, 161, 258
- Iranian 3–5, 93 f., 251
- Iraqi 251, 258
- Jordanian 3, 109, 237
- Lebanese 34
- Moroccan 3 f., 16, 83, 230, 251, 258
- Pakistani 106, 109
- Palestinian 3 f., 58, 60, 109, 268
- Saudi 39, 237
- Tunisian 3
- Turkish 3 f., 16
Modesty, clothing, and nudity 13, 17, 88, 180, 185, 185–187, 208, 213, 215, 237–243, 247–267
Motzki, Harald 59
Mourning rituals, *see* Burial and mourning practices
Muḥammad (Prophet) 13, 26–31, 211–213, 215–217, 219–221, 228, 232, 234 f., 237, 253, 260, 264 f., 274
- *see also* Prophetic medicine
Musallam, Basim 6 f., 10, 14, 31 f., 134, 201, 280

Najāsāt (impure substances) 212, 227, 230 f., 257, 266, 269

Nawawī, Muḥyī al-Dīn (d. 676/1227) 46, 51, 66 f., 85, 238, 240, 243
Non-Muslims
– *see* Christians and Christianity; Jews and Judaism
Nu'mān, Qāḍī (d. 363/974) 252
Nutrition 10, 59, 61–65, 146, 215
Nuwayrī, Shihāb al-Dīn Ahmad (d. 733/1333) 170 f.

Oaths 17 f., 76 f., 80–82, 88. 90, 98 f., 112
Orphans 66, 85 f.
Ovaries 132–136

Parents, relationship with married daughters 55, 102–104, 107, 253–255, 261
Paternity 2, 4, 68, 83, 90, 112, 278
Paul of Aegina 49, 124 f., 157 f., 179 f.
Peirce, Leslie 60, 103 f., 109
Pessaries 119, 139, 145 f., 160, 171, 194, 200
Pharmacists 11, 149, 177, 184, 218, 225
– *see also* Medicines and pharmacy
Phlebotomy, *see* Cupping and phlebotomy
Pleasure and sexual arousal
– among boys and eunuchs 245, 250
– as a prerequisite for conception 117, 133, 140, 150, 156, 161
– as a medical need 117, 123, 130, 150, 154, 203
– as a purpose of marriage and marital right 36 f., 39 f., 43, 95, 111
Poisons 184, 212, 216, 227
Polygamy 2–4, 20, 26 f., 32–34, 57, 94–97, 100, 105, 112 f., 162, 278
Pormann, Peter 176, 229 f.
Powers, David 77, 79
Pregnancy
– enslaved women 1, 84–89
– legal claims 68, 80–84, 90–92, 112
– *rāqid* (sleeping fetus) 72, 83–84, 90 f, 106 f., 112
– tests 132, 168–171
– *see also* Childbirth
Privacy 78, 85, 224 f., 239, 244, 247 f., 251
Prophetic medicine 6, 19, 207 f., 213–219, 221 f., 227 f., 233
Puberty 7, 59–67, 86–87. 129 f, 239–243, 250, 277
– *see also* Menstruation; Minors
Pulse-taking 176, 182, 197, 281

Qalyūbī, Shihāb al-Dīn (d. 1079/1659) 70, 239–241, 250
Qarāfī, Shihāb al-Dīn (d. 684/1285) 46, 48, 89
Qazwīnī (d. 682/1283) 170
Qur'ān 27, 78, 83, 94, 112, 118, 120, 141, 215, 219, 233–235, 245, 248, 261
Qurṭubī, 'Arīb ibn Sa'īd (d. ca. 370/980) 168, 170 f.

Ragab, Ahmed 210
Ramadan, *see* Fasting
Rapoport, Yossef 65 f., 95, 102, 104, 106 f.
Rāqid (sleeping fetus), *see* Pregnancy
Rāzī, Abū Bakr Muḥammad ibn Zakarīyā (Rhazes) (d. 311/923) 48 f., 60, 119, 123 f., 127, 132, 134, 143, 147, 149, 152, 157 f., 160, 162, 167 f., 176, 195–197, 229, 249
Ruhāwī, Isḥāq ibn 'Alī (fl. 3rd/9th century) 123, 162, 176, 184, 202
Ruqya 215, 233

Saffārīnī, Muḥammad ibn Aḥmad (d. 1188/1774) 223, 227, 231, 233
Saḥnūn (d. 240/854) 89
Sait, Siraj 110
Sakhāwī, Shams al-Dīn (d. 831/1428) 65
Saqatī, Muḥammad (d. 7th/13th century) 88, 170 f.
Sarakhsī, Muḥammad ibn Aḥmad (d. ca. 490/1096) 13, 72, 84
Satan 211, 223, 253, 271–274
Savage-Smith, Emilie 172, 199 f., 213
Semen 117, 133, 136–138, 141, 145 f., 149, 153–155, 159, 161, 193, 280
– in women 149, 155, 159 f., 161
Shādhilī, Ṣadaqah ibn Ibrāhīm (fl. 8th/14th century) 199 f.
Shāfi'ī legal school
– dissolution of marriage 37–39, 42, 45 f.
– marriage and domestic life 45 f., 93, 107

– medical care and knowledge 213, 219, 237–242, 249 f., 269
– menstruation, *'idda*, and pregnancy 70, 73 f., 84
– *see also* Adhra'ī; Bulqīnī; Ghazālī; Marwarrūdhī; Māwardī; Nawawī; Qalyūbī; Shirwānī, Suyūṭī
Shāfi'ī, Muḥammad ibn Idrīs (d. 804/820) 42, 45, 74, 84, 107, 219, 222 f., 233
Shaham, Ron 89 f.
Shapland, Fiona 63
Shatzmiller, Maya 102 f., 108
Shī'ite thought 34, 96, 105, 252
Shīrāzī, Abū Isḥāq (d. 476/1083) 46
Shirk (polytheism) 232, 274
– *see also* God and piety
Shirwānī, 'Abd al-Ḥamīd (d. 1301/1884) 240
Slavery and slaves 1, 57, 73, 87–89, 123, 169, 178, 238
Soranus of Ephesus (d. 2nd century A.D.) 125, 134, 155 f., 166
Spellberg, Denise 28, 271, 275
Stephanus of Athens (d. 7th century A.D.) 124, 166, 174
Sterility (in men) 47, 54, 161
Surgery 49, 146, 165, 172, 179, 187 f., 191 f., 194, 199 f., 281
Suyūṭī, Jalāl al-Dīn (d. 911/1505) 171, 213, 219, 247

Ṭabarī, Abū Ja'far (d. 310/923) 94 f., 271–273
Ṭabarī, 'Alī ibn Sahl Rabban (fl. c. 246/850) 136, 143–149, 151, 156–158, 163, 167 f., 171, 197
Thousand and One Nights, The 3, 17, 98
Trousseaux 34, 55, 99, 102 f., 279
Tucker, Judith 88, 103, 111

Ullmann, Manfred 119 f., 122, 124–126, 149, 175, 281
'Umar ibn al-Khaṭṭāb (d. 23/644) 28–33, 39–43, 50, 71, 74, 107, 248 f., 282
Umm al-walad, see Slavery and slaves
Urine inspection 163 f., 176, 185
'Utbī, Muḥammad ibn Aḥmad (d. 255/869) 81

Vieille, Paul 4 f.
Violence 50–52
Virginity 28, 30, 34 f., 48–50, 58, 66 f., 86, 90, 130, 156, 158 f., 163, 170–174, 187–189, 243, 258, 280
Visiting the sick 252–257, 260 f., 268

Wansharīsī, Aḥmad ibn Yaḥyā (d. 914/1508) 37, 50, 56, 75, 80–83, 85 f., 89, 91, 103, 106 f., 256 f., 279
Waqf endowments 102, 106
Weddings 19, 90, 103, 173, 252–255, 258–261
Wetnurses, *see* Breastmilk and breastfeeding
Widows and widowers 58, 69, 80 f., 83, 90–93, 99–103, 105–109, 130, 155–160, 279, 284
Witnesses, *see* Legal testimony

Yazbak, Mahmoud 60 f.

Zāhidī, Najm al-Dīn (d. 658/1260) 73
Zahrāwī, Abū al-Qāsim Khalaf ibn 'Abbās (d. ca. 400/1013) 49, 146, 179, 187–189, 191 f., 197, 200, 281

www.ingramcontent.com/pod-product-compliance
Lightning Source LLC
Chambersburg PA
CBHW031757220426
43662CB00007B/439
9783110681628